Cambridge Studies in Social Anthropology

General Editor: Jack Goody

35

PARENTHOOD AND SOCIAL REPRODUCTION

DEDICATION

To Meyer Fortes, whose pioneering research in kinship first led me to work in West Africa, and whose sensitive ethnography and acute analysis have posed the question of *how* polity and economy affect family roles.

Parenthood and Social Reproduction

Fostering and Occupational Roles in
West Africa

ESTHER N. GOODY

Cambridge University Press

Cambridge
London   New York   New Rochelle
Melbourne   Sydney

Published by the Press Syndicate of the University of Cambridge
The Pitt Building, Trumpington Street, Cambridge CB2 1RP
32 East 57th Street, New York, NY 10022, USA
296 Beaconsfield Parade, Middle Park, Melbourne 3206, Australia

© Cambridge University Press 1982

First published 1982

Printed in Great Britain at the University Press, Cambridge

British Library Cataloguing in Publication Data

Goody, Esther N.
Parenthood and social reproduction. –
(Cambridge studies in social anthropology; 35)
1. Foster home care – Africa, West
I. Title
362.7'33'0966   HV887.A36   80-42177

ISBN 0 521 22721 6

Contents

v

Tables

Tables

Tables

Figures

Acknowledgements

The studies on which this book is based have extended over twenty years and would not have been possible without the help of many people. My debt to Gonja friends and assistants is irredeemable, and to mention them all impossible. A few, however, were particularly important in work related to kinship fosterage: in Buipe, Bomunana, Kofi Maman and Adamu Dari; in Bunsunu, Damba Yiri Wuritche, Supini Wuritche, Grunshi, Nyiwuleji, and Mahama Katanga; in Kpembe, Miama, Adama, Tcheraba, Dongitche, Kelli, Soale, Ewuntoma and Aladzi of Sabon Gida, Singbung Wuritche of Singbun, and the Kasoatche, the Limam and the NsoaWura as well as Adia from Sakpare. J. A. Braimah, the KanyasiWura, was a constant source of information and insight. Of those who helped directly with the formal aspects of the Kpembe study, Mr Zakaria Allassan and Mary Braimah carried out the TAT storytelling sessions with the children with tact and persistence without which this part of the study would have been quite impossible. Salifu Seidu, Asumani Damba, James Salifu, and Paul Dari were valuable members of the team. Anna Craven, who drew the TAT pictures and worked throughout the Kpembe Study in Kpembe with me, was indefatigable, despite ill-health.

A quite special debt is owed to Shiata Bawah, who, since I first knew her in 1957, has been an unfailing source of support and always ready to share her deep understanding of Gonja life. Shiata and her husband John Bawah have contributed much to my understanding of the differences between eastern and western Gonja, and of the meaning of Gonja hospitality.

The long and complicated analysis of the Kpembe material was made possible by a grant from the Social Science Research Council (UK), which allowed me to employ Ilma Scantlebury and Nicola Tahaney (now Dr Hart). Thanks are due to both for their patience and skill, and particularly to Dr Hart who designed a number of the codes. The computer analysis was done with the help of Janet Spedding, now Dr Spedding, whose gifted assistance was most timely.

Debts to teachers and colleagues are equally numerous. I first talked about the framework for analysis of parent roles to Max Gluckman's Manchester semi-

Acknowledgements

nar, whose joint insistence that economic factors must be more important than I had allowed for sent me back to the data. I must record here that they were only partly right about the basis of Gonja fostering, but in the larger sense I must agree with them. Professors Meyer Fortes and Terry Turner read more recent versions of Chapter 1, and I profited much by their comments. The persistent faults are mine, however. Professor S. G. Lee gave generously of his time in suggesting approaches to the Kpembe projective material. Had I not been determined to attempt an analysis which focussed on shared experiences (age, parents' divorce, membership of a particular estate...) I would have made more use of his suggestions. Professor Gustav Jahoda took the time to read through the full length Kpembe Report, and I am most grateful for his thoughtful comments. Professor Jerry Kagan looked at Chapters 2 and 3 while I was putting the final manuscript together. I am grateful to him for pointing out a major methodological problem of which I had been unaware. It was at this stage too late to remedy it, but his comments confirmed the wisdom of not publishing the Kpembe study itself as a separate volume.

It is impossible to specify debts to those with whom one works closely over a long period, and so I can only say that the joint authorship of Chapter 4 with Jack Goody indicates in a very small way how much my thinking owes to his wide-ranging work on northern Ghana ethnography and in kinship theory. Christine Oppong's MA thesis on Dagomba childhood (1964) was the first detailed material on fostering in northern Ghana after my early work on the Gonja, and made it possible to see that fostering was of far wider significance, and subject to very different forms of institutionalization, than what might be found in any one society. Horace Miner's early study on Timbuctoo pinpointed the practice of placing of children with Mallams and craftsmen. Although I had read this before first going to Gonja, it was not until I began to look again at material on traditional states that I realized how seminal his observations were. Without the corpus of ethnography on the Hausa initiated by Mike and Mary Smith, Chapter 5 would not have been possible. Here I must also record my gratitude to Polly Hill and Ibrahim Tahir for discussions which deepened my understanding of Hausa society, and cleared up a number of misapprehensions. I have had several helpful conversations with Enid Schildkrout, who also made detailed comments on the Hausa analysis.

The studies reported in Chapter 6 were made possible by the help of Dr D. K. Fiawoo and Mr Emanuel Mends of the University of Ghana, Legon, and the skill and energy of Gladys Azu in organizing and carrying through the Krobo survey. I hope the publication of the material at last will make clear the size of my debt to them. The task of coding the data from the southern Ghana surveys was ably carried out by Dr Jeremy Eades. The analysis in Chapter 7 owes much to talks over the years with Dr Margaret Peil, whose generous permission to use unpublished data is most gratefully acknowledged. Discussions with my colleague Carol MacCormack about patterns of parenthood among the Sherbro with whom she worked were particularly useful in gaining an impression of what might be called a situation of 'endemic fostering' on the Atlantic coast.

The study of West African student families in London was carried out in the field by Christine Muir (now Christine Groothues). She not only managed the survey phase in which a complicated sampling scheme required unusual patience of the inverviewers, but herself conducted the interviewing over 18 months of the 20 families in the 'in depth' phase of the study. It is more her study than mine. The comparison with West Indian immigrant families was made possible by Dr M. T. Spens who arranged and supervised the interviewing. It also owes much to Margaret Sanford's dissertation on Child Keeping in British Honduras (see Sanford 1971 and 1975). The analysis is, however, my own, and so are the shortcomings.

Martha MacIntyre's editorial endeavours are gratefully acknowledged; she is not responsible for persistent infelicities.

Field research in 1956-7 was sponsored by the Ford Foundation's Foreign Area Fellowship Program. The Kpembe Study was jointly sponsored by the Wenner Gren Foundation and by the Child Development Research Unit of the University of Ghana, Legon. The coding and analysis of the Kpembe Study material was supported by the Social Science Research Council (UK), who also funded the London Immigrants study. The African Studies Centre at the University of Cambridge has repeatedly rendered assistance on bibliographic and other matters. A Fellowship year at the Center for Advanced Study in the Behavioral Sciences at Stanford in 1979–80 provided time to rethink the earlier work and write new chapters. Without the pause of this year, a book would never have emerged.

Chapters and parts of chapters have previously appeared in the following places:

Part of Chapter 1 as 'Forms of pro-parenthood: the sharing and substitution of parental roles'. In J. Goody (ed.), *Kinship: Penguin modern sociology readings.* Harmondsworth, Middlesex. 1971

Chapter 2 in P. Mayer (ed.), *Socialization: the approach from social anthropology.* Published by the Tavistock Press, London. 1970

Chapter 3 is based on the final chapters of *The Kpembe study: a comparison of fostered and non-fostered children in eastern Gonja.* Report submitted to the Social Science Research Council, London. 1970

Chapter 4, with J. Goody first appeared in *Man* (NS)2, 1967

Chapter 7 and Chapter 11 are partly based on 'The delegation of parental roles in West Africa and the West Indies', first published in T. R. Williams (ed.), *Socialization and communication in primary groups.* Published by Mouton, The Hague. 1975

Chapter 10 with Christine Muir Groothues as 'The West Africans: The quest for education'. In J. L. Watson (ed.), *Between two cultures.* Published by Blackwell, Oxford. 1977

xii

Acknowledgements

Part of Chapter 12 appeared in 'some theoretical and empirical aspects of parent-hood in West Africa'. In Christine Oppong *et al.* (eds.), *Marriage, fertility and parenthood in West Africa.* Published by Canberra University Press, Canberra. 1978
Appendix 1 is also drawn from *The Kpembe study.*

Grateful acknowledgement is made of permission to republish these here.

Introduction

This is a book about parenthood and socialization which takes West Africa as its special focus. It is mainly concerned not with the early years of infancy and childhood, fascinating as these are, but rather with the years of later childhood and adolescence. It sees parents as confronted with a set of tasks that take the same general form in all societies: begetting and bearing, endowment with birth-status identity, nurturance, training and finally sponsorship into full adult status. Somehow these tasks must be performed if there is to be a succession of genera-tions of socially accredited adults. Yet the actual structure of a particular society – its political system, economy, settlement pattern, population density, patterns of inheritance and succession to office, all these will affect the manner in which the tasks of parenthood can be accomplished. Therefore the way in which parenthood is institutionalized must vary between societies – as indeed it does. If the tasks of parenthood are realized through different institutionalized forms, then the experiences of the child along the route to adulthood will inevitably also be different.

The central theme of the studies that are brought together here is the ques-tion of how parent roles and patterns of socialization are articulated with other aspects of a society. This is a question which has become increasingly apparent to me since the beginning of these studies in 1956. Thus it is implicit in the earlier chapters, becoming clearer in the later studies. My first fieldwork was among the Gonja of central Gonja (1956–7) and later in the divisional capitals of Kpembe (eastern Gonja, 1964), Bole (western Gonja, 1965) and Daboya (northern Gonja, 1974). In the Gonja work I looked at parenthood and sociali-zation in detail, in one particular society. But Gonja parental institutions are quite strikingly different from those which had previously been described for West Africa, particularly in Fortes' classic account of socialization among the Tallensi (1970). It was this contrast which generated the theoretical paradigm that frames all these studies (Chapter 1).

At first my concern was to document the Gonja pattern, particularly the institution of kinship fosterage whereby many children are reared not by their own parents but by relatives (1961, 1970, 1973). Chapter 2 describes the insti-tution of kinship fosterage in Gonja and asks whether the experience of being

1

fostered – reared – by a relative rather than in the parental household had a detrimental effect on the lives and careers of Gonja adults. This problem led to a detailed comparison between children being fostered and those growing up with their own parents which I carried out in Kpembe, in eastern Gonja (Chapter 3). The study of the social matrix of Gonja fostering, and its consequences both for other institutions and for the children themselves, forms the focus of Part I of this volume.

Part II is concerned with the prevalence of the delegation of parent roles elsewhere in West Africa. Once alerted to the practice of fostering children with kin, I began to look for references to apparently similar or related institutions in other West African societies. But at this time there was no detailed documentation of fostering apart from that in Gonja.[1] It became imperative to discover whether the sending of children to grow up away from their own parents was rare – a unique adaptation to the special circumstances in Gonja – or on the contrary was a common response to some general feature of life in West Africa. A survey of available ethnographies on northern Ghana (J. and E. Goody 1967 and Chapter 4) showed that the other states had patterns of sending children away from the natal home to be reared which were analogous to those found in Gonja. These centralized societies in the savannah area were also ones that placed little emphasis on unilineal descent groups, that is, on clans and lineages. On the other hand, in the segmentary societies which lie interspersed among these kingdoms, such descent groups play a very important role not only in kinship but in political, religious and economic affairs. And in these segmentary societies there was no institutionalized delegation of rearing roles. There appeared to be something about segmentary unilineal descent systems which promoted a unitary parent role and which we attempted to link to patterns of residence for women and to the stability of marriage.

The other side of the question is: 'What is there about states that leads to the delegation of parent roles'? In order to explore this further, in Chapter 5 I consider the data available on four savannah kingdoms. Two of these, the Dagomba and the Mossi, are similar to the Gonja in having only a limited division of labour with a few non-farming occupations; their political systems, though based on the rule of an invading group over the indigenes, did not have elaborate hierarchies of office or complex systems of taxation of individual production. The other states, the Hausa emirates and Bornu, already had an elaborate division of labour in pre-colonial times with most adults having one or more by-occupations in addition to farming; as well as wage labour, there was also taxation of individual production and an elaborate political hierarchy related to taxation. Chapter 5 seeks to describe the delegation of parent roles in these traditional kingdoms, and to relate this to economic and political complexity.

Thus far the picture is one of segmentary unilineal descent societies in which parental rearing roles are not delegated, and of traditional state systems in which delegation is institutionalized. But a perusal of contemporary Ghanaian literature

2

indicated that the rearing of children away from home was a frequent practice in the modern, cosmopolitan world of the south. In an effort to explore and document this practice, short, focussed studies were made in three small towns each belonging to one of the major ethnic groups in southern Ghana: the Ewe, the Fanti and the Krobo. Together with Gladys Azu's work on the Ga (1974) these investigations, made in 1964 and 1965, make it clear that various forms of fostering are regularly practised in these coastal societies (Chapter 6). A new complexity is introduced here by the fact that both matrilineal and patrilineal descent groups coexist with institutionalized fostering in these societies. So it cannot be the existence of unilineal descent groups in themselves which is responsible for the unitary parent role in the segmentary societies examined in Chapter 4. However the southern societies differ from the northern ones in two important ways. First, the southern societies are not segmentary in a political sense; they have a governmental structure based on the town, constituting what I have termed 'town-states'. Further, these town-states have long been involved in the world economy mediated by centuries of trade, and more recently by the colonial administration. Both politically and economically the southern societies are more complex than the segmentary systems of northern Ghana.

The detailed analysis of the states in Chapter 5 revealed two models for the delegation of parent roles. In the simple differentiated states of Gonja and Dagomba, fostering was nearly always done by kin. In the more complex hierarchical states (Hausa and Kanuri), many children went to unrelated pro-parents. Drawing on this analysis, it seemed probable that the delegation of parent roles was related not merely to the absence of strong unilineal descent groups which marks most of the states, but more positively to the economic and political complexity of these kingdoms. If this were so, then parallel levels of political and economic complexity in southern Ghanaian societies could be expected to generate forms of delegation of parent roles analogous to those found in the northern states. The data from the southern Ghana surveys in Chapter 6 relates to comparatively rural communities within the southern societies traditionally based on town-states.

Chapters 8 and 9 consider two more specialized forms of training for older children and adolescents that have emerged in the urban centres of coastal West Africa. These are modern apprenticeship, as found in the southern cities of Ghana and Nigeria, and the institution of 'wardship' in the Creole cities of Liberia and Sierra Leone. In Chapter 8 the proliferation of informal apprenticeship is related to the adoption of a highly elaborate division of labour characteristic of modernizing societies. In Chapter 9 socio-economic stratification and the emergence of a political elite are related to wardship as a basis for continuing patron-client relations among adults.

Anthropologists are always on the lookout for natural experimental situations. In the third major section of the book, the nature of the structure of parent roles is further explored by looking at the adaptation of West African

3

families to living in London (Chapter 10). This study provided an opportunity to see what happened to traditional patterns of parenthood under radically changed circumstances. The very striking finding here was that half of a sample of nearly three hundred families had sent their young children to live with English foster-parents. This study also indicated that traditional fostering in West Africa was not limited to Ghanaian peoples. For the great majority of the families were from Nigeria, mainly Yoruba, and many of the parents had been fostered as children at home in Nigeria. To add to the complexity of the picture, another Nigerian group, the Ibo, who traditionally did not practise fostering, placed their children with English foster-parents when living in that country. It seems clear that we are dealing with a very general paradigm of West African culture.

But how general is it? As a further probe, a pilot study was done on parent roles among West Indians in London. As immigrants, whose ancestors were African, this group encountered many of the same problems that led the West African couples to seek English foster-parents. Although they make complicated arrangements for the daily care of their children, West Indian parents reject the idea of placing them with English foster-parents. Chapter 11 discusses this material and seeks to explain this striking difference between the two sets of immigrant families.

Looking back over the range of descriptive and comparative material on traditional and contemporary patterning of West African parent roles, it is apparent that a simple dichotomy between unitary parental rearing and fostering is too crude. The concluding chapter seeks to examine the many different forms in which parent roles are delegated in relation to two quite different processes. The first is the very long-term progression from egalitarian segmentary societies through simple states with rudimentary social and economic differentiation to more complex hierarchical states based on trade and an elaborate division of labour. This progression appears to parallel a shift from parental rearing, first to fostering by kin, then to the placing of children with strangers in various forms of apprenticeship, wardship, and so on. The emphasis here is on the identification of the mechanisms which seem to produce the changes in parent-role model. And these are seen as anchored to the way in which different types of social structure determine what are the effective strategies for fulfilling the tasks attached to parent roles. Thus the key question becomes: 'What are the circumstances which make parental rearing adaptive, and what are those in which it is no longer adaptive?' The next question becomes: 'What are the circumstances which make fostering by kin adaptive?' And finally: 'What are the circumstances which lead to the rearing of children by strangers being more adaptive than either parental rearing or rearing by kin?' The distribution of West African societies between those which restrict parent roles to the parents themselves, and those in which their delegation is institutionalized, fits remarkably well with the pattern produced in the answers to these questions. By framing questions in terms of changes in parent-role strategies in response to the changing

4

social structure, it also becomes possible to understand the close parallels between the traditional states with complex hierarchies and the modern urban centres. Although the two sets of societies differ in their political and economic institutions, both are hierarchical and economically stratified, and thus pose similar problems for fulfilling the tasks attached to parent roles: in both, the major problem is how to secure for children the skills and resources necessary for differentiated and specialized adult roles. The proliferation of forms of delegation of parent roles in these complex systems allows maximum mobility; it does not restrict the children to the skills and resources controlled directly by their parents. Viewed in this light, the high incidence of fostering with English foster-parents by West Africans in this country becomes an extreme case of seeking to utilize the delegation of educational and nurturant aspects of the parent role in the interests of social mobility and of the attainment of advantageous, high status, adult roles. This is a different form of the institution of wardship in the Creole centres of Freetown and Monrovia where people from the rural areas place a child with an educated member of the elite in the city.

A second process occurs within the family itself. This is the dynamic – the balance of tensions and bonds, of ties and cleavages – which is generated in the course of carrying out the various tasks. As parent roles are differently allocated in different societies, so the tensions and ties will affect different actors. It is a central theme of the analysis that these role dynamics, systematically replicated, feed back into and become part of the wider social structure.

This concluding chapter returns to another theme from the initial analysis of the nature of parent roles. This is the critical nature of birth-status identity in systems in which parent rearing roles are delegated. Transactions in parenthood have a different meaning where birth-status identity is fixed and immutable, for they are then concerned with rearing and sponsorship and not with jural status. With this fact in mind, the attempt is made to confront the question as to whether this special West African attitude towards the delegation of parent roles is to be seen as a sort of cultural paradigm, consistently applied across a wide range of different situations, or whether it is better viewed as a pragmatic response, within the constraints as they are perceived, to problems presented in the fulfilment of parent roles.

5

1

A framework for the analysis of parent roles

Anthropological accounts of parenthood have tended either to concentrate on formal institutions – the transfer of bridewealth as securing rights in children, initiation rituals – or to concern the character of early emotional and 'caretaking' relationships and the learning of impulse control. Not only are these areas of special interest to the psychologist but, clearly, with the learning of language and the basic cultural repertoire of custom, gesture, and idiom, this period is a vital one for the formation of adult character in a given society. If, however, we are concerned with the technical skills and role structure of this same society, we must give more emphasis to the context of learning in later childhood and adolescence. Moreover, it seems clear that the pattern of expectations governing interpersonal relationships is not established once and for all during early childhood. In later years relations between parents and children are no longer dominated by physical dependency; these and the relations with peers only then begin to take the form which they will retain in adulthood. And it is during adolescence, with emerging self-awareness, that the individual's position in the wider kin group and the community comes to take shape.

All these elements must be included in any framework for analysing the nature of parent roles in West Africa. The difficulty in finding such a framework is to agree on a suitable theoretical basis for its derivation. I propose to resolve this by asking simply: 'What are the critical tasks which have to be dealt with in producing a society's new members, and rearing them so that they can effectively assume adult roles in society?' What, in very broad terms, must parents *do*? It is immediately obvious that there are many tasks which have to be done, but which in our society are carried out not by parents but by nurseries, schools, industry, the state, or even by the new recruits themselves. And it could be argued that tasks which are not performed by parents in our own society are not properly parental tasks. Logically this is a perfectly correct position, but I think it more fruitful theoretically to take the opposite view, and consider that the full range of problems involved in reproducing a new generation be treated together. If we find that in certain societies some of these tasks are carried out in the family, while others are the concern of wider groups or are left to the

6

maturing individual, then this tells us something important about the society concerned. In short, we must see parenthood as divisible into several different roles, each concerned with a different prerequisite for social replacement. It then becomes possible to see how these tasks are linked or distributed in different societies. What is of particular theoretical interest is the ways in which institutions external to the kinship system itself affect the allocation of parent roles.

Parent roles

Anthropologists have traditionally defined roles in terms of the rights and duties associated with them. This has the clear advantage of focussing attention on the interactive aspect of roles, for one person's rights are another's obligations. There have been some attempts to see parenthood in these terms, notably a paper, 'Transactions in parenthood', in which W. H. Goodenough acknowledges that physiological parenthood and what he calls 'psychic parenthood' have some significance, but proceeds to outline a framework for analysis which is limited to 'transactions in the rights, duties, privileges and powers of jural parenthood' (1970a:398). He suggests that an analysis must deal with *succession* to jural parenthood as a result of incapacity or death of parents; with *exercise* by others of *overriding rights* in the child; with *delegation* without actual surrender of jural rights; and with arrangements by the jural parents for *sharing* of some or all of their rights; and outright *transfer* of rights in the child (1970a:409). However, Goodenough considers that it is not possible to discuss the *content* of parental rights comparatively; this can only be meaningful in the context of a particular culture. In order to construct a definition of jural 'father' and 'mother' which will be applicable in all societies he defines motherhood in physiological terms (the jural mother is the woman who bore the child) while the jural father is the man married to the jural mother. The limitation of this approach, apart from its formality,[1] is that it seems to leave aside certain important features of parenthood. While jural rights in, and duties with respect to, children are clearly important, the affective ties between parents and their children, parents' role in socialization and education, and the claims which can be made in the name of morality are also highly significant, and they are certainly subject to a wide range of transactions.

I therefore suggest that content be restored to the relationship between parents and children by seeing parenthood as concerned with fulfilling the tasks involved in bearing and rearing children, and establishing them in their turn as effective adults. Parenthood is about social replacement. Such an approach includes transactions in jural rights, but is not limited to these. Viewed in this way we need not expect to find that a single distinctive feature (physiological paternity, marriage to the mother, jural authority) will always coincide with a particular relationship. The tasks of parenthood must be carried out somehow,

7

but not necessarily by a single set of 'parents'. Significantly, what I have called the tasks of parenthood appear to receive social recognition, as well as a patterned, institutionalized response, in all societies. For the present the clear candidates for universal problems of social replacement appear to be: i. bearing and begetting, ii. endowment with civil and kinship status, iii. nurturance, iv. training and v. sponsorship into adulthood. Each of these aspects of parenthood can, individually, be split off from the rest and made the object of one or more of Goodenough's transactions – delegation, sharing, succession, pre-emption and transfer. Such familiar institutions as ritual Godparenthood (*compadrazgo*), the wet nurse, the nanny, Roman adrogation, and fosterage can all be seen as institutionalized transactions concerning one or other responsibility usually associated with the parent role; as institutionalized transactions which may, but need not, concern jural rights and duties with respect to the children.

If we do look at the various tasks suggested as underlying parent roles, the question of how to define rights and duties, and how to decide whether they are shared, delegated or transferred is also simplified. For it is immediately apparent that it makes no sense to speak of all five areas as subject to the same *kinds* of rights and duties, which will become clear as each of the tasks of parenthood is considered in turn.

Bearing and begetting

Bearing and begetting are physiological facts which may be culturally endowed with different meanings, but which always seem to carry an irreducible connotation.[2] While it is possible to transact about the *consequences* of bearing and begetting by defining birth-status identity separately, or allocating responsibilities of rearing to others, the fact of physiological parenthood cannot be altered once conception has taken place. In most societies the correspondence of physical paternity and birth-status identity is considered desirable, and often a lack of correspondence affects assumption of full birth-status rights in adulthood. But begetting and bearing as physiological acts seem to have a significance of their own. Among the Tallensi of northern Ghana, for whom birth-status identity depends on the transfer of bridewealth cattle, there is no formal disability or stigma attached to a child begotten by another man before the mother's marriage, and subsequently legitimized as the child of the husband by the transfer of bridewealth. But still, Fortes writes, the Tallensi feel that the child's genitor ought to bring the cow of rearing to the step-father and the cow of redemption to the mother's lineage elders in order to secure social paternity of his child so that begetting and birth-status identity coincide (Fortes 1949b:27, 136). The transaction cannot be run the other way. That is, it is impossible to transfer the role of begetter to the mother's husband. In this sense there is no way to transact about – to socially manipulate – begetting and bearing. They are once-and-for-all physiological facts. The best that can be done is to transact about the socially constructed rights and duties linked to birth-status identity, to bring these into line with the physiological facts.

Some societies, like the Gonja and the Lozi, refuse to see any distinction between physiological paternity (which they perceive as an obvious process) and social paternity (which conveys full birth-status identity to the child). Thus the civic and kinship status of a Gonja child derives from his genitor and never from a mother's husband who did not beget him. However under certain circumstances the mother's husband could insist on retaining control over the person and labour of his wife's adulterine child. He justifies this by his prescriptive rights in the mother's sexuality (as his wife) and as his due for rearing the child. This situation is seriously out of balance from the child's point of view (he must accept the authority of the mother's husband, and work for him, but receives in return no civil identity or rights through him and indeed would always occupy a disadvantaged status in the household); it was recognized to depend on the superior power of the mother's husband. That is, it was chiefs and other powerful men who could succeed in controlling an adulterine child in this way. The son, on the other hand, was expected to abscond to his genitor as soon as he was old enough to escape, and could expect to be welcomed and receive full birth-status rights once recognized by him. Although defended by the proverb 'A thief does not own the thing he steals', the control of the mother's husband over an adulterine child was likened to a form of slavery, as both depended on force. The problem arises in Gonja because jural rights depend on physiological paternity, and there is no way that this can be *socially* manipulated.

It is of course possible to construct special meanings for the physiological facts of bearing and begetting, in the realm of ideas. The Ashanti say that a mother and her children are 'of one blood' while the father and his offspring share a spiritual force, the *ntoro*. The Gonja share with many other peoples the conviction that the child is built up from the father's semen, while the mother holds and feeds the foetus, but does not contribute directly to its physical formation. The Trobrianders take an extreme view in recognizing the possibility of resemblance between father and child but denying that it could be due to any physical link between them. In nearly all societies there are culturally elaborated expressions of the physical link between parents and children. It is particularly interesting that despite the intimacy of the link between mother and infant, there are cultures in which the physiological nature of this link is not given ideological recognition. The Zulu, who liken the mother to a field in which seed is planted by the father, are strongly patrilineal, and it might be supposed that such a denial of the mother's physiological role was an expression of patrilineal ideology. However the Gonja, who describe the mother as 'like a basket, simply holding the baby', are not strongly patrilineal, and indeed have certain beliefs and institutions which are characteristic of matrilineal societies, such as the over-right of the mother's brother to sell a child into slavery, regardless of the father's wishes. However estate membership, and with it rights to political

9

and ritual office, is transmitted from a genitor to his children, and perhaps it is this fact that is reflected in the way conception is perceived. It seems more likely that the conceptualization of the mother's contribution to creating an infant in terms of holding it safely, and feeding it, are drawn from two other sources; on the one hand, the foetus grows within her and emerges linked by a chord to the placenta, which is often likened to congealed menses; and on the other hand, her role during infancy and childhood is that of nurse and source of nurturance. (And indeed a woman's continued role is as preparer – and often provider – of food.) The social structure is clearly one source of models for explaining how babies are created; but observation of parent roles also can play a part, as can observation of animals. And, as the Gonja ideas indicate, the resulting models can conflict with other apects of the social structure.

A number of societies seem to have split beliefs about paternity into beliefs about spiritual and physical paternity, the former being the task of gods or spirits, and the latter the province of human males (e.g. the Murngin of Arnhemland). Significantly, when this happens it is usually civic and kinship statuses that are determined by (or determine) spirit paternity, with the rights and obligations of physiological paternity being linked to the rearing relationship. Occasionally spirit paternity is reserved for rare cases of beings that are wholly or in part supernatural, as in the theologies of ancient Greece, Christianity and Hinduism. In these cases, in order to validate the supernatural character of the offspring – their difference from normal human beings – physiological paternity by a human father *is* denied.

In attempting to tease apart the component elements of parenthood it is analytically preferable to treat begetting and bearing as physiological facts which may be given different social recognition (denied, linked with spirits, linked exclusively to the genitor). Once conception has occurred, transactions concerning bearing and begetting are limited to the realm of ideas; they are essentially cultural rather than social. In terms of Goodenough's transaction series, it is impossible to delegate, share, succeed to, or transfer physiological parenthood,[3] for this is an accomplished fact. It is of course possible to manipulate socially the *consequences* of this fact, that is, to transact about rights and duties held by and in respect to the child. The distinction may seem an unnecessarily fine one, but it is nevertheless of great significance, as shown by the strenuous efforts made by adopted children in Western societies to discover their 'real' (i.e. physiological) parents, despite having full jural status through adoption.

Status entitlements and rearing reciprocities

The remaining four aspects of parenthood can be divided into two sets. On the one hand are those in which reciprocal rights and duties are conditional on or arise from performance of the role obligation (nurturance, training and sponsorship). Of an entirely different nature is endowment with civil status which in all societies is defined in terms of rights and duties conveyed by birth under specified conditions. Gough (1959) uses the concept of 'birth status identity' to mean 'all the social relationships, property-rights, etc. which a child acquires at birth by virtue of his legitimacy, whether through the father or through the mother' (1959:32). Usually, but with significant exceptions, this means birth to parents who are recognized as married. There are a few societies, mainly matrilineal systems and a few cognatic ones, in which these rights are based on physiological parenthood (i.e. no distinction is made between physical and social paternity), and they do not depend on the parents' marriage. They are, nonetheless, defined in terms of who the parents, genitor and genetrix, are. It is the designation of adult status rights in terms of the parents' position in the social system which I refer to as birth-status identity or civil/kinship identity.

In a matrilineal system, birth status identifies the child with the lineage of its mother, and through this identity conveys entitlement to rights of inheritance and succession. Typically, bestowal of birth-status identity follows from the formal identification of the mother's genetricial powers with her lineage in an 'initiation' or 'puberty' rite and may not depend on her marriage.[4] Occasionally this mechanism is utilized by a patrilineal group which thus provides for a daughter to be kept, unmarried, at home to bear children to perpetuate her father's descent group, as among the Krobo (Huber 1963).

In a patrilineal system birth status identifies one with the lineage of the man who fulfils the conditions of social fatherhood, however these may be defined in relation to rights in genetricem over women, and in relation to ideas about paternity. In a cognatic or bilateral system birth-status identity either may be linked to the kin groups of one or both parent or may simply be specified in relation to the parents themselves. In either case it is a matter of filiation – of direct links with individual parents – and of rights and duties in respect of those parents and their estates. Where cognatic kin groups hold significant resources, rights to membership must be established by virtue of links of filiation to the parent concerned.

However a given society defines the conditions of its transmission, full birth-status identity carries with it rights and obligations (a share in, or management of property, worship of shrines, often involving the burial and worship of the previous status-holder) which may be termed *status reciprocities*. These rights and obligations pertain to a status in a system of statuses; as such they are critical in placing the individual in the status system of his society. In contemporary Western society the significance of parental status placement has greatly diminished. It can be argued that the clearly demonstrable difference in opportunities associated with parents' class and occupation are a function of material resources rather than status placement *per se*. However I believe this to be only partially true, since attributed status affects the opportunities open to a person as well as a person's perception of these opportunities. In addition, birth-status identity is still critical for the establishment of citizenship which in turn controls freedom

11

to move between countries and the right to hold a job. Recent legislation in England has linked birth-status identity to the right of a woman to bring a foreign spouse into the country. It should also be noted that some hunting and gathering systems may represent exceptions to the general rule that birth-status identity is critical in determining adult status.

In many societies the stress on legitimacy underlines the function of endowment with birth-status identity in bestowing on the child a recognized position in the socially constructed world into which it has been born. If not born 'according to the rules', then it cannot participate as a full member. There are two kinds of reasons why these rules are so often expressed in terms of the recognition of the parents' marriage. In the first place, in the vast majority of societies rights to property, office and citizenship are vested in kin, and rules about marriage control recruitment of new members. It is surely significant that where there are sub-groups within a society which appear not to care about the rules for marriage and legitimacy, these groups lack resources and indeed often have limited civil status.[5] In Western folk usage legitimacy is a condition of an individual, based on the legal relationship between his or her parents. But it takes its meaning from the power of kin and community to acknowledge membership rights of new recruits. That this is still partly effective is shown by the inclusion until very recently of evidence of legitimacy on the birth certificate needed for entry into jobs and for passports (dependent on citizenship) throughout life. Further, while an illegitimate child can be given full jural status in an adopting family, he cannot 'create' such a status by himself.

The other reason for the close link between parents' marriage and full civil and kinship status arises from the tasks of parenthood themselves. While it is possible to separate these analytically into several parent roles, it is empirically the case that all, or nearly all, of them are usually filled by the biological parents. Social recognition of the parents' conjugal union acts as a sanction on their meeting these obligations of parenthood. Both marriage and parenthood are, as it were, being played on the public stage.

The reciprocities of rearing

In the remaining three aspects of parenthood, reciprocal rights and duties are not conveyed at birth, but are generated in the performance of the role, and take quite different forms in each case. Nurturance in infancy and early childhood creates close affective bonds between caretaker and child. The child is totally dependent for survival on the caretaker, and able to do very little in return. It is of course difficult to separate the rights and duties arising from nurturance in distinction to, say, civil status or training. But where this is possible, as for instance where custody over children changes on legitimation by the subsequent marriage of their parents, there is typically a recognition made of the work of nurturance. Fortes notes the inclusion of the 'cow of rearing' as part of the payment made if an adult man wishes to transfer his civil status from the lineage of his mother's husband to that of his genitor (1949b:27, 136), and Ruth Goodenough reports that on Truk, if the real parents wish to take back a child which has been reared by others, they must reimburse the adoptive parents for the care they have given (1970:328). These rules make clear the recognition of the work done in nurturance. By making a payment, the parents can be seen to cancel any claims on the child by the foster-parents built on a sense of obligation to them. It is even more difficult to isolate the reciprocal obligations which the nurtured child is felt to incur, but typically they concern care in old age. The Gonja are beautifully explicit about this; they say: 'In infancy your mother and father feed you and clear up your messes; when they grow old, you must feed them and keep them clean.' Significantly, the main sanctions for these rearing reciprocities are informal, and are based on the very affective ties which the close relationship engendered. I know of two cases of middle-aged Cambridge people, a man and a woman, who for several years regularly visited and helped to support an elderly nurse – not because of any legal obligation, but out of a sense of affection and obligation based on the care given to them in early childhood.

While in many societies fathers spend considerable time playing with infants and young children, and may assist in looking after them, there is to my knowledge no society in which the role of the father is so defined as to include the major responsibility for care, feeding, cleanliness and perpetual attention which is essential for rearing young children. Nor is any other man expected to do this. Nurturance is everywhere seen as the primary responsibility of women; and there are always rules specifying which woman has responsibility for a given child. This task may be shared, delegated or transferred to someone else, but primary responsibility is recognized as belonging to one particular woman. An obvious but often overlooked consequence is that both boys and girls are initially reared by, and dependent on, women, which contrasts strongly with the sex-role patterning in the rearing of older children.

As a child matures, its abilities and needs change, as does its participation in the world outside the family. The training which accompanies nurturance in early childhood is, roughly speaking, the same for boys and girls: the learning of language, impulse control, and cultural gesture and idiom is broadly similar for children of both sexes. But older children become increasingly conscious of sex roles, and are increasingly expected to develop according to the norms appropriate for members of their own sex. This empirical observation is entirely consistent with the process of social replacement which requires that two kinds of adults, men and women, are needed to reproduce the social system. In pre-literate societies the consequence is that the training of boys is undertaken by men, and the training of girls falls to women. This allocation is not the result of conscious arrangement so much as of the intimate link between training for adult roles and increasing participation in the domestic and subsistence economy. While young boys may be given women's tasks to do, as they grow older, larger

13

and stronger they are pulled into the male economic sphere. There their role models are men, and the tasks which they learn are central to adult male roles. Girls begin very young to help their mothers and the other women of the household with both domestic chores and childcare. As they approach maturity they may take over some of these tasks entirely so that on marriage they are already skilled and confident in these core aspects of a woman's adult role. In systems where the domestic group is not divorced from productive activity, older children of both sexes are expected to contribute substantially. At the same time, if the child's contribution is to be useful, it will have to be guided and disciplined. It is this aspect of the process of social replacement that makes the parental task of later childhood focus on training or education. Both in order to make effective use of the child's increasing contribution to the labour force, and in order that he or she later be able to perform adult roles, especially occupational roles, effectively, the young girl or boy must be trained, however informally. The consequence of the sexual division of labour in pre-industrial societies is that it is the mother, or other women, who train girls, and the father, or other men, who train boys.

Many, probably all, societies consider that one of the major responsibilities of parents is the moral education of their children. Training in adult economic role skills is important, but it is not sufficient. Moral education is based on precept, parable and proverb which specify how a 'good Gonja/Ashanti/. . . man/woman' ought to behave. Here both parents play a part, though the parent of the same sex is seen as having the major responsibility.

Whether training occurs within kinship roles or outside them, it involves constraint, authority and discipline which are irksome to the child. This control is balanced to a varying degree by the child's growing sense of competence in adult skills. The training relationship inevitably is characterized by ambivalence, and how this is handled depends very much on how the teacher–pupil role is related to the other parent roles. If it is part of a multiplex parent role, then there are constraints of affect built up in the nurturance relationship, as well as the constraints arising from the control the parent has over access to critical resources, which may be linked either to birth-status entitlement (but controlled by the parent) or to sponsorship. If training is delegated and thus separated from the other parent roles, then as in many formal schools discipline may become a dominant feature; it is striking how regularly discipline is a central aspect of the teacher's role.[6] Where training is delegated, the labour of the child is sometimes seen as reciprocating the teacher's efforts. In other systems the child is not considered as capable of, or himself responsible for, compensating his teacher. In societies of the latter sort, it is the parents who must reciprocate, usually financially, if they delegate the training of the child.

Sponsorship is the most variable of all the parental tasks, since it is concerned with providing the resources and 'certification' necessary to take up a full adult role in a given society. Exactly what resources are required varies extremely

14

widely, and hence sponsorship takes a range of different forms. In some systems birth-status identity itself is the major requirement for full participation. One thinks here of Australian multi-section systems in which marriage depends on section identity, though here initiation combines education with certification – that is, a youth who has successfully passed through circumcision (and often sub-incision) and the related ritual is held to be fully adult, ready to marry and to take a place in community affairs. In this process it appears usual for an Australian youth to have a specific ritual sponsor, not necessarily his father.

Initiation often carries the dual function of training and sponsorship, a linking of knowledge and readiness for adult roles that is found in many societies, including, of course, our own. Indeed, sponsorship in modern society often takes the form of provision for advanced education which in turn provides the young person with both occupational qualifications and access to middle-class status. Sponsorship is perhaps sociologically the most interesting aspect of parenthood since it provides a control mechanism by which adults may limit access to occupational and status positions. Typically the return exacted for sponsorship is the allegiance of the young adult to his sponsor, which may have economic and political implications for both. This control function is very clear in situations where the sponsor must provide basic resources from his own reserve to establish the youth. Bridewealth cattle and farm land are perhaps the most common examples, but marriage and full adult occupational role are often linked. Where the establishment of an individual depends on his sponsor relinquishing some resources, as in the traditional pattern of marriage and farm inheritance linked with the retirement of the father in rural Ireland, sponsorship into full adult status may be delayed by the parents as long as possible (Arensberg 1959).[7]

The protégé in return is usually expected to acknowledge himself subordinate to his sponsor, perhaps expressing this by living with him, or by contributing economic assistance. Or it may suffice that he serve his sponsor by granting him public respect or political allegiance. As this suggests, the sponsor–protégé relationship not only provides for the transition between minority and adulthood, but extends the filial relationship into the adult world, into the external system. For the protégé enters the wider social system by making use of a share of his sponsor's resources and position in it.

It is very often the case that the status identity conveyed through the pater carries with it the rights to position and resources needed to achieve full adulthood. Here the role of sponsor and pater are merged. But there are a number of societies where this is not so, usually because birth status is narrowly defined. In Euro-American society, for instance, the training received in adolescence determines to a large extent the position to be occupied in adulthood, and the intervention of a well-to-do sponsor, whether an individual or the state, can completely transform the opportunities available to a working-class youth by providing for a good education. This same phenomenon is seen in present-day Ashanti where either the father or the mother's brother may pay for secondary

15

schooling and university which enables a man to enter the educated élite. Significantly, in Ashanti, the protégé incurs an obligation to support other members of the family later on. Or to take a somewhat different case, a Yakö youth who lives with his mother and her kin has the right to farmland which enables him to marry, despite the fact that land is usually reserved for agnates. But he may use this land only so long as he lives with and assists his matrikin (Forde, 1963). Perhaps the Tallensi case is the clearest of all. Here too a man can live with his maternal kin, and farm on their land. But so firmly is status identity tied to social paternity that he may never 'own' this land nor serve the ancestors of his mother's lineage. He has these rights only in patrilineal land and ancestors. Matrikin can sponsor him socially and economically, but they are unable to make him fully one of themselves (Fortes, 1949b).

The nurturance, training, and sponsorship aspects of parenthood, then, generate characteristic patterns of reciprocal obligations, and transactions about these aspects of parenthood are about the right to enter into a relationship which implies more-or-less self-enforcing reciprocities. It is quite a different situation with transactions about status entitlements. The distinction between sharing or delegation on the one hand, and outright transfer on the other applies differently to the parent roles characterized by status entitlements than to those which generate reciprocities within the rearing relationship. Birth-status identity may be subject to outright transfer, as in adoption and adrogation, but not to sharing or delegation outside the group. Rights based on the provision of rearing services, on the other hand, are directly linked to these services. If more than one person provides a given service, then both will share in the resulting rights; similarly, the performance of a given parental task may be delegated to a non-parent, and by the performance of that task, the pro-parent establishes the associated claim – to support, labour or allegiance. In other words, sharing and delegation of parental role tasks which are characterized by performance-linked rights can occur independently of any alteration in civil status, since what is at issue is specific behaviour linked to a particular task of parenthood, and relevant to a given stage of the child's maturation.

The definition of parenthood

If parenthood consists of the tasks of bearing and begetting, nurturance, training, sponsorship and endowment with civil birth status, how then are we to define *parents*? For, clearly, who carries out these tasks varies from one society to another, and often several people are responsible for different aspects of rearing the same child. Goodenough suggests that in order to have a universally applicable definition it is necessary to combine biological and social criteria: maternity being defined biologically, and paternity as depending on marriage to the mother. Quite apart from the inelegance of combining classes of criteria in this way, this sort of definition doesn't seem to work, either in fitting the empirical data or in focussing on the critical issues. The difficulty in finding a universally applicable definition of parents seems to have obvious parallels with the celebrated difficulty in defining marriage and the 'family'.[8] In both cases several sets of rights and obligations are associated with the institution. For marriage these are linked with sexuality, reproductive capacities, domestic services, economic services and the legitimation of children. For parenthood there are the 'tasks of parenthood' as outlined above. But in each case they can be combined in different ways according to the institutions and ideology of the given society. Leach (1961) has proposed that rather than continuing with unsuccessful attempts to find a single criterion for defining marriage (with each proposal eliciting at least the necessary single contradictory case) we accept that there is a small, specifiable, set of criteria among which societies select one or more. For the Nayar exclusive sexual rights are not relevant, but the *tali* ritual and a high caste genitor are; for the Gonja, marriage does not convey rights of paternity over all the wife's children, but it is linked to her exclusive sexual and economic services; for the Nuer, marriage conveys prescriptive rights of social paternity, but domestic and sexual services may be withdrawn or waived. Marriage is about the holding of some kind of exclusive rights, but which rights are critical varies between societies.

If parenthood is best considered as a set of roles which may be allocated to different people, how are we to define the 'real' parents? It is significant that such a question should even arise. Why should one feel the need to be able to say of a child 'These are his "real" parents'? This question is partly anchored in our own cultural experience. For us it means 'Who are the physiological parents?' While this aspect of parenthood carries very different weight in different societies, I doubt that there is any society in which it is impossible to ask the question in a meaningful way. But 'real' parenthood may be linked to different combinations of parental roles in different societies. Very often it is defined in physiological terms. But in many societies the 'real' parents are seen as those through whom civil/kinship status is transmitted. And there are a few societies, like the Tununermuit Eskimo (Rousseau 1970) and at least some poor urban black communities in the United States (Stack 1974) in which 'real' parents are defined by the rearing relationship itself.[9] It would be analytically elegant to be able to say that in every society 'real' parents are defined as the adults through whom a new member of the society receives social identity, social placement. But the well-known cases of matrilineal systems highlight the fact that such a definition will exclude the physiological father in a significant number of societies, including those like the Ashanti and the Trobriands in which he is considered to have a special and important relationship to the child which we immediately recognize as characteristically paternal.

We are left in the position of having to recognize that there are 'kinds' of parenthood – physiological, jural, educational – which are differently weighted in different societies. This weighting is not arbitrary, but a response to a balance of cultural and institutional features in a given social system. In any particular society there are terms for male and female parent, and there are rules about how these terms should be used. These 'father' and 'mother' terms are very often used in a classificatory manner. Where this happens there is usually (perhaps always) a special way of addressing and referring to one's own parents. That is, it is felt to be important to be able to distinguish between one's 'real' and classificatory parents.[10] Pragmatically it is not difficult in actual practice to discover whom a person treats as his or her parents. The difficulty is an analytic one arising from attempts at comparison across societies, since different societies have grouped the parental roles in different ways.

Rather than selecting one of the constituent parental roles as the basis of 'real' parenthood, it seems preferable to retain a dual approach to the problem of a universally applicable definition of parenthood. On the one hand, we must take very seriously indeed the emic definition of parenthood in any given society. It provides critical information about the structure and values of the kinship system. At the same time we need to be able to compare the way parental roles are managed across societies. This can be done by mapping the distribution of parental roles. The notation proposed makes it possible to show how the five parental-role tasks are allocated in any particular system. The anchoring of the notation on P (Parents) is based on the physiological bonds of bearing and begetting. This reflects the empirical fact that this bond is everywhere given some form of recognition and is not subject to transfer or abolition. In most societies it is normal for a woman to nurture the children she bears. The correspondence between physiological paternity and the other parental roles is more variable, but, as Goodenough points out, the emic definition of fatherhood tends to link it to the husband of the physiological mother because of his pre-emptive sexual rights over her. However, by mapping the allocation of parental roles, the anchoring of Parents on physiological parenthood does not distort the analysis, since for any given society the model shows which of the other roles, if any, are also filled by the genitor or genitrix. It is also perfectly possible to produce an emic model of parenthood using the same notation, but anchoring the Parents on the particular constellation of parental roles significant in that society.

In most societies, most parental roles coincide for most children most of the time. This overlapping of the analytically separable parent roles constitutes an *overdetermination* of parenthood, such that the resulting multiplex role is culturally distinctive, though not always including exactly the same component elements. It is this clustering of parent roles which tends to attract distinctive 'father' and 'mother' terms, particularly when it includes physiological parenthood and the role which conveys civil/kinship-status identity.

The factoring of parenthood into the five roles associated with the tasks of social reproduction has been the result of my attempts to find an analytical framework within which a wide range of child-rearing institutions made sense.

18

However it is more than an analytical exercise. It suggests one kind of solution to the problem of a universally applicable definition of parenthood. And it also suggests certain substantive properties which differentiate the several parental roles. For it seems that for each of these there is a characteristic kind of relationship, and a particular type of reciprocity which binds the members of the role dyad: the bonds of bearing and begetting, status reciprocities, and the reciprocities of rearing.

In the final section of this chapter the focus is shifted from the identification of the tasks of parenthood which together provide for social replacement, to a consideration of some of the implications of the divisibility of parenthood. I want to look very briefly at a number of institutions which build on the allocation or delegation of parent roles to more than one set of parents. I use 'allocation' of parent roles to describe the culturally normative distribution of these roles in a particular society. The term 'delegation' implies that rights and roles originally vested in one set of parents are, by them, transferred to another set. This in turn implies a norm that assigns these roles initially to a single set of parents. The burden of my argument has been that there is no necessity for all the tasks of parenthood to be dealt with by the same parental figures. But I have also made the point that in fact, in any given society, parent roles tend to cluster, though exactly which tasks go together may vary. Nevertheless it would be wrong to suggest that genitor and genetrix 'normally' hold all the other roles and delegate them according to social or cultural arrangement. Thus while allocation refers to the culturally prescribed distribution of parent roles, delegation is used to describe the transfer of one or more roles to pro-parents when this is not culturally pre-empted, but occurs in culturally standardized ways. For example, a matrilineal society *allocates* the endowment of birth-status identity to the genetrix and her matrilineal kin; in Latin America and many Mediterranean societies ritual sponsorship is *allocated* to god-parents. On the other hand, in Gonja the genitor and genetrix are also mater and pater (conveyors of birth-status identity) and they normally also nurture, train and sponsor their children. At the same time there is a norm which specifies that one or more children of a union should be reared by other kin. In this case the genitor and genetrix, who are also pater and mater, agree to the transfer – i.e. they delegate – the rearing roles which they would otherwise fill themselves.

Allocation and delegation of parent roles

The most common situation is for all five of the parent roles to be played by the same persons. When this happens the bonds of bearing and begetting between genitor/genetrix and biological offspring are combined with the status reciprocities linking *pater* and *filius*, with the reciprocities of rearing which unite child with nurse, and, later, with his/her tutor, and finally, with the ongoing obligations of subordination and assistance required by the sponsor of his protégé.

19

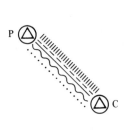

Where P ⃝ = parents*   ~~~ = birth-status identity

  C ⃝ = child*   - - - - = nurturance reciprocities

             · · · · · = training reciprocities

——————— = bonds of bearing / begetting |||||||||| = sponsorship reciprocities

* For some purposes it is necessary to differentiate between parents and/or children by sex.
Where this is not critical no distinction is made for the sake of clarity of presentation.

Figure 1-1. The complete set of parent-role tasks vested in one pair of parents: Analytical model

This is the 'ordinary' parent–child relationship, and it is very strongly cemented indeed (Figure 1.1).

It is probably the very overdetermination of the ordinary parent–child relationship which accounts for the widespread occurrence of pro-parental institutions. For one or more elements of the total set can be split off and used to create a supplementary parent–child tie without dissolving the remaining links between original parent and child. And indeed, in many of these institutions it is the continued existence of the links between original parent and child which give meaning to the reassignment of other parent roles. Which of the possible roles is transferred and which retained will determine the type of links between original parent and child, and between pro-parent and child. Together with other factors, such as their respective positions in the wider social system, the distribution of parent roles will also determine the relationship between original parent and pro-parent themselves.

The fundamental question here is 'Why should the allocation or delegation of a given parent role come to be institutionalized in a society?' This question underlies many of the studies which are presented in this book, and I do not wish to anticipate their conclusions here. In the accounts of ritual sponsorship and adrogation in the latter part of this chapter, and of Gonja fosterage in Chapter 2, these institutions are taken as 'given' in that they are culturally defined and enjoined in their respective societies. I am not here concerned with how this came about but rather with these as examples of how the allocation and delegation of parent roles can vary and how these variations work in practice. However it is clear that at some level the participants find role delegation advantageous. The model of the parent-role set can be used to describe the transactions which manifestly accompany the various sorts of institutionalized role delegation. This is relevant because these transactions can be shown to depend in part on the particular character of the reciprocities associated with the different parent roles. The notation of the Parent/Child/Pro-parent model is a convenient way of representing the allocation and delegation of parent roles in these examples. It is also useful later (Chapter 12) as a means of translating several functionally specific West African pro-parental institutions into the more general terms proposed in this framework. Transactional process is only one of the important levels of analysis, but because it recurs in the actors' descriptions of these institutions it is important to make it explicit.

Balancing transactions

The theory of transactions derives in part from games theory, and requires that either all parties to the transaction consider that the gains at least outweigh the costs, or (an often ignored alternative) that there be a power imbalance such that one party is forced against his will to accept a situation in which costs outweigh gains. Another possibility is that the calculus is based on different time scales for the various participants, such that one party is willing to accept a temporary deficit in hopes of a larger deferred reward. There is no need for all parties to base their accounting on the same 'currency'. One may 'pay' in labour and receive as recompense a wife, while another 'pays' with deference, for political advantage. And so on.

I have described thus far a model of parental roles which would allow consideration of allocation and delegation, and sharing of the rearing reciprocities and transfer of status entitlements, that is civil status. And it has been suggested that these roles represent rights and obligations involved in meeting a series of problems encountered in the bearing and rearing of children, in social replacement. While from the analyst's point of view these problems of social replacement can be seen as problems for the society, from the actors' point of view they are problems for those directly responsible for the child. If the pro-parent sees his function as helping the parents to meet their obligations, this must be a special case, due to some commitment to the parents' welfare, or that of the child, the most usual reason being common kinship. Normally, the pro-parent's motivation will be different from that of the parent, though complementary to it. Pro-parents may balance their efforts in nurturing, training or sponsoring a child against the rearing reciprocities which they create – for instance, against the obligation of the child to return care in their old age, or against the labour

21

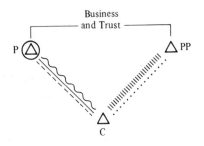

Business
and Trust

P △ △ PP

C △

Where P △ = parents

C △ = child

PP △ = pro-parent

────── = bonds of bearing / begetting

∿∿ = birth-status identity

─ ─ ─ = nurturance reciprocities

· · · · · = training reciprocities

ⅠⅠⅠⅠⅠⅠⅠⅠ = sponsorship reciprocities

Figure 1-2. Alliance–apprentice fosterage in Ibadan (A. Cohen 1969)

which the child contributes to the domestic unit, subsistence agriculture, petty-commodity production or trade, or against the political support of the child in adulthood, or of his parents in the present. Cohen has given us an elegant description of a training and sponsorship arrangement among the Hausa of Ibadan in which a long-distance trader may place his son as a foster-child with his Ibadan landlord, thereby ensuring his credit and securing future opportunities for the youth in the Ibadan trading world. For the landlord the foster-son provides a hard-working assistant who can be trusted (he has his way to make) and who, unlike his own sons, is not contesting his control over business resources (A. Cohen 1969). The point is that the model must reflect the transactions from the point of view of the parent, the child and the pro-parent.

In the example of the Hausa child placed with his father's Ibadan landlord, the distribution of parental roles would be as shown in Figure 1-2. Cohen describes the relationship between parent and pro-parent (the Ibadan landlord) as one of long-term business association and mutual trust. If the fostered son gets on well with the landlord and proves adept in the business, he may be married to a daughter of the landlord, converting a rearing relationship into one based on the more permanent tie of affinity, and ultimately of kinship through the grandchildren. The parent and pro-parent then become co-parents-in-law, thus giving formal recognition in kinship terms to the long-standing relationship between them.

A framework for the analysis of parent roles

Hausa fostering, of which the Ibadan example provides one type, is a relatively complex institution (see Chapter 5). Both training and sponsorship are sought from an unrelated business colleague in a position to assist both father and son. While in this form it is advantageous to each of those concerned, it is not culturally enjoined. Among the Gonja of northern Ghana it is expected that one or two children of each marriage will be sent to be reared by kin. Here the rearing task, and the reciprocities arising from it, are defined as the right and the responsibility of kin of both parents.

Fosterage

The verb 'to foster' is derived from the Old English root *fod*, for food. To foster is 'to nourish, feed, or support; to cherish; to bring up with parental care' (*Shorter Oxford Dictionary*); another early meaning of 'nourish' was 'to educate'. In the present context fosterage can be defined as the institutionalized delegation of the nurturance and/or educational elements of the parental role. Thus we would expect the ties which link foster-parent and foster-child to be essentially affective and moral in character, based as they are on the reciprocities of rearing.

For some purposes it is also convenient to distinguish between fostering which is initiated of necessity (crisis fostering), typically because the natal family of orientation is unable to fulfil these roles due to illness, death or divorce, and fostering entered into voluntarily. Such a distinction has nothing to do with which parental-role elements are delegated, but is only concerned with the basis on which the original decision to foster was made.[11]

A further distinction turns on the difference in nurturance requirements of infants and young children on the one hand and older children and adolescents on the other. In the first case rearing means providing food and care and early socialization in control of impulses and bodily functions. This can conveniently be termed nurturant fosterage. The older child also requires food and shelter, but the primary task of foster-parents at this later period is training in adult role skills and the values of the society. Here the terms educational or apprentice fostering are appropriate, depending on the emphasis given to the institution in a given situation. The institution of the wet-nurse in medieval Europe is a type-instance of nurturant fosterage; while apprenticeship as commonly practised in the same period provides an illustration of educational fosterage which merges in many cases with sponsorship in the way I have defined it.

Equally important in defining fosterage is the designation of what it is not. As used here, fosterage does not affect the status identity of the child, nor the jural rights and obligations this entails. Fosterage concerns the *process* of rearing, not the jural definition of status or relationships.

23

The wet-nurse in Europe: fourteenth to eighteenth centuries

While references to wet-nurses occur in very early written sources such as the code of Hamurabi, it is impossible to tell from this type of source whether the use of a wet-nurse was common, or mainly in response to crises when the mother's death or illness prevented her from feeding her own infant. However recent studies of infancy in Italy in the fourteenth to sixteenth centuries (Ross 1974: 184ff.), England in the fifteenth and sixteenth centuries (Tucker 1974:243) and seventeenth century (Illick 1974:308ff), and France in the seventeenth and eighteenth centuries (Marvick 1974:263ff; Flandrin 1976:201–6, 216–17; Donzelot 1980:10ff., 28) describe the frequent employment of wet-nurses by healthy mothers. Their use was apparently very common among the upper classes and the urban elite in all three countries. At least in France it had spread to the urban working class by the middle of the seventeenth century.[12]

In Europe at this period the wet-nurse commonly took the child home with her, often into the country, where it stayed until around the age of two. Payment was usually by the month. Reasons for placing an infant with a wet-nurse were complex. It was believed that a nursing mother could not have sexual relations without endangering the infant; yet Flandrin shows clearly from the French material that the Church held that it was a wife's duty to 'pay her conjugal dues' to her husband (1976:206). Thus delegation of maternal nurturance

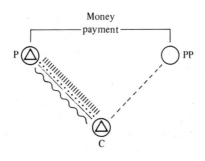

——— = bonds of bearing / begetting	· · · · · = training reciprocities	
∿∿ = birth-status identity	‖‖‖‖‖‖ = sponsorship reciprocities	
– – – = nurturance reciprocities		

Figure 1-3. Nurturant fosterage: European wet-nursing

24

was seen as 'necessary' if a woman was to fulfil her sexual duties as a wife. This choice also enabled a woman of quality – i.e. of noble birth or wealth – to avoid the tiring and demanding care of young children, thereby also preserving her figure and youthful looks. It is unlikely that these reasons weighed very heavily with the small shopkeepers and silk weavers of Lyon, nearly half of whom lived and worked in one room (M. Garden 1970:408, quoted in Flandrin 1976:95). A contemporary observer describes the misery of wives of working men who were forced to place their children with wet-nurses 'because they really must begin to feed themselves' (quoted in Flandrin 1976:205), either by serving in the family shop or as textile workers. Significantly, another contemporary French writer said of the attitudes of parents employing wet-nurses 'They regard themselves as justified on the grounds of example and custom' (Moheau, quoted in Flandrin 1976:204). Here a pattern of parental-role delegation has become customary among the elite in response to one set of pressures, and has been adopted as legitimate partly on their example by another segment of society impelled by a different set of constraints.[13]

Whatever the rationale, the use of wet-nurses was very common in Italy, England and France at this time. The children who survived infancy returned to their natal families, usually around the age of two, on the conclusion of this initial period of nurturant fosterage. Contemporary commentators, particularly doctors and midwives, discuss the importance of the wet-nurse's influence on the child, but characteristically this is seen as passing through her milk, whether it is a matter of physical health or of character and temperament. The relationship is defined as highly functionally specific. On the other hand there are also accounts of the affection felt by nurses for their foster-children, and by adults for the woman who nursed them in infancy. The rearing relationship, even in infancy, creates affective ties in both nurse and infant.[14]

In the context of the divisibility of parent roles it is striking to see that none of these studies describes the integration of the returned two-year-old as a problem. While such difficulties may well have occurred, but not been recorded for the twentieth-century analyst, it would appear that this was not *seen as a problem* at the time.[15]

Kinship fosterage in Gonja

The fostering of children by kin is very common in Gonja, and this institution is described in detail in Chapter 2. For purposes of comparison with other forms of parental-role distribution the model is presented here (Figure 1-4).

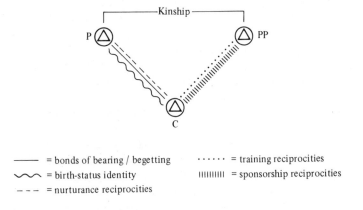

—— = bonds of bearing / begetting	······	= training reciprocities
⌇⌇⌇ = birth-status identity	|||||||||	= sponsorship reciprocities
− − − = nurturance reciprocities		

Figure 1-4. Kinship fosterage in Gonja

Ritual sponsorship

The historical development of ritual co-parenthood (*compadrazgo*) has been well documented by Mintz and Wolf (1950) who also consider the various functions of this institution in Europe and Latin America. They see co-parenthood as the creation (by ritual and legal fictions) of obligations similar to those imposed by parenthood. Essentially these involve the conversion of non-kin relationships into quasi-kin ties complete with constraints on marriage and sexual relations, the prohibition of quarrels and the obligation to provide economic assistance. The selection of ritual co-parents from among existing kin serves to impose specific obligations where previously diffuse ones obtained. Mintz and Wolf point out that co-parenthood can be based on lateral ties within a single social stratum in such a way that cohesion within the group is reinforced. But it can also be used to create a lien on a member of an adjacent stratum. The latter form allows the development of links between otherwise independent elements – farmer and shopkeeper, field-hand and foreman. Here an element of status imbalance is involved, deference being traded for social and economic advantage.

26

A framework for the analysis of parent roles

A second characteristic of ritual co-parenthood is that the effective ties are between parent and co-parent, with their common child a relatively passive member of the triad. This illustrates well the manipulative aspect of the institution. Ostensibly its purpose is to ensure the ritual well-being of a child. Yet it has repeatedly been elaborated in such a way that the child is the least important person involved. What element of the parental-role complex is being used here? Clearly there is no alteration of the identity status of the child, and the central status reciprocities are not affected. Similarly, unless the parents cease to be able to care for the child, neither the nurse nor the tutor element is delegated. The child remains with the biological/social parents who raise it, and with whom the affective and moral obligations of the rearing reciprocities are generated. There remains the role of sponsor. The special characteristic of this role is its mediation between the child and the external system. Originally meant to mediate between the child and the supernatural, there appears to be a recurrent tendency for the link between ritual co-parent, the child, and its own parents to be extended into other spheres. Economic cooperation is common between co-parents, and so also are claims to respect, importance and assistance. Here the prominence of the co-parents and the passivity of the child become more understandable, for children cannot operate effectively in the external system, although others can and do so, on their behalf.

Like fosterage, co-parenthood seems designed for working in the gaps between the formal elements of the system. Neither institution affects jurally defined status identity, yet both make use of elements of the parental role to create reciprocities which form the basis of links between individuals and groups.

Ritual sponsorship in the Balkans: komstvo

A recent analysis of ritual sponsorship in the Balkans (*komstvo*) by Hammel (1968) provides an illustration of how the links based on sponsorship can be institutionalized to form continuing links between families. As Hammel describes it, *komstvo* has significance in determining the relative status of local kin groups, in that a sponsor is sought from an equal or higher status group, never one of lower position. Further, the 'giving' of *komstvo*, that is, the offering of the sponsorship role, conveys prestige; at each occasion on which the sponsor is present, he is greatly deferred to and given precedence in ceremonies (especially in southern and eastern Serbia). Hammel is further able to show that *komstvo* links tend to be repeated in successive generations and are seen as affecting relations between kin groups in the same sort of way as ties of marriage and of descent. However, in *komstvo*, as with the *compadrazgo* complex, sponsorship, and indeed only *ritual* sponsorship, is the single parental-role element to be

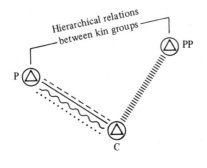

———— = bonds of bearing / begetting   ······ = training reciprocities

∿∿∿ = birth-status identity ||||||||| = sponsorship reciprocities

– – – – = nurturance reciprocities

Figure 1-5. Ritual sponsorship in the Balkans (Hammel 1968)

transferred to the pro-parent; only by means of this link are joint interests created and maintained between the two sets of parents. And even more clearly than with *compadrazgo, komstvo* relations are extra-domestic, affecting as they do the relative statuses of local kin groups (Figure 1-5).

Adrogation

The final parental-role element to be discussed is the provision of status identity. In order to avoid confusion, I suggest that the Roman term *adrogation* be used where the main purpose of delegating parenthood is the substitution of a new status identity in place of that which was acquired at birth. An extreme, and a very clear, example of this sort of delegation of the status-bestowing aspect of parenthood occurs in the 'adoptions by will' which were accepted practice among the Roman nobility. It was in this way that Augustus became the 'son' of Julius Caesar. Technically this may have been considered as 'inheritance on condition of taking the testator's name' (Crook 1967:112). But in any case it illustrates how status identity can be altered without affecting the other elements of the role set.

Roman 'adoption' and alliances based on adrogation

'Adoption' in Republican and Imperial Rome was basically a legal and ritual transaction by which a person passed from one *potestas* (legal authority) to another. 'It had nothing to do with the welfare of children' says Crook, but was

28

'the characteristic remedy for a family in danger of dying out' and 'those adopted were often adults' (1967:111). Elsewhere it has been argued that 'mainly the institution [adoption] was one whereby the great families provided themselves with heirs to their property and worship, successors to office or a political following' (J. Goody 1969:60).

The evidence for 'adoption' in ancient Rome concerns the nobility almost exclusively. They had not only vast fortunes to transmit, but also the splendid reputations of their ancestors, whose wax effigies were celebrated at each new funeral and to whose descendants the consulship was effectively restricted. Under such circumstances it is hardly surprising that there were fathers willing to lose their sons in adoption. That it was a loss is indicated by the fact that the son ceased to be a legal member of his natal family and, should the other members all die, the 'adopted' son could not return to save it from extinction.

Yet there were advantages. In a study of party politics at the end of the Republic, Taylor writes: 'To unite families, adoptions were as important as intermarriages . . . By such adoptions the two (noble) houses were brought closely together, and the man adopted was thought to belong to both families. Thus the younger Scipio Africanus, son of Aemilius Paullus . . . speaks of *both* his fathers, and is proud of the family tradition of both his houses (1966:34).

There is an apparent contradiction in these accounts, for on the one hand both Taylor and Crook speak of the fact that the 'adopted' son must renounce any legal or religious link with his natal family, and yet both refer to the use of 'adoption' to create an alliance between two noble houses. The key to the problem lies in the fact that, as both writers again note, 'adoption' often concerned adult men rather than children. In terms of the distinctions we have been using, the reciprocities of rearing, and of course the bond of begetting, are already firmly forged between the son and his natal kin. There remains the transfer of status identity so explicitly arranged by the Romans, and in some cases the sponsorship of the young adult.[16] The bonds of parenthood are again split between two families, in this case in line with the distinction we have made between jural and moral reciprocities. Significantly, the adopting father did not seek an infant or young child with whom he might expect to fill a complete set of paternal roles. Instead he often appears to have preferred a son for whom, since he was already adult, the nurturant and educational aspects of parenthood were closed. Such a son combines in his person loyalties to two great families; his adoption secures the basis for a lasting alliance as well as an heir to name, traditions and estate.

The characteristic feature of Roman 'adoption', then, is the concern to substitute one legal status for another. 'Adoption' of a jurally independent person, one whose father and father's father were dead, was referred to as *adrogation*. For adrogation meant the disappearance of the separate identity of the adrogee and his descendants, and each instance apparently required a special law (Taylor 1966:88, 91). There was not a direct correspondence between adrogation and the

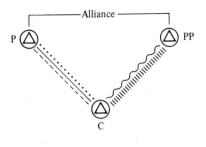

——— = bonds of bearing / begetting   ······ = training reciprocities

∼∼∼ = birth-status identity ||||||||| = sponsorship reciprocities

– – – = nurturance reciprocities

Figure 1-6. Adrogation in Imperial Rome

physical adulthood of the new son in ancient Rome, since children might be orphaned. However the term does correctly emphasize the substitution of status identity independently of the reassignment of other parental roles. In addition, in Roman usage, it was commonly adults who were 'adopted', and their persisting ties of affection and duty towards their natal kin were utilized to forge alliances central to political life, while their recruitment to the adopting family insured the legal continuity of its reputation and estate.

Because of this quite explicit splitting of parental roles between natal and 'adoptive' family, adoption as here defined is an inappropriate term for the Roman transfer of civil status in adulthood. This becomes clearer if we consider the nature of 'true' adoption.

Adoption

Adrogation is seldom institutionalized, as the special conditions which render it advantageous are relatively rare. It is far more often the case that where an heir to office, property or shrine is needed, those concerned hope also to find a child whom they may rear and train, and who will love and respect them as well as observe the legal formalities of status reciprocities. While the bond of begetting is not transferable, we have seen that the remaining parental tasks may be filled by others besides the biological parents. I suggest it is where the complete set of available parental-role elements is transferred from natal to pro-parents, that the term adoption is best employed. This has the advantage of consistency with popular usage. But more than that, it allows us to distinguish institutions which depend for their effectiveness on the *sharing* of parental-role elements, from the case where 'total parenthood' is renounced by one couple and assumed by another, i.e. adoption.

The adoption of a young girl as a future bride for a son in the Taiwanese institution of *sumpoa* provides a fascinating example of what I would see as true adoption (Wolf and Huang 1980). The girl, often from the age of 2 or 3, is reared by the pro-parents, takes their name, and observes formal mourning as for true parents. If, for whatever reason, she does not eventually marry a son of the pro-parents, they arrange her marriage as they would for a daughter born to them. In other words, the pro-parents take over the remaining tasks of nurturance, training and sponsorship as well as becoming the locus of civil and ritual status identity.

The incidence of adopted daughter-in-law marriage found in the Taiwan study was high, ranging from 44 per cent to 25 per cent, for the women born between 1891 and 1920 (Wolf and Huang 1980:125). As such it must be seen, not simply as a cultural option, but also as a response to significant structural constraints. What were these? Two factors stand out. The high rate of adopted daughter-in-law marriage may initially have been a response to the imbalanced sex ratio of the pioneer period of settlement from the Chinese mainland when it was difficult to find a girl to marry. Although the sex ratio has since evened out, poverty is widespread, and makes it a worrying expense to rear daughters only to then marry them off. At the same time, parents of a boy face the difficult problem of raising the necessary money for marriage expenses for their son. The adoption of a daughter/daughter-in-law resolves the problem for both sets of parents. For while a girl cannot marry her own brother, she may marry an adoptive brother. Thus the adoption of a daughter-in-law relieves her parents of the expense of rearing a daughter, and at the same time allows her adoptive parents to avoid the expense of bringing in a bride from outside the family.

The second constraint to which this institution is a response is the friction between mother-in-law and daughter-in-law. Quarrels between the two women are frequent and serious in this patrilineal, virilocal society. The new wife is subject to close daily control by her mother-in-law and finds that, if there is a dispute between them, her husband invariably takes his mother's side. The mother-in-law fears that her son's wife will alienate his affections for her, and even threaten the filial piety he owes her by persuading him to establish a separate household elsewhere. The interests of the two women are clearly opposed. However where the bride was adopted as a child, and reared by her future mother-in-law, their relationship is very different. It is based on affective bonds built up through nurturance and dependency, and later the adopted daughter's training in and growing contribution to the domestic economy. Wolf

31

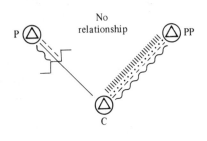

= bonds of bearing / begetting   ······ = training reciprocities
〜〜 = birth-status identity ||||||||| = sponsorship reciprocities
– – – = nurturance reciprocities   ∧∧ = break in relationship

Figure 1-7. Adoption

and Huang report that there is much less friction between a son's wife and her mother-in-law when the wife was raised as a daughter. Indeed, the wife may receive from her adoptive mother/mother-in-law support and companionship that Chinese women often fail to get from their husbands.

In the institution of *sumpoa*, the reciprocities of rearing have been manipulated so as to provide a counter-balance to the tensions built into the mother-in-law/daughter-in-law relationship by a strongly patrilineal, virilocal system. The transfer of the jural identity of the future bride to the family of the future husband, by her adoption in her childhood, replaces the transfer of potestas over her at marriage which, altering as it does an established adult identity, must be elaborate, public and expensive.

Of course 'total parenthood' is not transferable. For the fact of physiological parenthood is not open to social manipulation. But the desire for a total transfer can be inferred with respect to adoption in Western society from the efforts made to keep the identity of real parents secret. Writing about contemporary America, Carroll remarks on the concern with secrecy lest the natural parents try to reclaim their child from its adoptive parents (1970:4). But he goes on to speak of the lengthy jural processes which, once completed, render such an attempt illegal. The adoptive parents appear to fear that the bonds of bearing and begetting may prove stronger than both the moral and affective ties arising out of child-rearing on the one hand and the legal claims of status reciprocities

32

on the other. Thus adoption, as it is practised in our society, provides no basis for the sharing of parental-role elements, just because adoptive parents are seeking to fill all these roles themselves. They want a whole child, not part of one.

Adoption among the Tununermuit Eskimo provides another instance of an institutionalized preference for the total transfer of parental roles. Despite the difficulties of rearing an infant apart from its mother, adoptions were ideally arranged during the pregnancy and completed shortly after the child's birth. When, as sometimes happened, an older child was orphaned, even close relatives were reluctant to adopt it (Rousseau 1970:5, 40). As with Western parents, the Eskimo make every effort to secure rights to the adopted child in infancy, thus preventing the development of affective ties between natural parents and their child which might later weaken the attachment to the adoptive parents.

It is not always necessary to avoid or break off relations between own and adoptive parents. When a brother's child is adopted in order to continue the direct line of descent, as in China and India, the links between the brothers remain in force, as do any affective bonds already forged between the adopted son and his own parents. However, where in China a man assigns a son to continue the line of a dead brother, it is clearly adrogation of civil status only which is taking place (Wolf and Huang 1980).

The care of orphans and destitute children

The definition of who is obligated to care for whom is a function of both legal and moral norms, and these in turn are based on rights in property and in persons. But, inevitably, the definition of what should be done to care for deprived children is related to the existing modes of delegating parental roles. Thus, in Gonja, where fostering by kin is voluntarily arranged, fostering is also used as a way of caring for children if their natal family of orientation disperses. Kin who have a *right* to claim a child in purposive fosterage, have a *duty* to accept the role of foster-parent in a crisis. But in both cases it is the roles of nurse, tutor and often sponsor which are assumed. Since these roles are separated from that of pater/genitor in voluntary fostering, there is no reason to redefine the child's jural identity when fostering is necessitated by family crisis. In Gonja, rearing children has no effect on *who* they are.

A similar situation typically obtains where one finds institutionalized co-parenthood. The privilege of being a ritual sponsor carries with it the obligation to provide assistance in crisis if this becomes necessary. Ordinarily the co-parent is concerned only with partial sponsorship, and not with either jural status or rearing. Should the protégé be orphaned the sponsor may take over his care and full sponsorship obligations if kin are not available to fill these roles. But the main function of the sponsor in crisis is to be an interested party, to see that suitable arrangements are made, and to ratify these as being appropriate. Again there need be no question of redefining the jural identity of the orphan,

33

although this may be done for other reasons: for example, if the role of pater is vacant and the sponsor would like to fill it.

Where jural status only is altered, adrogation does not serve to provide for the care and training of an orphaned child. Selection of an orphaned adult for adrogation does, however, mean that there will be no persisting affective ties to parents to act as the basis for claims on the adrogated son.

We have defined adoption as the transfer of all available parental roles. As such it is clearly an effective way of providing for the various needs of destitute children. But there is a special sense in which adoption is appropriate in such cases. For, by definition, where the parents are dead or have actively rejected the child, they present less of a threat to the adoptive parents' monopolization of parental roles. Adoption brings together those who need parents and those who need children. But, more than this, adoption of orphans and illegitimate children brings together those who lack someone to fill key parental roles, and those who wish to pre-empt these roles completely. Potential conflict between natural and adoptive parent is thus eliminated or minimized. Such a rigid separation of natural and adoptive parents is the antithesis of the pattern found in the institutions of kinship fosterage, ritual sponsorship and adrogation, which depend upon the continuity of prior bonds to create a link between parents and pro-parents.

Because in our own society parental roles are largely concentrated and are regarded as most appropriately filled by the biological parents within the nuclear family, we tend to see this constellation as both right and necessary. Yet these roles are potentially available for sharing not only among kin but even with unrelated neighbours, with friends or with the state. Sharing is one way of spreading the task of caring for deprived children. But it is also an effective way of forging links between adults – parent and pro-parent – and between generations – child and parent, child and pro-parent. Where sharing of parental roles is institutionalized, as in the giving of foster-children and in ritual sponsorship, such links are systematically created. To understand these simply as ways of coping with crisis situations, or of arranging to cope with them should they occur, is to fail to recognize the way in which many societies make use of the unique strength of the bonds between parent and child.

PART I

Parent roles in Gonja

2

Kinship fostering

Among my first Gonja field notes is a reference to '*kabita*, a girl given to someone'; '*kayeribi*, a boy given to someone'. It is indicative of the centrality of
fostering in Gonja that this should have penetrated the confusing impressions of
those first few days. For indeed, many of the children in Gbuipe were not living
with their own parents but with relatives. After a few months this seemed
entirely normal to me, but at first it must have struck me as strange – a true
ethnographic fact. I had not encountered descriptions of such an institution in
reading about West African societies, though with hindsight I can see that there
were clues. There are now accounts of analogous practices for the Bariba, the
Mossi, the Songhoi, the Hausa and the Dagomba.[1] My own material on the Gonja
of northern Ghana illustrates how the delegation of training and sponsorship
works in one society. The first part of this chapter is devoted to a description of
kinship fostering in Gonja. In the later sections I shall turn to a consideration of
some indices of the effects of fostering on the adjustment of adults. In Europe
and America such practices are often felt to be harmful to children. Here I want
to consider what the consequences of growing up with foster-parents are in a
society in which this is considered perfectly normal, and to look at it from the
standpoint of both the senior and the junior generation.

The institution of kinship fostering[2]

The Gonja form a weakly centralized state to the north of the Ashanti. The ruling
group claims descent from Mande conquerors who invaded the country from the
south-west probably during the sixteenth century. With the Mande horsemen
came a group of Muslims whose descendants still live in the divisional capitals as
advisors and traders. The third element making up the Gonja polity consists of
the various commoner groups, speaking a number of Gur and Kwa dialects.
Rulers, Muslims, and commoners alike are farmers – the freeing of the slaves,
the end of war and the reorientation of trade have removed the major sources of
economic differentiation between them. Estate membership is through paternal
filiation, though some offices go to sisters' sons. Marriage between all three

37

groups is constant and assumed as normal; this is perhaps encouraged by the absence of unilineal descent groups in all three estates.

The traditional marriage payment is 12 shillings and 12 kola nuts. This amount is distributed among the kin of the girl as a 'witness' (*anyishi*, lit. the eyes) that the marriage has taken place. There are additional gifts and observances which vary in different parts of Gonja (E. Goody 1973). Money gifts are now sometimes made to the girl's parents, particularly in the eastern parts. However, traditionally the Gonja avoided accepting money in arranging marriages because people felt this was too much like buying a slave. 'A wife should be a free woman in her husband's house', I was told. Marriage gifts are in practice non-returnable.

Associated with this absence of the transfer of wealth to the girl's family is the absence of the transfer of rights in a woman's children to the husband. Paternity is reckoned strictly biologically, and adulterine children are not subject to the social paternity of their mother's husband. A man is the father of those children he begets whether with his wife or outside of marriage. That is, rights *in genetricem* are vested in the biological parents and their kin.

As rights *in genetricem* are not alienated by the girl's family at her marriage, they are in a sense retained, and her siblings and parents claim rights in her children. But the extension of rights over children is not limited to the mother's kin. The father also has rights in his children and these are shared with his siblings and his parents. This claiming of rights in children is expressed in the institution of kinship fostering that is prevalent thoughout Gonja, taking somewhat different forms in different parts of the country. The institutionalized pattern is for a daughter of the marriage to go to a father's sister and a son to the mother's brother.

A man who wishes later to claim a particular boy as a foster-child can insist on paying the barber who shaves off the 'ghost hair' on the seventh day when the baby is named. It is the mother's brothers who have the right to do this (if they do not, it is the father's father or elder brothers who automatically assume the responsibility). The boy remains with his parents until the age of five to eight, when his foster-parent (*nyinipe*) comes to claim him. From then on, except for visits, he lives in his foster-home until he is old enough to marry, when his foster-parent should in theory offer him the choice of a horse, a wife, or a gun. After this he is free to return to his father's house. That men do return to their father's house is insisted upon in discussion. But in fact the regularity with which this occurs varies in different parts of Gonja together with other aspects of the social structure.

Although descriptions of male fostering usually refer to the foster-parent as the mother's brother, in the ruling estate it is held to be a good thing for 'brothers' to bring up one another's sons, so that father's brothers are often found as foster-parents.

The father's sister has certain duties towards her brother's wife, both in the sequence of rites which establish the marriage, and when children are born. Her right to claim a daughter as a foster-child is seen as directly related to this involvement in the affairs of the couple. And as she is often the one to bathe the new-born infants in the medicine which ensures their health and sturdy growth, she is in an excellent position to ask this favour. Alternatively, if she is living at a distance, the father may send her a message telling her of the birth of a daughter and announcing that when she is older, the girl will come and serve her. Thereafter the future foster-parent (*tchepe*) should send the first string of waist beads which mark the transition of the naked infant to the status of little girl, and she will also bring small presents when she comes to visit.

In eastern Gonja there is another formal claim made by a woman on the third child of her married daughter. If a woman bears two children, then the husband is expected to agree to send the next girl as *kinyipo pibi* (child of the breast) to his wife's mother as a foster-child. As she grows, she will assume the domestic tasks in which the daughter used to help her mother; moreover she is expected to make a marriage in the same village where her foster-mother lives, thus remaining nearby to look after her in her old age. Her husband will also have special responsibilities towards his wife's foster-mother in supplying food and shelter; according to the formal expectation, he will be a kinsman.

Incidence of fostering

But formal norms are only a part of the picture. We need also to ask how often people actually send children to be fostered, and whether fostering takes the form it is said to.

Although it varies in form and incidence in different parts of the country, fostering is a common practice in Gonja. If we take the percentage of children currently reared as foster-children, the figure for central Gonja is 18 per cent, with an even balance between boys and girls; for eastern Gonja it is 26 per cent, with a preponderance of girls. It is useful to compare these figures with Fortes' findings for a Tallensi sample of 170 children: only 2 per cent were living with neither parent; all of these were orphans (Fortes, 1949b:136).

A figure that represents the proportion of all children currently fostered inevitably excludes infants and young children who will later be fostered. If we take instead the percentage of adults who were fostered in childhood, the figure is considerably higher. In a sample of 72 adults from northern Gonja, 53 per cent of the men and 64 per cent of the women had been fostered as children. Of a western Gonja sample of 166 adults, 53 per cent of the men and 56 per cent of the women had been fostered. With the exception of eastern Gonja, where the incidence of male fostering is much lower, all the adult samples in Table 2-1 show over 50 per cent of both men and women as having been fostered for part of their childhood.

Another measure adopted for its usefulness in making comparisons between societies is based on the full sibling group. In the western Gonja sample, four

Parent roles in Gonja

Table 2-1. *Rearing experience of adults in six Gonja samples*[3]

	Rearing experience					
	Fostered		Reared by parents		Total	
	No.	%	No.	%	No.	%
Northern Gonja						
Men	16	(53)	14	(47)	30	(100)
Women	27	(64)	15	(36)	42	(100)
Western Gonja						
Men	41	(53)	36	(47)	77	(100)
Women	50	(56)	39	(44)	89	(100)
Central Gonja						
Men	15	(52)	14	(48)	29	(100)
Eastern Gonja						
Men	6	(15)	33	(85)	39	(100)

Note: The absence of adult women's samples from central and eastern Gonja is unfortunate. However, female fostering is certainly no less prevalent than male fostering in either of these areas. My impression is that girls are fostered slightly more often than boys in Busunu (central Gonja). In eastern Gonja (Kpembe) girls are fostered very much more often than boys.

sibling groups in five had at least one member fostered in childhood. I would suggest that the significance of fostering for socialization lies in part in the position of the socializing agents – parent figures and peers – in the social system. That is, if the adolescent gains his view of himself in relation to the society through his participation in primary groups, and his primary groups differ from those of his siblings, though overlapping with theirs, then for both fostered and home-reared siblings experience is widened. The fostered child is at home in two domestic families, and his siblings become familiar through reciprocal visiting with members of the fostering family as well.

To put this in another way, the sibling group is, under these conditions, an open group. Where first and second cousins, indeed all kin of one's own generation, are called either 'older sibling' (*nda*) or 'younger sibling' (*nsupo*), it is a matter of some members of the full-sibling group living with one set of brothers and sisters while another, perhaps more than one, lives with a different set. And in western Gonja four-fifths of the sibling groups are split up in this fashion.

Fostering always means a change of residence. The fostered child sleeps in the

40

room of the foster-parent (girls) or with the youths of the foster-parent's household (boys). Meals are provided by the foster-parent and eaten with other children of that compound. It is in the domestic and subsistence economy of the foster-home that the child participates increasingly as he matures. If he is still living in the same village as his own parents, he will see them regularly and may spend some of his leisure with the play group of his early childhood. However, fostering frequently means moving to a new village as well as to a different household. In these cases the break with the natal family of orientation is more radical and the dispersal of the sibling group is emphasized by the intervening distance. The proportion of cases in which fostering involves a move to a different village varies from one part of the country to another. In central Gonja, where the population density is low and villages are scattered, residence in a different village from the parents is very common. In an eastern Gonja sample of 79 currently fostered children, 49 (62 per cent) were living in a different village from both parents.

But does fostering actually take the form it is said to? This is really two different questions. First, do foster-children go to father's sisters, mother's brothers, and mother's mother – the traditional foster-parents? Second, are they sent in the circumstances specified by the formal norm? The brief answer to the first question is that in fact foster-children go to a wider range of kin than is formally specified. In the Buipe sample of currently fostered children (central Gonja), the father's sister and the mother's mother were the most common foster-parents for girls, in that order. But together they accounted for less than two-thirds of all cases. The single most common category of boys' foster-parents was father's maternal siblings and matrilateral cousins, followed by mother's brother and mother's father. In all, 19 out of 34, or 56 per cent, went to a real or classificatory sibling of the parents, while the remainder went to a real or classificatory parent's parent. These same 34 foster-children were evenly divided between maternal and paternal kin (16, or 47 per cent, were with maternal kin, and 18, or 53 per cent, with paternal kin). This is confirmed in the (very small) figures for the second central Gonja sample. The proportions for western Gonja show a bias in favour of maternal kin. Girls in the northern Gonja sample went about equally to maternal and paternal kin, but there is a bias in favour of paternal kin as foster-parents for boys in this group. There were no cases of boys fostered by maternal kin in the eastern Gonja sample (Table 2-2). These variations are all consistent with differing emphases on maternal and paternal lines in each area, which it is not possible to examine here. However, overall it is clear that, with the exception of the fostering of boys in eastern Gonja, children of both sexes are sent to maternal and paternal kin. That is, successful claims are made by kin of both spouses on the children of a marriage. They are, however, made more often than the norm suggests by the grand-parental generation.

Table 2-2. *Distribution of foster-children between maternal and paternal kin in seven Gonja samples*

| | Foster-children sent to: | | | | | | | | |
| | Maternal kin | | Paternal kin | | Others[a] | | Not known | | Total | |
	No.	%	No.	%	No.	%	No.	%	No.	%
Northern Gonja										
Boys	6	(38)	9	(56)	1	(6)			16	(100)
Girls	13	(48)	14	(52)					27	(100)
Western Gonja										
Boys	18	(44)	9	(22)	8	(20)	6	(15)	41	(101)
Girls	28	(56)	19	(38)	3	(6)			50	(100)
Central Gonja										
Busunu boys	4	(25)	5	(31)	5	(31)	2	(13)	16	(100)
Buipe girls and boys	16	(47)	18	(53)					34	(100)
Eastern Gonja										
Boys	none		5	(83)	1	(17)			6	(100)

[a] 'Others' include those reared by own full siblings, by parent's master or mistress (i.e. children of ex-slaves), by a chief, or by a Koranic teacher.

Voluntary and crisis fostering

The second question to be raised about the fit between the formal picture of fostering and the actual practice concerns the circumstances in which children are sent to foster-parents. According to the actors' model, foster-parents ask for a particular child at birth and then, when he is old enough to 'have sense', come and collect him from the parents. However, if fostered children are compared with other children, a disproportionate number of them are found to be from homes where the parents' marriage has been broken by death or divorce. In the Buipe sample, 40 per cent of all children and adolescents are from broken homes, but, of the foster-children, the figure reaches 74 per cent (25). Here two modifying factors should be mentioned. In the first place, some of these children were sent to be fostered before their parents' marriage ended; I know this to be so for some, but lack information on others. Second, only in two of these 25 cases were both parents dead. In the remaining 23, the child could have lived with the surviving parent rather than with a foster-parent.

It seems that the institution of fostering provides a charter which can be employed in placing children at the time of the dispersal of the original family of

Table 2-3. *Crisis and voluntary fostering among men and women of northern and western Gonja*

	Form of fostering:							
	Crisis		Voluntary		Not known		Total	
	No.	%	No.	%	No.	%	No.	%
Northern Gonja								
Boys	12	(75)	4	(25)			16	(100)
Girls	18	(67)	9	(33)			27	(100)
Western Gonja								
Boys[a]	16	(43)	21	(57)			37	(100)
Girls	26	(52)	23	(46)	1	(2)	50	(100)

[a] These data are taken from a different sample from that used in Tables 2-1 and 2-2 (in which there was insufficient information to distinguish between crisis and voluntary fostering).

orientation. While each parent may keep one or two children on divorce, and some children may stay with the surviving parent following a death, the dissolution of the conjugal family tends to bring about the placing of some or even all of the children with foster-parents. It should be emphasized that this is a culturally patterned alternative, not a necessity, except in those few instances where both parents are dead. Where fostering follows the dissolution of the conjugal family, I use the term 'crisis' fostering to distinguish it from 'voluntary' or 'purposive' fostering, which is initiated while the parents' marriage is intact. In the western Gonja sample reported in Table 2-3, 43 per cent of the cases of male fostering and 52 per cent of the cases of female fostering were associated with the disruption of the parents' marriage by either death or divorce. For the northern Gonja sample, the proportions were even higher – 75 per cent and 67 per cent, respectively

Specific functions of fostering

The care of children in crises is an example of a functionally specific use of fostering. There are a number of other specific functions of this institution as well as the more diffuse, but equally important, functions that concern the maintenance of links between kin. Specific functions can be discerned at several levels: with respect to the moral and technical education of the child concerned; with respect to the foster-parents; and with respect to the parents themselves.

Although there is a certain amount of variation, it is generally held that children should not be sent for fostering until they 'have sense' – between the ages of five and seven. The period of the next ten years or more during which they live with foster-parents is one of training in the skills specific to each sex as adults – cooking and other domestic tasks for girls, and farming for boys. It is the foster-parents' task to provide precept and model for these skills, and they are felt to be in a better position to do so than a child's own parents because they will not hesitate to use disciplinary measures when necessary, as would a parent. Conversely, it is held that the child fears and respects a foster-parent where he might take advantage of the affection and lenience of his own parent. In other words, parents are not expected to be good teachers for their own children, and fostering is seen as one way of making sure that child gets a good education. The foster-parent is held responsible for the moral as well as the technical education of the child, and difficult and proud children may find themselves sent to foster-parents who should be able to teach them respect (*jirma*) and perhaps strengthen a wayward character (*da*).

Functions of fostering for the foster-parent are varied. There is no doubt of the value of a girl to the domestic economy from an early age: fetching water, washing dishes and clothes, minding children, sweeping the compound, running errands, selling bits of condiment and produce around the town, and eventually cooking and gathering firewood – all these women's tasks are readily shared and even taken over by the older girls. Boys are useful at a later age, although they can run errands and scare birds from ripening grain when still young. However, in discussing these 'economic' functions of fostering one needs to remember that the children would have been equally useful at home. There are cases in which an only child is sent to a foster-parent who has children of her own; and there are boys who do nothing whatever on the farm of the foster-parent. This is not the place for a detailed analysis of the Gonja economy: in the 1950s and 1960s it was a relatively simple one based on hoe agriculture, with ample land, owing to a willingness to farm several miles from the permanent villages. There was little ownership of resources other than a few cattle. There is no evidence that economic necessity is a decisive factor in the allocation of foster-children. If the labour of youths was at a premium, one would expect to see stepfathers making more effort to retain their wives' sons to farm with them. This is very rare.

Where old women are concerned, the companionship of a foster-child is reckoned as particularly valuable, and this is also true for childless women. However, the sending of children to barren women is not stressed by the Gonja – it certainly happens, but for them its importance is overshadowed by the other features of the institution.

The specific functions of fostering so far as the true parents are concerned are most evident in crisis fostering. It is assumed that a co-wife will not take the trouble to look after another woman's child, and, following the death of the mother or the parents' divorce, the safest place for young children is with a kinswoman. A woman does not like to enter a new marriage with several children, although she may take a daughter and any infants with her. There is a special

44

term, *angola*, for a boy living with his mother's husband and the relationship is compared to that between sexual rivals. They are enemies and each is expected to wish the other ill. So awkward is this situation that even young boys are said to run away to their father or a kinsman rather than live with a stepfather.

The advantages to the parents of voluntary fostering are less evident. Where there are many children, it is one way of reducing the number of mouths to feed. In this situation, too, there is danger of jealousy from childless women leading to attempts to injure the children through witchcraft and it is thought safer to disperse them. One youth I knew who had done very well in school lived with his classificatory mother's brothers in order to be safe from the supposed hostility of his father's wives whose own sons were less successful. The management of difficult children is often handed over to foster-parents much as an English child might be sent to a certain type of boarding school.

In view of the Mossi *pogsioure* (Skinner 1960), the Dagomba practice of sending the children of chiefs to court officials for training (Oppong 1973) and the Buganda custom of sending boys to court to serve as messengers and pages in the hope of later political advantages (Richards 1964), it should be noted that there does not seem to be any significant political function to Gonja fostering. There is no system of clientship in Gonja, and succession to political office is within the dynastic segment of one's father, so preferment can be only of an informal and limited nature. There is no important sense in which the child's family stands to gain by an alliance based on fostering.

There were a few cases in which a boy had been sent to cement the friendship of two chiefs, in much the same way that one might give the other a wife. This is done but not made much of by the people themselves – it is one special application of a general practice. Another similar application is the sending of a boy to live with his Koranic teacher. It is perhaps surprising how seldom this occurs, given the charter of fostering, but it does sometimes happen.

Nor is access to special skills gained by an apprenticeship based on the fostering relationship. In Gonja there are few such traditional skills: nowadays, iron-working, divining, weaving, and drumming just about exhaust the list. Of these the blacksmiths form patronymic groups, but not endogamous ones. They do exchange children in fostering, and in this way a sister's son may occasionally learn and practise the craft. But there is no systematic utilization of fostering for recruitment, and a man may train his own sons, his brother's, or sister's.

There is one kin group of diviners, the *ledzipo*, within which individuals are recognized as having special powers. However, selection within the group occurs by possession; it is held to be determined by the spirits, not by humans. Other forms of divination may be taken up because of possession by the spirit of a related dead diviner, in the course of treatment for illness, or by an adult seeking guidance from an expert.

The Kontunkuri drummer of the paramount, at Damongo, and the Mbonto-kurbi drummers attached to the divisional capitals of Kawsawgu and Mpaha, play items of traditional history (albeit in a form few can understand). The need to preserve these may have given rise to mechanisms to ensure sufficient players in each generation. I neglected to inquire into this point. However, in discussing the present situation with regard to the Kontunkuri, I was told that the only youth then learning was a brother's son of the drummer. As his interest was only lukewarm there were fears for the continuity of the drum history. The drummers who are found in all the divisions have a similar need to preserve traditional forms especially in respect of the Ntimpani drums (copied from Ashanti) which drum the titles and exploits of previous chiefs on Fridays and Mondays. Despite this, drummers insist that anyone who is so inclined may learn, and no special provision is made for continuity. There is some evidence that in the past Ntimpani drummers were slaves. Bintiri drummers, who led in war, might belong to either ruling or commoner estate, and were recruited on the basis of personal inclination.

Only in the town of Daboya is there weaving and dyeing of cloth for sale (rather than occasionally on commission). The Daboya weavers numbered more than 70 in 1974, and were organized in a number of sections which they referred to as 'companies'. All sons were expected to weave at least until they were old enough to marry, when some used their new independence to take up different work. But the weavers preferred not to teach their own sons, sending them instead to a close kinsman for training, even though this meant that the teacher rather than the father benefited from the youth's labour for several years. Although the weavers explicitly favoured marriages to close kin, in practice while their daughters married weavers, the sons married much more widely (there was a higher rate of polygyny among the weavers than in other commoner sections). Occasionally a man taught a relative's son from outside the section. Unless the apprentice came from another town, no change of residence was involved.

The purpose of detailing the specific functions of fostering to the main actors concerned has been to make clear what fostering does not do, as well as what it does. Those functions that are most evident, and most emphasized, in Gonja are such as must be involved wherever fostering occurs – training, service, and companionship. There does not appear to be any single institutional feature which is closely related to the sending of foster-children: economic and political advantages are limited, and certainly not stressed. What does seem to be the most outstanding feature of kin fostering in Gonja is its pervasive, widespread character. Except in eastern Gonja, something like 50 per cent of all adults in each sample had been fostered in childhood, and household censuses show no disproportionate concentrations of foster-children, apart from the households of important chiefs, which have larger numbers of attached residents of all sorts.

One final descriptive point might be made. While fostering of classificatory siblings' children does occur, and occasionally of classificatory grandchildren, what does not happen, or happens so rarely as to be inconsequential, is the sending of a child to an affine of a parent's sibling. The foster-parent/foster-child tie is a direct one, based on the reciprocal relationship of service and training with respect to tasks which are central to the adult sex-typed role in this society. Men take their kinsfolk's sons, women take their kinsfolk's daughters. The role-model is provided (as are discipline and instruction) by the child's kinsman or kinswoman, not by an affine.

Given the pervasiveness of the institution, and the general nature of the training which is its main rationale, I would argue that its major function lies in the way in which it reinforces ties between kin. Where, as in Gonja, marriage between members of different estates and different ethnic groups is common, and where there are no strongly corporate unilineal descent groups to organize rights and duties and claims on property, there is a constant centrifugal tendency among kin. This is most extreme in central Gonja where villages are relatively far apart and marriages across considerable distances add an element of spatial dispersion to the social and ethnic complexity. Under these conditions, rights in children assume the character of a joint resource. Claims on this resource are one way of expressing kin ties, for the kindred is not only unbounded, but there are strong pressures to keep it 'open'.

Children's responses to fostering

I now want to turn to the question of the effect of fostering on those most directly concerned, the children being fostered and the adults who were fostered in childhood.

When a group of fostered children were asked how they felt about it, the range of responses was very wide. Some said that they preferred to be with foster-parents because they got more attention, more food, and more goods to take with them on marriage, and because, if the foster-parent did not treat them well, their parents could intervene, whereas 'your own mother can do as she likes and no one will say anything'. Others said that they would rather be with their own parent because there they would not be forced to work, would not be disciplined so severely, and would get more food and more attention. Asked what they intended to do with their own children, the reaction was again mixed, although the majority replied that they would have at least one child fostered. Some of those who had previously stated that they would rather be brought up by their own parents said that they would send their child to a parent or sibling to be fostered. This would seem to indicate a sense of obligation to keep the system going, even at the age of six to sixteen. Interestingly enough, only a few of the fostered children spoke of sending a child to the person currently acting as their foster-parent. It is as though children currently being fostered see any obligation for the care given them as balanced by their daily work; in childhood the present is sufficient unto itself. However, when adult women who were fostered have their first child, they often return to a foster-parent rather than to

47

their own mother; moreover some send a daughter to a previous foster-parent. It might also be argued that, where so many are prepared to send a prospective child to their parent rather than their current foster-parent, there is a stronger attachment to parents, and a stronger sense of obligation to them than is felt towards foster-parents, despite the fostering relationship. This argument fits with the picture of the fostering relationship as an additive one, not replacing that between parents and children, but experienced as something different and additional to it.

The mixed feelings of the foster-children themselves raise the question of the effect of fostering on a child. What kinds of adult do fostered children become? It seems to me worth taking this question seriously because in thinking of fostering in our own society we assume that it is a makeshift arrangement made necessary by some crisis in the parental family. It is expected that it will be to the disadvantage of the child and it is thought likely that maladjustment in adulthood may follow a history of fostering in childhood. The implication is that only the parents can provide that mixture of affection and guidance which is necessary for healthy adjustment while growing up. We are not concerned with the problem of removing a child from his parents during the first four or five years. As Bowlby (1960) has shown, such an event may have special hazards and raises problems connected with development in infancy and early childhood which are not directly relevant to the Gonja situation where fostering normally is initiated after the age of five.

Any answer to the question as to what kinds of adult are created by Gonja kinship fostering presupposes a measure of adjustment. I have two such indices to offer. Neither is free from difficulties, but taken together they provide some corroboration for what must otherwise be a mere impression, that the fostered are not at a disadvantage compared with the non-fostered in their adaptation to the society in which they live.

'Success' in adulthood as an index of the effect of fostering

The first of these indices is based on the rearing histories of 'successful' men, and compares the incidence of fostering in this group with that among 'ordinary' men. The question here is whether successful men are more likely than others to have been fostered. If fostering is related to success, this might be either directly, though offering greater opportunity of appointment to and advancement in office, or by rendering such achievement more difficult; or more indirectly, through developing personality characteristics which either help or hinder success.

For the purposes of this inquiry, successful men have been defined as those holding positions in one of the three status hierarchies which operate in the two divisional capitals where these data were collected.

The traditional system is based on a hierarchy of chiefships. In Kpembe (eastern Gonja) these offices are open to men whose fathers were members of the ruling estate by patrifiliation. The ruling estate is divided into three dynastic segments – non-exogamous with only truncated genealogies, and thus not lineages in the full sense. Succession to a chiefship depends on the support of a man's own dynastic segment – his paternal kin. In the second capital, Bole (western Gonja), succession may be either by patrifiliation to one of the chiefships of the first rank, or by matrifiliation to the ruling estate - to a second-rank chiefship. In both divisions there are a few commoner chiefships, succession to which is by paternal filiation.[4] Most of the successful men in the samples from Kpembe and Bole held chiefships in the traditional system.

A second group of successful men was drawn from the officials in local government. These are achieved statuses, dependent for the most part on at least a middle-school education. This selection also introduced a bias in favour of the ruling estate, particularly in Bole which has had its own middle school for only a few years.

The third category of successful men was made up of those who were especially respected elders in their communities but held no office in either the traditional or the modern system.

In all, 29 'successful' men from Kpembe and 25 from Bole were interviewed about their rearing histories. On another occasion, random samples of men from these two communities were interviewed concerning marriage histories, and included in the interviews was a question on rearing history. If we compare the incidence of fostering in these 'ordinary' populations with that among the 'successful' men, it is possible to see whether successful men are more or less likely than others to have been fostered in childhood.

This comparison is made in Tables 2-4, 5 and 6. It is immediately clear from the figures presented that in neither the eastern nor the western Gonja sample is fostering negatively associated with success: successful men have been more often fostered as children than have those who hold no position. This difference is only pronounced for the eastern Gonja sample (Table 2-4a). Indeed, the straight comparison between ordinary and successful men for western Gonja (Table 2-4b) shows no difference. However, while eastern Gonja 'ordinary' men were

Table 2-4a. *Comparison of rearing experience of 'successful' men and 'ordinary' men from eastern Gonja*

Rearing experience	Ordinary men	Successful men
Fostered	6	10
Reared by parents	33	19
Total	39	29

$\chi^2 = 3.42$; $p = 0.10$

Table 2-4b. *Comparison of rearing experience of 'success-ful' men and 'ordinary' men from western Gonja*

Rearing experience	Ordinary men	Successful men
Fostered	41	13
Reared by parents	36	12
Total	77	25

$\chi^2 = 0.008$; not significant

Table 2-5. *Comparison of rearing experience of 'successful' men and 'ordinary' men of ruling estate: western Gonja*

Rearing experience	Ordinary men of ruling estate	Successful men of ruling estate
Fostered	10	13
Reared by parents	16	12
Total	26	25

$\chi^2 = 0.916$; not significant

preponderantly of the ruling estate and thus had access to political office, this was not the case in western Gonja where approximately one-third came from each of the three estates. In the latter area male fostering is more widely prac-tised by the commoner than by the other two estates. Yet if 'ordinary' men of the ruling estate (those who have attained no position) are compared with 'suc-cessful' men of the ruling group (Table 2-5), we again find that the successful men are more likely to have been fostered, although the difference here is not so pronounced as that in the sample from eastern Gonja. Thus it seems unlikely that the experience of being reared by foster-parents gives rise in any systematic way to men who are handicapped in comparison with their home-reared peers in the pursuit of adult careers.

This conclusion still leaves open the question of the ways in which fostering may be positively related to success. Is it through the conferring of direct advan-tage, or indirectly through the development of such characteristics as indepen-dence and achievement-drive which are an advantage in the struggle for position? To this question my material offers some clues, if no conclusive answer.

Fostering by paternal kin may operate to strengthen later claims to office by establishing personal links with agnates other than one's own father. This is how the Gonja themselves see it, and several of the chiefs in the Bole sample grew

Table 2-6. *Rearing experience of Bole 'successful' men related to type of position held*

	Reared by:			
Position held	Parents	Paternal kin	Maternal kin	Total
Chiefship of the first rank	6	4	0	10
Chiefship of the second rank	2	3	1	6
Achieved position	4	1	4	9
Total	12 (48%)	8 (32%)	5 (20%)	25 (100%)

up with father's brothers (real or classificatory) who were themselves chiefs and thus in a position to influence appointments to vacant skins (offices). However, judging from those instances I know well, the foster-parent himself is often not alive by the time a protégé seeks chiefship – at the earliest in his thirties. Nevertheless, if the foster-parent himself is no longer able to be of help, his sons and younger brothers with whom the protégé grew to adulthood are by then among the vocal members of the family council which determines who among the men of the segment shall be put forward for office. Thus it may well be that fostering by patrilineal kin serves to strengthen a man's position with the group of agnates whose support is necessary if he is to obtain a chiefship.

It is, of course, also possible that the experience of being fostered tends to develop characteristics which give a man some positive advantage in forming his career. Consideration of the cases of the fostering of successful men by maternal kin is revealing (Table 2-6). In the Bole sample there were six holders of sister's son chiefships, four of whom had been fostered. But only one of these four had been brought up by his maternal kin. For the other three men, fostering could not have led directly to chiefship (success as measured here) because, while they were reared by paternal kin, their chiefships were obtained through maternal connections. In the Kpembe sample there were two cases of successful men fostered by mother's brothers. One of these had been manoeuvred into a chiefship by his mother's brother. The other had been placed in a privileged position where he had minor jobs with the Medical Field Unit which led to his picking up a fair command of English. Now, in a different town and subdivision from that in which he grew up, and long after his foster-parent's death, his own initiative had brought him to hold the job of court interpreter, which placed him among the 'new elite'. So fostering by maternal kin does not necessarily lead directly to the holding of a sister's son chiefship, although this does occur. There are other factors at work, and at least some of the time they take the form of individual initiative. It is perhaps significant that in the Bole sample none of those fostered by maternal kin later succeeded to chiefships of the first rank (patrifilial chiefships) but four of the five did *achieve* positions of importance. In fact, of these four men, one was the member of parliament for the district and a government minister, and another the district commissioner.

It is clear from these data that the factors involved in successful careers are complex, and the role played by fostering is by no means plain. However, it does seem fair to say that fostering does not hamper achievement in either the traditional or the modern system.

Marital stability as an index of the effect of fostering

The second index concerns the relative frequency of divorce for women who have been fostered and for those who have been brought up by their own parents. In our own society divorce is considered to be both an indication of individual inability to form stable emotional relationships, and a response to pressures which render difficult the establishment of stable unions.

I have argued elsewhere (E. Goody 1962; and Chapter 4) that marriage in Gonja is unstable owing to institutional features - the strength of the sibling bond, the status of a woman in her natal home, the absence of widow inheritance, and the ousting of widows, all tend to precipitate a return of older women to their kin in what I have called terminal separation. These same features undermine marriage during the years of active childbearing - the middle years of a woman's marital career. Yet in this period there are counter-pressures supporting the maintenance of a marriage: affection, desire for children, and joint concern with the rearing of children and the domestic enterprise result in some stable unions of many years' duration. In comparing the divorce ratios of fostered and home-reared women, we are asking whether there is anything about the experience of being fostered that makes a woman more susceptible to the disruptive pressures which are built into the system. For it might be that the experience of being brought up away from home emphasizes instrumental relationships at the expense of close emotional ties, thus making it more difficult to establish a satisfactory conjugal relationship in adulthood. As one man put it, 'All foster-children become liars because they want to please their guardians and they fear their anger.'[5]

Even if the institutionalized pressures leading to terminal separation affect the two groups similarly, more stable marriages in the early and middle periods could lead to significant differences in their divorce ratios.

The material for comparison comes from Bole, in western Gonja, and from Daboya, in northern Gonja. Of a sample of 89 women from Bole, 44 per cent had been reared by parents and 56 per cent by foster-parents. This is an area with a somewhat higher incidence of divorce than central or eastern Gonja. For the Bole sample as a whole, the proportion of all marriages that ended in divorce

Table 2-7. *Comparison of the divorce ratios of fostered and home-reared women of two Gonja samples*

	Number of persons	Number of unions	Number of divorces	Divorce ratio 'C'
Western Gonja				
Fostered	50	79	26	38.2
Reared by parents	39	65	20	40.0
Northern Gonja				
Fostered	27	40	10	32.3
Reared by parents	15	19	5	38.4

Western Gonja: $\chi^2 = 0.034$; not significant
Northern Gonja: $\chi^2 = 0.176$; not significant

was 31.9 per cent. For all marriages except those ended by death, the proportion terminated by divorce, Barnes' ratio C (Barnes 1949), was 39.3 per cent. If fostering does in fact work to make settled emotional relationships more difficult in adulthood, we would expect to find that, within this situation of overall high divorce, fostered women would have proportionately more divorces, and home-reared women proportionately fewer. In fact the data show no significant difference between the divorce ratios of the two groups (Table 2-7). The 39 women brought up by their own parents had among them 20 divorces, giving a figure for ratio C of 40 per cent. For the 50 women who were fostered as children, there was a total of 26 divorces, giving a ratio C of 38.2 per cent. A comparison of the divorce ratios for fostered and home-reared women of northern Gonja shows slightly more divorce among those reared at home (a ratio of 38.4 as compared with 32.3 for fostered women). However this difference is within the range of variation to be expected by chance; the χ^2 is not significant. There is thus no basis for accepting the hypothesis that fostered and home-reared women have significantly different divorce ratios. While it cannot be suggested that fostering leads to an especially stable emotional life, it cannot be said to make divorce in adulthood more probable.

Conclusions

When these two indices, incidence of fostering among 'successful' men and incidence of divorce among fostered and not-fostered women, are taken together, they suggest that, in a society where fostering is positively valued by adults and viewed by fostered children with at least mixed feelings, it does not produce adults who are at a disadvantage with respect to success either in their marriage or in their career. Various features of the institution have been suggested which might be related to this conclusion; primary among these is, no doubt, the fact that foster-parents are kin, and that ties with own parents are usually maintained throughout childhood and adolescence. Parents are seen as taking a continued interest in their children's welfare, and as ready and able to interfere should things not go well. Also of importance is the definition of fostering as a situation involving service to the foster-parent and the training of the child. This view is held by children as well as adults; foster-parents are not expected to be indulgent, whereas parents are. Therefore, the increasing demands inevitably made by the foster-parent with the coming of later childhood and adolescence, are regarded by all concerned as legitimate. In any case, the frustrations attendant on giving up the freedom of childhood are, for the fostered, experienced not with their own parents but with other kin on whom they are not so emotionally dependent. Except in eastern Gonja, approximately half of all adults have spent their later childhood and adolescence living and working apart from their own parents. For them, this period of education and gradual entry into adult roles, although still mediated by kin, takes place outside the nuclear family. They are involved already with the wider world of kin and community.

3

The Kpembe study

The problem set by the Kpembe study was to observe and compare children who were growing up with their parents (father, *tuto*; mother, *niu, maa*), with those who had been sent to a foster-parent (male, *nyinipe*; female, *tchepe*). But how to do this? Dissatisfaction with the impressionistic observations of my fieldwork in central Gonja in 1956–7, led me to explore the possibility of more objective assessment. The choice of what to look at was determined by a few seminal books on the one hand, and on the other by the nature of Gonja fosterage itself, as I had understood it during the earlier study. Together these provided the basis for a number of hypotheses that were central to the design of the Kpembe study, and especially for the various techniques for eliciting from individual children their feelings, attitudes and ways of responding to the world. The major tools were a modified Thematic Apperception Test, a sentence completion schedule, a test of concepts, a set of moral problem stories, a self-picture drawn by each child, and an interview.

Study design and methodology

Originally it was intended to match fostered children with parentally reared children on the basis of sex, age and estate membership. However, the study design included the continued observation of two neighbourhoods, one of the ruling estate, and the other Muslim, in order to see children in their families and in their peer groups. These children of Ewurajipope and Nsoape were the core subjects. Finding others to match them proved impossible once the number of variables involved became clear (see Matrix A, Appendix I). Instead the sample was extended by adding fostered children from other neighbourhoods, in order to have a group large enough to allow comparison of subsamples at the analysis stage. The final sample contained 97 children, 51 girls and 46 boys.

An initial period of about two months was used for pretests and the organization of the procedures. The TAT pictures had been drawn in England using photographs made in central Gonja. During this phase several of the original pictures were rejected because of poor response; these were pictures without human figures or lacking activity. Also dropped were the moral dilemma stories, as well as an instrument for eliciting representations of time, distance, volume, weight, etc. The difficulty with these was in part to arrive at a vernacular version (using repeated back translations) which seemed valid, and related to this, concern as to the essential meaningfulness of these tasks to the Gonja child.

The neighbourhood observations were made by the author together with Anna Craven, a Cambridge anthropology graduate. We also interviewed each child on rearing history, family structure, early memories, and attitudes to fostering. The TAT was administered to each child alone, in each case by a local same-sex adult with whom they were familiar, in a neighbourhood room borrowed for the occasion. The whole TAT interview was tape recorded (in the vernacular), which allowed for spot checks on the interviewers' style, degree of intervention, and the quality of the interaction. Problems with the children's initial understanding of the task were discussed at length with the testors. After the difficulties with the other instruments I was surprised how readily the children understood and participated in the TAT sessions. This was almost certainly due to the fact that storytelling is a favourite pastime in which they vie with each other to recount traditional stories with flair. Once we had made it clear that we did not want the traditional stories but ones which they themselves made up, they quickly caught on and built up their story around the picture cues. Story tapes were transcribed by native speakers as soon as possible. The transcripts were then translated and checked mainly in Kpembe, though the task had to be completed during the following autumn when I was teaching at the University of Ghana.

Coding and analysis of all the data was done in Cambridge. The sentence-completion material proved too ambiguous to be meaningful. The self-drawings (a modification of the draw-a-man test suggested by Mundy-Castle) distinguished reliably only between those children who had been to school and those who had not; many of the latter felt unable to use pencil and paper, although they draw freely in the sand.[1] The Coding of the TAT stories (discussed in Appendix I) was done 'blind' to avoid being influenced by knowledge of particular children. Then a record was compiled for each child which included demographic data, rearing history, interview responses and TAT scores. The full analysis, too long to be included here, relates the TAT indices to several demographic indices (sex, age, estate of father and of mother, schooling, state of parents' marriage, whether parents are living, rank in sibling group). For the fostered children an additional set of variables was also used (whether crisis or purposive fostering, subsequent trauma, inclusive trauma, age when fostered, duration of fostering, distance of foster-home from parental home, by whom fostered). Matrices showing associations between demographic variables, fostering variables, and between the two sets of variables, are included in Appendix I. The full report is on file with the Social Science Research Council, London.

The original purpose of the study was to test hypotheses about the effects of fostering on Gonja children. It was hoped that with a relatively large sample one could use the indices coded from the stories, and other measures, not to learn more in depth about individual children, but rather to look at the systematic effects of fostering on Gonja children. But it was clear from the beginning that a definitive test was impossible for a number of reasons. First, earlier observations suggested that there were no major differences between children being fostered and those growing up with their own parents. If the analysis revealed no differences between the two sets of children, this could be because the early informal observations were correct and the two were substantially the same. Or it could be because of error either at the testing stage or in the analysis. Perhaps the indices do not really reflect the variables they were designed to represent; or perhaps these are not the best variables to consider in assessing the consequences of fostering. The differences could in fact be substantial, but not reflected in the indices we had chosen. In the Kpembe study this general problem was compounded by the fact that the TAT pictures had been drawn especially for this population and most of the indices were new; the stimulus material, codes and indices were all unstandardized. In short there are problems of validity at several levels. Nevertheless it seemed worthwhile to try and obtain some more systematic appreciation of the effect of fostering on the children of Gonja.

As is clear from the findings presented in this chapter, there are few differences between fostered and home-reared children. On the one hand, this result is consistent with the original observations made in central Gonja in 1956–7 and consistent with predictions made in the Kpembe study itself. On the other hand, for the technical reasons mentioned, the findings cannot be considered definitive.[2] There are two sorts of evidence that have prompted me to present this material nevertheless. First there is the experience during the field study, in which it soon became obvious that some of the attempts to elicit responses from Gonja children were not working. The experience with the TATs was very different. Testors were at ease with the procedure, children enjoyed the sessions, most children produced substantial stories which picked up the picture cues. The TAT storytelling seemed to make sense to the Gonja, children and adults, whereas several other procedures had mystified and confused them.[3]

The second sort of evidence has, I believe, important implications for the relevance of TAT-type procedures in anthropological research. This is the finding that both demographic and social factors are reflected in the data. Here one is not working with individual differences but with patterns of response which reflect experience common to all Gonja children, or to those of one sex, or those who share a particular position in the family. These effects are not different in kind from those hypothesized for the fostering experience. But they allow a different sort of cross-checking. The differences between Gonja girls and boys on our TAT indices of aggression fit with the pattern of sex differences found for Western societies where boys are consistently more concerned with aggression imagery than girls (Oetzel 1966:323–6; Maccoby and Jacklin 1974:228ff.).

Conversely, it is girls who show higher levels of concern with affiliation both in Western societies (Oetzel 1966:330-1) and among the Gonja. The fact that these sex differences on aggression and affiliation imagery in the Gonja TAT material correspond with the Western pattern of differences between boys and girls, suggests that the indices are in fact recording information about the motivational structure of Gonja children (the data on Gonja children's aggression imagery and affiliation imagery scores is presented in Appendix I).

Another sort of corroboration concerns imagery which reflects experiences that are culture-specific. I have written elsewhere on the high level of divorce in Gonja, and described the pattern of terminal separation by which older women leave their husbands and 'retire' to live with kin (E. Goody 1962; 1973). Because women come to live in the husband's town on marriage, divorce or 'retirement' to kin means the departure of the wife. For the Gonja child, the conjugal family is experienced as potentially unstable, even when his own parents remain together. I was also led to write about witchcraft in Gonja, although I went into the field with what almost amounted to a determination not to do so. I felt that the dynamics of witchcraft beliefs and accusations were well understood and did not pose a problem for me. However, fears of attack by witches, and repeated reference to witchcraft in people's accounts of their experience and their explanations for misfortune forced me to treat this as a topic which was problematic for the Gonja. The particular aspect of Gonja witchcraft beliefs which attracted my attention was the *de facto* distinction between good witches who were male, and evil witches who were female (E. Goody 1970c).

Among the six TAT pictures shown to each child was one in which a Gonja woman is ladling soup. This was included to provide cues linking women, food, hospitality and nurturance. I rather expected stereotyped stories about 'this is a woman making supper . . .' Instead there were two main themes: girls told stories centering around a woman, often a relative, who was a witch and was engaged in cooking the flesh of a child she had killed; and boys produced tales about wives who were either lazy about cooking, or who had in some way betrayed their husband.

What had seemed especially problematic to me about Gonja witchcraft beliefs was the fact that women also concurred that dangerous witches were women, 'because we women are evil' as one informant put it. What seems to be happening in the girls' stories to the 'woman cooking' picture is the expression *by girls* of deep concern about their own potential hostility; nurturant women are deadly dangerous and not to be trusted. Somehow, girls in this society have to come to terms with a culturally validated belief that women are evil and actively seek to kill close kin. The striking fact is that boys do not tell stories about witches in response to this cue. Instead they appear to be working through the problem their society presents to them: wives come and go. This is doubly problematic for boys since a wife is also a mother; a wife who leaves her husband is often a mother who thus leaves her son. Girls more often accompany their divorced mothers than do their brothers, and this may partially explain the absence of this theme in their stories. But of course a woman's view of unstable marriage is different from a man's, especially in a polygynous society. It is quite likely that girls' doubts about their mothers' faithfulness (to them as well as to their father) also receive expression in the witchcraft fantasies. Similarly, boys' fear of women as potential witches may be contributing to their view of women as treacherous. But for boys and for girls the picture of a woman cooking served as a cue for stories expressing one of the major conflicts which each must confront in taking on adult roles; and in each case the conflict is expressed in a cultural idiom. While I did not predict these responses, there is a sense in which they can be said to be 'structurally predictable' from Gonja kinship roles.[4]

Another example of structural prediction occurs in the stories of first-born sons. Fortes has written at length about the avoidance between a man and his first-born son among the Tallensi (1949b; 1959) and in many other West African societies (1974). He sees this as reflecting the conflict between a man and his direct successor in a situation in which the 'success' of the son must depend on the father's death or retirement. The avoidance customs between a man and his first-born son in Gonja are relatively mild in comparison with that described for the Tallensi, the Mossi and the Hausa (see Chapter 5); however, they are enjoined never to eat from the same bowl, lest the son's hand, in touching his father's, should draw from him his strength. One of the codes applied to the TAT material was based on Murray's Nurturance motive: nurturance was coded when a character was described as providing nourishment, protection, love, or aid. An incidental finding was that eldest and only sons practically never describe male figures as nurturant. For instance, no eldest male of a sibling group refers to more than a single nurturant male, and many refer to none; but two-thirds of the middle male siblings mention two or more than two (see Appendix I). Again, a finding not predicted in advance, but one which might well have been forecast on the basis of Fortes' prior writings on the subject.

There are a number of other structurally congruent patterns in the TAT imagery concerning school attendance, estate membership and morality. By themselves they do not tell us much about Gonja society. But in conjunction with other types of analysis, such patterns of response to apparently neutral cues do indicate that the analysis based on the observation of daily life and simple censuses also has a validity at the level of individual feelings and experience.

Finally, it is sometimes possible to relate an individual child's stories directly to what is known about their lives. In writing the report on the Kpembe study it seemed desirable to provide some examples of children's TAT stories in the appendix. Three boys and three girls were therefore selected to represent different ages and different rearing experiences. Each set of stories was prefaced by a sketch of the child and his or her background. Up to this point there had been no attempt to look at the stories of individual children as a set in relation to

59

other knowledge about them. I had been looking for systematic patterns of response related to common experience – fostering, divorce of parents, school, etc. It was therefore quite unexpected to find that a child's stories tended to reflect his or her immediate situation quite directly. For example, Afishata, 12, was living with her mother, who had an older foster-daughter Mariamu, 14, and also another foster-child of about four, newly arrived.[5] Of Afishata's six stories, three were directly concerned with a parent who favours one child over the other, one with a husband who favours one wife over the other, and another about a daughter whose mother spoiled her by not teaching her how to do domestic work. Looking back at my notes I find that the mother was being especially affectionate to the new foster-child about this time, holding her on her lap, and praising her for little things. This raises for me the question of the depth of the feelings tapped by story imagery. It is clear that Afishata was pre-occupied with sibling rivalry at the time of the study and that this was at least in part a response to the immediate situation of the newly arrived foster-child. However, she was not in any obvious way disturbed by the situation; indeed, she chose the older foster child in the household as one of two friends to accompany her on the hypothetical expedition to Salaga. Profiles of Afishata and the other teenage girls in the Ewurajipo section of Kpembe are given in Appendix I, and then assessed as to how they have adapted to the problems of this period of their lives, in relation to their rearing situation.

Moru, one of the three boys whose stories are presented as a set in the original report was living with his parents. The overwhelming problem in Moru's life is his crippled leg. At the time I was working in Kpembe his mother was away on a 'visit' to her relatives, but I later learned that she had left Moru's father and never returned. One of two recurrent themes in Moru's stories is the concern of a boy over having a woman to cook for him, and over having enough food. The other recurrent theme is hostility which is uncontrolled and gets men and boys into trouble. This is doubly fascinating, since Moru's father is known for his sharp temper; but in addition it seems possible that Moru finds it difficult to manage his own aggression. As a cripple, he cannot challenge other boys to fight and beat them, yet his stories are much concerned with boys fighting each other. The aggression theme reflects a long-standing problem in Moru's life; but the anxiety about a woman who is a source of food and love appears to be a response to the recent departure of his mother (see Appendix I for these two sets of stories).

I do not know enough about all the children to be able to say how often their stories mirror their current or long-standing problems as individuals; this was not the intention of the study design. But that this clearly does happen in some cases is significant in terms of the important question of the validity of story imagery in assessing response to life situations. At least some of the children were using their stories to express the problems in their lives. This conclusion makes it seem more legitimate to seek from the story imagery expressions of the shared problem of adaptation to the fostering experience.

If we are willing to concede this degree of congruence between individual imagery and socially produced conflicts, then it is perhaps reasonable to take note of the parallel findings on the absence of clear differences in imagery between fostered children and those reared by their parents. But given the multiple problems of both reliability and validity one can do little more than take note. The findings are consistent both with earlier unstructured observation and with the hypotheses formulated at the beginning of the Kpembe study.

Hypotheses concerning the relationships between fostering and the TAT indices

In framing the hypotheses I was concerned with several facets of adjustment. First, with anxiety level. Fostered children did not seem to be more anxious than other children, which would be one indication of easy adjustment to their new surroundings. Second, fostered children seemed to form similar kinds of relationships with the fostering adults of the same sex as they had previously had with their own parent; so ability to form effective relationships was a second variable to be assessed. Finally, the period properly covered by fostering is said by the Gonja to be that between the ages of five or six and marriage. Thus, while infancy and early childhood are excluded, some children spent the long phases of latency and adolescence entirely with foster-parents. The major developmental tasks of this period concern the learning of adult roles. In Gonja these tasks have at least three dimensions. The first of these is behaviour related to respect and obedience. Not only is the kingdom based on hierarchies of office but, within the family, the kin group and the village, it is important that men and women give respect and deference where it is due, and they in turn require these dues from their subordinates (E. Goody 1972).

Second, the economic roles appropriate to men and women, including domestic roles, must be mastered. Sex roles are partly defined in terms of respect relations, but an equally important dimension consists of role-related tasks and skills; domestic and child-rearing tasks for women, and the more obviously economic tasks of farming and hunting for men.

There is a third dimension of adult roles best seen as kinship roles; their components are behaviours defined, for example, as 'maternal', 'sisterly' and 'kinlike'. In addition, kinship roles include elements of deference of females to males, and elements drawn from role-related economic behaviour.

The more general hypothesis that fostered children do not differ markedly from those reared by their parents can now be stated more specifically in relation to these variables:

61

  (i)   Fostered children will not differ from those reared by their own parents with respect to level of anxiety.

  (ii) Fostered children will not differ from those reared by their own parents with respect to their ability to form effective relations with caretaking adults.

  (iii) Fostered children and those reared by their own parents will not differ in their learning of respect and deference behaviour.

  (iv) Fostered children and parentally reared children will not differ in their learning of sex-role tasks.

  (v)   Fostered and parentally reared children will not differ in respect to their learning of kinship roles.

Although the major hypotheses predict an absence of difference between fostered and parentally reared children, there were some areas in which some contrast might be expected to appear. These differences are the effects of ceasing to be solely dependent on own parents and siblings; that is, they derive from the extension of primary relationships to members of a second domestic group, often in a new community. Here, the predicted differences were in autonomy and in the scale and scope of perceptions. It was thought that those children who were fostered would use a longer time scale, have a broader spatial perspective, and would people their world with more individual actors. Thus:

  (vi) Fostered children will tend to see events in a longer time perspective than parentally reared children.

  (vii) Fostered children will tend to see events as happening within a wider spatial framework than those reared at home.

  (viii) Fostered children will tend to perceive more actors as relevant to the events they are concerned with than do parentally reared children.

These variables all concern the 'scope and scale' of perception, and the general hypothesis was that the effect of having not one but two families of orientation will be to broaden the frame of reference for the individual's perceptions and for the effective field of interaction. It was further suggested that under optimum conditions the same experiences, particularly the establishment of a secondary set of dependency relations, would lead to greater independence and autonomy.

  (ix) Fostered children, both boys and girls, will be more autonomous than those reared by their own parents.

These four hypotheses were not derived from any special body of general theory, but rather from 'middle-range' postulates, based on a mixture of observation and inference. There are, however, a few areas of theoretical interest on which predictions can be based. One of these is achievement-related motivation on which a great deal has been written (McClelland *et al.*, 1953, McClelland 1961, Atkinson 1958, LeVine, 1966). Indeed LeVine and McClelland have suggested that variations in the level of achievement motivation from one society to another may be significant for strategies of industrialization in underdeveloped areas. There is some reason to expect that fostering would enhance the achievement drive in that foster-parents are more likely to make demands for high performance and less likely to indulge children than are own parents.[6] And indeed this would certainly be the Gonja view. However, arguments based on the effect of the social structure on socialization (LeVine 1966) suggest that the overall level of achievement motivation in Gonja will not be high. The emphasis on obedience and deference, the present paucity of positions open to individuals on the basis of merit, together with a generally low value placed on success in farming, leave few substantive areas in which parents actively try to encourage achievement in their sons. And, indeed, success in competition for the offices available within each estate depends on seniority by age and the support of one's kin, at least as much as it does on individual initiative. The Gonja themselves also suggest that foster-children are often motivated to please rather than to conform to an inner standard of excellence. There is no evidence that a man sends a son to be fostered in order that he learn to value excellence of effort for its own sake. Indeed in this society we might expect that girls would be more highly motivated than boys to meet standards of excellence, for they are exhorted to learn to perform domestic tasks effectively in order to secure and retain a good husband. On the other hand, boys, especially of the Ruling group, grow up believing that farming and manual labour are signs of lack of success, of the inability to arrange for others to perform these tasks. There is, then, little basis for predicting a higher level of achievement motivation among fostered than among parentally reared boys, but such a pattern may emerge among the girls, where fostering is more directly associated with the learning of excellence in a valued set of skills.

(x)   There will be no difference between fostered and parentally reared boys on level of achievement motivation. Girls who are being fostered may be higher on achievement motivation than those living with their own parents.

Two more indices were of interest because they have been the subject of considerable attention by the psychologists concerned with developing standardized projective measures. The first of these is the motivation to affiliate, that is, to establish, maintain or restore friendship-like relationships. This is of interest here as a possible measure of concern with peer-group relations, an area of behaviour on which the fostering experience may be expected to impinge. The peer relations of foster-children are central for two reasons. In the first place, the child who is removed from his natal domestic group is at the same time separated from the children of his own age with whom he has spent his leisure time. True, if he is still in the same town these children are not inaccessible. But, if he has moved to a different part of town, they no longer form the group in which spontaneous play occurs and a new peer group will have to be forged. The other reason why these peer relations are important is that, if the foster-child does not find it easy to relate to his foster-parent as he did to his own parents, the peer group may be a refuge and a source of support. This is particularly likely to be a problem for a boy, since he may have very little contact with the wife of his foster-parent, that is, no real foster-mother. Both of these factors would lead us to expect that fostered boys would show a higher level of motivation to affiliate than those with their own parents. For girls the picture is slightly different because they tend to have one or two close friends rather than moving with a group of peers; and girls' friends are almost always those with whom they live and share domestic tasks. That is, girls do not move as freely as boys outside the compound and its immediate environment, nor do they separate work and play companions in quite the same way. In a sense, then, girls' 'friends' are ascribed, while those of boys are 'achieved'. In this girls are very vulnerable. If they are sent to a foster-home where there are no other girls of their own age, they can be very lonely. On the other hand, they seem quickly to form close associations if peers are available. If still in the same town, a fostered girl may retain her previous friendships, though the time spent together will now be limited to evenings and to those rare occasions when one of them can get permission to leave her own neighbourhood to pay a visit.

(xi) Fostered boys will be more concerned with affiliation than those reared by their parents. Fostered girls will also have higher affiliation scores than parentally reared girls.

The standardization of scoring of concern with hunger also makes it a potentially useful index. Atkinson and McClelland (1958) have shown that high scores on this index are related to whether their subjects were in fact hungry or satisfied. While there is nothing in my observations to suggest that fostered children are less well-fed than those being reared by their own parents, food is a subject of general concern to Gonja children, and thus one around which feelings of discrimination might well focus. For instance, children whose mothers are dead are expected to suffer hunger because it is said that no other woman will care enough to be sure they are fed regularly. What this really means is that orphans may not be the direct responsibility of any one woman. But a foster-child is: For a girl, it is her foster-parent, for a boy, a wife of his foster-parent. Thus any difference in concern over food between fostered and parentally reared children is likely to be the result of a difference in 'fringe benefits'. For instance, titbits which a mother will put aside for her child in the late afternoon, when the evening meal is still not ready, will perhaps not be so readily saved for a foster-child, though this is largely a matter of the relation between the individuals concerned. Here it again seems likely that the boys will suffer from the fact that they are placed under the care of a man and only indirectly that of a foster-mother in the person of the wife of the foster-parent. Here too the age at which a child is sent to the foster-parent is probably important. A very young child has a good chance of establishing the kind of dependent relationship within which special care will be extended, while the older child enters the foster-home as an ostensibly independent individual, less in need of special attention.

> (xii) Fostered boys are likely to have a higher level of concern with food than boys reared at home. This will be especially true of boys sent for fostering at a relatively late age. Fostered girls probably do not differ from those reared at home in their level of concern with food, but those fostered at a relatively late age may be higher on this variable than either early-fostered girls, or those reared by their own parents.

At this point I must stress once again the exploratory nature of this entire study. Although the formulation of hypotheses and the attempts to measure aspects of motivation are central to it, this procedure has been dictated by a desire to specify variables and processes in operational terms, rather than by the expectation that by so doing it would be possible to 'prove' any specific proposition in a definitive manner. There seems to be a paradox for the investigator in the fact that one does not want to claim a level of accuracy or finality for observations which are by their very nature tentative and preliminary. Yet to make these observations in a way that can serve as a basis for further work, requires an attempt at formalization. And this attempt can easily appear to be making claims to definitive findings.

In the present context, there are two possibilities in confronting the problem of fit between variables and the indices for their measurement. One can either decide that the situation is impossible, and give up further analysis. Or one can invoke the exploratory nature of the enquiry, proceed 'as if' the indices were the variables, and in evaluating the results keep the tentative nature of the identification very much to the fore. The latter course is the one that has been adopted, and the reader is urged to think of what follows as an exercise in the use of systematic procedures 'as if' they were warranted. Despite these limitations, such bases for the tentative testing of propositions cannot be worse than the impressionistic methods of arriving at conclusions usually adopted in the study of simple societies. It is hoped that in the course of the analysis insights can be gained into Gonja personality and social structure on the one hand, and the implications of fostering children and adolescents by kin on the other. If some of these insights seem important enough to test further, perhaps the present study can also contribute guidance on which methods are most apt to prove workable and reliable.

Indices selected for the evaluation of hypotheses

The following list matches hypotheses with the indices selected as most appropriate for each one; the nature of these indices is discussed in Appendix I. In most cases more than one index is used and where one of these is considered of special importance it is *italicized.*

Hypotheses	*Indices*
(i) Fostered and parentally reared children will not differ with respect to level of anxiety.	need *harmavoidance*; extreme aggression; denial of threat; incidence of failure.
(ii) Fostered and parentally reared children will not differ in their ability to form effective relations with same-sex adults.	*rejection by adults as sanction*; passivity/withdrawal; denial of male/female figures.
(iii) Fostered and parentally reared children will not differ in their attitudes to obedience and deference behaviour.	'proud child'; all adult sanctions; moral traits.
(iv) Fostered and parentally reared children will not differ in their orientation towards role tasks.	role task orientation; denial same-sex adult.
(v) Fostered and parentally reared children will not differ in their attitudes to appropriate sex roles.	girls: need affiliation; denial same-sex adult; boys: aggression cue responses; denial same-sex adult.
(vi) Perceptions of time: fostered children will use longer time perspective than parentally reared children.	no adequate index: child/adult orientation as an index of social maturity.
(vii) Perceptions of space: fostered children will use a broader perception of space than parentally reared children.	no adequate index: used Q. 6 from interviews.
(viii) Perceptions of significant actors: fostered children will use more characters than parentally reared children.	introduced characters.
(ix) Autonomy: fostered children will be more independent than parentally reared children.	anxiety nurturance; need nurturance, females and 'parents'; used Q. 10 on interview.
(x) Need achievement: there will be no difference between fostered and parentally reared boys on achievement motivation, but girls reared by foster-parents will have higher achievement scores than those with their own parents.	need achievement index.
(xi) Need affiliation: fostered boys will be more concerned with affiliation imagery than will those with their own parents; fostered girls will	need affiliation indices.

have more high need affiliation scores
than will parentally reared girls.

(xii) Fostered boys will have a higher level of
concern with food imagery than boys
reared at home, especially with boys sent
for fostering at a relatively late age. Fostered girls probably do not differ from
those still at home in their level of concern with food imagery, but those fostered at a late age may have higher scores
than either early fostered or parentally
reared girls.

hunger codes.

The testing of these hypotheses requires the setting of levels of significance.
Differences for which the p value is .05 or less are treated as reliable, while differences for which the value of p lies between .20 and .05 are considered as
trends. An additional criterion which must be met for a trend is that the difference reaches a percentage specified for each sample size. This is an *ad hoc*
attempt to take into account the greater ease with which reliable differences
may be identified in large sample. Where sub-samples are compared within a
sub-sample, as for instance with the scores for early- and later-fostered girls, the
number may drop to less than 10; in such a case very large differences are
required before a reliable result is achieved. I have also followed the convention
of rounding all percentages to the nearest 5.

There is a further factor which makes reliable differences difficult to
demonstrate. This is the obvious fact that motivation is susceptible to multiple
determinants, while projective tests are subject to many sources of error. Hence
the advantage in being able to discuss trends as well as reliable differences is that
it allows the analysis to go beyond the assessment of hypotheses as simply supported or not, and thus enables one to use more fully the indices derived from
the complex projective material. When working with the tendencies of samples to
differ no suggestion of finality is intended; I am merely making tentative suggestions as to the possible implications if such differences could later be shown
to be reliable.

The Kpembe study might perhaps be best described as a stage in an ongoing
process of trying to understand Gonja institutions and personality. The very
general impressions of a first period of field work, based on observation and a
few simple censuses, led to the conclusion that kinship fostering was prevalent
and on the whole positively adaptive. At the same time more specific ideas as to
how fostering affected children were generated by this first experience. The
Kpembe study was planned as a way of assessing these initial hypotheses in a
less subjective manner. In the process of codifying and analysing the projective
material, new insights have been gained, on a still more specific level, and these
led in turn to the clarification of key intervening variables (such as the age at
which children of each sex are sent for fostering). Hopefully these will in turn be
built into new attempts at validation.

Evaluation of hypotheses concerning the effects of fostering in Gonja

The hypotheses will be considered in three groups: original hypotheses concerning areas in which fostered and parentally reared children were not expected to differ; original hypotheses of areas in which differences between fostered and parentally reared children were predicted; and subsequent hypotheses based on previously standardized codes. Both reliable differences and trends will be discussed in each case.

Original hypotheses of no difference

Hypothesis (i): Fostered and parentally reared children will not differ with respect to the level of anxiety expressed in projective material.

Of the four possible measures of anxiety, only harmavoidance has to my knowledge been used in previous studies. Fantasies of extreme aggression (killing, severe injury, cannibalism) are included among possible indices of anxiety because they appear to be relatively free of culturally prescribed responses to aggressive cues. Thus as a group boys are higher on most modes of aggression than girls, in accordance with expectations of the Gonja themselves. However, where the sexes are compared on frequency of mention of extreme aggression, girls are actually higher on all three types of cue; and for response to the threat cue the difference reaches the level of a trend. Denial of threat was coded when the picture cue was threatening, but the story told about it does not refer to this fact in any way. This measure is a possible index of anxiety, if we are justified in assuming that the avoidance of any reference to the threatening situation was a form of defence against the anxiety it aroused. Finally, the simple frequency of mention of failure is a possible index of level of anxiety in that a high score shows preoccupation with failure based at least in part on responses to innocuous cues.

On only one of the 18 individual indices did a reliable difference between fostered and parentally reared children appear. But on this measure (extreme aggression), it is the girls being raised by their own parents who have the high 'anxiety' scores. Of the 7 cases in which a difference reaches the level specified for a trend, 5 show the children who are being fostered to be less anxious. The remaining 2 are harmavoidance scores for girls, and on these the fostered girls tend to be more anxious.

For boys there is some evidence that either fostering reduced the 'normal' anxiety level,[7] or there is something about being raised by one's own parents which raises it. For girls there are conflicting findings, with no clear indication as to whether fostering increases or decreases anxiety levels.

Conclusion (i): There is only one reliable difference on the indices of anxiety between children being fostered and those being raised by their own parents. This shows girls being reared at home to be more anxious. When trends are

68

considered as well, fostered boys are consistently lower on indices of anxiety, while fostered girls are lower on some and higher on others.

Hypothesis (ii): Fostered and parentally reared children will not differ in their ability to form effective relations with adults.

Three possible types of index of ability to form effective relationships have been suggested, all of them tentatively. Of these, perhaps the most direct are the indices of denial of male and female adults. No inferences are involved here, apart from the assumption that denial is motivated. References to the rejection of children by parent figures as a sanction on correct behaviour can also be seen as an indication of concern with parent–child relationships. A much less direct measure is the level of passive and withdrawal responses; those who scored on this variable failed to indicate either approach or avoidance in their responses but maintained a neutral or passive position which seemed to the coder inappropriate in the context of the situation described in the story.

Conclusion (ii): There is only one reliable difference between fostered and parentally reared children in their ability to form effective relationships. This finding suggests that boys being reared by their own parents may be handicapped in this respect. But the indices used were on the whole unsatisfactory.

Hypothesis (iii): Fostered and parentally reared children will not differ in their attitudes to obedience and deference behaviour.

The most direct index of the children's attitudes towards obedience and deference behaviour occurs in the coding of references to moral traits. One type of response by many children was to tell a story concerned, at least in part, with a 'proud' or 'naughty' child. The Gonja view disobedience and disrespectful behaviour by children as 'bad' and many of the children showed their concern with such standards in the story material. Other standards of behaviour were also mentioned, almost always in the breach. Thus boys in particular told of thieves, liars and lazy people, as well as of 'proud children'. The girls were almost exclusively concerned, so far as morality went, with the obedience/ respect dimension, though in absolute terms they were no more likely to mention 'proud children' than were the boys. The 'proud child' rating as used here is simple an indication of which individual subjects mentioned this trait. Some mentioned it repeatedly, but for immediate purposes a present/absent dichotomy is sufficient.

The other type of index relating to attitudes towards obedience/respect behaviour is the rating of references to adult sanctions on the behaviour of children. The rationale here is that a high level of concern with adult sanctions also indicates a concern with obedience, that is, with the circumstances in which sanctions are likely to be incurred. Three sorts of sanction are considered: 1 abuse and/or criticism – it was sometimes impossible to distinguish these and hence the two were combined in a single index of verbal sanctions; 2 rejection by a parent figure; and 3 severe physical punishment.

For girls none of the four possible indices indicate a difference between those being fostered and those living with their own parents. For boys, one of the four comparisons shows a reliable difference and one a trend. In both cases there appears to be greater preoccupation with criticism and punishment on the part of those living with their own fathers.

Conclusion (iii): Fostered and parentally reared girls do not differ in their attitudes to obedience/respect behaviour, but parentally reared boys are more concerned with obedience (in the sense of being concerned with punishment) than are those with foster-parents.

Hypothesis (iv): Fostered and parentally reared children will not differ in their orientation to role tasks.

Only two possible indices are available on orientation to tasks associated with adult, sex-typed, roles. They are, however, fairly direct, particularly the first one. This is role-task orientation and is a simple count of the number of times a subject mentions role-related tasks. No estimate being made of how the child felt about such tasks. The second of the possible indices is less direct. This is the frequency with which subjects fail to include in their stories an adult of their own sex when one is clearly present in the picture. Obviously, such a cue denial may be a response to a number of different aspects of the sex role, among which the role-specific task is only one. Unfortunately boys deny actors of either sex very infrequently, and thus this index is really only of use for comparing fostered girls and those reared by their own parents. On only one of these indices is there a tendency for those who are being reared by their own parents to differ from foster-children. Fostered boys tend to show a slightly lower level of concern with role-related tasks than do the other boys. This result is contrary to the Gonja expectation that fostering will provide better training in both character and role-skills. However, it does fit with the generally overall higher level of concern among boys being reared by their own parents which appears on these indices, though it is unfortunate that so few measures of this variable were available.

Conclusion (iv): Fostered children do not differ reliably from those being reared by their own parents on the available indices of orientation to sex-role related tasks. The only observable trend is for boys with their own parents to show a higher level of concern than those being fostered.

Hypothesis (v): Fostered and parentally reared children will not differ in their attitudes to appropriate sex roles.

This hypothesis differs from the previous one in being concerned with the extent to which children of each sex have adopted the motivational style which most strongly characterizes their own sex in contrast to the opposite one. Specifically, a comparison of the boys' and girls' responses over all the variables shows that boys differ from girls most strongly and most consistently in their aggression imagery. Boys respond to aggression cues and threat cues, *and* to aggression–neutral cues with higher levels of aggression imagery than do girls. Thus it seems reasonable to see aggression imagery as the culturally appropriate male response in a wide variety of situations. Girls, on the other hand, are consistently and clearly higher on affiliation imagery. In Gonja society (as in our own) this is the particularly female response to a wide range of social stimuli. Thus, in assessing the degree to which children have adopted motivational styles appropriate to their sex, it has seemed reasonable to look at the extent to which boys respond with aggressive imagery and girls with affiliative imagery.

For the purpose of comparing the aggression imagery of fostered and parentally reared boys I have used the four measures which rate responses to the aggression cue picture, because, while males are more aggressive in all contexts, it is in reponse to external provocation that aggression is most socially approved. Aggression imagery in responses to this picture cue (Picture V) was coded physical, verbal, supernatural or 'aggressive threat'. More than one mode of aggression could be coded for the story told about this picture if more than one was mentioned.

The comparison of affiliation imagery of the fostered girls with that of girls reared by their own parents was based on the scores of each of the six pictures for need affiliation. The seventh index is a summary score on need affiliation, and is therefore not independent of the other scores. The last of the possible indices of the girls' sex-role orientation is denial of female figure.

For neither boys nor girls are there reliable differences on any of the possible indices of orientation to appropriate sex role. For each sex, however, there is a single instance of a tendency to differ, and in each case it is the parentally reared children who show the stronger 'role-appropriate' score. However, the trend is neither a consistent nor a strong one.

Conclusion (v): There is no reliable difference between fostered and parentally-reared children in their orientation to the appropriate sex role, but there is a tendency for those reared at home to score higher on appropriate sex-related imagery on two of the eleven possible indices.

Original hypotheses of no difference: Conclusions

Of the 44 comparisons possible on the various indices of adjustment considered for the 'no difference' hypotheses, only three showed a reliable difference between fostered and parentally reared children. Two were comparisons of fostered and non-fostered boys and one was for the girls' sample. In all three cases, it was the children who were living with their own parents who had the more extreme scores. Fostered boys were significantly less likely to produce passivity and withdrawal reponses, and they were significantly less concerned about verbal criticism as a sanction. Fostered girls were significantly less likely to produce imagery of extreme aggression. The trends for the boys' responses were all in the same direction. Fostered boys tend to be less anxious, less concerned with physical punishment as a sanction, less concerned with role-related tasks, and less likely to identify with the male role, as measured by a high score on aggression.

These results of the comparisons of the boys' scores are not highly reliable, but they are consistently in the same direction. Fostering, instead of acting to accentuate anxiety, the tendency to respond passively, sensitivity to adult sanctions, and instrumental and affective identification with the male role, is associated with lower scores on these dimensions. It seems at least possible that fostering may have a liberating effect. In a society where parents place great emphasis on quick and unquestioning obedience, and where the family is a critical link with the community and the wider society, boys who grow up with kin rather than their own parents may even be at an advantage. For them, the learning of adult roles may be instrumentally defined, and divorced from the emotional relationships with the natal family.

The single reliable finding for the comparison of fostered and non-fostered girls is that the latter are more concerned with extreme aggression in their stories. Further, of the five trends, four are for measures which were used as indices of anxiety, and the fifth is probably best understood as a reaction to the threat produced in the picture cue. It seems that for girls there is a single dimension for which fostering is important: anxiety. Thus fostered girls do not appear to differ from others in their ability to relate effectively, in their concern with sanctioning behaviour, or with role-related tasks. There is a slight tendency for those who live with their own parents to have higher affiliation scores (though on one cue only) which we have suggested indicates a relatively high level of femininity; it may be that girls who stay at home are more feminine. As we have noted, they are significantly more likely to produce extreme aggression imagery. But for the measure of generalized anxiety, that is, the harmavoidance indices, it is the fostered girls who come highest. Clearly, whether a girl is brought up at home or sent to foster-parents does not make a great deal of difference on the measures we have been able to use, and the differences which do appear are not consistent.

Hypotheses predicting differences between fostered and parentally reared children

As a group these hypotheses have proved disappointing in the low level of confirmation, at least in part because of the difficulty experienced in finding suitable measures for the variables specified. Several attempts were discarded in the field at the pretest stage (a 'concepts' test and a 'moral responsibility' test). An

72

attempt to code the story material for degree of 'empathy' was not pursued, for technical rather than theoretical reasons. As a result, the evaluation of three of the four hypotheses turns on a single index. For the fourth hypothesis, concerning independence, it was possible to use four separate indices, and here alone reliable results and clear trends were obtained.

Hypothesis (vi): Fostered children will use longer time-perspectives than parentally reared children.

The only index considered relevant for the variable of time-perception is a very indirect one. This is the overall balance of all the stories told by a given subject in terms of orientation towards the world of children (all child actors, or a mixture of children and adults) or the world of adults (all adult actors). The rationale was that those who responded in terms of all-adult stories were using a fantasy world populated by adults; that is they were 'looking ahead' to the time when they themselves would be adults. It could also be argued that, for whatever reason, such children were very strongly identified with the adults in their lives so that for them 'the present' was lived in an adult world. In this sense the index of child/adult orientation is also an index of social maturity. Here, too, our reasoning would lead to a prediction that fostered children should be higher on adult-orientation than those who had remained at home. Whatever the interpretation placed on the index, there was no difference in the imagery used by the two groups.

Conclusion (vi): Fostered children do not differ in their time-perspective from those reared at home.

Hypothesis (vii): Fostered children will use a broader perception of spatial relations than those reared by parents.

The only relevant measure of spatial perception proved to be the responses to Question 6 of the Interview. Here the children were asked: 'If you could live anywhere at all where would you really like to live?' There is no difference at all in the 'ideal residence' of fostered boys and those with their own parents. For instance, about two-fifths of each group would live either in Southern Ghana or abroad. For the girls there is a slight tendency for parentally reared girls to prefer somewhere in northern Ghana (but outside Kpembe Division) more than do those who are with foster-parents. The latter group, however, has a slightly stronger preference both for Kpembe itself and for southern Ghana or abroad.[8] In effect, then, the responses of the fostered girls form a U-shaped distribution, with high frequencies at each extreme ('present home' and 'south/abroad'), while those of parentally reared girls are almost evenly distributed over these three categories. Thus it seems that fostered girls may have either relatively wide or relatively narrow perception of space in the context of this question, while parentally reared girls are less likely to stick close to home but also less likely to think in terms of really distant places.

73

Conclusion (vii): On the single index used, fostered boys do not differ from those reared at home in their perceptions of space. Fostered girls, however, tend to have either narrow or wide spatial perception, while those reared at home tend to fall in the intermediate range.

Hypothesis (viii): Fostered children will include more characters in their stories than do those reared by their own parents.

This hypothesis concerns a third facet of a general variable of 'scope' for which it was hypothesized that fostered children would be less narrow and restricted in their perceptions than would those reared at home. It was thought likely that fostered children would use more characters in their stories than those still at home. However, using the score of number of characters who appear in the stories of each subject but not in the pictures, there is no difference for either boys or girls by rearing experience.

Conclusion (viii): There is no difference between fostered and parentally reared children in the frequency with which extra characters appear in stories.

Hypothesis (ix): Fostered children will be more independent than those reared by own parents.

Autonomy, or independence, is not intended as a matter of perception, as were the other three variables in this set, although it is undoubtedly influenced by perception. Rather it is a motivational variable, concerned with the extent to which children feel dependent on, and 'need', in Murray's sense, nurturant or protective support; or, conversely, the extent to which they define situations in independent or autonomous ways. Four separate indices, three based on the TAT codes and one on an interview question, seemed relevant for evaluating this hypothesis. The scores on 'nurturant female' and 'nurturant parent figure' are simple counts of the number of times such figures appeared in the stories of each subject. The two scores are independent. 'Nurturant female' was coded only when a female figure was portrayed as nurturant, but not identified as a parent. These nurturance codes, as well as anxiety nurturance, are based on Murray's definition of need nurturance (1938). Since anxiety nurturance was coded from the same story material as the previous two indices, the measure is not independent. However, there were many references to nurturant parents or females which could not be scored as 'anxiety nurturance'.

The inverview question (No. 10) was phrased slightly differently for boys and girls but required them to select two companions (peers) for a leisure-time activity of some duration. On the basis of knowledge of the people named, this was subsequently coded into choices which reflected a high degree of independence (companions from outside the section, or if within the section, then not from an immediately adjacent compound); intermediate choices (companions from immediately neighbouring compound); restricted choices (companions from within same compound); and dependent and isolated choices (companions only from among own siblings, parents or other adults).

Together these indices cover two complementary aspects of 'autonomy'. On the one hand the nurturance indices are concerned with imagery expressing dependency, and anxiety about dependent relationships. On the other hand, while the scoring of responses to the Choice of Companions question also reflects dependence at one end of the scale, at the other end it classifies choices which are independent or autonomous in a positive sense. That is, those who make independent choices of companions, actually selected friends who were not living nearby. But for the nurturance codes, those who did not score on nurturance imagery made no positively independent choice, other than not being 'actively dependent'.

We find that for the boys there is no tendency for either fostered or parentally reared to make more independent choices. However, for the girls there is a reliable difference, with fostered girls making significantly more independent choices than those living at home.

If we turn to the other sort of index of autonomy, we find that on the various nurturance indices there is a regular trend in the predicted direction for comparisons between fostered and parentally reared boys. Those living with their own parents consistently score more often on these indices, and in this sense fostered boys appear to be more independent. For the girls the comparisons on the nurturance indices do not show any differences. Thus fostered boys are more independent if we use low scores on nurturance as an index of independence, and fostered girls are more independent if we use choices of companions as an index of independence. Although the indices which discriminate are different for both boys and girls, it is those fostered who score highest on independence wherever there are any differences.

Conclusion (ix): Fostered girls are significantly more independent in their choice of companions; fostered boys tend to be more independent in having lower need nurturance scores.

Hypotheses predicting differences between fostered and parentally reared Children: Conclusions

Only one index was found for each of the three attempts to measure scope of perceptions – in respect to time, space, and relevant actors. Of the six comparisons between fostered children and those reared by their own parents (three each for boys and girls), only one showed a trend that met the established criteria. Perception of space, as measured by the location of the 'ideal' place to live, did differ for fostered and parentally reared girls, with the former more often choosing somewhere close at hand, but also more often choosing a really distant town, either in southern Ghana, or 'abroad'. The preference of not-fostered girls for places in northern Ghana (but outside the Kpembe Division) might be interpreted as meaning that they are at once more free but less ambitious than their fostered peers.

However, on the whole these attempts to show a difference in perceptual style among fostered children and those reared by parents have not succeeded. I would be happier about rejecting the hypotheses had it been possible to find more, and more satisfactory, indices of perceptual scope. However, we must reject them on present evidence.

The other hypothesis in this set predicted greater independence for fostered children. In this case there is some support for the hypothesis to be found in the measures used, though there is also the finding that different kinds of measures discriminate for boys and for girls. On all three of the indices of nurturance, boys reared by foster-parents tend to be less concerned with nurturant parent figures than those living with their own parents. None of these nurturance indices differentiate between fostered girls and those raised by parents. When Choice of Companions was used as an index of independence, however, there was a reliable difference, with fostered girls significantly higher on independent choices. On this index fostered and parentally reared boys did not differ.

The finding of a reliable difference among girls for the Choice of Companion is similar to the only positive finding in the comparisons of perceptual scope, namely, the bimodal distribution of the responses of fostered girls to the question about the 'ideal place to live'. Some fostered girls were more stay-at-home, but others were more adventurous in the sense of venturing (in speculation) outside northern Ghana. This result would suggest that for some girls, but not for all, fostering does have a broadening influence. In conclusion it seems that there is no satisfactory evidence for believing that fostered children have wider perceptual scope than those reared at home. But the hypothesis that fostered children will be more independent than their parentally reared siblings is consistent with the findings.

Hypotheses based on previously standardized indices

The final set of hypotheses to be considered consists of three indices which have been the subject of varying amounts of research in laboratory conditions. These are the measures of motivation to affiliate, to achieve, and the hunger drive (or the need for food). Unlike the previous hypotheses, these were not formulated before the start of the Kpembe study. The first analysis of the TAT indices which I made was of the differences and similarities between the responses of boys and girls. It was in the course of working this out that the hypotheses concerning affiliation, achievement and hunger were formulated. So they draw on a knowledge of the overall level of response on each measure, as well as of the differential responses of girls and boys. As a result it has been possible to include a limited number of secondary hypotheses, which in turn allows for greater specification of relations between variables. Indeed, these secondary hypotheses tend to yield more definite findings than do the primary forms.

Hypothesis (x): There will be no difference between fostered boys and those being reared by their own parents in frequency of achievement imagery, but fostered girls will have higher achievement scores than those with their own parents.

In considering the possible effects of fostering on achievement motivation, it is first necessary to take into account the influences for and against a high level of this variable in children who are being brought up by their own parents. Only then can we ask how fostering experiences may be different. Davis (1944) distinguishes between the influence of original socialization patterns and later adaptive acculturation in personality formation. Since, except in very unusual circumstances, all Gonja children spend the first three years with their own parents, they share a single pattern of original socialization. Any differences between them occur later, in the phase of Davis' adaptive acculturation.

Gonja child-rearing practices tend to emphasize indulgent attentiveness in the early months, with the sharing of care-taking tasks between the mother and the other women or girls who are available to help. The baby is never left alone for more than a few moments, being tied to the back of the mother or her helper, resting on a hip, or sitting under a shaded tree where others are gathered. Slightly older children enjoy playing with a baby, and when the mother has time, she will sit down and tickle or sing to the child.

Weaning is begun at the age of four or five months by offering morsels of cooked food while the mother and older children are eating. It is said that the baby gradually loses interest in his mother's milk by the time he is two, and that this process is aided by her next pregnancy, likely to occur about this time, which causes her milk to dry up. Toilet training is also gradual, with little attention paid to occasional lapses, and once the child can walk, the older children lead him first to the outside of the compound and later to the refuse heap on the edge of the village. It is said that a child who continues to wet his mat at night after the age of five or six will be shamed by his parents in front of the others in the compound, and even outside it. However, I never saw this happen, though I once heard of a young man who could not keep a wife because of his incontinence.

Discipline is strict and arbitrary but it is often followed by affectionate treatment, as when a mother smacks her infant and then gives him her breast to stop his crying. However, the alacrity with which children from the age of four or five obey their parents is impressive. Obedience is employed in seeing that the children help with small tasks around the compound; later on the boys assist in the farm. This training begins very gently with requests to a toddler to fetch a bowl or cloth for his mother, but girls of six or seven are expected to be able to sweep the house and wash the dishes from the evening meal. Until they are ten or eleven, the tasks of boys in the farm are limited to fetching things and to scaring away the birds from the ripening grain. Even then a boy is at first only asked to clean the small weeds, to lay out the seed yams for the men who plant, or to follow behind putting the caps of grass on the yam mounds to protect them from the intense sun of the dry season.

In her study of the differences between mothers of boys with high and low achievement scores, Winterbottom (1958) found that those whose mothers made earlier demands on them for independence and mastery[9] had the highest achievement scores. These same mothers also set earlier but fewer restrictions than did the mothers of low-achievement boys. How does this relate to the treatment of her son by the Gonja mother? As we have seen, weaning and toilet training are not treated as serious problems and, so far as I can tell, children are not made to feel very strongly about the control of these functions. From the age of a few months, the young child is often entrusted to a sibling to look after. In the company of his nurse he has constant companionship and stimulation, but few if any demands for mastery are made upon him, and none for positive independence. Instead, he is praised for being gay, or appealing, or for not being a bother. Except when tears are the result of punishment, babies and young children are not allowed to cry. A nurse is expected to keep her charge from crying and mothers complain about those who bring the baby back too soon because it needs a feed.

Once children can run about easily, they are made the responsibility of an older sibling when out of the compound, but very much left to find their own amusement. Much of the play of the three- and four-year-old is autistic in the sense of sitting and watching others, or making designs with sticks in the dust. Slightly older children begin to fashion model cages and little lorries from sticks, play house, and join in any number of singing and ball games; they play hide and seek, and tag, and the boys engage in endless mumble peg.

In none of these aspects of early socialization is there an emphasis on mastery by adults. There is, however, steady encouragement to be independent; and, for the girls particularly, responsibility for younger children soon intrudes on freedom. How does fostering affect this picture? Quite differently for girls and for boys. For the former, the foster-parent is always a woman,[10] and while she is almost always delighted to receive her foster-daughter, she is also aware of her duties in training the girl. Furthermore, a foster-parent will wish to make use of the help a foster-daughter can provide, and I have seen instances where demands were made upon a girl of five or six which it is unlikely would have come from her own mother. In terms of early demands for mastery, fostering does make a difference for girls.

For boys the picture is different. In view of the norm, a surprisingly high proportion had been sent to foster-parents before the age of five (50%), but with only one exception they were described as the foster-child of a man. As the age at which boys are expected to begin to contribute to male endeavours (eight or

78

nine is probably the earliest) is in any case later than the equivalent for girls, these boys spent a minimum of four years as foster-children before any role-specific tasks were seriously expected of them. During this period they were fed and bathed, and sent on occasional errands by the women of the compound, but otherwise left very much to their own devices. Indeed, from the age of six or seven, all the young boys in the compounds find themselves places to sleep, for they are no longer welcome in their mother's room. Again, independence is approved though not actively encouraged. But mastery demands are not pressed until well past the age of eight, which Winterbottom suggests may be the critical period.

There is thus little difference in the kind of life led by a fostered boy and one being reared by his own parents, and in neither case are mastery or responsibility stressed at an early age. In Davis' terms, the adaptive acculturation of boys who are being fostered does not differ much from that of those who are not. For girls this is not the case, since earlier and more consistent demands are made by foster-parents than by a girl's own mother.

The other study which is suggestive of how aspects of parent–child relationships may influence level of achievement motivation is that of Rosen and D'Andrade (1959). Their findings indicate that fathers of high achievers tend to be relatively non-authoritarian, while their mothers tend to be relatively dominant and pushing. Both fathers and mothers of boys with high achievement scores tended to be warmer and more supportive, and to set higher standards for their sons than the parents of low achievers. Though I find such characterization difficult, I think Gonja parents of both sexes could be rated as relatively authoritarian and as not setting high standards. Fathers and mothers both vary in the amount of warmth they express to their children.[11]

I have no evidence that foster-parents behave in a more or less warm or authoritarian manner towards children than do their own parents, and I do not believe they explicitly set them higher standards. But the fact of being fostered does influence parent–child relationships by the very process of substituting the actors. For it seems likely that children feel differently about the affective sanctions applied by adults with whom they have not formed their primary dependent relationships. What does this mean in terms of the relationships that foster-children of each sex have with their foster-parents?

While a boy who is sent to a foster-parent is freed from the immediate control of a possibly authoritarian father, he is also removed from the support and encouragement which his mother might provide. One of the important differences in the way that fostering is experienced by boys and girls, arises from the fact that a child is placed in the immediate care of an adult of the same sex. Thus while a girl goes to live under the care and surveillance of a woman who can assume at least some aspects of the maternal role, a boy is sent to a man for training and guidance. If he is still small, his foster-parent will place him under the care of a wife, but to her the boy is an added burden and very little help.

While she will certainly feed the child, she will take less pains over him than her own children. If a boy goes to a foster-parent after the age of seven or eight, he is likely to see very little of any particular woman, as he will sleep with the older boys, take his meals with them, and spend little time in the compound.

It would seem that in terms of Rosen and D'Andrade's findings, a fostered boy has half the conditions for a high level of achievement, the absence of the authoritarian father, but lacks the other half, the dominant and pushing mother. The boy who is reared by his own parents, on the other hand, is very likely to have both a supportive mother and an authoritarian father. Thus he too has only half the conditions necessary for a high level of achievement motivation. Rosen and D'Andrade do not consider the effect on achievement motivation of girls of different styles of father–daughter and mother–daughter relationship. However, there must be important differences from the pattern they found for boys because, in addition to the affective relationship that exists between them, the mother is a model for the adult instrumental role *vis-à-vis* her daughter. To the extent that the same role-factors are operating for the learning of achievement motivation by girls, the fostered girl is in a very different position from a fostered boy. In her new home her closest relationship is with her foster-mother who almost without exception is pleased to have her company and her help. So, within the limits of the foster-mother's own personality, she is likely to be the kind of supportive and yet exacting, non-indulgent mother-figure found related to a high level of achievement motivation. In addition, the child's relationship with the husband of her foster-mother is likely to be casual, as well as emotionally neutral, very different from the authoritarian figure which her father may have presented.[12]

There is another factor that in my opinion is at least as important in attempting to unravel the problems of achievement motivation, namely, the effects of pressures deriving from the social system. Very briefly, these seem to lead to predictions of the same sort as do the psychological factors already considered: competence for girls is encouraged in the sphere of domestic skill which is directly related to the assumption and successful performance of her adult roles of wife and mother. There is immediate feed-back for successful achievement in these skills and she is led to believe that there is a long-term advantage as well. On the other hand, the adult male skills valued in this society are not those which a young boy or youth can attempt, let alone begin to master. His efforts are directed towards farming, yet for the ruling and Muslim groups this is a necessary but not an esteemed job. Slaves and followers of successful and important men used to farm for them. The valued adult skills are in the spheres of administration, adjudication, learning (for the Muslims), medicine and warfare. Today all of these, with the partial exception of a Muslim education, are remote from the experience or aspirations of a young boy.[13]

There is a final factor which affects male achievement orientation in particular, and which I suspect is largely responsible for the low level of achievement motivation in the imagery of all our subjects. This has to do with the link between competition and achievement, especially in those societies where deference and respect are major features in establishing and maintaining relationships between men. Open competition is a form of challenge, and as such is the direct opposite of deferential and respectful behaviour. If excellence is validated by success in open competition, then striving for excellence conflicts with obligations to defer to one's seniors. In traditional Gonja society girls move in the sphere of domestic and kinship norms and activity. Their excellence at domestic and maternal skills is not defined in competition with others, and does not represent a challenge to anyone.

The single exception here is fecundity; but, while success in bearing and rearing a large number of children may be a matter for jealously, everyone still regards it as directly associated with domestic and maternal skill to which all aspire, and for which all women are respected and admired. It is significant in this context that women who have managed to rear large families are not accused of doing so by illicit means – that is through witchcraft or the use of medicines. Rather, those who have failed to bear or rear children may be accused of trying to harm their more fortunate sisters in this way. Success in maternal enterprise is not seen as being at anyone's expense, as a result of competition. Failure, however, may lead to competition by illegitimate means. But while co-wives are rivals for their husband's affections, the Gonja emphasize this fact less than many African societies. This is probably because divorce is easy, and a dissatisfied wife is not forced to remain and suffer her rival's success in apparent unconcern.

For boys it is otherwise. Men are assumed to be in a state of competition with other men: for wives, for wealth and for office. It is widely assumed that all available means, overt and covert, will be employed to gain succcess. Yet it is often required of them that they outwardly respect and defer to these same rivals. Success is not openly celebrated unless a man is very sure of the strength of his protective medicines. For to do so is to claim precedence, to challenge the status of others as well as their competence in any single sphere. Such a challenge will bring reprisal, either through legal channels, informal sanctions or mystical aggression. The point here is not whether such reprisals actually occur, but rather that men believe they do (E. Goody 1970c).

In short, women can excel at female skills without seeming to compete, and thus without threatening the established hierarchy of respect. For they operate within the domestic domain within which subordinate relationships are permanently defined by sex and kinship status. Men cannot excel without being seen as competing and as intending a challenge to the established hierarchy. For they operate in an external domain in which relations between both individuals and units are seen as open to redefinition through the demonstration of superiority, whether this be by age, wealth, political office or mystical power.

Of course if women are seen to be employing skills and powers which give

81

them mastery within the external domain, that is, the male sphere, they are seen as competing and as threatening the 'proper' order of things. The Gonja believe that such women must be evil witches.

LeVine has analysed the relatively low achievement scores of Hausa youths (1966) in terms of the effect of a system in which achievement goals (offices, advantages obtained through patrons) are only to be held by submissive, compliant behaviour. He suggests that this operates through parents training their sons to be compliant and submissive, which in some way they sense is the way to succeed. My contention would be that in this type of society it is seen as dangerous to be openly competitive. A man who is not compliant will not succeed. But, in addition, if he appears to be openly competitive, he may invite attack, both direct and mystical.

However this may be, there is little basis for predicting a high level of achievement motivation among Gonja boys, whether they are fostered or reared by their own parents. For girls there are conflicting influences, and fostering may well tip the balance for some in favour of a relatively high level of achievement motivation.

The overall level of achievement imagery is low for both boys and girls. This is in part due to the code which requires an explicit concern with an internalized standard of excellence. Using the summary scores, there is no difference between home-reared and fostered boys. Fostered girls are slightly more likely to score on achievement imagery than those reared by their parents, although this difference only reaches the level of a trend.

Conclusion (x): Fostered boys do not differ from other boys in the level of achievement imagery in their stories, but that of fostered girls tends to be higher than that of those reared by their own parents.

Hypothesis (xi): Fostered boys will be more concerned with affiliation imagery than other boys. Fostered girls will have higher affiliation scores than others, but because of the generally high level of affiliation imagery for girls, the difference will appear in the proportion of each group which has high affiliation scores.

Any consideration of need affiliation scores must be in the context of the substantial (and reliable) difference between boys and girls in their need affiliation scores. Boys are more likely to have no score at all on affiliation imagery: 35 per cent of the boys compared to 20 per cent of the girls. And boys are very much less likely to have high scores; only 15 per cent of the boys average more than one reference to affiliation imagery in each story, while 40 per cent of the girls do so. The prediction is that, although in absolute terms boys are not particularly concerned with affiliation, fostering will make them more interested in making and keeping friendly relationships. Girls, on the other hand, are more generally concerned with affiliation, and have relatively high scores. The prediction is that fostering will be related to these high scores. Another way of looking

Table 3-1. *Need affiliation in relation to fostering: Modal categories*

	Need affiliation scores							
	None		Low		High		Total	
Parentally reared								
Boys	*(10)*	*55%*	(6)	30%	(3)	15%	(19)	100%
Girls	(2)	15%	*(7)*	*55%*	(4)	30%	(13)	100%
Fostered								
Boys	(7)	30%	*(15)*	*60%*	(2)	10%	(24)	100%
Girls	(9)	25%	(11)	30%	*(15)*	*45%*	(35)	100%
	28		39		24		N = 91[a]	

[a] Total is less than 97 because temporarily fostered children are excluded as in other tables.

at this pattern is to suppose that boys and girls start at different points on a need affiliation scale; fostering increases concern with affiliation, but the effect appears at different points on the scale for each sex.

For the boys the difference on the summary score for need affiliation reaches the trend level; there is at least a tendency for fostered boys to show more concern with affiliation imagery than do those reared by their parents. A straight comparison of fostered and parentally reared girls on the affiliation summary score gives neither a reliable difference nor a trend. However, the prediction for the girls was in terms of proportion of high scores. This information is presented in Table 3-1. Here we see that the proportion with low scores actually declines by 25 per cent for those being fostered, while the increase in high scores among the fostered group makes this the single most frequent category for them. The modal score for each group is indicated by italics in Table 3-1. For both boys and girls the mode of those fostered is one category higher than the mode for those being reared by their own parents.

Conclusion (xi): Fostered boys do tend to score more often on need affiliation than do those reared by their own parents. Fostered girls do not differ from parentally reared girls in the frequency with which they produce affiliative imagery, but the modal responses category for those being fostered is 'high' while that of those reared by their parents is 'low'.

Hypothesis (xii): Fostered boys will have a higher level of concern with food imagery than those reared by parents. Fostered girls will not differ from the parentally reared in their concern with food and hunger. For both boys and girls, those fostered after the age of five will show a higher level of concern with food imagery than those fostered earlier.

There are three different scales for imagery concerned with hunger which were each scored separately for stories to hunger-cue pictures (those containing graphic reference to food cooking or eating) and to hunger-neutral cues. The three scales rate stories on imagery about deprivation of food, food as a goal, and the 'deprivation minus goal' scores, which is similar to the need food score designed by Atkinson and McClelland (1958) who found it to be positively associated with hunger.

Fostering separates both boys and girls from their own mothers, whose strong and continuing concern with their nurturance could be relied upon. A fostered girl, however, has from the first a direct relationship with her foster-mother, and remains throughout childhood and adolescence in close contact with her, and with the domestic domain. The fostered boy has only an indirect relationship with that wife of his foster-parent to whose care he is assigned, and often lacks a firm base in the domestic group. The pull of peer-relationships and later of farm tasks, as well as the 'roaming about' to which all boys are subject, probably compensate for this in time, but the absence of a close relationship with any particular woman within the domestic unit led to the prediction that fostered boys would be more concerned with food than those reared by their own parents.

In fact none of the comparisons between fostered and parentally reared boys shows a difference in hunger imagery; there is no support for the initial hypotheses that fostered boys would show more concern with food and hunger imagery. The expected lack of difference is present between fostered girls and those with their own parents.

Further consideration of the situation of fostered children led to the secondary hypothesis that those fostered early would be better able to re-forge with the foster-mother the close dependency bonds based on nurturance which characterize the tie between mother and own child. Where a new set of dependency bonds has been established, the foster-mother is likely to take the same special pains a mother does to see that her foster-child does not go hungry. Here the prediction was that early-fostered children, both boys and girls, would be less concerned with hunger and food imagery than those fostered later (after the age of five). While the prediction is in the same direction for children of both sexes, the fact that girls work directly with food, and so have a chance to eat between meals, might lead to smaller differences in their case. Indeed the position of the later-fostered boys is in a sense extreme, for they move directly into the world of the men, and, while leaving behind their own nurturing mother, are unlikely to establish a close relationship with a fostering 'mother'.

For the boys, responses to both types of cue are consistently in the predicted direction. Four out of six comparisons result in differences large enough to meet the criteria of a trend. Responses to the hunger-cue pictures result in the greatest differences, two of these indices approaching the level of reliability with $p = .10$. The differences on hunger-neutral imagery are weaker, but consistently

Table 3-2. *Comparison of frequency of 'high deprivation'*
food scores for boys and girls by age of fostering: Hunger cues

	Age of fostering			
	Before five years		After five years	
High deprivation scores (4–9)				
Boys	0/12	0%	4/13	30%
Girls	7/8	85%	6/15	40%
			N = 48	

in the same direction. Later-fostered boys do tend to be more concerned with hunger and food imagery than do those fostered before the age of five.

The girls' responses on indices of hunger motivation are less easy to interpret. There is a consistent trend for the responses to hunger cues, with two of the three comparisons yielding either a tendency to differ (deprivation minus goal) or a highly reliable difference (deprivation index). However, these differences are in the direction opposite to that predicted. It is the early-fostered girls who show both the high level of concern with deprivation and a tendency towards more deprivation-oriented than goal-oriented scores. Unlike the boys, then, it is the early-fostered girls who appear to be most concerned with food and hunger imagery. None of the three comparisons of responses by girls to the hunger-neutral cues show either a trend or a reliable difference.

How are we to interpret the finding that for girls, early fostering is associated with a higher rather than a lower level of concern about food and hunger? Here again it is necessary to consider the 'absolute' level of concern of boys and girls with hunger imagery. In fact the straight comparison of boys' and girls' hunger imagery shows the latter to have much higher scores both for concern with deprivation of food and on the need food index. If this pattern is related to the effect of the age at which a child was sent for fostering, we find that there is no real difference in the hunger imagery of boys and girls sent for fostering after the age of five, but that early fostering has marked and very different effect depending on the sex of the child (Table 3-2).

It would appear that there is an unusual lack of concern among early-fostered boys about deprivation of food, but much concern, on the other hand, among early-fostered girls. There is no tendency for boys and girls fostered after the age of five to differ in the degree of concern with deprivation of food. Going back to the previous argument, this finding suggests that for some reason boys find it easier to establish a substitute dependency tie in the early years than girls do. The most likely reason for this that I can suggest derives again from the differences in role expectations. Fostered boys are expected gradually to move towards a relationship of apprenticeship with their male foster-parent, whose

task it is to teach them farming and other skills, as well as the behaviour asso-
cited with deference and respect. But men have very little to do with boys below
the age of six or seven except to fondle and play with them in the evenings. An
early-fostered boy moves into the world of women where few demands are made
on him either in early or later childhood; while the boy's socialization into
youth and adolescence is generally left to men. So an early-fostered boy is
entrusted to a woman whose only role in respect to him is a nurturant one.

For girls the pattern is similar, but the actor's roles are different. Thus an
early-fostered girl is also entrusted to a woman whose main role is nurturance.
But the same woman will increasingly make demands and place constraints in
the course of the training in domestic skills as well as in respect and deference
behaviour. Furthermore, as her instructor, the formal task of the foster-mother
is to ensure that the girl is obedient and reaches a high standard of performance
in role-related skills. This task is one of the main reasons for sending a child to a
foster-parent. So a woman is careful not to over-indulge the foster-daughter
whom she will later have to train and discipline. For the fostered girl, the spheres
of nurturance in early childhood and of training in later childhood and adolescence are not separated but merge gradually into one another. It seems very
likely, then, that women fostering very young girls are less indulgent and more
demanding than those fostering very young boys. I hesitate to comment on the
basis of my own observations, as I saw too few young foster-children. Of those
I did see, one little girl of five had demands made upon her that were far above
her capacity to meet. Another girl of four had just joined a foster-mother who
was clearly affectionate towards her, but who also was already beginning to
make simple requests that were easily within the child's competence. Of two
boys under five years, one was notoriously over-indulged by his grandmother
while the other was treated with erratic affection by a grandmother who, nearly
blind and scarcely able to move about, relied on him for more than he could
manage by way of companionship and service.

There is a further possibility which can be no more than speculation. Demands
made upon boys by women may be less threatening to them than demands made
by women on girls. In this society the absolute status difference between men
and women is clear to the youngest child; it may not threaten a young boy's
identity to be mildly constrained by a woman 'as a mother', because he knows
that as a male he is in one sense not vulnerable. A young girl, on the other hand,
is subject to the world of older women as well as to the world of men. A 'mother'
who constrains and demands places additional burdens on a developing sense of
identity and confidence. But whether or not this particular line of reasoning is
correct, it seems very likely that any difference between the food and hunger
responses of boys and girls will be related to the fact that for girls, food is at
once a source of nourishment and gratification, as well as a source of work. For
boys, and indeed for men, food always remains something which is procured by
them, but prepared and 'given' by women.

The Kpembe study

But such observations are far removed from the indices which occasioned them. Let us return to the main hypothesis about concern with food and hunger, namely that fostered boys would show a higher level of concern with food than those reared by their own parents, but that fostered girls would not differ in this respect. There is no confirmation of the hypothesized difference between fostered and parentally reared boys, but as predicted, girls do not differ. Fostering of itself, then, does not appear to affect a child's level of concern with food. However, we have seen that the age at which fostering is initiated is reflected in differential hunger scores, early fostering being related to low scores among boys, but to high scores for girls.

Conclusion (xii): Fostered boys are no more likely to be concerned with food than others. However, boys who are sent to foster-parents after the age of five show consistent tendencies towards high concern compared with those fostered earlier.

Fostered and parentally reared girls do not differ in their degree of concern with food and hunger imagery. However, early-fostered girls are significantly more likely to have a high level of concern with deprivation of food than are those fostered after the age of five.

Evaluation of hypotheses: Summary

The findings concerning the three sets of hypotheses have different implications. The first set of hypotheses predicted that fostered children would not differ significantly from those being reared by their own parents on various measures of anxiety, ability to form relationships, attitudes towards obedience and respect, and in orientation to sex roles, and sex-role prescribed tasks. There were only a few scattered differences on these measures, and no consistent and reliable patterns appeared. There were some hints that boys with their own parents might tend to be more anxious, more concerned with obedience and more concerned with role tasks. However, these were so weak that the most that can be said is that there is no clear evidence for difference, and no evidence at all that fostered boys are more anxious or more concerned with male roles. Nor is there any clear evidence for differences between fostered girls and those reared by their own parents. These findings do not permit the assertion that there are no differences between fostered and home-reared children; only that no differences have been shown to exist.

The second set of hypotheses predicted that fostered children would differ from others in their perceptual style and degree of independence. The attempts to measure perceptual style were consistently unsuccessful, most of them being rejected before the analysis was even begun. However, on the measures used there were no reliable differences, though it does appear that fostered children, both boys and girls, show more independence than those with their own parents.

Parent roles in Gonja

The final set of hypotheses were formulated after the analysis had started, and are mainly interesting because it proved possible to specify more exactly how fostering seemed to be related to differences in achievement motivation, affiliation and concern with food. I do not consider that these differences are in any way demonstrated, but would hope that the mechanisms suggested might be further tested on analogous samples. In particular it would be valuable to explore the difference in vulnerability of girls and boys between the ages of three and five.

*   *   *

In this section I first looked at the practice of kinship fostering in Gonja in terms of people's beliefs and the way it works in practice, exploring the question of the effects of fostering in a number of ways. In Chapter 2 men's careers and women's marital stability were found to be little affected by the experience of fostering, which was certainly no disadvantage. The analysis of projective imagery of a large sample of children in Kpembe produces nothing which alters these conclusions. Neither did my observations of children in their homes and neighbourhoods, nor the extensive interviews with them (some of which are summarized in Appendix I). Having examined this question on several different levels with consistent results, I want now to turn to an examination of the wider distribution of fostering and related institutions in West Africa, in both the 'traditional' and the 'modern' spheres.

PART II

Parent roles in West Africa

4

The circulation of women and children in northern Ghana

With JACK GOODY*

In this chapter, written with Jack Goody, preliminary consideration is given to some of the correlates of the movement not only of children in fostering, but also of women in marriage and divorce, in the societies of northern Ghana. In the following chapter I broaden the basis of consideration of the movement of children both geographically and institutionally.

As the result of fieldwork among the LoWiili and the Gonja we were led to compare a set of kinship factors. These are: the nature of marriage prestations (bridewealth etc.); the pattern of divorce; the presence of widow inheritance (or levirate); the extent of kinship fostering; the concepts of paternity; the kind of kin groups. The LoWiili and Gonja display two distinct clusters of these variables, and the same two clusters are found in all of the societies discussed, with some relatively minor exceptions. We seek to understand why these variables should be grouped in these two ways, what is their influence on residence, and offer an explanation for their occurrence.

The discussion of these interrelationships continues earlier lines of research on fostering (E. Goody 1961; 1966), divorce (E. Goody 1962), descent (J. Goody 1962; 1968) and cross-cousin marriage (J. and E. Goody 1966). Though it is specific in its ethnographical reference, the analysis relates to the general theme pursued by Radcliffe-Brown (1950), Fortes (1949a; 1950), Gluckman (1950), Leach (1957), Fallers (1957), Stephens (1962), Lévi-Strauss (1963), Lewis (1962) and many others concerning the relative strength of conjugal and sibling bonds. We are concerned with this problem not in the abstract but in so far as these ties are explicit in patterns of residence. We wish to make the general point that the residence pattern must be viewed not simply in relation to the post-marital residence of women (virilocal, uxorilocal, etc.) but as a whole, that is, over the entire life-cycle, so as to include the return to natal kin (by divorce) as well as the earlier separation from them (by marriage). It must also include an analysis of the factors determining the residence of the children of the union;

* We are grateful to Susan Drucker Brown and Christine Oppong for information on the Mamprusi and Dagomba; other material for this chapter was gathered during the course of our work in Ghana.

Table 4-1. *Kinship variables among the LoWiili and Gonja*

Set	Variable	Cluster A: LoWiili	Cluster B: Gonja
1. Unilineal descent groups		Present	None, except dynastic descent groups
	Ratio of sibling residence	Lower	Higher
	Widows	Levirate	Inheritance banned: widows ousted
2. Residence of women	Divorce prestations	Return of bridewealth	No legalising act
3. Residence of children	Divorce patterns	High→medium→low	High→high→high
	Marriage prestations	High	Low, virtually non-existent
	Paternity	'Social'	'Biological'
4. Residence of men	Fostering	None: occasional nurse-girls and care by substitute mother in crisis	Frequent
		Largely agnatic	Partly agnatic

for the bonds between siblings that have been loosened by marriage may be strengthened by bringing up (fostering) one another's children or by arranging marriages between them; indeed, we regard some forms of preferential cross-cousin marriage as just such an attempt to perpetuate the brother–sister tie in the following generation – the compensation for the incest taboo at one remove.[1]

Methodologically we set out to continue the tradition of limited comparisons (using a few societies) that has already proved itself of some value in furthering our understanding of divorce (Gluckman 1950; Leach 1957), witchcraft (Nadel 1952; Wilson 1951), cross-cousin marriage (Radcliffe-Brown 1930; Leach 1951), matrilineal systems (Richards 1950), incest (J. Goody 1956b) and a number of other topics. We then extend the scope of the analyses to consider the other groups in the area that have been the subject of detailed study, namely the Tallensi and the Konkomba. These intensive comparisons are aimed at illuminating the interrelations among the variables in each of the two clusters A and B, and their bearing on the questions of kin-group structure, sibling and conjugal roles, and shifts in residence (see Table 4-1).

Finally we test our conclusions by means of a systematic, inclusive, regional comparison, that is, against all the societies in northern Ghana on which reports, however fragmentary, exist. The purpose of this final exercise is to establish the distribution of the clusters observed in the intensive comparisons and hence to provide a local test of the firmness of the association. The results of the extensive comparisons are presented in Table 4-2, which is deliberately similar in construction to our earlier table showing the distribution of cross-cousin marriage in the same area, in order to permit cross-reference (J. and E. Goody 1966).

Kinship patterns in northern Ghana

	Pattern of divorce			Marriage prestations (total)	Fostering (other than crisis fostering)	Widow inheritance	Paternity (status of adulterine child)	Exogamous kin groups	Sources
	Initial	Middle	Terminal						
Type 1									
1. Isala				H (30 c or 2C)		+		+(P)	R 501, 505, 466
Awuna (Fra)				H (2 C+5 c)		+		+(P)	R.528, 529
Awuna (Nagwa)				H (3 C+25 c+s)		+			R 533, 536
Konkomba	O		O	H (£22 + Farming)	O	+	S	+(P)	Tait
2. Tallensi	H	M		H (4 C)	O	+	S	+(P+m)	Fortes
Namnam	H		L	H (4 C)	O	+		+(P+m)	G.f.
Nankanse	H	M		H (4 C)	+(?)	+		+(P+m)	R 283, 267; G.f.; Cardinall 74
Kusasi	H	M		H (2–5 C)	O	+		+(P+m)	R 388, 385, 375; G.f.
Builsa	H	M		H (2 C+2s)	O	+		+(P+m)	R 399; G.f.
Dagaba	H	M		H (30–50 c)	O	+		+(P+m)	R 414, 422; G.f.
Kasena	H	M		H (2 C)	O	+		+(P+m)	R 545, 539; G.f.
3. Lowiili	H	M	L	H (20 c+2–3 C+F)	O	+	S	+(P+m)	G 1956a
4. Lobirifor	M	M		H (3 C+F)	O (?)	+	S	+(P+M)	Labouret 279, 287; G.f.
Lodagaba	M	M	L	H (13–20 c+ 2–3 C+F)	O	+	S	+(P+M)	G.f.
Chakalle	H	H	H	L	+	O		+(P+M)	G.f.
Type 2									
5. Vagala	H	H	H	L	+	O		O	R 521, 520; G.f.
Safalba	H	H	H	L	+	O		O	G.f.
Degha	H		H	L	+	O		O	Tauxier 407; G.f.
Choruba	H	H	H	L	+	O		O	G.f.
6. Gonja	H	H	H	L	+	O	B	O	G. 1962
Dagomba	?	H	H	L (4 c)	+	O		O	R 460; Oppong f, 1973; Blair
Mamprusi	H	H	H?	L	+	+/O		(O)	Brown, S. D. f.; R 460, 463; Mackay
Wala				L	+	+		(O)	G.f.
Nanumba				L		O		O	G.f.; Amherst 38

Legend:
H = high
M = medium
L = low
+ = present
O = absent
Sources: R = Rattray 1932;

P = patrilineal descent group
M = matrilineal descent group
m = matrilineal complementary descent group
C = cows
s = sheep
G = Goody (J. or E.);   f = fieldnotes.

c = cowries (in thousands)
F = farming
S = 'social' legitimacy
B = 'biological' legitimacy

Parent roles in West Africa

We begin the analysis with a statement of the general differences between the LoWiili and the Gonja, and then examine certain features of their kinship systems which we see as interrelated.

The general contrast between LoWiili and Gonja

Political organization

Before 1900, the LoWiili had no chiefs, their social organization was segmentary in that the constituent units were relatively homologous and politically equal (Fortes and Evans-Pritchard 1940).

The Gonja were stratified into ruling, Muslim, commoner and slave estates, forming parts of a loose state that we have called an overkingdom.

Economic organization

Before 1900, the LoWiili were almost entirely agriculturalists, living in dispersed settlements and deriving their living from hoe farming.

The Gonja were farming on land which is in general less fertile but less populated than that of the LoWiili; some were also active in trade and crafts. The exaction of limited amounts of tribute, taxes on trade and labour services contributed to the support of chiefs, while the better-off owned slaves. They lived in nucleated villages, and in a few areas of concentrated political and commercial activity formed the kind of 'poly-ethnic town' found elsewhere in the western Sudan; indeed Salaga, the main commercial town of Gonja, was called the Timbuktu of the south and was the entrepot through which Ashanti kola nuts were sold to traders from the Mossi and Hausa states to the north and north-east.

Religious system

The LoWiili are 'pagan', that is to say, they lack any commitment to one of the major world religions.

The Gonja are religiously stratified, the commoners being pagan, the traders Muslim, and the chiefs accepting aspects of all faiths held by their subjects, though there is a mounting tendency for them to increase their commitment to Islam, a trend that earlier appeared among freed slaves.

Kin groups

The LoWiili place considerable emphasis on unilineal descent groups (UDGs), and both patrilineal and matrilineal descent groups are found side by side; only the patrilineal groups are property holding, i.e. inheritance takes place within the group and is thought of in these terms.

94

Among the Gonja, on the other hand, the ruling estate is organized into dynastic descent groupings of an agnatic kind that operate on the political but only marginally on the domestic level. Unilineal descent groups in the usual sense are absent and from the present point of view (although this problem requires a more detailed analysis) Gonja can best be 'placed' as a 'bilateral' system.

But both societies display a good deal of patrifilial emphasis (not necessarily patrilineal, by which we refer to social action associated with unilineal descent groups recruited agnatically). For example, marital residence in both is over-whelmingly virilocal, that is to say, when the conjugal unit constitutes a residential group, its location is determined by the husband rather than the wife.

We are concerned, then, with the contrast observed between the pagan, non-stratified, acephalous LoWiili where male agnates occupy neighbouring compounds in a dispersed farming settlement, and the Gonja, whose centralized, stratified, ethnically and religiously more complex organization is associated with a bilateral kinship system which links together individuals living in nucleated villages and towns, the latter supporting a somewhat economically diversified population.

The specific contrast between LoWiili and Gonja

The residence of married women

On the domestic level the first difference that struck us, again, moving between these two societies that we had known over a number of years, had to do with residence. We first want to consider (in schematic form) some of the factors that 'complicate' patterns of post-marital residence.

Complicating factors in residence

'Complex' residence patterns arise in two main ways, by the circulation (physical movement) of adults and by the circulation of children. The prohibitions on sex and marriage between brother and sister mean that in all but a few marginal cases, one or the other has to make a residential shift. In most systems this occurs at or during marriage and establishes the conjugal unit as a dwelling group.

Societies with patrilineal descent groups normally have a 'simple' pattern of residence and this is the case among the LoWiili.[2] Men usually live with their fathers (i.e. patrilocally) and women with their husbands (i.e. virilocally). The domestic unit thus contains a male core which persists over the generations, unless men go off to find new farmlands in other parts.

But in all matrilineal, and in many bilateral, societies the pattern is a complex one. If 'matrilineal' men circulate, then the differing pulls of their lineage and conjugal ties are likely to make for flexibility. In the course of his marital career a man has to split his available space–time between kin and conjugal roles. To do this he may reside alternately in the two places (e.g. Dobu), or he may make fre-quent visits between them (e.g. Hopi); in these cases the pulls work diffusely over the whole of his married life. On the other hand the effects may be concen-trated at quite different phases of the life-cycle, leading to a general shift from uxorilocal to virilocal residence (Bemba) after the marriage has matured. When the 'matrilineal' women circulate (i.e. by virilocal marriage), then it is the male children, not the male adults, whose residential loyalties are split. A lineage home can be maintained only by the institution of 'child return'; children circu-late in the opposite direction to women.

The residential patterns of matrilineal societies are invariably complex not only because of these different forms and their associated problems of bride, groom, and child removal, but also because in any one instance they are unlikely to follow a single 'rule'. In many cases the resultant distribution is a function of the strength of opposing forces at different stages in the domestic cycle (Fortes 1949a).

In those bilateral societies where claims to fixed resources are inherited through both sexes (i.e. that practise 'diverging transmission', see J. Goody 1962:317), a married couple is likely to be offered the alternative of residing with the kin of either the husband or the wife, and perhaps with the kin of their parents as well. Other factors, too, may determine the location of a marriage. A small bridewealth or a large dowry may give a woman and her kin the right to remove the groom or acquire his offspring. For the Bemba 'wealth consists of the power to command service' (Richards 1956:46); through his daughters a man obtained the services of a son-in-law. But property in land is perhaps the most important of the factors behind the determination of residence in what have been called (misleadingly in some respects) 'loosely structured' societies.

The residence of LoWiili and Gonja women

Among the LoWiili, women play primarily a wifely role; of course, they pay short visits to their natal kin, after seeking permission from their husbands, but such permission is reluctantly given and the visits are short. Occasionally a woman may be recalled by her kin to enforce a bridewealth payment or other debt. The LoWiili husbands see themselves as having obtained the right to have their wives living with them (the right of bride removal) through the heavy bridewealth payments and farming services which they have rendered. They also see themselves as having acquired the same control over their children, although the daughters, who in any case quit after marriage, may return to their mother's family as brides, if they marry the mother's brother's son.

In Gonja (and in the other states of northern Ghana) fixed resources are negligible, most land being free and unimproved. The residence of a couple at marriage is not at issue: a woman joins her husband. What complicates the pat-tern is 'woman return' and the circulation of children. A woman may return to her kin during or after a marriage, and then live as a sister rather than as a wife.

The circulation of women and children in northern Ghana

This happens, to some degree, in all societies, but the proportion of time spent one way rather than another is a significant variable in the comparison of societies. It is clear that a Gonja woman spends a very substantial part of her life not living with a husband.

The ratio of sibling to conjugal residence

The relative frequency with which a woman is found residing as sister and as wife we refer to as the ratio of sibling to conjugal residence and is to be distinguished from the divorce rate with which it is often confused.[3] It is a high ratio of sibling residence rather than high divorce as such that could be taken to indicate the strength of the relationship between brothers and sisters. In Euro-American societies, a divorcee does not normally return to live with her parents or her brothers; she either gets another husband or lives as a feme-sole, so that high divorce is not related to the strength of kinship ties. Among the LoWiili, the role of an adult woman (in residential terms) is as a wife; she leaves her husband when she wishes to marry another one and only the rejects (mainly witches) return to their kin for more than a short time. Among the Gonja a woman will have as many, if not more husbands as a LoWiili woman, but the former spends less of her adult life living as a wife and more as a sister.

The difference between these three basic situations (Gonja, LoWiili and Euro-American) is brought out in a number of ways: in the length of a woman's visits to her home, in the treatment of widows and in the patterns of divorce.

Patterns of divorce

We have not calculated any precise ratios for the LoWiili. But the pattern, if not the rate, is clear.[4] In the early stages of marriage, LoWiili wives quite often leave their husbands; girls who have been persuaded into a certain marriage may find a more congenial spouse. Since divorce is usually initiated by women throughout this area (polygyny means they are always in short supply), its frequency partly reflects the extent of the control exercised by male kin. For if a woman who wishes to end a marriage is not allowed to remain with her natal kin but is returned by them to her husband's house, incipient divorce is often smothered in the early stages. While her male kin may be willing for her to go to a new husband who will refund the bridewealth and so relieve them of embarrassment in this respect, such alternative spouses are less easy to find as a woman grows older, even though bridewealth would be reduced. For this reason, and because of the birth of children and the growing affection between the spouses as time goes on, the marriage becomes increasingly secure, until in old age it is virtually unbreakable. This we describe as a high (H), medium (M), low (L) pattern of divorce. It is associated with a low ratio of sibling residence. But it is not necessarily associated with the loss of control of a daughter by her natal kin-group. What often keeps a daughter not only in the married state but also in a particular marriage is pressure from her kin. Thus, in contradistinction to other writers on this subject, we do not necessarily see low (middle and terminal phase) divorce rates as linked with a detachment of a woman from the control of her siblings or other kin, much less her absorption or incorporation in her husband's clan. Low divorce may indicate a high degree of kin control; here we have 'strong' patrilineal descent groups in a sense other than is meant by Fallers, Lewis, and others. For this reason it seems advisable to use the idea of strong descent groups, as Lewis has recently concluded (1965), only with reference to specific criteria.

In Gonja, by contrast, divorce is common throughout a woman's life: before the birth of children, during the years of active childbearing, and later in terminal separation. This latter is the *de facto* dissolution of marriage on the initiative of the woman when childbearing is done and is very common among the Gonja. Between the ages of forty-five and sixty, women of the ruling and Muslim estates and, to a lesser extent, the commoners, make prolonged visits to their kin, usually a real or classificatory brother, from which they never return to the houses of their husbands. This is so common a practice that it is rare to find a woman of fifty-five or over living with a husband.[5] English speakers refer to this as 'retiring from marriage', but in Gonja it is simply said that 'because the woman was old she went to sit with her kinsmen' (E. Goody 1962). Terminal separation is a major contributory factor in the high ratio of sibling to conjugal residence among the Gonja, as is the high (H), high (H), high (H) pattern of divorce.

The residence of children

Among the LoWiili, children are brought up by their own parents,[6] and immediate kinship ties tend to be localized. If a LoWiili woman leaves her husband, she loses touch with her older children; although she may take very young children with her, they will be sent back to the father when old enough to look after themselves. When a man dies, his lineage makes a token bridewealth payment to the wife's kin to stress its continuing rights over the widow and her children. That such a payment is necessary makes it clear that the LoWiili woman retains a role – as sister and aunt – in her natal lineage, as well as of wife and mother among her husband's people. The difference is brought out by the fact that among the LoWiili the roles of sister and aunt have little effect on the residential pattern. Nuclear families are not broken up by the obligation to send children to other kin, nor by prolonged visits of a woman to her relatives.

In Gonja it is children as well as women who circulate. Great emphasis is placed on the institution of kinship fostering whereby from the age of about five, children are sent to be brought up by non-parental kin. Claims to a foster-child are formally expressed as the rights held by a man in his sister's children (more particularly, in their sons) and by a woman in her brother's daughters. But in practice children are reared by a wide range of kin and girls in particular are often asked to go and stay with a grandparent.

The circulation of women and children in northern Ghana

Fostering tends to split up the sibling group at an early stage and often over long distances. Social relationships in Gonja extend over a very wide spatial field. There, members of the ruling and Muslim estates in particular marry widely and therefore foster widely.[7] The institution of fostering seems to us most likely to be found in the absence of 'strong' unilineal descent groups, at least, patrilineal ones. For while kinship fostering could take place entirely within the unilineal descent group (we might then speak of 'descent fostering'), we know of no such limitation in practice.[8]

Easy and relatively frequent divorce also means that the nuclear family is always on the point of dispersal; most homes are (from the Western standpoint) broken homes. In fact, children are often living with non-parental kin. Since political status is given by the Gonja father, there is no real problem of the unilineal affiliation of the children and no great anxiety over their whereabouts. One consequence is that if a woman returns to her natal kin (and this is in many ways a praiseworthy act), she may well find a child of hers living there.

Adult brothers in Gonja are often widely separated, though they may come together at annual festivals and on 'family' occasions. There is not the constant interaction that exists in the joint agnatic household of the LoWiili (or any similar society); brothers are less often in each other's company, though they continue to have close ties which among the ruling group are manifest in political support (J. Goody 1967). The difference is also manifest in cross-sibling (brother-sister) relationships and in sororal ties. For LoWiili women, once married is always married, though not necessarily to the same man. But among the Gonja, a woman often returns to her kin (sometimes for many months) after the birth of her children, between marriages, and when she has given up marriage as a career. She can live as a sister, not only as a wife. And her brothers must find a room and food for her as long as she wishes to live with them.

Widows

In all peasant societies the aged have to be supported out of the current production of a kin group, which forms the basic productive unit. Indeed, this is equally true of all dependants, the young as well as the old, and women, too, unless they take part in productive or money-making activities.

For women the alternatives are support by the husband, by the brother or, at a later stage, by the children. Before the menopause there is no great problem, since the coital and usually the reproductive services of women are in effect exchanged for support (among other things) in the economic sphere, although there are clearly important variations in the dependence on 'kin' or 'affines', brother or husband, which are correlated with (among other factors) the inheritance of property. In northern Ghana virilocal residence at marriage is virtually universal; when the conjugal pair forms a residential unit, the wife joins the husband. Because of this, and because of the marriage age differential, the

99

problems of residence in old age centre upon women rather than men, on widows rather than widowers.

Among the LoWiili the rights which a husband (and his group) acquire by bridewealth payments persist after his death. All children born to the widow belong to the dead man, unless the bridewealth payment is returned. She is expected to make a leviratic 'marriage' and women in general accept this position. In 1965 we found the widows of Bonyiri still living in his compound seven years after his death (J. Goody 1956a:45). And fifteen years after the funeral of the late chief, Gandaa, a number of his widows remained in his house. There are certain advantages for these women. Nominally they are all leviratic wives,[9] but some in fact are certainly there because of their sons and grandchildren. 'He's not my husband', said one widow, referring to the dead man's brother who had become her leviratic spouse, 'my son is'. And a woman will possibly see more of her daughters, too, when she is living at their lineage home.

The contrast in the treatment of widows is most striking. For whereas the LoWiili encourage a widow to stay where she is, the Gonja in effect forbid it. Widow inheritance is banned; death dissolves the marriage and a woman is forbidden to marry any of her dead husband's close kin. Death divorces a woman from all her classificatory husbands. She has to return home to marry elsewhere, although in some cases her children may support her in her own compound. In any case, the ban on remarriage to her children's paternal kin means in effect that she has to quit her late husband's compound, where there is no role that she can easily fill. If she is of marriageable age she offers a forbidden temptation to her late husband's brothers. If she is past the menopause her place is with her own brothers. So the widow is ousted.[10]

Unless she goes straight to a new husband the Gonja widow returns to her natal kin where she settles down with a child (usually a son) or with another kinsman. Sometimes a widow establishes a compound of her own. When she does so it is usually sited near the house of a kinsman of which it is regarded as an offshoot. If a woman chooses to join her brother, even a classificatory one, he will find her a room and provide her with food. Indeed, in some parts of Gonja it is said that one reason an adult son may be living with his maternal kin is so that he can farm for his mother in her old age.

Marriage transactions

Among the LoWiili bridewealth is very high relative to a man's total holding of capital; the average number of cattle in a compound was 4 (one to every 2.5 persons in the community), while the bridewealth payments consisted of 20,000 cowries and 2 to 3 cattle. An investment of this kind cannot come out of what a young man makes by selling his surplus grain and cash crops. It has to come from 'corporate' funds, most usually from members of the senior generation, father and mother's brother, possibly from more distant kin; in this case a debt is contracted which is extinguished at death. Again, corporate funds are not sufficient to sustain many payments of this kind unless there is a counter-balancing intake from the marriages of sisters who are thus cattle-linked, although never in the specific sense of the Lovedu; a man is dependent either upon his sisters or upon the senior generation.

The out-going funds are not only – nor even perhaps primarily – for sexual (i.e. coital), domestic or economic services, but relate to the proven procreative powers of the woman. For the payments are not made in a lump sum but by instalments, as the children are produced. A barren woman earns no bridewealth, apart from the initial transfer, a fact which makes her barrenness a matter of concern to her brothers as well as her husbands. Bridewealth is largely child-wealth.

It is not surprising then that fostering should be uncommon in such a system. The co-resident corporation is always agnatically based in these societies, so that its core is formed by the males of a patrilineage. Its resident male members supply bridewealth for each other, bridewealth which is produced by the out-marrying females. Members have joint interests, financial and otherwise, in each other's marriages and in the offspring that result; they are unlikely to want the care and control to pass into the hands of other, non-lineage, kin. There are of course always a certain number of sister's sons living with maternal kin, but this is refuge (or crisis) fostering. Children are rarely, if ever, sent to maternal kin by their parents, but occasionally run there to get away from them; or young children accompany their mother when her marriage is dissolved.

Among the Gonja a man's outlay at marriage is basically the wedding expenses, a matter of entertainment and display, plus bridal gifts and presents to in-laws, which are rarely recoverable in the event of divorce.[11] There is little incentive to accumulate property for marriage; young men are less dependent upon their parents' wishes and do not need to farm for kinsfolk in order to get help with marriage payments. Not that Gonja youths are unsolicitous of their senior kin, but filial piety is more relaxed, less complicated by pecuniary considerations, and dead ancestors do not play the central role in an individual's life that they do among the Tallensi or the LoWiili.

There may be family pressures on women, formerly supported by force, to marry the children of close kin, either cross-cousins or occasionally (among Muslims) paternal parallel cousins. Such marriages were often sanctioned by supernatural forces too, since the close ancestors, particularly the maternal ones, are concerned to ensure that their descendants do not fall out. But a woman is held neither to a particular marriage, nor to marriage in general, by a background of heavy transactions which have to be repaid in the event of divorce.

It will be seen that the presence of high, fixed bridewealth, like infant betrothal (e.g. among the Konkomba), places considerable restraints upon the junior generation in making marital arrangements. Unlike the Gonja, the LoWiili find it very difficult to raise the bridewealth themselves. Unless they depend upon kin, they have to work in the south in order to acquire the necessary funds or migrate to an area where land is more plentiful.

Divorce transactions

Important here is the nature of divorce transactions, by which we mean the counterpart of marriage transactions. Bridewealth, dowry, wedding gifts - are these returned or retained on divorce?

Among the LoWiili bridewealth relates to the whole period of the marriage; if this is dissolved the prestations are returned, perhaps with some deductions for the expended portion of a woman's marital career. It is not surprising that, given the nature of these transactions, LoWiili divorce rates should display the kind of pattern that Fortes notes for the Tallensi: initially high, then medium, then low, a pattern that is almost the inverse of the scheme of bridewealth payments (Fortes 1949b:85-7). For the return of bridewealth is an enormous charge on a brother's funds. The LoWiili cannot afford to have their sisters around their compounds, not if they want partners themselves. The only occasions on which this happens is when a man with few children discourages his daughter from marrying until she has produced a child on his behalf; this is the 'house-child', who has at once a privileged and an underprivileged status (J. Goody 1956a:62; 1962:223). A woman sometimes lives with kin when she is divorced by her husband; but if the husband initiates divorce, he loses the right to claim the return of bridewealth, so that examples of this are rare.

In Gonja gifts are not usually returned in practice. They are made once and for all, to please in-laws, to initiate intercourse and to secure the removal of the bride. Thus a father is under no economic pressure to persuade his daughter to 'try again', nor, on the other hand, to recall a daughter from a man who has been slow with his bridewealth payments. Consequently affinal relations, particularly with the senior generation, take on a different quality and do not display the same pattern of deep respect that is reported for the LoDagaa and the Tallensi. One can hear a woman refer to a son's wife as her 'grandchild' and treat her in the joking manner appropriate to this category of kin. However, the easy relationship with mothers-in-law may also be affected by the fact that they are seldom found in the same compound as their sons' wives: even if a woman is still living with her husband, her sons are likely to have moved out of their father's compound by the time they marry. But it is all affinal relations, not only those between mother and daughter-in-law, that are more diffuse, more relaxed. So the presence or absence of high bridewealth appears to have considerable ramifications for the whole set of kin relations.

Paternity

One further aspect of the contrast between the LoWiili and the Gonja associated with this set of variables concerns the concept of paternity. The critical case here is the fate of the adulterine child. Among the LoWiili, as in other societies with 'strong' unilineal descent groups, a man's jural father (pater) is his mother's jural husband, no matter who is the actual genitor. Among the Gonja a man's jural father is his genitor; if a chief's wife sleeps with a commoner, then the child is a commoner; as in earlier England, it becomes possible to bastardize the off-spring of a married woman and thus exclude him from the enjoyment of the property and status of his mother's husband. Although the Gonja affirm that 'a thief doesn't own the thing he steals', it is seldom that an adulterine child is accepted by his mother's husband; a boy is usually forced to seek out his genitor. A husband's rights are in no sense exclusive even over his legitimate offspring, for they are shared with maternal kin. Traditionally it was the mother's brother who had the right to pawn or sell the children into slavery, not the father. This provides the charter not only for claims on particular children for fostering, but for the strongly held sense of 'ownership' of, or rights in, one another's children which characterizes the groups of both full and half-siblings. Clearly, overlapping claims are present, for siblings of both parents feel that they share rights in the same children. This idea is sometimes expressed by saying that half the children (the first, third, fifth etc.) belong to the father's side and half (the second, fourth, sixth etc.) to the mother's, but no such strict allocation is in fact adhered to. One reason for this lack of exclusiveness, as some of the actors themselves explain, is the nature of the marriage prestations.

Among the LoWiili the corollary of the fact that bridewealth transfers rights in a woman's procreative powers to the husband's lineage is the idea that a woman's natal kin have the exclusive ownership of children before these pay-ments are made. 'House-children' are not in fact illegitimate; rather their legiti-macy (albeit restricted) resides in their natal lineage. A man may deliberately use his daughter to produce children on his behalf; these are what the LoWiili refer to as *yirbie* and the Nankanse as *yi-yeen bia*, 'the children of the house'. 'This is not a marriage', writes Victor Aboya, 'It is only a sowing of seed' (Rattray 1932:I, 161-2). Among the Gonja, on the other hand, a man has a claim upon his children by an unmarried girl, for paternity and 'ownership' are not deter-mined by bridewealth, nor, indeed, by 'marriage'.

Unilineal descent groups

Table 4-1 summarizes the main differences between the LoWiili and the Gonja in terms of the two clusters of kinship variables. Logically consistent with these is the fact that the LoWiili have 'strong' (i.e. multifunctional) unilineal descent groups, the Gonja none; indeed, apart from the dynastic descent groups of the ruling estate and the residual patronymic groups of the Muslims they can hardly be said to have boundary-maintaining kin groups (as distinct from kin ranges) at all.

Low marriage payments, the prohibition on widow inheritance, a high ratio of sibling residence and 'biological' paternity (cluster B), all fit with the absence of unilineal descent groups. Whereas high marriage payments, the levirate, a low ratio of sibling residence (rather than a low rate of divorce in itself) and 'social' paternity (cluster A), all these are consistent with 'strong' unilineal descent groups.

Other intensive studies

The other intensive sociological studies of communities in northern Ghana are of the Konkomba and the Tallensi. In terms of the institutions we have been isolating, the Konkomba represent a more extreme case than the LoWiili. The stability of marriage, writes Tait, is regarded as absolute and is in fact 'remarkably high' (1961:180). Inheritance of widows (and even betrothed) is very frequent as a result of the disparity in age between husband and wife. Because of this children often have to be redistributed at the death of the father, a situation that is dealt with by a special form of 'crisis fostering' where the orphans are looked after by close agnatic kin of the deceased.[12] In his discussion of the development of the household, Tait writes of the assignment of orphaned adolescents and young adults of both sexes to reinforce the existing members of a newly established household on the farm and in housework. This is essentially an allocation of the labour available to a minor lineage after the death of a male member. There is no question of control of either widows or children passing outside the lineage that has acquired rights in them; both are physically retained within the unilineal descent group, or rather, the lineage home.

Bridewealth payments and services are relatively high among the Konkomba. In 1952 Tait estimated their total value at £32, while marriage to a woman of the neighbouring Kabre tribe involved an outlay of 4 cows, at a value of £40 to £50. A major difference exists in the kind of transaction that was made; internal marriages between Konkomba involve the transfer of perishable foodstuffs (guinea-corn) rather than cattle or cowries. The payments of grain, however, could be commuted (on some traditional system of reckoning which was clearly not keeping up with contemporary inflation) to cash payments amounting to £6.[13] While the average annual cash income of a compound head was less than £10, this sum could be accumulated by two weeks' work on a farm in the south (Tait 1961:95). It would appear that the outlay on brides was formerly considerable, but that labour migration has led to an easing of the situation.

There does not seem to be any return of marriage payments in the event of divorce, perhaps because the latter was so rare and the former so perishable. In any case runaway wives had to seek some distant haven where such claims were unlikely to be effective. If she goes back to her natal home her brothers 'accept her for a short period only and will then return her to her husband' (Tait 1961: 183); for nearly every Konkomba marriage is an arranged marriage, since girls are betrothed in their infancy to men already of marriageable age; and when the time comes for them to join their husbands, 'all are reluctant to go, most of them seek to delay their going, and in the end they go weeping bitterly' (1961: 182). The pre-emption of sexuality involved in infant betrothal leads to a maximization of parental control and Tait concludes that 'the low rate of broken marriages is due to the controls exerted over both spouses and is in no way due, in the early years of marriage, to happy and close personal relationships' (1961: 182). This control is exercised in a wife-providing (and wife-getting) direction, rather than in the retention of rights over women as sisters.

The Tallensi case is most illuminating on this subject and its value is particularly high because of the depth of Fortes' fieldwork and analysis. These people display the same set of characteristics as the LoWiili and Konkomba; widow inheritance, absence of fostering, high bridewealth. Marriage tends to be 'unstable in the initial stages' (Fortes 1949b:84), but 'despite these initial pitfalls of marriage, families do get established and remain stable' (85). In the absence of precise rates it would be difficult to say that the Gonja situation was much different up to this point, although we have rated Tallensi divorce in the middle stage as medium and Gonja as high. But in the final stage the contrast with Gonja is clear, for when a woman has borne two or three children this link through the offspring becomes 'a really effective force in maintaining the marriage' (87).[14] Moreover, a father is under a similar sort of pressure as his LoWiili counterpart, i.e. partly 'economic', to encourage his daughter to remain in the married state.

Extensive comparison

In Table 4–2 we present the information we have been able to gather from published material, unpublished papers and fieldnotes on the peoples of northern Ghana. The initial classification, on the basis of the presence and type of unilineal descent groups, we do not discuss at length here since we do so in another paper on cross-cousin marriage (J. and E. Goody, 1966:347).[15] We simply point out that the horizontal subdivisions 1, 2 etc. have the following significance:

1. Patrilineal descent groups.
2. Patrilineal descent groups plus unnamed matrilineal descent groups (e.g. Tallensi *soog*).
3. Patrilineal descent groups plus matrilineal descent groups, but property is only inherited within the first.
4. Patrilineal descent groups, plus matrilineal descent groups, both corporate with regard to property, i.e. double inheritance (transmission down both lines).
5. Patrilineal descent groups, of limited significance (ethnic groups of commoners within centralized societies).
6. Unilineal descent groups absent, or very limited, except in a dynastic context (centralized societies).

In the two latter cases, the unilineal descent groups (in so far as they exist at all) have few functions, although in group 6 dynastic descent groups control eligibility to high office. So we speak of them as 'limited' or 'weak'. Moreover, group 6 consists of centralized states and group 5 of linguistically distinct peoples subordinate to those states; the same is true of at least one part of the Chakalle, a people about whom our information is minimal. With the possible exception of the Chakalle, groups 1, 2, 3 and 4 all consist of stateless societies.[16]

The two clusters of variables that emerge from the intensive studies are also found in the societies which have received less attention from sociologists. For example, writing of the Vagala, Rattray mentions a system of 'adoption' which is in fact precisely the same as what is here called fostering. It is the only society of the 'Gonja' type with whose domestic organization he deals and he specifically remarks upon adoption and widow remarriage, linking this with the bridewealth transactions, viz., 'The position of widows regarding re-marriage is unusual, but in keeping with the fact that brideprice was not paid for them on marriage. The heir may not take them . . .' (1932:2, 521).

There are three cases in the table which do not altogether fit the Gonja and LoWiili models. In Mamprusi, according to both Rattray and Mackay, widow inheritance is allowed; however it seems to be rare, treated with ambivalence and absent from some Muslim groups (Brown, private communication). The greater stress placed here on persisting rights over women may be related to the somewhat greater emphasis placed on unilineal descent groups; segments of the royal dynasty are exogamous up to a depth of three generations, A similar situation obtains in Wa, which was probably an offshoot of the Mamprusi kingdom.

The case of the Chakalle of the eastern Wa district (group 4) is possibly anomalous because of the nature of the available material. This ethnic unit consists of a western group, speaking Dagaari (Wala), who have undergone much Muslim influence and were under the hegemony of Wa; and an eastern group, speaking Chakalle (a Grusi language), who are predominantly pagan and were under Gonja domination. The information on these people was collected during the course of several brief visits and the apparent inconsistencies may be due to differences between the two groups which certainly require further investigation.

Finally, there is the case of the Nankanse. Of these Victor Aboya writes that some children are brought up by their paternal grandparents and some by their mother's brother. This situation is very different from that obtaining among their immediate neighbours, the Tallensi, where out of 170 children under sixteen, only 2 per cent were not living with at least one parent and these were all orphans. Fortes is very clear on this point: the vast majority of Tallensi children grow up with their natural parents (1949b:136). However, the Nankanse appear to send children to be socialized not only to parental grandparents but also outside the lineage, to maternal uncles.[17] We offer no further explanation for this apparent anomaly, although we would add that our own enquiries reveal a situation much closer to the Tallensi pattern.

The circulation of women and children in northern Ghana

With the possible exception of the Nankanse, the situation found in northern Ghana can be seen in terms of the presence and strength of the unilineal descent group. The 'descent' societies retain residential control over their wives at the expense of seeing their sisters; if they prevent their wives from spending much time with kin, then they in turn will see little of their sisters. Control over the wife carries with it control over the children, who are rarely sent out in 'voluntary' fosterage. But although control of women as wives is linked to the control of women as sisters, the roles are not substituted for one another at marriage; rather, the role of wife, and later mother, is an incremental addition to a woman's status.

Discussion

The issue of general theoretical relevance which this material raises has to do with the relationship between bridewealth (or brideprice) and divorce.[18]

In pointing out that a high bridewealth enables men to control the movement of women (or at least of their genetricial rights), we see such payments as helping to sustain not so much a low divorce rate as a low rate of sibling residence. However frequently women circulate in the high bridewealth groups, they do not stay long with kin. In these same societies in northern Ghana there is also a relatively low divorce rate, particularly in the middle and later stages of a woman's marital career. We recognize that this is not a universal correlation; Gluckman (1950) and Lewis (1962) cite a number of examples to the contrary, though we think these need examining to differentiate those cases where the bridewealth is a. returnable; b. jurally high (i.e. fixed at a high amount relative to total resources); c. not simply part of the wedding celebrations or an indirect endowment of the bride.[19] A jurally high bridewealth, such as we find among the LoWiili and similar groups in northern Ghana, is linked (by the actors and by regional comparison) with the transfer of genetricial rights in the bride to the husband's lineage; it defines the status of children in relation to a series of unilineal descent groups; it is a form of childwealth.

Conclusions

From the standpoint of marriage transactions, fostering, paternity, divorce, widow inheritance and kind of kin group, the societies of northern Ghana display two main clusters of variables which are summarized in Table 4-3.

Type 1, e.g. Tallensi (or LoWiili). These societies have patrilineal descent groups, high (returnable) bridewealth, low fostering, 'social' paternity, increasingly stable marriage, high ratio of conjugal residence, and widow inheritance.

Type 2, e.g. Gonja. These societies have no unilineal descent groups (or only weak, non-exogamous ones), low (non-returnable) marriage payments, 'biological' paternity, high fostering, consistently high divorce, high ratio of sibling residence, and no widow inheritance.

107

Table 4-3. *Summary table: Kinship variables in northern Ghana*

Unilineal descent groups	Marriage prestations	Pattern of divorce	Widow inheritance	Paternity	Fostering	Exogamous kin groups	Exceptions
Type 1: Unilineal descent groups present							
1	A	A	A	A	A	A	
2	A	A	A	A	A	A	? Nankanse fostering
3	A	A	A	A	A	A	
4	A	A	A	A	A	A	? Chakalle
Type 2: Unilineal descent groups 'weak' or absent							
5	B	B	B	B	B	B	
6	B	B	B/A	B	B	B/A	? Mamprusi ? Wala

Note: The anomalous cases are discussed in the text.

As they affect residence, these variables form two overlapping groups, those primarily influencing the circulation of women, and those bearing on the circulation of children.

Residence of children

In societies of type 1 bridewealth serves to transfer rights in children and legitimacy is automatically conferred upon all offspring a wife bears; children live with their parents, or on their deaths, with lineage proxy-parents. In societies of type 2 low marriage prestations are not associated with any transfer of rights in genetricem, and there is no distinction between 'social' and 'biological' paternity. Rights over children are diffused among the kin of both parents and kinship fostering is widespread. Just as in societies of type 1 the relatively low divorce rate of fertile marriages makes for continuity in the nuclear family, so the high divorce rate in societies of type 2 often gives a wide dispersal to the children of one man or one woman.

Residence of women

In societies of type 2 a high divorce rate throughout life and the ban on widow inheritance are associated with a high ratio of sibling to conjugal residence. Women live with their kin at intervals throughout their lives and nearly always return in old age. The opposite pattern is found in societies of type 1 where the increasing stability of marriage, the refundability of bridewealth and the inheritance of widows are all linked with the virtually fixed residence of women with their husbands and sons in the agnatic extended family. The ratio of sibling to conjugal residence is markedly low.

These two groupings are obviously not themselves discrete. Apart from the duplications of particular variables in both sets, the residence of children clearly affects the residence of adults, and vice versa. The point is that in societies of type 2, the physical circulation of members begins at an earlier phase in the developmental cycle and hence has different implications.

Any attempt to explain the incidence of these two clusters of interlocking variables must also take into account non-kinship factors, such as we have listed at the beginning of this article. We note that all the 'bilateral' groups form part of a stratified state, and that these states have all been influenced in varying degrees by Islam, whose family law greatly modifies the organization of descent groups (Greenberg 1946; Trimmingham 1959). The advent of Islam had important social implications: paternal parallel cousin marriage and diverging devolution modifies the system of descent groups, making them 'weaker' in some senses. But here we would give more weight to the nature of the centralized systems. These are conquest states, established by one ethnic group over another, under a situation of open connubium (free and frequent intermarriage between status groups).

Given the incorporation of structurally diverse groups associated with frequent intermarriage, the result is a mutual adjustment of domestic institutions (the area most directly influenced). This tends to produce a kinship system based on the lowest common denominators and results in the kind of 'bilateral' system found (for much the same reasons) in other centralized poly-ethnic African states – the Hausa and Nupe of northern Nigeria, the Dagomba of northern Ghana and the Ngoni, the Nyakyusa and the Lozi of Zambia – all of these have incorporated groups of widely different social structures. Indeed the evidence on these state systems suggests the presence of a set of kinship variables very similar to those that we have isolated among the Gonja.[20]

5

Traditional states: responses to hierarchy and differentiation

The comparison of societies in northern Ghana showed a clear pattern of association between centralized political systems and delegation of some aspects of parental roles. I now want to look further at a number of traditional West African states to try to isolate these processes. Besides the kinship variables, three main features emerge as central to the nature and extent of parental-role delegation: Islam, the extent of the division of labour (as determined by involvement in the market and by occupational differentiation), and the elaboration of the political hierarchy. The Mossi and the Dagomba, like the Gonja, are instances of 'simple differentiated states'. Their politico-economic systems are characterized by only a moderate level of occupational differentiation and involvement in cash economy, and have relatively weak forms of centralization. The Kanuri and Hausa represent more elaborate occupational structures and both had wage labour in the pre-Colonial period, reflecting a considerable level of market involvement. Both Kanuri and Hausa had complex political hierarchies based on taxation as well as tribute. Such states can be characterized as 'more complex hierarchical systems'. Occupational differentiation and political hierarchy both appear to be linked, in different ways, to the delegation of parental roles. Where these features are less highly elaborated, parental roles are mainly delegated to kin. In the more complex hierarchical systems, training and sponsorship are also delegated to political superiors and to specialists in craft and trade. The Mossi have some characteristics of both types and their patterns of parental role include delegation to political superiors as well as to kin, but not, apparently, to traders and craftsmen.

The aim of this chapter is to build up a picture of how the management of parental roles responds to increasing occupational differentiation and political hierarchy in the two types of complex system. For this purpose, the analysis of type cases is sufficient, especially where the patterns are confirmed from different sources and indicated as applying to further examples. It is not possible here, for reasons of availability both of material and of space, to attempt the sort of systematic comparison presented in the previous chapter in which all known examples within a specified geographical area are considered. Here, however, I am concerned to concentrate on parental roles and to delineate pattern and process rather than to establish their extent.

110

Traditional states

Simple differentiated states

The Dagomba

As neighbours of the Gonja, with a centralized political structure but with a quite separate historical and linguistic background, the Dagomba are important for comparative purposes, and merit consideration in more detail. Fortunately there is an excellent study of Dagomba childhood by Christine Oppong (1973) which allows us to analyse parental roles in the context of political, economic and kinship institutions.

Whereas the Gonja trace their political traditions to the Mande kingdoms of the northwestern Sudan, the founders of the Dagomba state came from the north and speak a Mole-Dagbane language. As with the Mamprusi kingdom immediately to the north and the Mossi states of Upper Volta, with all of which the Dagomba are said to have a common origin, they differ from the Gonja in mode of succession to political office. Eligibility to office is restricted to those whose fathers held office of an equal or higher position in the hierarchy which culminates in the paramount, the Ya Na. Thus the grandsons of a Dagomba chief whose fathers failed to hold office are themselves ineligible, and there is a constant sloughing off of descendants of officials from the select group of nobles. Since there is substantial polygyny among chiefs, there are many sons who do not hold office, and hence the number of grandchildren who are not recognized as eligible members of the ruling group constitutes a large and constantly replenished pool. Together with open connubium, this has led to a merging of junior branches of the ruling elite with the commoner population, a process further facilitated by their common language.

Thus neither ruling group nor Muslims constitute distinctive major subdivisions of the population, apart from those who hold chiefship and their immediate families, and those who are active followers of the Prophet. Links are more particularistic among the Dagomba, more categorical among the Gonja. Available accounts of the Dagomba political system describe the ranking of chiefly titles, and the struggles for appointment and promotion, but there does not appear to have been a well-developed system for the levy and collection of taxes (apart from a local annual levy of foodstuffs and market taxes) nor an elaborate judicial hierarchy.[1]

Yendi, the Dagomba capital, was in pre-colonial times a large market and centre for long-distance trade with the Songhai, Mossi and Hausa states to the north and northeast. The occupational roles and statuses based on trade have, however, long ceased to be important, and it is not possible to reconstruct their place in Dagomba life. Today, the capital, the major towns, and the villages of more important chiefs act as centres for some specialists. A few, like warriors, drummers and fiddlers, are dependent on the court. Others, like barbers, butchers

111

and blacksmiths, draw their clientele from among the people of the village as well as serving the chief and his followers. However, most villages have neither fiddlers nor specialist drummers, and they lack both leather-workers and weavers. Muslim priests and teachers are found in the main population centres; and butchers also are concentrated in the larger towns, as a relatively large population is necessary to make regular slaughter economic. The occupations of diviner, barber and blacksmith appear to be more widely dispersed. As in Gonja, most specialists are also farmers. There are a few more specialists among the Dagomba – the Gonja nowadays lack leather-workers and fiddlers, and very few towns are large enough to support butchers. This slightly greater degree of occupational differentiation among the Dagomba is probably related to their generally higher population density.

The widest kin group recognized by the Dagomba is the *dang* which traces membership through both males and females. As men tend to live in or near the father's house, while women join their husbands' households on marriage, the residential group has a patrilateral bias on the ground. As with the Gonja, bilaterality is modified by patrilateral emphasis on male roles and prerogatives. A father is said to 'own' his children, is responsible for their misdemeanors, debts and moral failings and should be obeyed implicitly. The rights of the father are subsumed in those of *his* father, so long as he lives, and after his death by the authority of the eldest brother in the sibling group. The senior male supervises family matters, arranges and sanctions marriages, distributes inheritance between heirs, and in some cases names, rears and trains junior members' children. Dagomba fathers have stronger claims on their children than their Gonja counterparts, since on divorce a Dagomba wife may take with her only unweaned children, and even these the father may claim when they are old enough to leave the mother. The clearest indication of the different balance is the absence of the right, supernaturally sanctioned, of a mother's brother to rear his sister's child. In Dagomba only the *lunsi* drummers have this right which is enforced by a ritual transfer of one son (selected by divination) to his mother's brother.

The patrilateral bias is clearly expressed in the transmission of rights to office; there appears to be no counterpart to the Gonja Sister's Son chiefship. Craft skills also follow this pattern in that they are considered to be reserved for and practised only by men, and are taught by men to the boys of the descending generation. If fathers teach their sons, the *de facto* pattern is one of agnatic transmission. However many Dagomba children are reared not by their own parents but by the kin of the mother or the father. Boys continue to be reared by men; girls by women, so that the sex-linked transmission of roles remains central. Where boys are reared by their father's kin, they will learn the skill particular to the men of that group. But where the mother has married into a kin group whose men practise another occupation, a son sent back to her kin will learn not his father's craft but rather that of his mother's people.

Traditional states

In his survey of the peoples of the Northern Territories of the then Gold Coast, Rattray wrote that 'parents are not even thought to be the best or most competent people to bring up their children, and should not keep all of them' (1932:263). But he went on to note that it was held that children could not be 'taken' by the father's side 'because they were already there' although a father's brother or father's father might in fact take a boy to live with and be trained by him. Daughters often went to father's sisters. Less often a mother's brother or sister would take a child. In a sample of 370 children, Oppong found that 35 per cent of the boys and 17 per cent of the girls were not living with their own parents. These were not evenly distributed among kin of both sides, however. Among the boys, 23 per cent were with father's relations, and only 10 per cent with mother's kin. For the girls there was less of an imbalance, with 10 per cent with paternal kin, and 7 per cent with those of the mother.

Oppong's data are particularly interesting because they can be further broken down by occupational specialization. And here it turns out that the patterns are very different for the different groups. It is most often the chiefs, drummers and musicians, who effectively claim rights in sister's and daughter's children. The Dagomba, unlike the Gonja, have a special paradigm for the rearing of the children of chiefs. This assigns sons, not to the mother's kin, but to other royals and to court officials who were often in a special relation of service-clientship with the chief. The children of a chief were thought to be especially susceptible to spoiling both by their parents and by courtiers if they remained in their father's household. Eldest sons were also thought to be particularly vulnerable to the malice of their mother's co-wives, who sought preferment for their own sons. They were usually placed with titled officials who lived outside the capital; formerly these were eunuchs, who by definition would have no sons of their own. The royal tutor was called *mba*, 'my father', by the prince and was expected to rear him to be respectful, modest, and diligent. There is an element of austerity in accounts of chiefly childhood which reflects this stress on the building of a strong character. If royal princes went to paternal kinsmen, it was not apparently to their father's own male siblings; hardly surprisingly, since these were his closest rivals. Nor were they sent to the commoner households of maternal kin as has been reported for some kingdoms such as the Shilluk. This suggests that with such groups political alliances based on the rearing relationship were feared as potentially disruptive. On the other hand, the entrusting of the chief's heir to a titled eunuch placed him outside the kinship system, with a tutor whose allegiance was to the chiefship itself.

Chief's daughters were placed with their father's sisters. These women could not themselves bear heirs to fill the highest offices, and indeed became increasingly identified with their brother's political role as they grew older, usually returning to live at his court or to take up a Princess chiefship over a village. The fostering of the chief's children seems to have been designed to strengthen bonds

113

between the chief and particular officials, providing the children with a safe and relatively rigorous childhood, while avoiding entanglement with factions outside the ruling family.

But if chiefs sent their sons and daughters to others to rear, they also tended to attract many foster-children to their own households. In the household of one divisional chief 10 out of 15 boys present were sons of his brothers or sisters. Chiefs are said to have greater control over their sisters' children than commoner brothers. There are obvious reasons for this, in terms of both present power and future prospects. These same considerations lead to the placing of children of unrelated followers in chiefly households as personal servants and to help with the time-consuming care of horses. The rearing relationship often matures into a patron–client bond expressed in terms of quasi-kinship, or is converted through marriage into one of affinity.

Loyal servants may be also sons-in-law, and 'foster children'; for client and slave families are often linked to the royal line of the chief they serve by ties of marriage, upbringing and fictitious kinship. . . For the chief may give female wards in his charge to followers [as wives] in return for their loyal services and they in turn may later give him the offspring of such marriages, the girls to be given in turn by him in marriage, the boys perhaps to come and serve him either as grooms, personal servants or musicians. (Oppong 1973:26–7)

Not surprisingly there appears to be a higher proportion of fostered children in chiefly households than in others. Here fostering is clearly being used to establish reciprocal claims on loyalty and support, a pattern which might be called 'alliance fostering'.

Households of men recognized as experts in their occupations – drummers, barbers, fiddlers and butchers – have a mixture of sons, siblings' children, and children of distant relatives or friends who have been sent to them for training. The *lunsi* drummers who chant the exploits and genealogies of chiefs, have the most elaborately institutionalized fostering of sister's children. When a woman of the *lunsi* marries, the men of her paternal *dang* have a right to claim one of her children to be taught drumming. Since only men play the drums and learn the chants, if possible, a boy is selected through divination. If there are only daughters, a girl will be taken and later given in marriage on the condition that one of her sons return to be a drummer. A special ritual is then performed for the ancestors after which it is impossible for the chosen child to return to the father's people. Ill-treatment, which would normally lead to the child's return to its own parents, is believed to bring death to the foster-parent. This ritually sanctioned transfer of a woman's child is known by the special term *zuguliem*, and only occurs among the *lunsi* drummers. Oppong treats *zuguliem* as 'adoption' because of the element of compulsion and the sanctions against return in childhood. But she elsewhere mentions that *lunsi* recruited through women do not necessarily remain with their maternal kin in adulthood, and that they retain the right to inherit in their paternal *dang*. The transaction therefore would

Table 5-1. *Relationship between status and occupational recruitment, and rights over kins-women's children: Dagomba (based on Oppong 1973)*

	Explicit belief that children should be reared by kin[a]	Named pro-parental institution[b]	Occupational roles hereditary: Restricted to kin	Supernaturally sanctioned rights to:		Male child obliged to learn father's occupation	Occupational role taught to non-kin
				Rear daughter's child[c]	Train daughter's child		
Chiefs	Yes	No	Yes	No	No	No	No
Lunsi drummers	Yes	zuguliem	Yes	Yes	Yes	Yes	No
Fiddlers	Yes	No	Yes	No	Yes	No[d]	No
Diviners	Yes	No	Yes	No	Yes	No[e]	No
Blacksmiths	Yes	No	Yes (?)	No	No	?	No (?)
Butchers	Yes	No	No	No	No	No	Yes
Barbers	Yes	No	No	No	No	No	Yes
Mallams	Yes	No	No	No	No	No	Yes

Other occupations mentioned by Oppong for which detailed information is not available are weavers and leather-workers.

[a] Oppong implies that this belief is shared by all Dagomba, whatever their occupational kin group. I have therefore attributed it to each of the occupational groups even where there is no direct information.
[b] 'there is no term for fostering by the paternal relatives' (Oppong 1973:45). Nor is any term other than *zuguliem* mentioned for fostering by maternal kin. Rattray, whose knowledge of the Dagomba was based on a much briefer study than Oppong's, says that *zuguliem* is practised by all classes of the Dagomba. There is nothing to indicate that Rattray was aware of the special usage given this term by *lunsi* drummers; what is clear is that rearing of relatives' children occurred 'among all classes of the Dagomba' (Rattray 1932:576).
[c] There appears to be the possibility in all groups that parents will curse their child for failing to give them a grandchild to rear (Oppong 1973:44).
[d] 'Tendency for all fiddlers' sons to learn to play but not obligatory' (1973:58).
[e] ' "God gives the diviners' bag to someone" . . . The power of divination is inherited within the *Dang*, the bilateral kindred, so that a man may inherit it through his mother or his father.' Only those 'caught' by divining spirit must learn; initiation occurs 'comparatively late in life' (1973:59–60).

seem to concern rearing and training rights which lead to an adult occupational identity with maternal kin, but not to a loss of paternally defined rights concerned with birth status.

There do not seem to have been any rules specifically forbidding the fostering of drummer's sons outside the paternal kindred, but it is believed that all sons must learn their father's skills. This would be virtually impossible if the boy were living with a mother's kinsman in a village where there was no *lunsi* drummer. Since failure to learn carried the threat of death or madness, presumably any fostering arrangements are either with men who are themselves drummers or with men in a village where *lunsi* drummers are present.[2]

Oppong specifically notes that, while all sons of fiddlers seem to learn to play the instrument, many never actually become fiddlers in adulthood. There is even less pressure on sons of barbers and butchers to follow their father's trade, though many do so.

The variation in fostering among the several Dagomba status and occupational groups is indicated in Table 5-1. Other occupations mentioned for which there is no specific information on rearing are weaving and leatherwork. There is no discussion of patterns of parental-role allocation among commoners who comprise the bulk of the rural population.

Discussion

As Table 5-1 shows, only the *lunsi* drummers are positively required to learn the father's occupation; most sons of fiddlers seem to do so. It is interesting to consider the specially strong dependence of chiefs on *lunsi* drummers and fiddlers. A chief's son who succeeds in entering the political arena is first appointed to the chiefship of a different village from that in which he grew up. He must move his family there and live among his subjects, where he is considered a stranger. Although he is supported by his position in the political system of the Dagomba state, he must also establish his authority over the villagers. To do this he depends partly on the presence and support of those followers who, attracted by his prospects or linked by ties of clientship, fosterage or affinity, have accompanied him. But his importance is greatly augmented by the public, ritualized chanting by the drummers of the exploits of his ancestors and of the pedigree that legitimates his position. He is further dignified by the praise-singing of the fiddlers who attend him and can turn even a minor audience into a state occasion. A successful chief is promoted to successively larger and more important villages, where each time he comes as a stranger and must repeat the process of establishing his authority.

The central problem of the *lunsi* drummers is the preservation of an unbroken continuity of the traditions and genealogies they preserve in their chants. Given the high level of infant mortality and the demographic accident in the sex of children, the rights to train a daughter's child may well be crucial for particular families who guard the traditions of the many branches of the royal line. But the loyalty of drummers to 'their' branch of the royal line is ensured by their total identification and by the dependence of their distinctive occupational position upon it. For the fiddlers who deal in constantly re-invented praise songs, on the other hand, continuity is not a problem. Further, their loyalty may not be taken for granted, since their praises can celebrate one chief as easily as another. Here it is the chief who must endeavour to establish particularistic claims on specific fiddlers. For it is just when his fortunes appear to be on the wane that he most needs their support. It is striking that the only occupational group mentioned by Oppong as having a high level of intermarriage with chiefly familes is that of the fiddlers. She reports that half of the fiddlers' wives are royals while one-quarter of their daughters are married to members of this group. Fiddlers' sons who have mothers of the ruling line may then be reared by their chiefly uncles, further strengthening the links between them.

Conclusions

Among the Dagomba the sanctioned rearing of sisters' and daughters' children appears to have become formally institutionalized only where there is some special pay-off for a status or occupational group, or as a consequence of the interdependence of two such groups.[3] All Dagomba seem to share the belief that it is often better for children to be reared apart from their natal families. But the patrilateral bias of the kinship system is such that, other things being equal, children are kept within the father's kin group, with fathers' brothers or more distant relatives. Children are sent to matrikin most often when occupational specialization becomes linked to political power in some way.

The Mossi of the Upper Volta

Some two hundred miles to the north of the Dagomba and Gonja kingdoms was located Ouagadougou, the capital of the most important of the Mossi states. The rulers of these states, like the Dagomba, trace their traditions back to the Mamprusi, from whom they split off many centuries ago; it is their descendants in the male line who fill the most important chiefships at the present day. Particular groups of patrilineal kinsmen provide the chiefs for offices at the national, divisional and local level, though junior branches could be deprived of their access to chiefship (*nam*) and replaced by a branch or individual more in favour with the senior chief. But there was a good deal of local autonomy, with the kingroups of the village chiefs interacting with commoners, both autocthones and the descendants of chiefs deprived of chiefship, marriages taking place between all groups. These commoners placed less emphasis on agnatic kinship, which was closely linked to claims to office, and more on geographical proximity (Skinner 1964:20).

117

Parent roles in West Africa

In the nineteenth century, subsistence agriculture apart, the Mossi lived by warfare and pastoral production rather than by manufacture and commerce. Visiting the area some years before the French conquest, Binger remarked that he particularly noticed that they were 'en retard comme industrie' (1892:i, 495). There was not a great deal of weaving, though the districts of Béri and Koupéla did manufacture a rough white cloth (*koyo*) some of which was exported to Wale-Wale in Mamprusi. But finer cloths ('les autres tissus, que l'on peut appeler fantaisie') came from Dagomba or from Hausaland, the latter often through the great Gonja market of Salaga, where slaves and donkeys were exchanged for cloth, mainly because of its portability, which then had to be sold at less than cost price to compete with the local produce. The imported cloth was also of better quality and more varied; Binger reports finding only two dyers in Ouagadougou, both strangers.

There was some smithing of iron, copper and silver, as well as some basketry. And, in a state that placed so much emphasis on cavalry, saddles, bits, bridles, stirrups, all had to be locally manufactured, but Binger's comments show that this was done mainly on a made-to-order basis; he found no stock waiting for sale.

As in other states of the area, there were a number of occupations of a service kind, drummers, barbers, butchers and so forth. But commerce as a whole, declared Binger, prospered no better than manufacture. The markets, held every three days, sold no European goods, and mainly dealt in local produce, especially beer, cooked food, and medicines; sometimes a merchant would come with two or three slaves. Outside the market, there was a light but continuing traffic in salt, donkeys, horses, and above all slaves 'which are at the basis of every transaction in Mossiland. They are its only product' which they used to buy horses, salt and kola (1892:i, 498).

The description, no doubt somewhat biased by Binger's experience with the court, is of a country geared to the production of donkeys and slaves, with the bulk of the population involved in agriculture for their own consumption. Neither manufacture nor commerce were highly developed, but the chiefs did receive taxes on trade and markets.

How did the political and economic situation affect the delegation of parent roles? We have reports of three types of such arrangements.

Firstly, there was the sending of children to maternal kin, and in particular the separation in this way of fathers and their eldest sons. Secondly, there was the sending of girls and boys to chiefs as *pogsioure* and pages. These children worked in the chief's household, and the girls were bestowed as wives on the chief's clients (Skinner 1964:42).

Thirdly, there was the delegation of parental roles within the large multi-family compounds, and possibly outside, as described by Lallemand (1976) for the present day.

There is no indication of any of the kind of occupational fostering reported

118

from Dagomba, which may be linked to the earlier lack of craft production noted by Binger, or may simply be a lack of information.

With regard to residence with maternal kin, Skinner reports that the rights and duties of a sister's child include residence in the maternal home 'during childhood' (1964:21) And he speaks of the obligation of a man, even a stranger, to allow his eldest son to be reared by his mother's patrilineage, an experience which often leads them to stay. A woman may take her child 'to be reared in her own patrilineal village during the lactation period' and if her first child is a boy, custom directs that she should leave him there to be brought up (Skinner 1961:56). Skinner interprets this custom, following Mangin (1921:35-6), as a sign of potential conflict between the generations, centering on the inheritance situation.

If the youth's maternal kin controlled the chiefship of a local area, then he could improve his social and economic position by remaining with them, and nobody could evict him. Further, he was entitled to get a wife through them, and could use their resources. On the other hand, the son of a noble man and a commoner woman 'seldom attached himself permanently' to his maternal kin, unless he had had some trouble with his father's people.

Even children of the paramount himself were sent, together with their mothers, to their maternal kin. Unlike other Mossi women, the wife of the Mogho Naba was sent away from court when she became pregnant to avoid the possible dangers from her co-wives. The young prince remained outside the court, educated by servants sent there for the purpose. He was also reared away from the court because of the Mossi father's 'traditional anxiety regarding those individuals who would benefit by his death' (Skinner 1964:48). Indeed, even the younger sons of the paramount often remained with their mother's kin until they were old enough to be assigned district chiefships (p. 49). Sons of other chiefs also appear to have taken up residence with their mother's brothers (p. 58).

The second type of role delegation is that associated with the sending of boys, to court to act as pages, and of girls, who are later distributed as wives. Much of the domestic work of the court was carried out by these pages, each of whom was 'adopted' by a royal wife. Like the boys, the girls were given to the chief by his subjects as a mark of respect and in hopes of future preferment. The chief in turn bestowed them as wives on the condition that the husband return to him the eldest daughter as a future *pogsioure*. Nobles received wives from their chief; chiefs received wives from their district chief (who received women from most of the groups in his district as well as outside it). District chiefs and nobles sent women to the capital and received others in return. Boys were also sent to chiefs as pages and personal servants. When they became adult, they might be given a *pogsioure* wife and sent home, to replenish the supply of wives and pages in their turn. The effect of this system was to concentrate in the chiefs' control a large number of girls who were available for allocation as wives, thus establishing a continuing relationship of client/in-lawship between the family of the bride and the chief on the one hand, and that of the chief and the groom on the other.

It is not clear at what age girls were sent as *pogsioure*, but they were placed in charge of the chief's wives whom they assisted in the demanding task of providing hospitality for visitors as well as feeding the large household maintained by chiefs in order to assert their importance (Skinner 1960).

Where a young man succeeded in obtaining a *pogsioure* wife from the chief, he not only was able to join the ranks of fully adult men by establishing his own household, but the direct client/in-lawship tie now existing between him and the chief must have weakened the authority of the head of his own kin group. If on the other hand the chief bestowed a *pogsioure* on an elder, his position was strengthened. If the elder then bestowed the girl on one of the junior members of the kin group, then the groom was indebted to him; if he married her himself, then his own household was strengthened. The ability of the chiefs to enter the micro-politics of the patrilineal group through the bestowal of *pogsioure* underlines both the strength and the weakness of kin organization within a centralized system.

Lallemand (1976) has shown how this principle of control by the elders has been taken over by women married into the compound in arranging the fostering of the children of younger wives. These younger women are seen as loosely and unreliably attached during the early years of marriage and it is held to be dangerous to allow them control over their children who belong, not to their mothers alone, but to the whole kin group. Some time after weaning, between the ages of 3 and 6, children are placed with an older woman who has finished childbearing, usually one whose husband's position re-inforces her own within the compound hierarchy. This 'second mother' is called by a special term, *roogo ma*, which Lallemand glosses as *educatrice* or *tutrice*. The child leaves her own mother's courtyard (within the larger compound) to join the household of the *roogo ma*, and it is there that she begins to participate in domestic tasks and farm work. Only the educatrice, and not the genetrix, is allowed to punish the child – apparently a jealously guarded prerogative. Girls remain with the *roogo ma* until they marry; boys until just before puberty, at which time they join the other unmarried youths and young men of the compound. While there is some indication that a child may be placed with foster-mothers outside the lineage compound, there is no specific information about this process. Presumably, as we have seen, one or more children are still sent to chiefs as *pogsioure*, and some to maternal kin as their parents' first-born, though it is also possible that the fostering within the compound which she describes serves this function as well. We are told that the mother does not release her first child for fostering until a second has been born – indicating that the first child is part of the system which she is describing. If this is so, fostering within the compound may possibly have partly absorbed the types of fostering discussed under the first heading.

What is particularly interesting in Lallemand's account is that boys are placed with foster-mothers only until 'just before puberty'; at the time when sex-linked occupational roles begin to assume central importance, they leave her household to join other youths and young men in an all-male domestic group. These youths form the core of the agricultural labour force, but there is no indication that they learn specialist economic roles (apart from those of the smiths' caste).

We have seen how accounts of role delegation among the Mossi have been related to intergenerational conflict, especially with the first-born son, and it seems essential here to place the discussion in the context of Fortes' important work on the subject.

The first-born

In a recent paper (1974), Fortes ranges widely over the ethnographic literature to show that there is a very widespread pattern of avoidance between parents and their first-born children, especially of children and the same-sex parent, with the most frequent and highly elaborated form being the avoidance between a father and his first-born son. He sees this avoidance as reflecting the unease felt by a parent at the prospect of being replaced, indeed dis-placed, in the course of time by his own children. The ambivalence of this feeling is due to its complexity. Children are greatly desired in nearly every society, and also much enjoyed for their own sakes, as playful and lovable. But rearing children inevitably brings with it frustrations and often serious inconveniences, if not actual sacrifices. When these frustrations are combined with the quite human anxiety about growing old, losing one's health and strength, and in very many societies, also losing one's social significance, the negative feelings can be considerable. Fortes suggests that these sentiments tend to become focussed on the first-born because his arrival marks an irreversible transition, not just of role, but of generation. These hostile feelings have often been met in West Africa by institutionalized patterns of avoidance which structure the interaction between parent and first-born, and in some cases are so extreme that they remove the first-born altogether from the parental household during infancy and childhood.

The link between this extreme form and the delegation of rearing roles is a direct one, but it is important to stress that first-born avoidance often takes strongly institutionalized forms even while parent and first-born are living within the same household. Thus, among the Tallensi the first-born son grows up in his parents' household but is subject to a number of rigidly observed prohibitions which last until his father's death. First-born sons do not eat chicken; they may not wear the father's smock or hat, or carry his bow or quiver; they may under no circumstances look inside the father's granary while he is alive; and from adolescence they must not meet face to face in the doorway of the compound. Finally, and this constitutes a daily reminder of their separation, a first-born son may not eat from the same bowl as his father, even though his younger brothers freely do so. Many of these prohibitions are ritually reversed as a part of the father's funeral ceremony. The son is made to wear the smock and hat, made to hold the bow and quiver, and gently pushed to look into the granary. Only the avoidance of chicken persists throughout his life to remind him of his special status. Yet Tallensi first-born sons remain in their father's households until adulthood. Indeed, if they did not, there would presumably be little need constantly to re-enact their essential separateness.

There are many facets to the fascinating problem of why some West African societies elaborately surround this relationship with prescribed avoidances, while others either ignore it, or settle for a mild form of avoidance; and why, of those that practise extreme avoidance, some manage this through ritualized behaviour while others physically remove the child from the father's household. In line with Fortes' view that it is the replacement of the parent in his social roles which the imagery of prescribed avoidance acts out, it would seem likely to be those societies in which paternity is most closely linked to the central male roles that had the greatest problem with containing parental resentment of replacement. Among the Tallensi, a son's full adulthood depends on his father's death and translation into ancestorhood, thus providing the ancestor shrine his son needs to take an independent ritual role in both household and community. Among the Gonja, on the other hand, a son is allowed to inherit neither property nor office directly from his father; both must first pass to a father's sibling or to an older half- or classificatory sibling. If there is no close father's brother or no older sibling, second or third cousins will be found to inherit rather than allow the property to pass directly to a son (E. Goody 1973:230–1). Ancestor shrines do not directly mediate with important supernatural forces in a way that supports kinship authority, as happens among the Tallensi. Thus the Gonja son does not in fact directly replace his father in central social roles, which is certainly consistent with the casual attitude towards this avoidance.[4]

It may well be that a different set of factors determine whether extreme avoidance is managed through ritualized behaviour within the household or by sending the first-born to be reared elsewhere. If parental-role delegation is present in other forms, then the same practice can be utilized to manage the avoidance between the father and his first born. If there is no model of role delegation to follow, then other means must be developed instead. The Mossi practice of sending first-born sons to grow up in the mother's parents' household (Skinner 1961) could be seen as another elaboration of the politically motivated practice of sending sons to serve as pages in the chief's court, and daughters as wives. The same might well be said of the type of fostering discussed by Lallemand. On the other hand these institutions of dispatching the child to be looked after by others have much wider consequences for the political, economic and indeed the kinship scene, as we see in comparing the practices among the Dagomba and the Mossi.

Dagomba and Mossi

Both the Dagomba and Mossi have a strong patrilineal bias to the local residential and production unit. In both cases, some of the political functions of the descent or local group have been taken over by a superimposed hierarchy of chiefs from which strict patrilineal reckoning excludes both commoners and all but the immediate descendants of office-holders in the ruling group. Each system has responded by developing certain patterns of parental-role delegation which mesh with the particular problems produced by the political structure. Both sets of rulers secured the safety and the education of their successors to office by placing them with officials outside the competition for power, an adaptation to a system in which failure to achieve office permanently disqualifies all descendants of other sons. Where the stakes are so high, there are no rules of combat. Chiefs also need followers to serve them and demonstrate their importance when they come as strangers to assume new village chiefships, which happens frequently in Dagomba. Both the fostering of their own siblings' children, and fostering and intermarriage with specialist occupational groups, particularly the vital fiddlers, are used to build and secure such a body of supporters.

The Mossi on the other hand do not move their chiefs through a succession of village headships, but instead most villages, districts and provinces have a ruling family which customarily provides the chief, although new rulers may be sent out from the centre. Under these circumstances it becomes important to both chiefs and subject to establish dependable claims on one another, and, in the *pogsioure*, the idiom of in-lawship has been elaborated in association with sending children to grow up in the chief's court. The chief thus has links of co-parenthood with the parents of the many children sent to him, and later used these children to establish links of combined clientship and in-lawship with those to whom he gives the girls as wives.

However, both the Dagomba and the Mossi also re-allocate the educational aspect of parenthood among descendants of a common father or father's father, and their wives. Lallemand considers that this allocation not only allows the older wives to benefit from their position within the extended family, but that it also provides a way of linking together the sons to the agnatic core rather than allowing them to identify too closely with mothers who may later leave their husbands. It also means that where an elder has been forced to agree to his son establishing a separate unit of production, as the foster-parent he can gain the economic services of his grandsons for his own. Lallemand claims that the son's assertion of his right to economic independence is considered by the Mossi to be a recent phenomenon, linked to the opportunities during this century for young men to earn money by migrant labour in the south. Both migrant labour and successful secession from the production group of the extended agnatic family are in turn linked reciprocally with the relative ease of divorce today. For it is only men who have been able to secure a wife and thus establish a domestic unit and produce children, who can meet the requirements imposed by the division of labour on the maintenance of an economically independent household. Lallemand implies that the placing of sons with a *tutrice* may also be a recent pattern. If so, it provides an unusual glimpse of the mechanisms involved in the elders' attempts to retain authority despite loss of effective sanctions. It would seem that rights over minors, as expressed in claims to rear children's and siblings' children, are more durable in the face of socio-economic change than rights over adults, whether as sons or as wives. This durability may be due to claims over children being expressed in affective, non-instrumental terms, whatever their latent consequences.

The next set of traditional societies to be considered combines greater political centralization, with more complex occupational and socio-economic differentiation. The Kanuri (of Bornu) and the Hausa emirates were closely linked to long-distance trade routes, but unlike the states already discussed, they contained substantial numbers who were engaged in market-oriented activities, in both production and distribution.

Complex hierarchical states

Bornu

The ancient kingdom of Bornu was situated in the northeast of present-day Nigeria, and across the border into Chad. The invading Safawa dynasty intermarried with the local people and imposed their language on the farming population, who today live in large villages. In addition, Fulani pasture their herds in the open countryside.

The major source for the following analysis is the corpus of ethnographic work by Ronald Cohen, especially R. Cohen 1961, 1967, 1971. The political system has a complex hierarchy beginning with the headmen of wards and villages (known as *bullawa*), who are subordinate to the headman of the major settlement in their village area, known as *lawan*. The *lawan* ratifies land transfers, adjudicates disputes, and is responsible for the collection of taxes. He is appointed by the emir's government at the capital, either by recognizing the heir of the previous holder, or, if local politics so decrees, by selecting a client of the district head or an even higher official. Above him is one of the 21 district heads who translate government policy into action at the local level. At the capital, now Maiduguri, live the Shehu and his councillors. Formerly the fief holders (pre-colonial equivalents of district heads) were required by the Shehu to reside in the capital, their control over their villages being delegated to their representatives.

The Kanuri nowadays have an active market economy. There are weekly markets – held in different villages for each day of the week – which form a network throughout the country; and in the large towns, permanent markets. But, more significantly, no household produces all that it needs, and so all are dependent

124

on market transactions. In turn this means that all households must have a source of cash. Whether as cause or consequence, nearly everyone in rural villages has an occupation in addition to farming. There are three categories of primary occupation in which some men do not farm at all: traders, political specialists, and religious specialists. But even these usually have farms worked by others which provide for some of their consumption needs. Even in towns many have farms, though some manage to earn enough at craft and service occupations to support themselves without farming. Men dye, build, work metals, tan animal hides, work leather, buy, sell and slaughter cattle and smaller livestock, tailor, embroider, make hats and musical instruments, trade in a wide variety of imported commodities, weave mats and work as labourers. There are also religious specialists, barbers, and carpenters, and, today, a variety of modern jobs ranging from mechanic and clerk to teacher and civil servant. It is the craft and service occupations which a man considers to determine his identity – farming is a necessary, but incidental, sideline. Men who have no specialist skill enter the market arena through agricultural wage labour, working on a seasonal or day-to-day basis. While the situation has obviously changed over the last 70 years, the economy seems to have been more differentiated than that of the Gonja, Dagomba or Mossi. According to R. Cohen, 'It is part of both the traditional and contemporary Kanuri conception of getting ahead in the world that personal advancement is not to be found in farming. Achievement in Bornu is seen as stemming out of profitable social relationships and more recently western schooling' (1967:78).

Although the structure of the political system has changed in its exact constitution over the centuries – with the change of dynasty in the nineteenth century, again with the imposition of colonial over-rule, and finally with Nigerian independence – there are major continuities. For comparative purposes the two critical continuities are the several levels of formal authority between the individual commoner and the Shehu in his capital; and the shadow, informal, political system which operated through the clients of the various officeholders. The informal system works in two different ways. The district head and the *lawan* brought with them on appointment their personal clients who acted as totally loyal private informants and enforcers of their edicts. Thus when a *lawan* reported that he could not raise the tax required of his villagers by the district head, the personal followers of the latter moved in and collected by force 50 per cent more than the stipulated amount (R. Cohen 1967:100–1). In this way legitimate authority is re-enforced by the *de facto* power which is available to those in high office because of the benefits their position allows them to bestow on personal followers. The second aspect of the exercise of informal political power is again through links of clientship. It appears that at all levels, from the household through the ward, the village, the village area, and the district, to the bureaucracies of the capital, individuals attempt to bypass or circumvent the authority of those immediately above them by appealing to personal claims on other individuals in still higher positions. In this way, formal power and influence are balanced – sometimes re-enforced and sometimes undermined – by particularistic ties of reciprocal obligation between patron and client.

Cohen relates this pattern of individual ties between patron and client to the norms underlying family relationships. He writes that

the Kanuri are quite clear . . . that the rules governing social relations in the family and household are the essential guides to the successful operation of the larger-scale organizations in the economic and political life of their society. Thus many social relations in Bornu have a kin-like quality or are spoken of using the idiom of kinship, even though the persons involved clearly recognize that they have no kinship with one another through genealogical, descent group or affinal relations. The most important of these relations is the *borzum* or discipline–respect relationship closely modelled on, and usually spoken in terms of, the father–son relationship (1967:46).

In this *borzum* relationship the father (or the classificatory father) gives his son (or classificatory son) protection, security, food and shelter, status in the community, or an occupation; he may help him to arrange a marriage and represent him in the adjudication of disputes. In his turn the son must be completely loyal, obedient and subservient to his father and work for him in whatever way the latter feels necessary. While the fundamental *borzum* relationship is between a father and his own son, it is extended in several ways to others, both kin and non-kin.

(1) A child must, above all, learn the meaning and importance of *borzum*. If he resists, he may be sent away to a relative's household to 'understand respect'.

(2) Whoever succeeds the father as head of the household on his death is entitled – and obligated – to receive *borzum* in return for protection and support. All senior relatives, older siblings, paternal uncles, and indeed older people in general, are entitled to respect, but not to the duties and total obedience and subservience due to the man who is head of the household.

(3) When a youth is sent to live with a senior male relative, so that the older brother or uncle is now his compound head, the latter is entitled to the same extreme shame-avoidance-respect as is the father himself.

Bornu is an 'interwoven set of economic and political hierarchies, and this relationship of *borzum* serves as the chief mechanism for the proper functioning of these complex relations between superiors and their subordinates' (1967:48).

Recruitment to political and occupational roles

The Kanuri have elaborated many different ways of delegating parental roles. In some cases children are given to grandparents, to other relatives, or to friends to be raised. Cohen observes: 'Sometimes the reasons are political, and the parents try to place the child in a very important person's household so that the child may grow up knowing and associating with people who can help him later on in life' (1967:62). At other times the reason is kindness to a friend or to the child's grandparents. But 'Whatever the reason the child lives during his early years in a compound other than that of his own parents.' Although this remark refers to a child's early years, other comments indicate that children probably are not 'given' in this way in infancy and early childhood, but at a later age when they do not require much care and can begin to contribute to the household.

Boys sometimes go after the age of six or seven to live with a religious teacher in order to learn the Koran and the beginnings of religious theology. In adolescence they may travel to join learned men for more detailed study. The relationship to the religious teacher (*mallam*) is a particularly reverent and respectful one, and it is said that 'Your mallam exceeds your father' – that is in the degree of authority and respect required towards him (1967:62).

All young boys learn farming in the household if they are living in a rural area. But nearly all Kanuri men have a dry-season occupation, which is normally learned in adolescence. It may be learned from the father, but such occupations other than farming usually involve some apprenticeship, especially for young boys. The nature of apprenticeship varies with the skills involved. For high-status occupations, or for those promising a high return in adulthood, a longer period of apprenticeship is required, and the master may demand a payment. Drivers – high status, good income – and butchers – low status, but good income – both demand long apprenticeships. Terms are looser if the master is a relative; if he is unrelated, there may be hard bargaining over the terms.

In general the boy must live in the master's house for a stipulated period helping with all the work of the household, the farming, bringing grass for the horse if there is one, running messages, and helping in the occupational specialization of his master. He is *tada njima*, or son of the house, and refers to his new household head as *abba njima*, or father of the house. He is supposed to act in the situation in the same way as a son acts towards his father (R. Cohen 1967:67).

A master who is also a kinsman will use the appropriate kin term towards his apprenticed relative and the training may begin early in the boy's life. A number of men reported they had had difficulty terminating their apprenticeship when they wanted to move out and become independent.[5] One barber of about 20 had moved out of his master's household but still considered himself *tada njima* to him, still carried out chores for him, and gave him about half of what he earned. There were still difficult operations that the apprentice could not perform himself and further training was necessary before he could become fully independent, though even then he would still owe his former master respect and give him gifts from time to time.

But if the diffuse nature of the relationship with a master presents problems in gaining independence, it is often felt to be easier than the relationship with one's own father in this respect. Some apprentices living with strangers were practising the same craft as their fathers but had chosen to live and train away from home, because they felt more free and because they wanted to travel to places while they were young.

Significantly, when Kanuri craftsmen estimated their earnings and discussed reasons for their productivity rising or falling, much the most frequently cited factor was the loss or gain of helpers either within the household or living close by. Thus the work, including farmwork, of an apprentice is seen by craftsmen as making an important contribution to their income.

The *tada njima* relationship is as important in the establishment of trading careers as it is in crafts. In trade there are specific skills to be learned concerning not only the sources of commodities and how to sell them, but about establishing relationships with potential suppliers and avoiding losses through bad debts. Central to trading is the need for capital, both to purchase stock and to tide the trader over until he can collect from creditors. *Tada njima* relations, often begun in childhood, are used both to gain these skills and to establish the trust necessary in securing credit from non-relatives. A merchant may take a number of boys into his household and observe them in their daily work. To those he finds most competent and trustworthy he will extend credit, helping to establish them as semi-independent traders. After they marry they may establish independent households but continue to work with their former master, either on commission or else on a fifty–fifty basis. One prosperous trader living in the capital had 13 such clients, mostly not kin, who among them buy millet in the countryside for resale in the city, sell cloth and onions in the countryside, buy fish on Lake Chad and sell it in the capital, buy natron for resale, buy cattle in Bornu for resale in Kano and in Makurdi, buy butter from Fulani and sell it in the capital, and sell kola nuts in the countryside, using the proceeds to buy groundnuts for resale. This whole complex enterprise is organized not with the aid of secretaries and banks, but through carefully established relations with dependants which are explicitly modelled on the father–son respect relationship and are often initiated by apprentice fostering.

The Hausa Emirates

The Hausa emirates consisted of a number of more-or-less independent states, under the over-rule of the Sultan of Sokoto. I shall utilize the accounts of Zaria and Kano, since these contain the most details for our present purposes.

Like Bornu and the other Hausa emirates, Zaria had a complex political hierarchy, established by the Fulani conquest over the Habe at the beginning of the nineteenth century. The Emir expected his local appointees to collect taxes; these chiefs, with their personal followers (*barori*) and administrative staff dealt with the headmen of villages and wards to carry out the policies of the central government. These offices were associated with a complex set of titles, acquired through kinship, clientship, and gifts of greeting (*gaisuwa*).

128

Traditional states

In the Fulani period in the nineteenth century, the elaborately hierarchical political system in Zaria depended increasingly on slave estates, which produced both the subsistence base and various craft products for trade, but also gave rise to continual warfare to recruit additional slave labour. The economy which resulted from this was, for West Africa, specialized and market oriented. M. G. Smith's data on the economy relate to the mid-twentieth century (1955). At this time (and perhaps in the nineteenth century) taxation served, and may have been intended to serve, as a force propelling men into production for sale or into selling their labour. They had to find the taxes. The long dry season left men without agricultural work for at least six months of the year. One common strategy was for the men of a family to leave in search of work, thus reducing the consumption of valuable food supplies at home. Even if they returned with nothing in their pockets, they would have fed themselves. Thus wage labour was an integral part of the economy. At a later period, in rural Kano, Hill found that in the same community, there were families forced to sell their labour and buy food from day to day; and there were families hiring extra labour and producing surplus grain for sale (Hill 1972).

Added to the variation in degree of subsistence self-sufficiency through farming is the fact that most men had non-farming, subsidiary occupations. Here Smith's occupational census of four rural Zaria communities is very revealing (Table 5-2). Of a total of 292 men, only 37 had no subsidiary occupation. Some, indeed, have two or more subsidiary occupations. Thus, among dyers, one was also a cornbroker, buying grain in the village and selling it in the city, and another owned a donkey which he used to transport goods for payment; among mat-weavers, there were the men who also acted as brokers, a long distance dry-season trader, a seller of cloth and hoe-blades, a blind drummer, and a Muslim official who slaughtered cattle. In these four communities, the men practised crafts, traded and sold their labour; only 8 were not also farmers.

Although the equivalent table for women cannot be reproduced here for lack of space, it is worth noting that of a population of 421 adult women, not one was without some form of subsidiary occupation, and over half had two or more. Their main occupations were the selling of cooked food, spinning, and weaving on the broad 'women's' loom. Smith's assessment is that 'The first striking character of the modern economy is its unusually varied combinations of production for household consumption with production for exchange. Aggregate budget data for all seven rural communities give a subsistence production ratio of 46 per cent of average total income, cash income accounting for the remaining 54 per cent' (1955:38). He is also at pains to emphasize the extremes in proportion based on subsistence production which such an aggregate figure masks. The range is from 75 per cent subsistence production to 5.7 per cent. Here even the highest proportion of subsistence production still leaves 25 per cent to be realized from cash transactions. Clearly it is no exaggeration to hold that every household must participate in the market to some degree, and most

Table 5-2. *Sample occupational census of adult men in 4 communities in rural Zaria (A, B, C, D) (taken directly from M. G. Smith 1955:242–3)*

Occupation	Community				
	A	B	C	D	Total
Farmers	49	89	12	137	287
Non-farmers	–	5	1	2	8
Crafts					
Dyeing	2	1	–	24	27
Mallams, inc. Koran Schools	4	8	2	18	32
Tailors (hand)	5	1	–	12	18
Tailors (machine)	–	3	–	–	3
Mat-weavers	–	1	1	12	14
Butchers	1	1	–	8	10
Barbers	–	3	1	4	8
Weavers	8	3	1	4	16
Builders	4	3	–	4	11
Thatchers	3	3	–	3	9
Maroka (Eulogists, singers)	3	4	1	3	11
Slaughterers of animals	?	?	–	3	3 (?)
Leatherworkers	–	1	–	2	3
Beater of cloth (dyeing process)	–	–	–	2	2
'Sarauta' – (Officials)	1	3	–	2	6
Ropemakers	?	?	–	1	1 (?)
Blacksmiths	2	1	–	1	4
Potters	–	–	–	–	–
Drummers	1	7	1	1	10
Tobacco-grinders	2	–	–	1	3
Hunters and Fishing	2	1	–	?	3 (?)
Carpenters (European type work)	–	–	–	1	1
Carpenters (Hausa)	–	–	–	–	–
Sellers of firewood	–	1	–	1	2
Trainers of horses	–	–	–	1	1
N.A. Mallams (Schools, Vet., etc.)	–	8	–	–	8
Alkali and his Scribes	–	4	–	–	4
Herbal medicine sellers	–	1	–	–	1
Beekeepers	–	1	–	–	1
Others	–	2	–	–	2
Totals	38	61	7	108	214
Labour, etc.					
Cotton-market, forestry, etc.	–	9	–	–	9
Kodago (paid farm labour)	9	5	1	2	17
Clothes-washing	1	–	–	1	2
Carrying trader's loads on *fatauci*	–	–	–	1	1
Bara (attendants)	1	31	–	2	34
Fadanci (errands for V.H., etc., agency)	1	23	–	3	27

Table 5-2 (*cont.*)

Occupation	Community				
	A	B	C	D	Total
Traders					
Kerosene	?	?	—	1	1 (?)
Buying groundnuts (for firms)	—	—	—	1	1
Buying hides and skins (for firms)	—	—	—	2	1
Buying cotton for local market	—	2	—	—	2
Tobacco	2	3	—	1	6
Cigarettes	—	3	—	1	4
Sugar-cane	—	2	—	1	3
Kolanuts	2	6	—	6	14
Salt	2	—	—	3	5
European cloth	—	—	—	1	1
Perfume	—	1	—	3	4
'Dankoli' (cottons, needles, etc.)	—	1	—	4	5
Palm oil	—	—	—	1	1
Raffia – palm	—	—	—	1	1
Cycles for hire	—	1	—	—	1
Trades in groundnuts locally	—	1	—	—	1
Brothel-keeper	—	1	—	—	1
Others	—	2	—	—	2
Fatauci (Men who go on Dry-season trading expeditions every year)					
Palm oil	—	—	—	1	1
Mats	—	—	—	1	1
Locally-woven cloth, and dyed thread	—	—	—	25	25
Talla (Boys who sell goods for traders, on commission)					
Cloth	?	?	—	2	2
Kolanuts	1	—	—	4	5
Brokers					
Cotton blankets (woven by women)	1	2	—	4	7
Foreign cloth (Yoruba, European)	—	—	—	1	1
Grain and other Farm Produce	1	3	—	—	4
Other Brokers	—	2	—	2	4
Summary					
Men with no Craft	22	64	7	50	143
Men with 1 Craft	15	27	5	71	118
Men with 2 Crafts	8	4	1	14	27
Men with 3 Crafts	2	3	—	1	6
Men with 4 Crafts	—	—	—	—	—
Men with more than 4 Crafts	—	—	—	—	—

Table 5-2 (*cont.*)

Occupation	Community				
	A	B	C	D	Total
Men with no Trade	?	?	?	?	?
Men with 1 Trade	4	10	–	16	30
Men with 2 Trades	1	–	–	–	1
Men with 3 Trades	–	2	–	1	3
Men with more than 3 Trades	–	1	–	1	2
No. of Subsidiary Occupations					
0 (Farmers only)	9	16	6	6	37
1	23	52	5	91	171
2	12	22	1	33	68
3	3	7	–	2	12
4	2	–	–	1	3
5	–	–	–	1	1
Total adult males	49	97	12	134	292[a]
(Some engage in Craft and Trading, some in several lines of Trade, some in several crafts)					

[a] Discrepancy in totals in original.

to a very high degree. We cannot say what the proportion would have been in pre-colonial times, but the emphasis on craft production clearly differentiates this area from the states we considered earlier.

Smith has little to say about recruitment to subsidiary occupations, apart from commenting that previously a son inherited his father's occupation, but that men changed subsidiary occupation if this seemed advantageous. There are two different words in Hausa which distinguish 'inherited occupations' from those which have been independently taken up. This linguistic fact would seem to suggest that the possibility of taking up a different occupation from one's father had been recognized for some time and was not a very recent innovation.

Any account of the occupational structure must be set in the context of Hausa views about social status and the relationship of prestige to occupation and to wealth. True wealth is what all Hausa admire and strive for, but few attain. Under mid-twentieth-century conditions it could be acquired through either trading or a political career; in the period of Fulani rule, the ownership of many slaves could also be the basis of wealth. But 'true wealth' is not simply the possession of a great deal of money (despite its extremely high value to the Hausa). Rather, true wealth depends on a combination of money with ownership of land, numerous offspring, and social prestige, plus influence and 'the political good fortune of adequate protection' (through clientship). It depends on good fortune, and may go as mysteriously as it came. It cannot, for instance, be transmitted to one's children; this they must be able to achieve for themselves, through

that fortunate combination of circumstances as well as individual effort, acumen and personal charm [that] are together the essential prerequisites of *arziki* [true wealth] . . . Wealth is thus not the goods consumed, since this process is fleeting; but rather the conditions necessary to secure the ability to consume. For to the Hausa, who ponder these matters deeply, a man is not fortunate because of his wealth, but *vice versa*. Thus *arziki* is a principle capable of social elaboration as a criterion to distinguish groups of different occupation and status (M. G. Smith 1955:15).

Arziki is conceptually associated by the Hausa with occupation since, in precolonial times too, occupations provided the means to wealth. The elaboration of the cash economy (already underway in the nineteenth century) has resulted in clearly distinguished occupational specializations which are socially ranked in terms of the *arziki* of each. But such a ranking is complex. Thus Koranic scholars and teachers, who may and do undertake to live mainly by alms, are for reasons of religious prestige superior to butchers, who, in features apart from birth, prestige and learning, have more *arziki* than mallams. Similarly, however wealthy he might be, a slave ranked lower than a freeman. For each occupational status, there is an appropriate type and degree of *arziki*. For mallams, knowledge and substantial alms; for Fulani nobles, appropriate office, timely promotion, and loyal followers; for merchants, commercial success, a large family, many dependants, adequate political protection through clientship, and generosity – and so on. Not only is there a different form of good fortune appropriate to each occupational class, but, for each occupational class, the *arziki* of another would be absurd; the merchant living on charity would have no one's esteem. Within this framework, Hausa occupational classes are roughly ordered in terms of prestige as follows:

> *Sarakuna na asali* – the aristocracy by birth
> **Masu-sarauta* – aristocracy by appointment to office
> *Mallams* and Koranic students
> *Attajirai* – successful merchants
> *Masu-sana'a* – craftsmen other than those mentioned below
> *'Yan kasuwa* – smaller traders
> *Dillalai* – brokers
> *Manoma* – farmers with unimportant subsidiary occupations
> *Makira* – blacksmiths
> *Maharba* – hunters
> *Maroka* and *Makada* – musicians, drummers and eulogists
> *Mahauta* – butchers

* The term *masu-sarauta* includes *sarakuna*, but also office holders who are not of noble family.

Slaves, among whose descendants today are the majority of butchers, are not included here, since by their legal status they were private property; if captives they could be alienated or killed at their owner's will, and were not full members of the community (M. G. Smith 1955:16).

Rearing of children by kin

Smith's analysis of the detailed censuses of two rural communities in Zaria includes some information on 'adopted' children. Both communities were old and well-established, one having been a slave plantation in the nineteenth century, and the other a market on an important trade route. Both were currently agricultural in the sense that nearly all men had farms as well as subsidiary occupations.

In community 'A' (an ex-slave village) there were 22 'adopted' children in 30 compounds with a total population of 403. The data are not given in a form which allows the calculation of 'adopted' children as a percentage of all children, but they constitute 5.4 per cent of the total population. In community 'B' (an old market village) there were 28 'adopted' children in 87 compounds, or 3.6 per cent of the total population. For comparison with figures from Ghanaian populations, the 28 'adopted' children in community 'B' represent 10 per cent of the 268 children under 15. Girls were 'adopted' more frequently than boys in a ratio of three to two. Fostering parents were grandparents, and father's and mother's older siblings. Normally men 'adopted' boys and women took girls. There appear to be no cases in either community in which a child was living with a non-kinsman (M. G. Smith 1955:19–24); Unfortunately, the numerical data on three urban communities, including the capital of Zaria, do not include information on the rearing of children or on the training of adolescents in adult occupational roles. Thus we can only say that in rural areas the rearing of children by non-parental kin is recognized and often practised.

Although Smith's quantitatively focussed study only touches briefly on parenthood and adult-role recruitment, the classic autobiography of the Muslim Hausa woman, Baba, as told to Mary F. Smith (1954), provides an unusually rich account of the meaning of what Hausa refer to as *tallafi* or *rana.* This is the practice which M. G. Smith translates as 'adoption'. Since in none of the many instances discussed is there a question of the *tallafi* relationship changing jural links and entitlements through the real parents, adoption does not seem to be the appropriate term. In Abrahams' *Dictionary of the Hausa Language, tallafi* is defined as the 'act of giving education and bringing up'. Although in each case Baba describes the child as 'hers', what she describes are relations of nurturance and training, and in some cases the arranging of the child's first marriage (sponsorship). The length of the period during which Baba looked after 'her' children varied from the two weeks required to wean a boy to the whole childhood of the three girls whom Baba reared and for whom she partly arranged the marriages. Of the six boys Baba speaks of as 'hers', one, Usuman, was already a young man when he was freed from his slave status; at this time he was 'given' to Baba as a son, her husband taking the role of father. She helped to arrange his marriage, and considered his child to be her grandson. All the rest slept in her room in childhood, three for relatively short periods (one for two weeks, one intermittently for two years, but he died). The fifth was a pupil in her husband's Koranic school whose parents lived in another town. When he finished his studies his parents came for him and there is no further mention of him in her story. The last of the boys 'given' to Baba was a son of her co-wife. She appears to have looked after him throughout his childhood until she divorced his father, at which time she left the compound – and her foster-son. In short, the giving of a boy to a foster-mother seems in these examples to be tied to their continuing residence in the same place. The mother–child nurturant relationship is delegated to or shared with a foster-mother, but the father–child relationship remains unchanged. Baba never had any children of her own, and was probably given foster-sons so that there would be men who felt an obligation to look after her in her old age, as is a son's duty.

Baba's foster-daughters, on the other hand, remained with her until they married, living in her room, helping her and learning women's household tasks. Two were the children of kin, a half-brother's daughter (his only child) and a full sister's daughter. The third was the daughter of a friend whose marriage to her own husband Baba was instrumental in arranging. It is significant that the co-wife later wanted to take back her daughter, but their husband refused to agree. When the marriage of a foster-daughter is arranged, the real mother and father are consulted and gifts shared with them. Through her foster-daughters, Baba feels that she too has grandchildren, but again this relationship is not exclusive; the real mothers also claim these grandchildren.

There is no doubt that the large number of foster-children whom Baba reared was due to her own failure to bear children. However, M. G. Smith's data on the incidence of foster-children in two rural Hausa communities, and the fact that both Baba and her only full sibling, Diji, themselves were fostered, indicates that this practice was not reserved for childless women but is a regular feature of parenthood among the Hausa. Nearly all of the cases which occur in Baba's story involve the rearing of children of close kin; a few were co-wives' children. But in the case of the Koranic pupil of Malam Maigari, included by Baba among the children 'given' to her during the years she spent in this marriage, one can see the adaptation of kinship fostering to other ends. By assigning the unrelated child to one of his wives, Malam Maigari ensured that he would be regularly fed and washed, and have a secure place of his own in the busy world of the compound. At the same time, this assignment helped to fill the hut of a childless woman. As for the boy himself, here was a mother to whom he could turn in times of unhappiness or illness, and through whom he could relate to the kinship-defined world of the compound. The adoption of the ex-slave Usuman shows another instance of assimilation to quasi-kinship status. Baba describes him as 'our eldest son', and insists that he was like a son in every way except that he would not inherit. This assimilation was not a purely altruistic act, however. There were no adolescents or young men in the compound at that time to take over certain duties like handing out grain from the granary, and Usuman stepped neatly into these tasks, which required a level of trust best ensured within the kinship idiom. Incidentally, Usuman had been bought as a child of 7 and reared in the household, so he knew no other family and had no other kin. As a freed slave he would have been extremely vulnerable in Hausa society without such support.

Accounts of the arrangements for fostering girls among Baba's kin show quite clear patterns. The recurrent relationships in which claims to foster-daughters are successful are those of mother's mother (mother's mother's sister) and father's sister. In several cases the girl's mother was against the arrangement, but it proved impossible to deny the rights of a senior kinswoman. Baba does not suggest that there was a fear of supernatural sanctions, only that these women had rights which could not be denied. There is a tendency to foster children of broken marriages and those whose mother has died. Here Baba contrasts her own Habe practice with that of the Fulani, who she says 'have no humanity' but leave the children in the dead mother's hut to be looked after by the father and by co-wives who do not like them. Given the high rate of Habe divorce, and the probability of remarriage, there are clearly aspects of crisis management in the reallocation of rearing roles to foster-parents. But many of the instances in Baba's account were not responses to crisis, notably the sending of her sister, Diji, to their mother's mother, of Baba herself to their mother's sister, and Baba's rearing of her co-wife's child.

What stands out in the accounts of the fostering relationship is the pleasure taken in caring for children and in their gaiety and games. Although fostered girls do help with household chores, it is only in the account of Baba's maltreatment by her 'grandmother' that there is any stress on this aspect. And this is the only example of a fostering arrangement terminated by the parents because of the child's unhappiness. It seems likely that the labour contribution of a girl is taken for granted, and is not expected to differ if she is living with her own or a foster-mother. There are, however, indications that the women in a secluded compound do care very much about the right to assign tasks to a girl. If a mother and foster-mother live in the same compound (as when they are co-wives) it is the foster-mother who has this right.

One way of seeing the importance of fostering children for Hausa women is in terms of the centrality of the maternal role. While personal attractiveness and a satisfactory sexual relationship with a husband are of great importance to a woman's sense of identity, so also is being a mother. This is portrayed in several ways, from the care and attention a mother pays to the physical welfare of her child, to a woman's delight in having her hut full of children who love and depend on her, to the advantage of having another pair of hands for the endless household tasks like fetching water and grinding grain. Again and again Baba uses as a criterion of her rights in a child the fact that she helped to arrange his or her marriage. This process seems to be largely in the hands of women, in the sense that there are informal enquiries to be made before any public act occurs. The child's paternal kin, especially the father, must be consulted about the suitability of a prospective husband, and must agree if the marriage is to be a marriage of alms-giving, in which no substantial gifts are given by the groom. But women appear to take the active role, both in negotiations and in the ceremonies themselves. Thus it was very important to Baba that she arranged the marriage of the freed slave, Usuman. This showed publicly that she was acting as his mother, that she had a 'son'. She says of the children she reared in the house of her second husband, Malam Maigari, that they returned to their parents before it

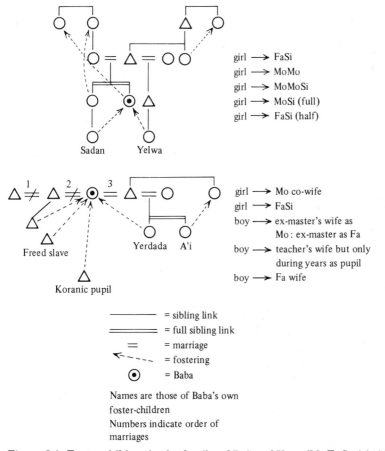

girl ⟶ FaSi
girl ⟶ MoMo
girl ⟶ MoMoSi
girl ⟶ MoSi (full)
girl ⟶ FaSi (half)

girl ⟶ Mo co-wife
girl ⟶ FaSi
boy ⟶ ex-master's wife as Mo : ex-master as Fa
boy ⟶ teacher's wife but only during years as pupil
boy ⟶ Fa wife

———— = sibling link
===== = full sibling link
= = marriage
←---- = fostering
⊙ = Baba

Names are those of Baba's own foster-children
Numbers indicate order of marriages

Figure 5-1. Foster-children in the family of Baba of Karo (M. F. Smith 1954)

137

was time to marry them. Thus fostering by no means always involves sponsorship as well as rearing roles. But it may do so, and, when it does, the relationship is felt to be stronger than when only the reciprocities of rearing are involved.

Baba and her family were not city folk; she several times repeats that her people were only farmers. Her second husband organized a Koranic school for young boys, and travelled during the dry season from village to village taking students as he went. And the third was a minor follower of a minor chief. So it is necessary to turn to other sources to see what parental strategies appear among the long-distance traders and the elite of the city.

In his study, *Scholars, sufis, saints and capitalists in Kano* (1976), Ibrahim Tahir gives biographical material on a very wealthy merchant, B. B's affairs were extremely complicated and were managed not through formal contractual relations but by manipulating a number of long-term personal relationships. Reference to Tahir's discussion of the elements of traditional Hausa clientship will make this clearer.

Many merchants have *abokan arziki*, friends in good fortune, or business associates, among other merchants. With them they exchange information, advance credit, place goods for sale, gain access to sources of supply, and learn of opportunities. 'Ideally these were one's closest friends' says Tahir. Such friendships were confirmed by the exchange of reciprocal services such as the rearing of one another's children. The wealthy men of Kano distrusted the bringing up of their children in their own homes, which was believed to inculcate *sakalci* or *shagwaba*, ill-discipline, softness and dependence. *Abokan arziki* exchanged children in order to avoid this. But the merchant, B, preferred to place his children with trusted slaves. An aged ex-client of his boasted that no child of the family was ever fostered except with kinsmen or slaves. In this way B avoided entering into reciprocal relations of service with other merchants. Significantly, his own marriages followed the same policy. He had long-term conjugal relations with six women. Four were daughters of his own slaves, and two were close relatives (one a father's brother's daughter, the other a mother's brother's daughter).

B avoided relationships based on equality such as *abokan arziki*. But he cultivated those in which he could take the dominant role. One type of unequal relationship was *jinga*. *Jinga* involves stable, contractual relations based on the extension of credit. B had *jinga* relations of this kind with families of dyers in four towns including Kano, and also with master tailors in Kano city. He put out his cloth for the dyers to dye, and also supplied them with cloth which they dyed and sold themselves. B also purchased their own independent output of dyed cloth for resale. Payments in *jinga* relationships were calculated, credits and liabilities balanced against one another. But the relationship was seen as one of the benefactor and beneficiary, with B as the benefactor. A person using craftsmen on a regular, large-scale basis was always their superior, and furthermore the craftsmen were always in B's debt. He was their *hanyan arziki*, their path to good fortune.

In direct contrast to *jinga* relations were *ciniki*, strictly commercial, relations. Other craftsmen sold B their products for cash, and bought materials, 'eastern goods' (imports) or kola nuts from him. Although there might be delay in paying in such transactions, so that debts were involved here too, there was no question of other considerations influencing payment. *Ciniki* relations were seen as mutually exploitative, each party attempting to make the best possible deal.

But both *jinga* and *ciniki* relations depended on credit; 'credit between two parties was interminable'. Both relations therefore depended on *amana*, professional integrity, trust, honouring one's bond. Failure to do so meant loss of credit-worthiness, and invited supernatural retribution. *Amana* was essentially based on long-term relations. Where long-distance trade is involved trust becomes particularly critical since transactions take place far away, and there is little means of checking up on an agent's honesty. Long-distance trade means dealing with strangers, and it means long delays between investing capital and seeing a return in the form of goods which can be sold locally, or perhaps traded even further from their source, thus increasing the profit. There had to be strict observance of *amana* in transactions involved with expeditions. The organizer of the expedition was entitled to one-third of the profits but had to take his agent's word on this. B employed as agents one of a small set of semi-independent clients (*yara*) in whom he had special trust. Ideally, *yara* were recruited young and trained at first within the family, given menial duties and sent on errands.[6] That is to say, they were foster-children in the patron's family. The patron watched to see how they took responsibility, and whether they were honest. When they were older, they were trained, together with the children of the family, by becoming apprentices to experienced *yara* and kin who were traders. In this way they gained experience in more limited trading operations while they were being judged for future trustworthiness.

B had seven major *yara* and several minor ones. Two of the major ones were relatives, a sister's son and a mother's brother's son. One was an ex-slave who gradually took more and more responsibility, and was given more and more trust. The other four had been early trading contacts. Tahir sees *yara* clientship as asymmetrical because each client could have only one patron, while the patron had as many clients as he needed. Even experienced *yara* clients were not used repeatedly on the same trade routes, lest they learn too much about them and usurp the patron's control over the expeditions. There were also difficulties in using close kin. Elder sons were anxious to inherit, and relations with them were awkward. Neither they nor other kin could be taken to court if they misused trust. The trust which was critical in *yara* clientship seems to have been based partly on the rearing relationship and partly on a careful calculation of the relative advantages to both sides.

Another side of the pattern of fostering children appears in a study by Hill (1969) and in Schildkrout's recent enquiry into women and children's work in contemporary Kano (1978; 1979). Because purdah is strict and women may not

139

go outside their compounds to buy provisions or to trade, they are totally dependent on having someone to do these things for them. In wealthy homes there are servants, but most households depend on children. A woman who has no children, or whose children are grown, can fill this gap with a foster-daughter. If a woman trades, or engages in sewing, embroidery or other home production, she must have someone to fetch the raw materials and to sell the finished goods. Again, a foster-child may be the only solution. Schildkrout found that women with a child to help them earned about three times as much as those who had none.

This same problem, and the same response, appear in A. Cohen's study of the Hausa in the town of Ibadan in southern Nigeria (1969: 65-6, 86-90, 219). The use of fostering in building trusted relations of clientship in long-distance trade is here seen from the other end, as it were. Significantly, the section which includes the discussion of male fostering is headed 'Investment in primary relationships', and follows a detailed account of the complexity of commerce where long distances, perishable goods, erratic communications, large sums of money, and a myriad of conflicting interests are involved. Cohen focusses on the affairs of the major *masu gida*, or landlords, who acted as middlemen between the traders from Hausaland in the north, coming either to sell cattle or to buy kola nuts, and the local Yoruba butchers and kola dealers. Risk-taking and the ability to sustain long-term credit are the key determinants of the landlord's success. His major problems centre on his need to work through many other people, commission agents, landlords, dealers and buyers; and on the absence of effective courts for dealing with theft, embezzlement and default. An important mechanism in such circumstances is the building of personal relations in which moral imperatives will act in lieu of judicial constraints. An obvious solution would be to restrict transactions requiring trust to close kin. But a man's sons are bitter competitors for his favour and his assets, especially where they are sons of different wives. And, further, the very strong avoidance between a man and his first-born son makes close cooperation with him virtually impossible. Not many of the important landlords employ their sons as assistants. One response has been to develop ways of creating the moral obligations characteristic of kinship, and the fostering of the sons of a brother or of a client is used for this purpose. Three-fifths of the boys fostered by men in a random sample of 120 fostered children were of this type.[7] A fostered son does not inherit from the foster-father, but rather from his own father, so their close relationship is not complicated by holder–heir tensions. There are various sources of foster-sons. As a man in Ibadan becomes successful in business,

his brothers and sisters in the North will try to send one of their children to his care so that the child will grow up in a well-to-do house and will learn a lucrative trade. In other cases the Sabo landlord is under obligation to 'relieve' his brother or sister of the first born son. At the same time, the more successful the landlord is in business the more inclined he is to foster male children. . . . There is hardly a landlord [in the Hausa quarter] without a number of fostered sons (87).[8]

140

Traditional states

But Cohen points out that sons and fostered sons together can account for only a small proportion of clients whom a landlord needs in his work. As these other clients will not be kin, the landlord must use other means to build with them the relationship of trust on which he depends. The most important of these is the client's marriage. A landlord urges young clients to marry, for they are thought to then be more responsible. Landlords often try and arrange for a young client to marry a 'daughter' of their house – their own daughter, a foster-daughter,[9] or a foster-daughter of one of their wives. But whoever the client marries, the landlord provides the expenses of the marriage, as well as the room for the bride in order to establish the new household. When the couple have a child, the landlord often fills the role of close kinsman in taking the first-born as a foster-child, or placing it with one of his wives.

This will create a new set of complex relationships between client and landlord. In one respect this kind of fostering constitutes an indirect financial help to the client, as the landlord will feed, house, and clothe and educate the child. Secondly, as it is almost an obligation between close kin to foster the first-born child of one another, the landlord will be linked to the client as a kinsman by virtue of the fostering. Thirdly, fostering is always regarded as an act of friendship between equals. Finally, the foster parent will inevitably benefit financially in the future when the fostered child begins to help in business. From the point of view of the client this last aspect of fostering is seen, not as an exploitation of his child by the fostering parent, but as an important measure of security in the future for the child (A. Cohen 1969:89).

From the foregoing analysis it might seem likely that there would be more fostered boys than girls. In fact the random survey of fostered children produced a ratio of one male foster-child for every three fostered females. Married women are very eager to foster girls, especially before their own children are old enough to help them, and after their own children have grown up, because wives are secluded within the compounds and not allowed to go out to market or to conduct their trading affairs. Virtually all married women are small-scale traders or sell cooked food. Together they provide the food for 'thousands of bachelors' as well as for the transient traders bringing cattle and buying kola. But to do this they must have helpers to buy supplies and to sell their products. And for this purpose fostered daughters are critical. Cohen also notes that a woman's status (expressed in the number of enamelled pans she has amassed) will determine her ability to attract foster-daughters, just as a man's business success draws foster-sons to him.[10] Women recruit foster-daughters from their own siblings' children, later from their children's children, and often from their husband's kin and clients.

Conclusions

In each of the four kingdoms considered in detail in this chapter, the delegation of parent roles has been institutionalized, though in rather different ways.

141

The Dagomba send children almost exclusively to kin, and the most formalized role delegation is linked to the teaching of occupational skills defined in terms of the kin group. Among the Mossi, first-born sons were often sent to maternal kin to rear, and recently the systematic reallocation of rights to train young children from genetrix to *tutrice* within the compound has been reported. These are forms of delegation within the kinship domain. Formerly the institution of the *pogsioure* extended rights over the rearing and the labour of children into the political domain, where it was used to convert ties of clientship into ties of kinship. The accounts of Hausa and Kanuri stress an elaborate occupational differentiation with clear antecedents in the nineteenth century. Today political and economic clientship flourishes at all levels, and is often initiated by alliance-fostering or by apprentice-fostering. There appears to be a shift in these more complex hierarchical systems from claims on the right to rear children to a balancing of benefits for parent, pro-parent and child, which is characteristic of the rearing of unrelated children. But claims continue to be pressed for the children of kin, especially by women in seclusion.

In the following chapters the focus shifts from areas of the traditional kingdoms of the savannah, where Western influence is relatively recent, to coastal West Africa which has been responding to contacts with traders and missionaries for centuries, though the pace of 'modernization' has greatly increased since the Second World War and the coming of independence. The pro-parental institutions which have emerged in the south have many similarities to those in the more complex traditional kingdoms, particularly in the more rural areas where there is a mixture of kinship fostering and apprentice fostering. In the urban centres more elaborate forms have emerged in which the kinship element tends to disappear, relations between pro-parent and child become more functionally specific and instrumental, and contracts and money payments appear.

6

Contemporary patterns in southern Ghana

Modern Ghanaian literature provides lively descriptions of the role of fostered girls. In Joe de Graft's play *Sons and daughters* we meet Adwoa ineptly carrying the slops through the living room. This is not intended as a commentary on the servant girl in question. Rather the character is used to show, with economy of exposition, that the family is sufficiently well off to have a housemaid, and that the son is self-conscious about the niceties of sanitation proper to their position. It is true that de Graft does not tell us much about Adwoa; but she is listed in the cast of characters as 'a maid-servant' and is clearly not Aaron's sister.

A rather different model is presented by the heroine of the novelette *The adventures of Esi Kakraba* (Odoi 1964). Esi leaves the remote village where she was born to stay with a woman trader who lives in a busy regional centre. There, along with the trader's niece, she learns the business of selling cloth as well as doing all the domestic chores. After five years, at about the age of fifteen, Esi's foster-parent takes her to Accra where she is apprenticed to a seamstress, the foster-parent arranging for her lodging and paying for the sewing classes.

The appearance of Esi Kakraba and Adwoa as stock characters in fiction suggests that the role of housemaid/helper is a familiar one in southern Ghana today. These references in modern writing and in newspapers to children living and working away from home in southern Ghana led me to wonder whether some form of institutionalization of fostering was a common feature of West African social systems, not only in the savannah states. I was therefore pleased to be able to carry out brief surveys in two southern communities, one Fanti and the other Ewe, during a period as visiting lecturer at the Institute of African Studies at the University of Legon. Later it was possible to add two Krobo samples. Using these data, and with the information from Azu's excellent study of the Ga (1974), it is now possible to discuss patterns of parenthood in four societies in southern Ghana.

This chapter has two main purposes: To present the empirical material on parent roles in these societies, and to examine the data in the context of the political, economic and kinship structure of these societies. It is also important

143

to place the communities from which the survey interviews were drawn in relation to the traditional states discussed in Chapter 5 on the one hand, and in relation to modern West African cities like Accra, Freetown and Lagos, on the other. It should then be possible to raise the question of how forms of parent-role allocation in the northern states are related to those in contemporary southern Ghana.

While the northern states of the Sudan rose and declined through the centuries in response to political, economic and religious forces, they were not directly exposed to European colonialism until the end of the nineteenth century. It is therefore possible to speak of 'traditional' institutions and 'modern' forms. However, on the coast of West Africa, European trade and politics have been important for five hundred years. The polities flourishing there in the nineteenth century had been shaped by these influences and continued to respond to the more radical pressures of the colonial and post-colonial periods. There is no clear break for these southern states between the 'traditional' and 'modern' periods. However, until the British formally assumed power over the countryside beyond the trading forts, these societies were politically individuated, if constrained in varying degree by external factors, both British and indigenous. What sort of societies were they?

The nature of the coastal polities

The coast of southern Ghana was first visited by the Portugese at the end of the fifteenth century, and the following centuries saw the building of trading forts by Portugese, Dutch, Danes and British. These forts and the trade for which they became the focus acted as catalysts for the establishment of small communities of indigenous merchants and middlemen who often represented the rulers of small states centered a few miles inland. The coastal communities became cosmopolitan, incorporating descendants of the local families of European traders, some of whom were sent to Europe to study at an early date. Despite their strategic position between the gold and slaves of the forest and savannahs to the north, and the European maritime traders, who were also the source of cloth, metal and later of guns and gunpowder, the coastal states continued to depend largely on agriculture and fishing.[1]

The four societies of concern here all adapted to this position by forming miniature states. Some of the Fanti and Ewe and all of the Ga states lay directly on the coast. Other Fanti states, the Krobo and most of the Ewe states lay in the savannah or forest just back from the sea.

In the nineteenth century the Krobo state was based on twin towns clinging precariously to the cliffs of Krobo mountain. These mountain towns acted as the political and religious centre for a people who farmed on the plain in times of peace but in times of trouble retreated to their rocky heights (Huber 1963). The Ga polities also seem to have been based on farming settlements stretching inland from a coastal capital to which all retreated in times of raiding by their inland neighbours. The Fanti states were similar in that each was governed from a capital in which the chief and his elders lived, and from which justice and military protection were organized. The Fanti states varied greatly in size.[2]

The Ewe were similar: 'Until the arrival of the European powers the Ewe never formed one political unit. They lived in autonomous groups. The smallest politically independent units consisted of single villages, while the largest, such as the Anlo, contained many large settlements and covered very wide areas' (Nukunya 1969:1). In 1906, Spieth listed 120 independent units, which Nukunya refers to as tribes. Ewe tribes differ widely in their political and kinship structure. Nukunya describes the traditional political system of the Anlo as 'centralised', since 'it provides for a constituted executive authority, and administrative machinery and judicial institutions'. There is a paramount chief, who lives in a sacred spot, and below him three senior chiefs who commanded the main sections of the fighting force when Anlo men were mobilized. Below these senior chiefs were the town and village chiefs, drawn from the senior patrilineage in each community. The elders of the other patrilineages formed a governing council with the chief, a political structure which Lloyd (1965) has characterized as a form of representative government.

The four peoples considered in this chapter speak languages of three different language groups of the Kwa complex (Westermann and Bryan 1952:76-96). As polities they have in common an origin in the meeting and amalgamation of peoples of different ethnic and linguistic stock. Significantly, all these societies retained unilineal descent groups as the basis of the political structure, incorporating intrusive elements within the same idiom of unilineal descent, even when this meant a switch from matriliny to patriliny. Through their appointed representatives (often elected from a designated lineage segment) descent groups formed the building blocks of the political structure. Among the Ga and Ewe, offices often alternate between two different lineage segments, lineages, or clans.[3] Typically, ritual offices have a political role as well, and political offices a ritual aspect. Certain chiefs were designated to lead the army in times of danger. Their titles, and perhaps the organization of the forces themselves, were based on those of the powerful and feared Ashanti. The Fanti had a permanent military organization, the famous *asafo* companies, which recruited their members through patrifiliation in this otherwise matrilineal society.

Although it is still possible to discern the role of descent groups in the precolonial political systems of these small-scale states, it is many decades since their representatives were able to wage war on their enemies or pass judgement on criminal cases. Descent groups have been further undermined by the increasing differentiation of wealth and style of life among their members. Few rights to corporately held resources still exist and the dispersion of members around the country in the modern occupational structure had deprived the lineage of a core of men who represent and guide its fortunes.[4]

145

Traditional ritual, economic and kinship institutions and parent roles

The polities of southern Ghana do not fit neatly into the framework used in Chapter 4 which contrasted unilineal descent groups and centralized states governed by a ruling elite. They were small-scale states in which offices were linked to unilineal descent groups which thus played an integral role in the 'centralized' political and ritual system. Hence the descent groups obviously played different roles than in acephalous systems where the ties and oppositions between the lineages as independent entities constituted the basis of the political organization. Their presence certainly affected the constitution of the southern states since offices and military duties were vested in them; at the same time, both polity and kinship were strongly affected by the fact that these states were involved in trade with the European powers on the coast.

In order to discuss parent roles in the present we have to place the problem in the earlier historical context. At the same time we need to draw attention to certain traditional institutions which have a direct bearing on ideas about parent roles today, in particular ritual sponsorship, pawning and fostering.

Ritual sponsorship: Circumcision and puberty rituals

The practice of male circumcision marks a sharp difference between such peoples of the south of Ghana as the Ga, Krobo and Ewe, and the Akan groups (such as the Fanti). Fanti boys are never circumcised; Ga, Krobo and Ewe boys always are. Although this is consistent with the presence of matrilineal and patrilineal descent groups in these societies, circumcision is not made a part of male initiation into age grades or secret societies. Rather it is an individual affair, usually done in infancy or early childhood. Nevertheless, Huber stresses that for the Krobo it is only through circumcision that a male becomes a 'real' Krobo, and indeed this was required of all refugees who wished to join the community. For unless circumcised a man could not go before the shrines of the Krobo gods from whom the people received health and protection.

Formerly there were puberty rituals for Ga boys also. These were necessary in some lineages before a man was allowed to approach the most sacred shrines. In Nungwa, only after puberty rites could a youth enter the forest of the god Gbøhu, marry, join the military company, fire a gun, have a man's share of rum, and have a full funeral (Field 1937:192). Without such rites it was believed that a man 'would be stupid'. Unlike the puberty rites for Ga girls, of which there were at least six different types (each with a distinctive ethnic origin), the boys' rites appear to have been the same in all the Ga lineages, except in Kpong. While each lineage was responsible for establishing the adult status of its own new male members, this similarity suggests that it was also important to provide a common

146

civil status in which, as adults, they had wider responsibilities to the members of the other lineages who formed the town.

Circumcision was a prerequisite to adult status, but not the only one. This is clearest from accounts of Ga socialization where the father's duty to teach adult economic skills to his sons, or to arrange for others to do so, is quite explicit. The father is also responsible for his son's first marriage. With an occupation and a wife, and as a recognized member of his descent group and of the wider polity to which it belongs, a youth becomes a man.

Ritual sponsorship for girls was necessary in all four societies before a girl could marry and bear legitimate children. In striking contrast to the lack of ceremony in the circumcision for males, even though it marked entry into the politico-ritual community, rituals associated with menarche for girls are elaborate in Krobo, among some Ga lineages, and formerly for the Anlo Ewe (Huber 1963:165ff.; Field 1937:185ff.; Nukunya 1969:79). Data on the Fanti *obrah-yia* suggest that it closely resembles the elaborate Ashanti menarche ritual. The Krobo puberty ritual for girls is known as *dipo*, and the Ga lineages which also practise this rite are said to be descended from Krobo immigrants. Until the British forceably prevented them in 1892, Krobo girls undergoing *dipo* rites spent a year on Krobo mountain with the priestess and her assistants. The Ga *dipo* of the 1930s was much briefer, but also involved several girls going through the rituals together. Both Fanti and Ewe girls appear to have undergone the ceremonies individually. These were considerably more elaborate among the matrilineal Fanti than for the patrilineal Ga.

Sponsorship for girls focusses on puberty rituals and marriage. Whereas the Ga and Ewe rituals are either forgotten or falling into abeyance (Nukunya 1969:79; Kilson 1974:61-2), Krobo and Fanti girls still appear to undergo them. Marriage also serves as a major gateway to adulthood, although how and whether it was celebrated differed between these four societies and has changed greatly in recent years. For girls, entry into adult status involved the allocation of sexual rights and rights over children, as well as the provision of sufficient capital for independent economic enterprise, albeit on a small scale. The extent to which these rights and obligations were vested in her natal lineage, in a husband and his lineage, or shared between them, varied greatly between systems, and also has changed over time. The general point to be made is that in each of these societies puberty ceremonies provide a public statement of the girl's sexual and reproductive maturity, thus preparing the way for further allocation and assumption of rights which establish her adult status.

The parents who convey birth-status identity are the ones who must arrange for girls' ritual sponsorship. However, where a girl is betrothed already the parents may be aided by the fiancé with the expenses, or are able to reclaim part of these from him. Here the close link between marriage, legitimate fertility and full adult status for women is expressed very clearly.

Parent roles in West Africa

Pawning

There is a widely reported practice in West Africa of using children (and sometimes adults) as security for loans, referred to in English as 'pawning'. The person pawned goes to live with the creditor and must work for him until the debt is repaid. Where children were sent as pawns this had the effect of removing them from the authority of their parents and transferring both rights to their labour and the responsibility for training in adult role tasks to the creditor. There is very little information on decisions about the choice of creditor with whom to pawn a child. However, Fadipe suggests that among the Yoruba a child was sometimes sent to a craftsman from whom he could learn a skill while working for him (cited in Koll 1969, see Chapter 8); Field mentions a youth who had worked as a pawn with a fisherman for ten years.

There are frequent references to pawning for three of the societies being considered here. Of the Krobo, Huber writes:

In the case of a bigger loan asked for perhaps to cover funeral, marriage or other ritual expenses, the petitioner first brought a bottle of rum . . . If the loan was granted, he gave one of his children, more often a boy than a girl, as hostage or security to his creditor. This hostage was to 'serve him . . .', i.e. to work for him up to the day when the money was returned. This practice was called . . . 'you give your child as security' or simply *awøba*. On the appointed day the debtor brought back the amount he had borrowed, together with another bottle of rum . . . , and the child was free to return home. At times, however, the boy would stay for some more weeks or months which his master would reward by giving the boy a cutlass and some other gifts, at the end of this period (Huber 1963:69–70).[5]

The Ga also used children as security for loans, sending them away in childhood, where they remained until the loan was repaid, even as adults. The work they did was counted as the interest on the debt, not as contributing towards its repayment. This distinction is seen very clearly for the Ashanti, where, if the person serving as security ran away without due cause, the debtor had to begin paying interest on the loan (Rattray 1929:50, 54). Unlike the Krobo, the Ga preferred to send daughters rather than sons as pawns, 'for it usually works out more profitably in the end' (Field 1940:57). Any suitor had to pay the original debt to free the pawned girl, and, if she was seduced by the creditor or a member of his family, then the debt was cancelled.[6] Writing of the mid-1960s, Azu speaks of children currently living as pawns; such a child is treated as a foster-child but is usually overworked (Azu 1974:46).

The transfer of children to the household of a creditor as security for a debt is recognized by the Fanti; indeed a myth relates the origin of matrilineal inheritance to a wife's refusal to allow her child to be pawned so that her husband could get a loan, while the sister agreed to let her child be sent. In gratitude the man left his property to the child of his sister rather than to the child of his wife

148

(and of himself). Both boys and girls were placed with creditors as pawns (*aho-baa*), a boy going to a man and a girl to a woman. As among the Ga, if a pawned girl became pregnant by her master the debt was cancelled. Christensen encountered cases of pawning during his fieldwork in 1951-2 (1954:40-2).

In relation to the conceptualization of parenthood and the delegation of parental roles, pawning is significant as involving an explicit distinction between the transfer of rearing, training and labour on the one hand, and the retention by parents and the lineage of rights concerning jural identity and the identity of any children a pawn might bear. Rights to a pawn's labour remained with the creditor until the original debt was repaid, even if the pawn had become an adult. But, however long the pawn remained with the creditor, his or her jural identity did not change; nor could the creditor convert a pawn into a spouse without cancelling the debt and going through the proper rites.

The delegation of training through fostering

For two of the four southern Ghana societies it is possible to say something about the earlier pattern of parental-role delegation through fostering. Huber's detailed account of the Krobo first describes what he calls 'full adoption'. This is the transfer from a man to his childless brother of the rights and responsibility for a child. However, as both the father and the father's brother have jural status by virtue of membership in the same minimal descent group, no change in the child's birth-status identity is involved. Rearing reciprocities, education and sponsorship link the child with his father's brother. Presumably the child would be the only heir to the pro-parent's property, since he had no other children. In any case brothers and their sons have joint rights in most of a man's property. The transfer of rearing roles serves to provide the childless brother with a personal heir, rather than securing the inheritance of assets by the brother's children instead of by an outsider.

Apart from this compensation for childlessness, Huber writes that

from ancient times there has been the practice of sometimes giving a child to a relative or friend 'as a messenger boy' . . . Good training or correction of a boy's or girl's character are the objectives of such temporary adoption. The guardian (*n hiEl*) preferably a man of practical wisdom . . . and personal experience, is expected to give good care and education to the child who, on its part, does messenger's or other personal jobs for him. If such a boy or girl is respectful towards his guardian, the latter shows his appreciation at the end of such training by making some presents to him or her, or by giving his own daughter to him in marriage (Huber 1963:86).

From the practice of ending the period of training with the presentation of a bride it would seem that the 'temporary' nature of the 'adoption' corresponds to the period of later childhood and adolescence. The term 'educational fosterage' seems appropriate here, and to the extent that marriage for a youth

149

marks his transition to adulthood, sponsorship is sometimes involved. However, there is no information about the relationships between children and their foster-parents, nor as to the frequency of its occurrence.

Azu's material on the Ga of Labadi (the La) is the most detailed available on the nature and the delegation of training for any of the four societies. From the moment the Ga boy moves into the men's house at the age of 7 or 8, he begins to help his father with his work, at first accompanying him and observing, perhaps carrying his tools. Some sons follow the father's occupation, gradually participating more and more until they master it. However, it is unlikely that all of a man's sons will follow his occupation, so the duty of every father is to place his son in an occupation of the son's choice, provided he can afford the training expenses; and sometimes it is the father who suggests the occupation to his son. Besides farming and fishing, the occupations favoured by La youth in the mid-1960s were as carpenters, drivers and fitters.

A father first solicits the help of his father and brothers and later his wife, to look for someone who is qualified in the trade the son intends to take to, from any of the four major lineages. [That is, from the major lineage of the father's father or mother and the mother's mother or father.] If they are unsuccessful, they then look elsewhere for such a person. This is done because the apprentice fee will be small and often negligible where the master is a relative.

Accompanied by a brother, the father makes his intentions known to the master. A bottle of gin is given to the prospective master when the boy is brought to him. The acceptance of the drink signifies the desire of the master to take the boy on as apprentice. However, the boy is accepted on probation for some time. If the master becomes satisfied that the boy is teachable, he further asks for 'drink' . . . This is given in the form of money. There is no fixed amount. It is the master who decides what to ask for. All the same, the minimum known to have been requested is five pounds.

The learning of a profession may entail changing residence and living with the master. In fact it is the main channel for fostering of male children or youths in the traditional set up; for in addition to the professional training he gets, the boy is expected to perform household duties such as laundering, sweeping and fetching water for the master. These form part of his character training. Thus before he is sent to the master, the elders in the [men's] compound meet, call on the ancestors and commit the boy to their protection. The boy is advised to behave at his new home and learn his profession diligently (Azu 1974:42-3).

Significantly, this professional qualification also makes the Ga youth eligible to marry. It constitutes both training and sponsorship in terms of the paradigm of parental roles set out in Chapter 1. If a Ga boy learns farming from his father, he must still demonstrate that he can farm on his own. After this his father gives him a gun and a piece of land. The young fisherman must show that he can paddle, and thus qualify to receive a share of the catch instead of just being given a few fish for helping to draw in the nets. Once the youth has demonstrated his proficiency in his chosen occupation, his father 'marries a girl' for him, paying all the expenses. The father might or might not have selected the bride; nowadays this would be unlikely.

Contemporary patterns in southern Ghana

The socialization of a girl involves less discontinuity, since she remains in the compound of her mother, who teaches her domestic skills, together with either trading or farming, unless she is fostered. Whereas the Ga boy may wish to follow an occupation that his father is unable to teach him, a girl's mother is believed to know the domestic skills that will enable her daughter to be a good wife and mother. However, says Azu,

There is a general belief that parents are not the best suited people for the up-bringing of their children; that they tend to pamper their children, making it impossible to exercise that little bit of hardness, if not harshness, that Ga believe to be an essential ingredient of the socialisation process.

For this reason children are often sent to relatives or non-relatives for training – *tsøsemø*. It is preferable to send the child to someone of the same sex for train-ing, and, although this is not always followed, it is less often the case that a boy is fostered by a female than that a girl is fostered by a male. A girl may be sent to a paternal or maternal relative who has no children of her own, or to a grand-mother to help her in the house. She may also be sent to an educated relative or non-relative 'to learn to be a lady'. The girl goes at the age of seven or eight and may live there until she marries, save for occasional visits to her parents. A girl so sent out participates in the performance of household duties, and sometimes in trading. Where the foster parent is educated, she may be taught sewing as well. She is given food and clothing and where she is dutiful, she may be given money with which to start trading (45).

The provision of capital with which to start trading constitutes sponsorship into her adult economic role. The foster-parent also plays a part in her first marriage (sponsorship again) in that she receives the first approach from the sui-tor's kin, and directs them to the parents. She is also expected to give her foster-daughter new clothing when she leaves, according to her means. Azu notes that because of the Ga residential pattern, fostering does not always involve a change of residence. A woman may give her daughter to her mother, or to a sister living in the same women's house. The foster-mother will be responsible for all the girl's actions, as well as for finding her food and clothing and teaching her cook-ing and childcare. Similarly, a man may give a son to a father or brother in his own men's house for the purpose of teaching him a trade. When one was expec-ted to marry within the maximal lineage, most foster-parents of both boys and girls would have been in the same lineage, though many would have been in different sub-lineages from the fostered child.

Any foster-child may be reminded in small ways that he or she is not the adult's *real* child. If the child does something wrong, the foster-parent may say: 'If you were my child I would have beaten you',[7] and a foster-child is often the one called to do small jobs while the other children play. Significantly, she suggests that whether a foster-child is well-treated or not also depends on his character.

The discussion of traditional Ga fostering concludes with the observation that fostering is mainly used between kinsmen to redistribute the advantages held by various members of the compound and of the wider lineage. 'A woman with many children sends one to live with another relative who has none; a poor or illiterate man sends one of his children to a rich or educated kinsman; and finally a "professional" brother or relative trains some of the young boys of the lineage in his art' (46). But she also declares that 'Fostering of boys is mainly connected with the learning of a trade' (45).

Contemporary patterns of parental-role delegation in southern Ghana

Fostering among the Ga of Labadi

The field work for Azu's study was done in the mid-1960s, so it represents the same period in Ghana as my surveys of Fanti, Ewe and Krobo fostering. She presents data on three sets of fostered children; on the informants who were themselves fostered, on the informants' own children who were fostered, and on the children fostered by her informants. The proportion of informants who were fostered is slightly lower than that for the Ewe, Fanti and Krobo samples discussed later: 24 per cent for males and 17 per cent for females. The relationship of the child to the fostering adult is shown in Table 6-1. Of the boys fostered 25 years or more ago, half went to a parent's sibling, and one-third to a grandparent. Only two went to a sibling, and 10 per cent to non-kin. Of the more recently fostered boys, the proportion with grandparents remained at one-third, but those with parents' siblings dropped to one-quarter. However, the number with full or classificatory siblings more than doubled, while those who went to non-kin reached nearly one-third of the fostered boys. For girls fostered 25 years or more ago, a third also went to grandparents, but nearly two-thirds to mother's or father's siblings; no girl went to a foster-parent of her own generation, and only one to a non-kinswoman. For the recently fostered girls, the proportion with both grandparents and parents' siblings has dropped; there are now two girls with a sibling, but the proportion with non-kin has risen dramatically from 4 per cent to 18 per cent, probably because these girls are likely to act as housemaids. Five of the girls being fostered by informants were housemaids; significantly, these were from two of the ethnic groups covered by the survey, namely, Ewe and Fanti.

The data for Ga fostering can also be considered in terms of the lineality of the relationship to foster-parents.

Azu comments that the patrilineage is now greatly weakened by the spatial dispersion of its male members. This takes two forms. Locally, many men no longer live in the lineage men's compounds, primarily because to have their wives with them is difficult if not impossible in the men's compound, even when they make a separate entrance which allows accesss from outside. But many men are no longer living in La, or even in the Accra area, as modern occupations often require mobility. A further factor weakening the patrilineage is the undermining

Table 6-1. *Relationship of child to foster-parent (by generation). Comparison of recently fostered with those fostered 25 years or more ago: Ga (from Azu 1974:94)*

Foster-parent generation of:	Fostered 25 years ago				Fostered within the last 25 years			
	Male		Female		Male		Female	
Grandparent	13	(34%)	9	(33%)	13	(33%)	10	(22%)
Parent	19	(50%)	17	(63%)	10	(26%)	25	(56%)
Sibling	2	(5%)	0	–	5	(13%)	2	(4%)
Non-kin	4	(10%)	1	(4%)	11	(28%)	8	(18%)
Total	38	(99%)	27	(100%)	39	(100%)	45	(100%)

of the elders' authority by younger men who have been educated and moved into professional jobs, often with very high salaries by La standards. When these men wish to have a voice in lineage affairs it is impossible for the elders to refuse. In addition to these recent pressures on the patrilineage, it clearly no longer plays the central political role in local affairs that it did in the traditional system. If the elders' authority were still backed up by the control of critical political and economic resources, the men of the patrilineage would make the effort to keep in touch and to fulfill their lineage obligations. For instance, where the lineage still controls land, its members make sure to press their claims.

The shift in the pattern of sending children to paternal and maternal kin during the last 25 years cannot be understood apart from the declining role of the patrilineage. Of the boys fostered 25 years ago or more, 45 per cent went to paternal kin. This figure has been halved in the past 25 years. The proportion of

Table 6-2. *Recency of fostering in relation to lineality of relationship to foster-parent: Ga (from Azu 1974:94)*

Related through:	Fostered 25 years ago				Fostered within the last 25 years			
	Male		Female		Male		Female	
Maternal kin	14	(37%)	12	(44%)	14	(36%)	30	(67%)
Paternal kin	17	(45%)	13	(48%)	9	(23%)	5	(11%)
Lineality unknown	3	(8%)	1	(4%)	5	(13%)	2	(4%)
Non-kin	4	(10%)	1	(4%)	11	(28%)	8	(18%)
Total	38	(100%)	27	(100%)	39	(100%)	45	(100%)

girls sent to paternal kin has dropped even more dramatically, from one-half to one-tenth. Where are children sent now, if not to paternal kin? The proportion of boys going to maternal kin has not changed. But the proportion with non-kin has nearly tripled. For boys, the role of the father in training for an occupation has greatly declined, because of the much wider diffusion of education, and because many jobs which do not require literacy cannot be learned from kin whose traditional occupations are farming and fishing. The very striking shift for girls from 48 per cent to 11 per cent with paternal kin cannot be accounted for on the basis of occupational training alone. The increase of girls going to non-kin, mainly as housemaids, accounts for less than half of this decrease. However, unlike their brothers, girls are much more frequently going to maternal kin (an increase from 44% to 67%). This change would seem to be linked to the declining power of the wider kinship system in constraining mothers to send daughters to their husband's kin. It also shows a tendency for matrilateral kinswomen to cleave together when traditional institutions do not exert contrary pressures; this also appears in the survey data on Fanti, Ewe and Krobo fostering.

Finally, in the earlier fostered group, more boys were fostered than girls, though the proportional distribution among kin was roughly the same. In the more recently fostered group, more girls are fostered, and there are sharp differences in their allocation to kin. Perhaps the most interesting finding in these data is that despite the very considerable changes in external conditions as well as in the pattern and function of fostering (i.e. the near-disappearance of pawns and the introduction of housemaids), fostering continues to be widespread. This is so despite the fact that school is now widely recognized as important, and the rate of attendance in suburban Accra is high. Yet despite the schools taking over part of the training function of parenthood, and despite the inevitable drop in the amount of time a schoolchild can contribute to domestic or other chores, fostering continues to be prevalent.

One further finding is precisely borne out by our study of West African families in London (Chapter 10). Highly educated, professional families do not send their children to be fostered, because: 'Educated parents prefer to bring up their children themselves, for they feel that they are better able than anyone else to train them'[8] (Azu 1974:94). The La data are not analysed in relation to parents' education, nor in terms of parents' residence in the traditional or modern section of the town. However there is a comparison of attitudes towards fostering held by members of the two sections. This shows strong disapproval (84%) among the residents of the modern section. It is hard to know just how to interpret this finding in view of the evidence that fostering continues to be frequently used, even among professional people, under certain circumstances. The disapproval expressed by the 'moderns' is almost certainly a partial reflection of their adoption of the nuclear family ideal as a basis for residence and for the definition of conjugal and family roles. It also reflects the fact that there are, for this group, few if any kinsfolk who are in a position to 'train the children better than their own parents'. However, parents' assessment of educational advantage for their children is highly relative to the opportunities available, as is very strongly brought out in the delegation of parental roles among West African immigrants in London.

Survey data on parental-role delegation from Fanti, Ewe and Krobo communities

The four survey communities were selected from three different southern Ghanaian societies, one matrilineal with complementary patrilines (Fanti): one clearly patrilineal (Ewe), and one, the Krobo, which, while patrilineal, has a relatively high level of assimilation of daughters' children, giving it a bilateral bias. Sibling groups of adult informants were chosen as the unit for data collection because while working in Gonja I had found that if material was collected on all members of a full sibling group, rather than only on the particular respondent, information was automatically available on such factors as position in the sibling group which might influence decisions about rearing arrangements. At the same time by talking to one person it was possible to gather information on the rearing histories of several others, full brothers and sisters. While indirect information is always open to inaccuracies, the full sibling relationship is close enough to provide reasonably reliable information concerning the period of joint childhood.[9]

Characteristics of survey communities

All four communities in which the interviews were conducted were large villages or small towns rather than farm hamlets. The Fanti town of Anomabo is an old established port with a fort still bearing the marks of slave chains. Its Christian graveyard contains headstones dating from the nineteenth century. A modern mansion built by a successful migrant looks down on the town from the cliffs to the west. The house of the traditional chief lies slightly to the east of the main town, beyond the new market. And along the shore, slender, gaily painted fishing boats are beached. Most of the dwellings lie on the seaward side of the main east–west coastal road, and are further divided by an invisible line separating the compounds of fishermen from those of farmers. But most either fish or farm; Anomabo is not urban in the sense that its people work in either industry or service occupations. Tefle, the smallest of the survey towns, lies inland from the ocean, but near the banks of the Volta River, and on a major east–west road. It is this strategic position for transport and trade that accounts for most of the non-agricultural employment of its people.

Odumase is the Manya Krobo 'capital' and Somanya the centre for the Yil Krobo. The people return to these 'home towns' for annual festivals. Too far inland for fishing, they lie on the Accra plain, some distance from the cocoa farms where many normally live and work. There are many family houses in

155

which a representative of the lineage segment lives, often with children sent to stay there while going to school. Odumasi and Somanya are less rural than Anomabo, for fewer of the inhabitants farm or fish for a living, and more work in local services, in white-collar jobs, or as teachers.

Another way of placing these towns is to look at them in relation to the indices used in the Ghana census. Where do they fit among the communities of modern Ghana? None of the four survey towns is a city as geographers use the term or according to the definition employed in the census (1960). With populations ranging from 1,469 to 9,258 they do not even reach the status of 'large towns' (populations of over 10,000). These are not urban communities.

But a more difficult and interesting distinction remains to be made, for neither are they rural. I sought them out for the survey because they were in each case not only well-recognized towns, but towns that were identified politically and culturally with the Fanti (Anomabo), the Ewe (Tefle), and the Krobo (Odumase and Somanya) respectively. A town had a special significance in the pre-colonial coastal societies as the focus of a small-scale polity. The rural/ urban distinction of sociology does not easily allow for this intermediate position. However, there are two concrete criteria by which it is possible to compare the four towns with more rural areas, in a way that indicates the nature of their differences. Three of the towns have 50 per cent or more of the adult population engaged in occupations classified as non-agricultural. In the fourth, Anomabo, many men are engaged in fishing for the market, which is classified with agriculture in the census. These are not rural communities in the sense that the majority of the adults are directly involved in the market economy either producing food for sale, working for wages, or engaged in craft or trade.

The second criterion is the proportion of the adult population which has attended school. In the four survey communities, between 29 per cent and 47 per cent of the men had some schooling.[10] In the surrounding rural areas, between 17 and 35 per cent of the men had some school experience. Figures for women are much lower in both the towns and rural areas: between 9 and 13 per cent for the towns and between 1 and 4 per cent for the rural areas. There is clearly a concentration of literate and partly literate adults in the survey towns compared with the rural areas surrounding them.[11]

Occupational differentiation, the existence of a variety of different jobs and the educational facilities available are central to participation in the modern economy and the emergent social stratification of the independent countries of West Africa. They are also critical to the ways in which parent roles are allocated in these rapidly changing societies when parents try to secure for their children the conditions of entry to new occupations and statuses. The four survey communities, while very different from teeming West African cities like Lagos, Kumasi, Accra and Freetown, differ in their turn from the rural hinterland where most people are farmers, and few have gone beyond primary school. Thus the allocation of parent roles found in the survey data reflects neither a response to urban conditions, nor yet the pattern of truly rural areas. They are the responses of people in small but thriving towns to changing demands of the twentieth century.

Incidence of fostering

Among the 106 sibling groups from the three communities studied, 83, or 78 per cent had at least one member reared apart from the parents. In just over half of these, a single child was fostered; in the rest two or more children were reared by pro-parents. The proportion of sibling groups having no member fostered is surprisingly similar for the Fanti, Ewe and Krobo sample communities, 20 per cent, 25 per cent and 23 per cent. The major difference between these three samples is that in nearly 60 per cent of the Krobo cases only one sibling was recorded as fostered, while in the Ewe and Fanti samples, about one-quarter of the sibling groups had only one sibling fostered. For multiple fostering the position is reversed, and sibling groups containing two or more foster-children were more than twice as many among the Fanti and Ewe (57% and 50% respectively) as among the Krobo (20%). Taking the three samples together, there were 509 individual siblings, of whom 153 had been fostered as children, exactly 30 per cent. There is only slight variation by ethnic group. Thirty-six per cent of Fanti siblings were fostered, 29 per cent of the Ewe and 27 per cent of the Krobo.

Sets of children studied

The interview was designed to learn not only about the rearing history of the respondent and his or her siblings, but about who raised the respondent's parents, whether the parents had reared anyone else's children, and whether ego and ego's siblings had reared each other's children. In short there are several sets of children for whom some rearing information is available. Taken all together, these cases of fostered children constitute a second population, which is termed the Fostered Sample to distinguish it from the Sibling Sample. When it is important to discuss the characteristics of fostered children, normally the Fostered Sample will be used. In order to compare children reared by their own parents with those who were fostered, the Sibling Sample must be used.

Characteristics of fostered children

(i) Sex of fostered children. Of the fostered children, 49 per cent were boys and 51 per cent girls.[12] However, this exact balance is misleading. Among the matrilineal Fanti, more boys than girls are fostered, which almost certainly indicates the legitimacy of claims by matrilineal kin on 'their' male children. For the patrilineal Ewe the balance is the other way, with a preponderance of girls fostered. Here the patrilineages appear reluctant to lose control over boys; this conclusion is confirmed by the distribution of fostered children between maternal and paternal kin shown in Tables 6-5a and 6-5b. The third ethnic

157

group, the Krobo, shows an even distribution of fostered children between both sexes.

If the Sibling Sample is taken as the basis for analysis, both the Fanti and the Krobo foster children of both sexes in equal proportions. The Fanti bias towards fostering boys in the Fostered Sample is no longer apparent. It is clearly a less robust difference than the Ewe preference for girls, which is just as strong in the Sibling Sample.

(ii) Age at fostering and length of fostering. The implications and consequences of growing up apart from their own parents will obviously be different depending on the age of the child when sent away from home, and on the length of fostering. Indeed, the duration of fostering is in part related to the age at which it was initiated.

In terms of the different elements of the parental role, the time of beginning fostering is critical. A child sent at birth will establish ties with the woman who nurtures it, and with whom it builds up initial dependencies and creates patterns of reciprocal response. A child reared by its own mother through infancy and early childhood builds these ties with her. Perhaps because the institutionalization of fostering is less formalized in these southern groups, I did not come across any explicit norms about the age at which a child should be sent to foster-parents; the Gonja say that it is better to wait until after the age of five or so when a child 'has sense'. However, the pattern for the Fostering Sample is clear, though it differs in interesting ways among the three ethnic groups. Infants are seldom sent to foster-parents, probably only when a family crisis makes this necessary (2% of the total sample). Indeed few children leave their parents before the age of 6 (6% for the total sample, but higher – 15% – for the Ewe).[13] Unfortunately, for about half of the fostered children, the exact age at fostering is not known, only that the child was old enough to do simple tasks around the house. We can only confidently report the general feeling that children are unlikely to be fostered before the age of 6, which may have influenced estimates where the actual age was not known. Except among the Ewe, people believe that children are fostered mainly in later childhood.

Taking only those children over 6 whose age at fostering is known, the great majority are sent to foster-parents before the age of 12. This differs somewhat among the three ethnic groups, with the Fanti sending over 90 per cent before the age of 12, the Ewe roughly the same proportion, while the Krobo send nearly 30 per cent after that age. It seems probable that the Krobo are using fostering in a somewhat different way than the other two groups. The data on crises during childhood suggest that these occur more frequently among the Krobo; since these presumably occur over a longer span of childhood, the times for initiating crisis fostering may be later.

One of the most important categories of response to enquiries about how long a child stayed with a foster-parent was 'until she or he was grown up'.

About 30 per cent of those who could answer this question first gave this reply. But of course the response means very different lengths of time depending on when the child was first sent to the foster-parent. Among all three ethnic groups, short-term fostering is rare. Fostering for less than three years' duration accounts for no more than 14 per cent of any of the three groups, and for only 7 per cent among the Fanti and the Ewe.[14] The relatively shorter duration of Krobo fostering fits with the substantially higher proportion of children sent to foster-parents after the age of 12. These would often be sent to learn an occupational skill, as there is a tendency for instrumentally specific apprenticeship to begin later than those oriented to more diffuse goals, such as character training or companionship. Among the Fanti and the Ewe, most fostering lasted for more than six years (72% and 83% respectively). For the Krobo, many of whom join foster-parents after 12, half the cases were of between three and six years duration, while one-third were over six years.

(iii) Relationship to foster-parent. To whom are children sent for fostering? To whom are parental-role tasks delegated? The most detailed information available is from the Sibling Sample. This material has the further advantage of including every choice of foster-parents made by a given set of parents for their children. It must therefore take into account the full range of responsibilities toward kin as well as the interest and ambitions of parents and children. If one daughter is sent to a lonely grandmother, the other may be free to learn baking from a father's sister. In order not to give a misleading sense of simplicity to this material, it seems best to begin with fairly detailed descriptive tables, and only then to condense and simplify these as analysis requires.

In the grandparental generation, all four grandparents appear as foster-parents, though surprisingly the mother's father does not appear to have reared any of the boys in these 106 sibling groups. Perhaps this omission is best understood in the context of very low fostering of boys by men of the grandparental generation. Only 2 out of 80 fostered boys were reared by a father of either parent (in both cases the father's father); nor does a matrilineal kinsman of this generation rear any boys. Why are these experienced mature men not selected to assume parental rearing responsibilities towards boys? As senior men in their descent groups, and no doubt respected members of the wider community, grandfathers would seem to be in an excellent position to provide male role models and give advice, particularly for those youths who were fostered 'in order to improve their characters'. This problem will be considered in some detail in the next chapter; here I only wish to point out the pattern in the reasonably representative sample based on the sibling groups.

Grandmothers, on the other hand, are a frequent choice as foster-parents of girls. The mother's mother is the second most common individual foster-parent from any generation, with a total of 12 cases. The father's mother falls far behind with only 3. Here it is hard not to see affective links between mothers

Table 6-3a. *Child's relationship to foster-parent: Sibling Sample – girls. (A relationship term in inverted commas indicates that it is a classificatory relationship.)*

	Fanti	Ewe	Krobo	Totals
Grandparental Generation				
Father's mother	1	1	1	3
Father's mother's mother			1	1
Father's father		1		1
Mother's mother	7	5		12
Mother's mother's brother		1		1
'Grandfather' – not clear if maternal or paternal			1	1
Parental Generation				
Father's full brother	1		1	2
Father's full sister	3	1	1	5
Father's paternal half-sister			1	1
Mother's full brother	3	1	4	8
Mother's full sister	9	5	9	23
Mother's maternal half-sister			1	1
Mother's 'sister'	1			1
Siblings' Own Generation				
Own full sister	1	2	6	9
Own full brother	1	2	1	4
Maternal half-sister		2		2
Paternal half-sister			1	1
'Brother' on father's side (father's brother's son, father's sister's son)		1		1
'Sister' on father's side (father's brother's daughter, father's sister's daughter	1	1		2
'Brother' on mother's side (mother's sister's daughter's husband, mother's sister's son)			1	1
'Sister' on mother's side (mother's sister's daughter, mother's brother's daughter)	2		3	5
Unrelated Foster-Parents				
Woman to whom apprenticed		1	2	3
Woman for whom a housemaid	2		7	9
Unrelated woman		1		1
Unrelated man		2	2	4
Identity of foster-parent not ascertained	1			1
Totals	33	27	43	103

and their daughters and the daughters' daughters as exerting an important pull, particularly when the pattern is just as clear between mothers and daughters of the patrilineal Ewe as of the matrilineal Fanti. The fostering of a grand-daughter by the mother's mother is the most prominent pattern in fostering by this generation; it is echoed by the striking frequency with which mother's full sisters foster girls (23 instances, or nearly one-quarter of all fostered girls). This pattern is prominent for all three ethnic groups, proportionately somewhat more so among the matrilineal Fanti. And again, in the fostering of daughters by the parents' generation, the father's female kin fall far behind those of the mother, with 6 cases, compared to the 25 of the mother's kin (including here classificatory as well as full sisters).

Table 6-3b. *Child's relationship to foster-parent: Sibling Sample – boys*

	Fanti	Ewe	Krobo	Totals
Grandparental Generation				
Father's mother	3			3
Father's father		2		2
Mother's mother	4			4
Parental Generation				
Father's full brother	4	2	9	15
Father's full sister	1			1
Father's maternal half-brother			1	1
Father's paternal half-brother			1	1
Mother's full brother	10	2	8	20
Mother's full sister	4		1	5
Mother's maternal half-brother			2	2
Mother's paternal half-brother			1	1
Brother's wife's father			1	1
Siblings' Own Generation				
Own full sister			5	5
Own full brother			4	4
'Brother' on father's side (father's brother's son, father's sister's son)	3	1	2	6
'Brother' on mother's side (mother's brother's son, mother's sister's son)	2			2
Half-brother – not ascertained if maternal or paternal			1	1
Unrelated Foster-Parents				
Teacher – while attending school	1		1	2
Creditor of mother – female			1	1
Unrelated man	1		1	2
Unrelated woman			1	1
Totals	33	7	40	80

Parent roles in West Africa

Looking at the fostering of boys by the parental generation, two relationships stand out. For the three ethnic groups together, the mother's brother is the most frequent foster-parent (20 cases) and only half of these instances are from the matrilineal Fanti where the mother's brother has a strong 'legal' claim on his sister's children. The next most frequent choice of a foster-parent from the parents' generation is the father's full brother. Although this occurs also in all three ethnic groups (15 cases), the matrilineal Fanti prefer maternal to paternal siblings of parents by a ratio of 3:1.

In the siblings' own generation, a *full* sister is the most frequent foster-parent for girls, and the second most frequent for boys. Indeed, this is the only female foster-parent of boys in the siblings' generation. It would seem that only the binding nature of the full sibling relationship can compensate for the problems raised by a woman rearing a boy of her own generation. Full brothers appear as foster-parents for both sisters and brothers in four cases. Again the claim of a full sibling is clearly a strong one. For girls, however, the most frequent foster-parent of their own generation after the full sister is a classificatory sister from among the mother's kin (5 cases). It seems likely that these women are often considerably older than the full siblings; they would be likely to be daughters of the mother's older sisters and thus are rather more like parents' siblings than members of the foster-child's own generation. Among the fostered boys, classi-

Table 6-4a. *Generation of relationship to foster-parent: Girls of the Sibling Sample*

	Fanti	Ewe	Krobo	Totals
Grandparents'	8 (24%)	8 (30%)	3 (7%)	19 (18%)
Parents'	17 (51%)	7 (26%)	17 (39%)	41 (40%)
Siblings'	5 (16%)	8 (30%)	12 (28%)	25 (24%)
Unrelated	3 (9%)	4 (14%)	11 (26%)	18 (17%)
Totals	33 (100%)	27 (100%)	43 (100%)	103 (99%)

Table 6-4b. *Generation of relationship to foster-parent: Boys of the Sibling Sample*

	Fanti	Ewe	Krobo	Totals
Grandparents'	7 (21%)	2 (28%)	0 —	9 (11%)
Parents'	19 (57%)	4 (57%)	24 (60%)	47 (59%)
Siblings'	5 (15%)	1 (14%)	12 (30%)	18 (22%)
Unrelated	2 (6%)	0 —	4 (10%)	6 (8%)
Totals	33 (99%)	7 (99%)	40 (100%)	80 (100%)

ficatory brothers on the father's side seem to play a similar role; with 6 instances, this is the most frequent fostering relationship for boys within their own generation.

If the several relatives who acted as foster-parents are grouped together by generation, the overall patterns are clearer (Tables 6-4a and 6-4b).

Considering the two tables together, the parental generation provides the largest number of foster-parents in each ethnic group for both boys and girls, with the one exception of Ewe girls where parents, siblings and grandparents are chosen equally. The sibling category is for the Krobo the second most frequent for both boys and girls. For Ewe boys and for both sexes among the Fanti, grandparents are chosen slightly more frequently than siblings. The Krobo are striking in almost never sending children to grandparents; only 3 out of a total of 83 fostered siblings. Finally, girls are twice as likely as boys to be sent to unrelated foster-parents. The difference between the sexes is exactly accounted for by the girls who went to serve as housemaids (9 out of 19, see Table 6-3a). Many of these girls were Krobo, and Krobo boys also went to unrelated foster-parents in 10 per cent of the cases. The Krobo seem to be substituting unrelated foster-parents for the grandparental generation.[15]

Finally, in order to look more closely at the differences between the three ethnic groups, the data have been ordered in terms of the lineality of relationship between foster-parent and child (Tables 6-5a and 6-5b).

The interesting finding in Table 6-5a is that, regardless of the descent system, girls are sent very much more often to female kin of their mothers than to any other category. This figure is most surprising perhaps for the patrilineal Ewe and Krobo where the jural claims of the agnatic kin might have been expected to result in a higher proportion of daughters being sent to father's mothers and sisters. In fact this proportion is the most consistent across the three ethnic groups for any of the tables concerning relationship to foster-parent.

Table 6-5a. *Lineality of relationship to foster-parent: Girls of the Sibling Sample*

	Fanti		Ewe		Krobo		Totals	
Maternal kin								
Male	3	(11%)	2	(10%)	5	(21%)	10	(14%)
Female	19	(70%)	12	(63%)	13	(54%)	44	(63%)
Paternal kin								
Male	1	(4%)	2	(10%)	2	(8%)	5	(7%)
Female	4	(15%)	3	(16%)	4	(17%)	11	(16%)
Totals	27	(100%)	19	(99%)	24	(100%)	70	(100%)

Lineality bears more of a relationship to the selection of a foster-parent for boys. The patrilineal Ewe sent 5 out of 7 fostered boys (71%) to paternal kin,

Table 6-5b. *Lineality of relationship to foster-parent: Boys of the Sibling Sample*

	Fanti		Ewe		Krobo		Totals	
Maternal kin								
Male	12	(39%)	2	(29%)	11	(45%)	25	(40%)
Female	8	(26%)	0	—	1	(3%)	9	(14%)
Paternal kin								
Male	7	(22%)	5	(71%)	13	(52%)	25	(40%)
Female	4	(13%)	0	—	0	—	4	(6%)
Totals	31	(100%)	7	(100%)	25	(100%)	63	(100%)

while the matrilineal Fanti exactly reversed the pattern, sending 20 out of 31 (65%) to maternal kin. The Krobo occupy an intermediate position, sending almost exactly half the fostered boys to kin of each parent. This finding is particularly intriguing in relation to the Krobo tradition of a girl's father raising her first son, often born before his mother's marriage, as his own. Although it must be said that none of the Krobo respondents gave this as a reason for fostering, Huber noted that 20 per cent and 37 per cent of the members of two descent groups were 'women's children' (1963:84–5). Table 6-5c further combines the data in Table 6-5b, making this pattern even clearer. For boys, the descent system further structures the choice of foster-parent, while for girls it seems to make little difference, either in strengthening claims of paternal kin or in weakening those of maternal kin.

Table 6-5c. *Summary of lineality of relationship to foster-parent: Boys of the Sibling Sample*

	Fanti		Ewe		Krobo		Totals	
All maternal kin	20	(65%)	2	(29%)	12	(48%)	34	(54%)
All paternal kin	11	(35%)	5	(71%)	13	(52%)	29	(46%)
Totals	31	(100%)	7	(100%)	25	(100%)	63	(100%)

Political and economic status of descent group

In planning the interviews for this survey the role of the descent group in fostering was not directly addressed, but information on the parents' descent groups was collected. Given the political nature of descent groups in the town-states of southern Ghana, I particularly wanted to examine the possible relationship between office-holding descent groups and patterns of fostering. It seemed possible, for instance, that boys in descent groups with rights in political office would be reared within the descent group both to retain control and to enable them to learn traditional skills and knowledge associated with their future role. On the other hand they might follow the Dagomba model in which princes were sent to foster-parents outside the capital. Or an important descent group might seek to establish and maintain an alliance through the fostering of children. Questions on this were never asked directly, but in relation to each case of fostering we sought to establish what the informant thought had been the reason for arranging it. In none of the interviews was a political motive ever mentioned for sending a child to a foster-parent. Of course this tells us very little about what might have happened in pre-colonial times when these town-states were independent polities fighting amongst themselves and against the European trading entrepôts for political and economic advantage. But today fostering does not seem to play an overt role in local-level politics in these southern Ghana communities.

Nevertheless, when patterns of fostering are examined in relation to whether the descent group holds rights in an office or valued skill there are certain trends which would be worth further investigation. Among the siblings themselves, a slightly higher proportion of families belonging to 'important' descent groups sent no children at all to be fostered, but these families were more willing to rear both boys and girls. The 'commoner' descent groups more often sent only their daughters for fostering. These daughters may have been the girls most often sent to work for unrelated women as housemaids, but it has not been possible to address this question directly given the way the data are coded. If the rearing of children by the parents of the Sibling Sample is considered in relation to rights in office, those whose descent groups held no office or skill were less likely to rear other people's children, and if they did so, less likely to look after more than one child. Parents in descent groups holding traditional office or skills were more likely to rear foster-children (55% did so compared to 39% of the non-office-holding group). And parents from office-holding groups were more likely to rear more than one foster-child (25% compared to 12% of the non-office-holding group). In short, there does appear to be some indication that children are sent to, or sought by, members of 'important' descent groups more often than by others.

Of course this factor, the importance of a descent group in the community, may be linked to others, for instance economic status. Informants ranked as 'high' in economic status were overwhelmingly members of 'important' descent groups. The opposite relationship, however, does not hold; that is, siblings who were ranked 'low' in socio-economic status were members of the office-holding and non-office-holding sets of descent groups in roughly the same ratio in which these sets were represented in the total sample.[16]

On the basis of the link between high estimated economic status and membership of an important descent group, there is likely to be an association between the number of foster-children reared by the parents of individuals in the Sibling Sample, and the parents' economic status. However, it is worth noting that only

165

14 out of 81 respondents were estimated to be of above average economic standing.[17] Therefore such a link cannot be present in a very high proportion of fostering arrangements, though it clearly does play a significant role in some.

Fostering as a response to crisis

Sending children to relatives is an important way of arranging for their care should the family of orientation break up. Of course it is not the only solution. On divorce both parents remain potentially able to care for the children. And even where one parent has died, the other remains to provide a home for them. But there are often reasons which make it difficult to keep the children with a parent. It is rare for a man to undertake the care of very young children, and on divorce they are apt to go with his wife, or, should she die, to her mother, sister or another female relative. A man is often reluctant to entrust children to a wife other than their own mother; co-wives are rivals for the husband's affection and support, and may be bitter enemies. If the mother marries again, children from a former marriage may be unwelcome in her new home. This is less of a problem in matrilineal societies where women may in any case be living with their own matrikin rather than with the husband, but even here the new husband may be reluctant to provide support for another man's children.

Crises in the Sibling Sample

The sources of information on the sibling groups were individuals who told about their own childhood and that of their brothers and sisters. Often the person interviewed had not himself been fostered but a sibling had. Thus the most interesting question to ask of this sample is 'How many sibling groups experienced a crisis in the family of orientation during childhood?' and 'How is this crisis history related to fostering?'

In comparison with the northern Ghanaian centralized societies, the frequency of divorce is low. It is probable that in about half of the sample Christianity or an Ordinance marriage may have exerted pressure against divorce. Whatever the reason for it, divorce was only reported as creating a crisis in 8 per cent of these families. Problems in the interpretation of the data on divorce are discussed further in Appendix II. However, I have concluded that if grown children reported their parents as not divorced (when they may well have been separated) and did not see their own or their siblings' fostering arrangements as made necessary by this sort of crisis, then there is a kind of truth here. Perhaps the best that can be concluded is that family life was not as smooth as the figures for divorce would suggest, and that the instances of crisis fostering under-represent the actual number where family conditions were a contributing cause.

If divorce is reported as infrequent, the death of a parent was a common experience, suffered by 43 of the sibling groups, or 40 per cent. Most reported

166

crises involved the death of a parent. Fifty-one per cent of the sibling groups experienced neither sort of crisis during their childhood.

What is the effect of a family crisis on the likelihood of a child being reared by foster-parents? While some fostering is undoubtedly due to family crisis, it is also undertaken for many other reasons (Table 6-8). Overall, family crisis does not seem seriously to alter the pattern of fostering. Thus if the proportion of families which experienced no crisis and sent no foster-children (21%) is compared with the proportion of 'crisis' families (i.e. those experiencing either death or divorce) sending no foster-child (19%), the result is virtually the same. However, this comparison masks one trend, namely, the greater likelihood that divorced parents will keep their children with them (33%) either compared to intact families (22% keeping all children), or compared to families disrupted by a parent's death (16% fostering no child). The converse of this is that families disrupted by death are more likely to send a foster-child than the others. Significantly, families suffering a parent's death are not found to send several foster-children with any greater frequency than other families. This is presumably related to the fact that some of the children will have already grown up before a parent dies, and thus their rearing arrangements are completed, while other families have produced only one or two children before being disrupted.

The relationship between family crisis and decisions about rearing arrangements for children can also be considered for the different sets of fostered children covered by the interview. These include three generations of children: the siblings' parents, other people's children reared by the parents of the Sibling Sample, and children of the siblings themselves. Each of these samples is independent of the others, and of the Sibling Sample itself. It would be an oversimplification to equate the generations of the sets of children with particular time periods. In fact the ages of those interviewed ranged from 18 to over 80, so that the childhood of the parents of the youngest informants coincided with the childhood of the children of the oldest sibling groups. The conditions concerned in the rearing arrangements for informants' parents would not have been as well-known to them as those of their own childhood. The same uncertainty attaches to conditions involved in arrangements for the children fostered by the parents of informants, many of them before the latter were born or while they were still infants. So it is not surprising that crises were only reported for 27 per cent and 30 per cent respectively of these two sets of fostered children. However, informants would be fully informed about the conditions surrounding the fostering of the children of their own full siblings. Yet here, too, only one-third of the children involved were fostered because of family crisis.

The clearest way to consider the differences in pattern of crisis and purposive fostering between the three ethnic groups is to use the Fostered Sample. A fostered Krobo child was much more likely to come from a family of orientation that had experienced crisis than was an Ewe child; Krobo crisis-fostering is 58 per cent of all fostering; Ewe crisis fostering is 14 per cent of all fostering.

The Fanti fall in between with 37 per cent of fostering cases due to crisis. This is consistent with the fact that the Krobo reported proportionately more parental divorces than the other two groups; Ewe reported no divorces. Krobo parents were also less often Christians, which would place fewer constraints on parental divorce. The substantially higher frequency of parents' deaths in the Krobo sample may be due to sampling error, or there may be some systematic factor of which I am unaware, such as a later age of men at marriage. But, even in the Krobo sample, 40 per cent of fostered children were reared apart from their parents for reasons other than family crisis.

The purposes of purposive fostering

The reasons given for sending a child to grow up with foster-parents are surprisingly varied. In all samples there were instances of fostering due to the desire to 'strengthen his or her character'. This reason was quoted and defended at length by a Krobo friend at the University of Ghana, who said that he had placed his daughter with his brother (a man less professionally qualified than he) because she was becoming too 'proud', and they, the parents, found it difficult to discipline her. The concern of professional parents that their children lack the proper respect for their elders is quite widespread.[18] It raises two different questions. Why should the children of professional people show less respect towards their parents and other elders? And why are the parents so concerned about this behaviour? These would seem to be real and interesting questions, whether or not the children are actually particularly disrespectful, a point almost impossible to verify. Perhaps this concern parallels the preference for rearing Dagomba princes by their father's courtiers away from the capital as well as the preference for wealthy and successful Kano merchants of the nineteenth and early twentieth century for placing their sons with clients and favourite slaves. In each case the particularly successful members of the community take pains to arrange that their children grow up away from what may be an indulgent and especially favoured environment.

Another frequent, but potentially ambiguous reason for sending a child to live away from home is 'so he or she can go to school'. Of course there are many communities without a secondary school and, in earlier years, there were many without good primary schools, or with no schools at all. In these cases a child was often sent to live with kin or with parents' friends in the town where the school was located. Other cases of 'school fostering' appear to happen when there are in fact schools available in the child's home town. Here the parents may be seeking an environment which they feel will be especially favourable to success in school. Many children are sent to live with a school-teacher on the grounds that he will help the child with homework. Sometimes a child is sent to a kinsman who has himself succeeded in secondary school or even university, but who is not a teacher. Here the household of an educated person is expected to provide the child with the right incentive for effective study, and with the

168

opportunity to meet other educated people. A particularly clear example of this sort of arrangement is reported by Fiawoo (1978) who describes how many children of successful Accra women traders are sent to live with Christian families in a certain village outside Accra. The village has a good secondary school and a reputation for piety, which stands in sharp contrast to the sort of environment a busy Accra trader can provide for her son in the midst of the city.

(i) Fostering and school attendance. The relationship between a child's rearing arrangements and whether or not he or she attends school is complex. Some children are fostered with educated relatives in order to benefit more from schooling or to be able to attend a particularly good school. Other children are fostered in order to receive special training that does not involve school, and which often makes school impossible for them. Others, particularly girls, are sent to help with housework and the care of small children while the mother is away from the house. Again, school is impossible for these 'housemaids'.

However, the first question to be asked is the pattern of school attendance among fostered children. About 60 per cent of this sample of people fostered in childhood attended school. While only half of these went as far as middle school, this in fact is a high figure for southern Ghana, particularly as most attended school in the interwar years, before the great increase in educational opportunities associated with independence. There is considerable variation between ethnic groups. Fifty per cent of the Ewe had not attended school at all, but only 40 per cent of the Fanti and 30 per cent of the Krobo fell in this category.[19]

In order to compare the school attendance of fostered children with those reared by their own parents, it is necessary to turn to the Sibling Sample. There is a very slight tendency for male siblings who attended school to have been reared by their own parents, and for those who did not attend school to have been fostered. But the total number of cases is low, and the differences slight. Even this difference disappears in the girls' data.

It is interesting to find that even when children are reared by their own parents, other kin sometimes contribute to school fees. Only one of the five sibling groups in which another kinsman paid school fees for children living with their parents was from the matrilineal Fanti group, despite the fact that in matrilineal systems the mother's kin have responsibilities towards her children which may include payment of school fees. The fact that both Krobo and Ewe relatives also contribute to fees for others besides their own children is consistent with the joint responsibility of close kin where descent solidarity is patrilineally defined.

However, it is clear that for a girl to be helped with school fees by anyone but her parents is closely linked to fostering. Where her education (in the broad sense) is the clear responsibility of the foster-parent, and where she is also a contributing member of the domestic workforce, a relative may pay for a girl's education, though Table 6-6 shows that parents still paid fees for nearly half of the fostered girls attending school. Parents were even more likely to pay fees

Table 6-6. *Arrangements for paying school fees for children in Sibling Sample*

	Who paid for schooling?	
	Males	Females
Not fostered		
Parent paid for all	21	14
Parent paid for some, another paid for some	2	
Another paid for all	3	
Fostered		
Foster-parent paid	9	8
Parent paid	8	2
More than one fostered child: parent paid for one, foster-parent paid for one	5	4
Total	48	28

for boys with foster-parents. This probably reflects two things: boys make less of a contribution to the domestic economy than girls (though they often do a great deal); and a parent who is keen to place a son with an educated family may not be able to ask them to meet the fees. Comparable information is available for some of the individuals in the Fostered Sample. Here again it is clear that sending a child to live with a foster-parent does not automatically mean that the latter will take responsibility for school fees. It is important to distinguish between the financial responsibility for education and the technical and moral responsibility. The latter may be delegated in fostering while the parents still retain responsibility for the former. (Just as another relative may take on the financial responsibility for paying school fees, while the parents retain the practical and moral responsibility for rearing the child.)

(ii) Apprenticeship. The diffuse conception of education, which includes moral training and the child's contribution to domestic work also holds for training in manual and technical skills. Apprentice carpenters, tailors and drivers' mates are expected to help with domestic chores, run errands, and often to sleep in the shop at night as a watchman. It is all part of learning the job. If the boy is from a different town his master will either provide him with food or give him 'chop money'. Arrangements for apprenticeship are extremely varied, partly in terms of whether the master is a kinsman, but also between trades, in different parts of the country, and in different West African countries. The nature of modern apprenticeship is discussed in Chapter 8.

(iii) Housemaids. Commenting on a survey of Accra she made in 1958, Ione Acquah stressed the importance of housemaids and noted that 'where the housewife is gainfully employed outside the home she may rely entirely on the services

of a girl to attend to all the domestic work, preparation of meals and care of the children. As the majority of women are engaged in petty trading . . . they are away from home for the greater part of the day' (1958:75). In the context of an extensive survey of Sekondi-Takoradi, Busia wrote: 'a significant feature of homelife in the town is the indispensability of the housemaid'. He adds that while sending daughters to respected neighbours or kinsfolk to be trained in domestic skills is a long-standing tradition, 'it is now justified primarily on the grounds that the housewife must have assistance with her domestic duties, either because her duties are many and exacting, or to set her free for earning money' (1950:34).

Many factors no doubt contribute to the increased dependence of women on housemaids. Towns are much bigger now, and the separation of home and economic activities more pronounced. More women are now trying to contribute to the support of themselves and their children away from their home towns where they could make joint arrangements with female kin about housework and the care of children. In cities like Accra and Sekondi-Takoradi, indeed, wherever a domestic family is not in the home town of either spouse, a married woman is likely to be the only adult female in a household, and must therefore take responsibility for all the necessary tasks, whereas in an extended household based on several wives or on several sisters (both common in traditional communities), sharing is built into the pattern of daily life. And of course where girls attend school, a woman has no longer the complete control over the labour of her own daughters that used to be the case. Not only are girls away for the main part of the day, but the parents are apt to be anxious about their completing homework assignments and are therefore reluctant to insist that they do much about the house. Foster-parents are unlikely to be so lenient.[20]

(iv) Summary: Purposes of fostering. A relatively large proportion of respondents did not know whether or why their fathers or their mothers had been fostered. It is often the case that children know few details about their parents' childhood, particularly younger siblings; parents seem to take pains to tell their older children, but then to leave it to them to tell the younger ones. This is probably particularly true of those whose parents died when they were young. For the same reasons, the accuracy of the information about the fostering of parents is sometimes doubtful. As a consequence the data in Table 6-7 about why parents were fostered cover only 25 men and 16 women. For these parents, however, information was reasonably detailed and hence dependable. All of the towns sampled have had at least primary schools for a number of years, which may partly explain why none of the parents were apparently sent to foster-parents in order to attend school. This is very different for the set of fostered children made up of children of the siblings in the Sibling Sample, Table 6-8.

Although one reason only was coded for each respondent, in three interviews there was more than one situation which led to fostering. In one such case, three children were fostered so that they could attend school, and a fourth to learn

171

Table 6-7. *Reasons why parents of Sibling Sample were fostered*

	Father		Mother	
Reasons why fostered:				
Kin begged for him/her	9	(40%)	8	(50%)
Kin needed companionship	1	(4%)	0	
Sent to improve character	1	(4%)	4	(25%)
Sent to learn craft or skill	3	(12%)	0	
Sent as security/interest on debt ('pawn')	3	(12%)	0	
Sent to non-kin as housemaid	0		1	(6%)
Sent because of family crisis	8	(32%)	3	(19%)
Totals	25	(100%)	16	(100%)

carpentry. In another, one boy was fostered to learn carpentry, another because of a parent's death, and two others because their mother was unmarried. In the final instance, one child was fostered to attend school and another 'for good training'. This last is a particularly clear example of the contrast between formal and informal education. 'For good training' could mean either 'to improve the child's character' or, if a girl, for general training in domestic skills.

The difference between the generations in references to fostering for schooling is marked; there are no such instances in parents' fostering histories, while 24 per cent of siblings' children who were fostered went for schooling opportunities. The difference is particularly interesting because schools were much more widely available as the twentieth century progressed, and thus one might have predicted a decline in the need to send children away to secure formal education. What is being reflected here is almost certainly the sharp increase in significance of schooling for adult occupational opportunities. When only a very few went to school, and there were very limited opportunities for them in adulthood unless they managed to secure further professional training, schooling did not enter actively into the ambitions and plans of ordinary parents. As the occupational structure became increasingly differentiated and opportunities multiplied, parents sought the advantages of school much more actively.

Parallel with the absence of 'school' as a reason given for parents' fostering, is the absence among the siblings' children of generalized reasons based on kinship obligations. These accounted for half the instances of fostered mothers, and 40 per cent of fathers. In coding the reasons given for fostering siblings' children, the three comparable cases seemed at once so individual and so different from one another that they were grouped together as 'other reasons' (see note to Table 6-8). It has often been claimed that the strength of kin ties is declining in contemporary West Africa. These findings are certainly consistent with such a conclusion. On the other hand, it may be the case that the reciprocal bonds of these full siblings were so immediate, representing debts laid down in a common

Table 6-8. *Reasons given for having fostered a sibling's child*[a]

To attend school	11	(24%)
To help in house, assist kin	4	(9%)
To help out parent	5	(11%)
Sent to improve character	1	(2%)
To learn skill/profession	3	(7%)
Other reason[b]	3	(7%)
Crisis in child's family	15	(33%)
NA	4	(9%)
Total	46	(102%)

[a] Other children of these parents may have been fostered by kin other than their parents' siblings, or by non-kin. Respondents were only asked about reciprocal fostering between siblings in this part of the questionnaire.

[b] These 'other' reasons were: (1) Reciprocity: the foster-parent had been raised by the mother of the foster-child, and sent her a child in return. (2) The foster-parent was childless. (3) The child was fostered as a mark of love for the sibling. All these reasons would have been subsumed under 'kin begged for child' or 'kin needed companionship' in the code for reasons for parents' fostering. But the codes were developed from the interview responses, and such diffuse kinship reasons were infrequent among the siblings. Perhaps they were generally taken for granted.

childhood, that to class these ties with 'kinship obligations' is to miss the point. They are obligations to closely related and intimately known individuals, not to a generalized collectivity such as a kin group. It seems likely that both conclusions are in a sense valid. For there were no responses couched in terms of general obligation, as was the case for the parents' generation, and as might have been expected in a situation in which kin group obligations were widely accepted as legitimating such choices, as we found in northern Ghana.[21]

In order to consider the relationship between ethnic group and the reasons for fostering, it is best to turn to the Fostered Sample as a whole, with the qualification that there will be a large number of instances in which the necessary information was not ascertained. Table 6-9 summarizes the available information on training (other than school) by ethnic group.

In comparison with northern Ghana, the most striking finding is the absence of instances in which fostering was utilized to train youths for traditional roles such as diviner, court linguist, drummer, herbalist, or for chiefship itself. Nor was fostering utilized to train youths for traditional crafts which have elsewhere been described as limited to the descent group (blacksmithing and goldsmithing). As we have seen, the Gonja do not use fostering in this way,[22] but the neighbouring Dagomba do.

173

Table 6-9. *Type of training other than school, by ethnic group: Fostered Sample*

	Fanti	Ewe	Krobo	Totals	% of totals
Housework/farming	2	2	15	19	14
Fishing[a]	8	1	0	9	7
Traditional craft	0	0	2	2	1
Modern craft	10	0	17	27	20
Trading	10	3	1	14	10
Seamstress/tailor	11	2	8	21	15
Bread-baking, beer brewing, selling cooked food	4	3	3	10	7
Hereditary professions: drumming, divining, herbalist, etc.	0	0	0	0	–
Hereditary craft: goldsmith, blacksmith	0	0	0	0	–
Job demanding literacy	6	0	0	6	4
'To train character'	6	0	22	28	21
Totals	57 (42%)	11 (8%)	68 (50%)	136 (100%)	99%

[a] The Fanti community sample was partially composed of fishermen. The Ewe community was on a major river, and many men fished. The Krobo do not fish.

This failure to utilize fostering for training for traditional offices or in 'closed' traditional crafts is echoed by the very low incidence for training in 'open' traditional crafts such as weaving, boat-making, wood-carving and house-building. There appears to be no need to make special arrangements to learn such crafts – perhaps because practitioners are usually found in every village. A parallel explanation can be offered for the low figure for training in 'jobs requiring literacy' since shools largely take over this task – but not always, as six instances were reported for the Fanti, mainly shopkeepers, where accounts of a simple sort were necessary.

In contrast, the popular modern occupation of sewing clothes (tailors for men; seamstresses for women), and modern crafts such as masonry, carpentry, driving, and mechanical repairs to cars, together account for one-third of the cases of training. The 17 per cent who were trained as bakers, sellers of cooked food or beer, or traders, were all girls. Training here includes a large component of productive labour, as an assistant is virtually indispensable for success in these occupations. As with the modern trades and crafts, the training received by the fostered child is balanced by the assistance he or she renders to the teacher. Together these categories of occupational training account for 50 per cent of the instances in the Fostered Sample. Another 21 per cent is covered by training in the basic subsistence skills involved in farming, fishing and housekeeping. It is significant that this is seen as training, since in fact such skills can be learned from parents as well as from foster-parents, in the sense that they are practised by all. The one possible exception would be fishing and farming in the Fanti community, where they were practised by only certain families. If a boy's father came from a farming family and he wanted to learn fishing he might be able to do so from his mother's kin. But in general, a boy or girl is reported as having been training in farming or in housework by a foster-parent, because of growing up with the foster-parent and learning the normal adult skills.

The other major category is what modern Ghanaians refer to as 'character training'. Since I have discussed this above, I need only remark on the relatively high proportion of cases in which this is given as the main reason for fostering. The absence of this reason in the Ewe sample is probably due to its small size. The Krobo may be more concerned with character training than the other two societies because of their tendency to send children at a later age. Alternatively, this response may simply be a culturally accepted explanation for fostering where there is no specific instrumental purpose.

Finally, Table 6-10 shows the relationship between school and other forms of training for the Fostered Sample as a whole. However, by definition, in this sample all the children were fostered. What is the relationship of special training to being fostered? That is to say, is fostering the only circumstance under which children are trained in occupational and more general skills? To answer this we must turn to the Sibling Sample, and compare fostered and non-fostered siblings.

Table 6-10. *Summary table: formal and informal training reported for Fostered Sample*

	Number	Per cent of those ascertained	Per cent of total sample
Fostered, and attended school[a]	119	47%	32%
Specific informal training in subsistence or occupational skill	108	42%	29%
Character training	28	11%	8%
Not ascertained, or no training reported[b]	118		32%
Totals	373	100%	101%

[a] This is not the same as 'fostered in order to attend school'. Information on whether a fostered child attended school is available in more cases than on whether school attendance was the reason for the child's being fostered.
[b] Where there is no information on this item, it is not always possible to tell whether the question was asked.

Table 6-11 raises two issues. In the first place, there were a substantial number of sibling groups in which no one was given any special training. Here subsistence skills were not considered as special training (nor, of course, was character

Table 6-11. *Proportion of sibling groups with members of each sex, and whether special training was provided for one or more children of that sex*

	Males		Females	
No sibling of this sex in the sibling group	13	(12%)	14	(13%)
No sibling of this sex received special training in this sibling group	45	(42%)	43	(40%)
One or more siblings of this sex received special training in this sibling group	48	(45%)	49	(46%)
Totals	106	(99%)	106	(99%)

improvement), so that those learning housework, farming or fishing would fall into these sibling groups. Such groups may well have contained fewer siblings, and thus offered fewer chances for training, but this question was not asked of the data. It remains interesting that for 40 per cent of the sibling groups, special training was not thought necessary. And it is also interesting that in those sibling groups where special training was arranged, this was often done for more than one child of the same sex; in 23 sibling groups two or more males were trained; in 28 sibling groups two or more females received special training.

The second issue (raised by Table 6-11a) is the relevance of fostering to special training. For both boys and girls, about half of those trained were fostered and the other half not. Some light is thrown on this pattern, which appears to contradict the relation between fostering and training in special skills, by comments written into the interviews. In many cases siblings not fostered began their training after the age of 15, which we had set as the end of 'childhood', that is, the end of the period during which parental training obligations towards children could be delegated. It is revealing to look at some of these comments.

> Informant (f) lived with two different women between the ages of about 18 and 22. From the first she learned dressmaking, from the second, trading.

> Informant (m) went to a non-relative at the age of 16 to learn carpentry, and stayed for 9 years

> Informant (m) lived with a distant relative by marriage to learn carpentry. He went when he was 20, and stayed 4 years.

> Informant (f), a brother and a sister each went, around the age of 16, to live with different people for training 'of various sorts'.

These responses were in fact made in the context of enquiries about residence ('and then where did you live?' . . . 'and then where did you live?' . . .) and thus do not reflect training undertaken while living at home.

176

Table 6-11a. *Individual siblings who received special training, in relation to whether fostered or not*

	Males		Females	
Fostered, and received special training	35	(46%)	46	(55%)
Not fostered, and received special training[a]	41	(54%)	37	(45%)
Totals	76	(100%)	83	(100%)

[a] For girls special training refers to some skill other than housework, such as baking, sewing or trading.

Further, if it is recognized that in these towns considerable occupational differentiation already existed, then it becomes likely that children could receive special training from a parent or parent's sibling living in the same house, or very near by. Such an arrangement does not require a change of residence, nor a change in the allocation of responsibility for rearing which is involved in fostering. This pattern is very clear in Azu's account of training of boys among the Ga whose home towns lie in and around old Accra.

Conclusions

Interviews with adults from small towns in southern Ghana show that during the middle years of this century it was very common to send children to be brought up by kin. Which relatives they were likely to go to varied with the descent system, though mothers' female kin had a disproportionate share in all three societies. While these arrangements were sometimes a response to family crises, between two-thirds and 40 per cent of the cases cannot be accounted for in this way. Nor is there any other single explanation which can be evoked. Children were often sent to kin 'in order to attend school'. But children who remained with their own parents were at least as likely to go to school. Indeed, school is more frequently given as a reason for recent fostering than in earlier cases when there were many fewer schools available. Conversely, informants' parents were said to have been fostered mainly in response to claims of kin (kin begged for him or her; or kin needed companionship) or to meet family responsibilities (sent as security for debt). There seems to have been a shift from sending children in response to claims by kin, to making claims on kin to take children so they can attend better schools, have the advantages of city life or learn new skills not available in a small town. There were no instances of children being sent to kin to learn traditional roles (linguist, chief), hereditary professions or crafts (blacksmith, goldsmith, diviner or herbalist) or traditional crafts (like wood-carving). In contrast, modern skills such as auto mechanics, tailoring, and driving were often learned in this way: modern skills account for one-third of the non-school training received by fostered children.

But what stands out is that most children went to kin. If girls were more likely than boys to go to unrelated foster-parents this is because they are being pulled into the service sector as housemaids. It is interesting that these figures for small-town fostering present a contrast with the urban Ga, where boys are more often sent to non-kin than girls, a fact that Azu links directly to the wish to learn occupational skills (1974:42, 94). The emergence of more formal occupational apprenticeships in the southern cities is discussed in Chapter 8. But first I want to compare the data from the southern small towns with those collected in northern Ghana where the effects of modern economic forces are less pronounced.

7

Fostering contrasted

This chapter compares the results of the surveys carried out in Gonja and in the four southern Ghana communities. These data show that Gonja children are more often sent to adults in the grandparents' generation while children in southern Ghana often go to adults who are real or classificatory siblings, as well as to non-kin. The difference in the generation of foster-parents has to be considered in relation to the functions of fostering in northern and southern Ghana.

Despite the relatively small number of West African societies for which there are detailed, numerical data on frequency and distribution of foster-children, it is now clear that this is a pan-West Africa phenomenon for which no locally appropriate functional explanation will suffice. While it is perfectly true that fostering 'fits' stratified societies such as the Hausa and Bornu because it is one avenue for the establishment of clientship relationships, it also appears between commoners in Gonja and among the relatively egalitarian Ga. Similarly, where wives are kept in seclusion by well-to-do Hausa Muslims in the north and in Ibadan, the need to have a child as a link between households and with the market is pressing; it is neatly met for those without children of their own by taking a foster-child. But fostering is also common among pagan and Christian Yoruba, where no such explanation is appropriate. Or again, in contemporary towns and cities, one often comes across children staying with kin, helping in the house and attending school. But African fostering cannot have arisen as a means of avoiding expensive boarding-school fees. I first came upon fostering among the Gonja of northern Ghana in a town with no school, and where indeed few children and scarcely any adults in the kingdom had had a chance to attend one. The neighbouring Dagomba make use of fostering to train a daughter's child in the traditional skill of the paternal kin group. The Gonja have many of the same skills as the Dagomba, and a high incidence of fostering, but only rarely do they use the institution as the basis of apprenticeship. In the west of the kingdom, the Gonja do, however, see the sending of a son to grow up with his mother's brother as one form of arranging for the care of the mother when she eventually returns to her natal kin in old age. A son who is already living there can provide a home and can farm on her behalf, in addition to the support which her brother is

179

morally obliged to contribute. The spatial distribution of marriage is narrower in eastern Gonja, and a wife's 'retirement' less likely to mean her departure to a distant village. Perhaps for this reason, the fostering of a son with his mother's brother is much less common in the eastern divisions.

One could go on citing similarities and differences between local variations of fostering in West Africa. The general point should be clear – there is a wide range of specific 'reasons' or 'functions' each of which makes excellent sense in its own context, but no one (or indeed combination) of which can be made to 'account' for the widespread occurrence of institutionalized fostering of children by kin in West Africa.

Yet if one considers other culture areas, this practice is rare enough to warrant some kind of 'explanation'.[1] Few Europeans or Americans would readily take a sibling's or cousin's child into their home for several years, or send their own son or daughter to an aunt or grandparent from the age of five until they were grown up. Purposive fostering with kin, the placing of children to fulfil one's obligations and at the same time gain for them the opportunity to grow up in a different family, often in a different town, does not seem to occur today in Indo-European societies. There are partial equivalents of a functional kind (*compadrazgo*, and other forms of fictional kinship) but not the actual removal of a boy or girl for the whole of childhood and adolescence, as we commonly find in West African societies.

Why is there this very general difference between the two sets of societies? What kind of underlying factor is common to all the various West African groups which have different particular reasons for fostering their children?[2] It must be a very general factor, because these groups differ widely in language, social structure, political organization and religious institutions. The simple answer is that fostering reflects the claims, rights and obligations, of members of an extended kin group. Given the norm that kin must share rights and obligations over resources, the fostering of children becomes only a special case of such sharing.

This view is entirely explicit for the Gonja of Northern Ghana. Rights of siblings over their children are expressed in the two models, one of which allocates the first daughter of a marriage to the father's sister while the other designates the second or third son as a foster-child of the mother's brother. In practice, a wide range of relatives serve as foster-parents, but these two models are the stated forms that act as charters for other claims. Siblings all say that they 'own' (*wǫ*) each other's children, which means both that they are responsible for them, and that they have claims over them. Unless there is some reason why the parents cannot manage their children, perhaps through poverty, lack of discipline, or the break-up of the natal family, the initiative in arranging fostering is usually left to the would-be foster-parent. Only when he or she presses the claim will the child actually be sent. Occasionally, a child is sent to an office-holder or to a Koranic teacher. In these cases the critical initiative is more likely to come from the parent.

180

Fostering contrasted

It is characteristic of West African societies that the 'sibling group' is not thought of as only the children of the same mother and father. This inclusiveness is usually reflected in the terminology, which designates the children of sisters (in matrilineal systems) or brothers (in patrilineal systems) or of brothers and sisters (among the bilateral Gonja) as themselves siblings. For instance, Fortes writes that in some contexts Tallensi brothers include all male members of the agnatic lineage of a man's own generation. In Gonja, all of a person's relatives of the same generation are either 'older sibling' or 'younger sibling'. Claims on the children of classificatory siblings are also made in Gonja, though they are not necessarily successful when the relationship is more distant than that of first cousins. It would seem to be in those cases where the terminology is open-ended, and the norms of siblinghoods very generally phrased, that the recognition of claims over children serves to define the limits of effective obligation. Rearing a sibling's child has this function because, in addition to the formal status obligation of kinship, the fostering relationship itself creates what I have called the 'reciprocities of rearing'. That is, specific, reciprocal, obligations of care and support are built up during childhood; the foster-parent is seen as looking after the child, feeding and training it, and these acts create a debt which the child must later be prepared to repay. Thus where second- or third-order relationships might cease to be considered binding in and of themselves, when they are reinforced by fostering a new set of obligations comes into play which is compelling in its own right. Furthermore, the fostered child grows up in a household of classificatory siblings (the children of the foster-parents) with whom he or she is on effective terms of full sibship, rather than the more diffuse relationship existing between distant kin who meet only occasionally.

In traditional West African societies, then, fostering depended on claims made against, and honoured by, kin. At the same time the sending of foster-children between elementary families served to strengthen the bonds by superimposing specific claims on the more general ones that tend to define the roles of distant relatives. An illuminating comparison might be with systematically practised cross-cousin marriage; indeed the diagram Yalman (1967) used to indicate the claims of cross-cousin marriage in a Kandyan village in Sri Lanka would serve

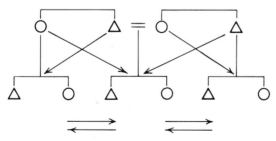

Figure 7-1. The interconnection and lateral extension of claims for foster-children (based on Yalman 1967:154)

181

equally well to illustrate the claims of fostering. As with cross-cousin marriage, it would be a mistake to expect that fostering will only occur between the children of primary kin (see Tables 6-3a and 3b).

Recent fostering in northern Ghana

In Table 7-1 data on relationship of foster-parent are given from four different studies, representing in all seven communities from eastern, central and western Gonja. The sex of the fostered child is given in parentheses for each study. Several points emerge from these figures. First, in all the studies, a very substantial proportion of foster-parents come from the parental generation (between 39% and 59%), which should be borne in mind for comparison with the West Indian pattern of fostering (Chapter 11). Next, if we compare the proportion of male and female foster-children resident with a grandparent (real or classificatory), we find that it is the girls who are much more likely to be sent (50%) compared to the boys (20%). This same pattern is found in some of the samples

Table 7-1. *Gonja (northern Ghana): Generation of foster-parent for four samples*

	Foster-parent is of:				
	Grand-parents' generation	Parents' generation	Child's generation	Not kin	Total N =
Data from:					
1. Buipe census[a] (children, m and f)	13 (38%)	20 (59%)	1 (3%)	0	34
2. Kpembe core[b] sample (children, m and f)	15 (48%)	12 (39%)	4 (13%)	0	31
3. Bole/Daboya[c] sample (adults, f)	39 (51%)	35 (45%)	3 (4%)	0	77
4. Men's marriage[d] survey (adults, m)	13 (20%)	37 (57%)	4 (6%)	11 (17%)	65
Totals	80 (39%)	104 (50%)	12 (6%)	11 (5%)	207 (100%)

[a] Old Buipe: 1956.
[b] These are all the fostered children in two sections of the divisional capital of Kpembe (eastern Gonja): 1964.
[c] The Bole sample consisted of all adult women in randomly selected compounds in the western Gonja divisional capital of Bole; the Daboya sample consisted of all the adult women in nine selected compounds in the central Gonja divisional capital of Daboya: 1965.
[d] This survey was carried out in three divisional capitals of eastern, central and western Gonja, and surrounding villages. The informants were all adult men in selected compounds: 1966.

182

from southern Ghana. The sending of girls to a 'grandmother' fits with training them in a domestic role, for they are expected to take over household tasks as well as provide companionship for the old women. Old men, on the other hand, are fed and looked after by their daughters or daughters-in-law, and a boy cannot be expected to fill a man's economic role. Finally, only in one of the four samples (the men's marriage survey), were any children sent to foster-parents who were not kin. These boys went either to join the household of a chief (6 cases) or to a Koranic teacher (5 cases, all in western Gonja). No girls went to non-kin in any of the communities studied.

Delegation of parent roles in southern Ghana

I must stress that the Gonja are a relatively remote group, on whom the industrial economy had made little impact when these surveys were carried out. The coastal peoples to the south have, on the other hand, been within the orbit of European trade since the sixteenth century. I have been able to do little direct work with coastal peoples apart from undertaking the surveys in four communities representing three different language groups in southern Ghana (Chapter 6). The following remarks draw on these surveys as well as on two recent books, Oppong's *Marriage among a matrilineal elite* (1974) and Azu's *The Ga family and social change* (1974), and on the studies of apprenticeship discussed in Chapter 8.

There appears to be a general tendency to shift from fostering by kin to analogous arrangements with strangers who can provide either a training in modern skills or a chance to gain familiarity with urban ways. In the Ewe, Krobo and Fanti communities I looked at in southern Ghana, daughters were sent to 'serve' women who baked bread for sale, to seamstresses and to traders; sons went to fishermen, carpenters, fitters and masons. Where such teachers were available within the kin group they were selected for preference, but in a number of cases they were not, and an arrangement was made with a friend or with someone of good reputation who could train the child. My impression was that the availability of a suitable 'master' could determine the choice of skill to which the child would be apprenticed. For Ga boys, there is a similar pattern of choice between a kinsman or a local expert of good repute (Azu 1974).

For girls, in addition to skills in sewing, baking and trading, there has evolved the institution of the 'housemaid'. I say evolved, because there does not appear to have been anything similar in the traditional societies of West Africa, with the possible exception of children who were lent to a creditor as surety for a debt.

The modern housemaid may be a relative of her master or mistress. This is preferred and is common (Oppong, 1974). However, many appear to be unrelated and to come for a sum of a few pounds per year paid monthly or annually to the parents of a young girl,[3] or when she is older, to the girl herself. Such girls tend to stay only a few years, and then either marry, or move on to some form of more remunerative employment, perhaps to an apprenticeship where they can learn a more saleable skill than housekeeping. There is a definite pattern of recruiting girls in rural areas to work as 'housemaids' in the cities of Ghana.

It would seem that as the skills and experience which parents desire for their children become more diversified, they begin to look beyond their kin to find someone to train them. Fostering by kin is gradually transformed into various forms of apprenticeship and domestic service. At the same time that kin are proving less able to meet these needs, there is a movement towards limiting the acknowledgement of kinship claims by those whose own education has led to a standard of living far above that of most of their relatives. While there is evidence that parents and full siblings still request and receive assistance in regular and substantial amounts, among the educated elite there is no longer the same pattern of honouring the claims of distant kin, even when made according to traditional norms (Oppong 1969).

Recent patterns in southern Ghana

The data in Tables 7-2 and 7-3 come from the surveys in southern Ghana which were discussed in Chapter 6. What I did not anticipate in planning these surveys was the shift from kinship to non-kin fostering. Hence when exploring the vocabulary of child-rearing in the vernacular in order to standardize the questions prior to interviewing I did not ask about how such apprentice-fostering was referred to. The figures in Table 7-2 particularly, on the non-kin fostering of boys, do not fit with observations on the sending of boys to learn such skills as carpentry, driving, 'fitting' (motor mechanics) and so on. While this may be a very recent pattern which does not appear when talking to adults about their own childhood, it seems more likely that informants did not consider these apprenticeships as 'rearing' when the 'master' was not a kinsman. Those few cases which do appear in Table 7-2 may be the ones in which a change of residence occurred as the result of apprenticeship, thus more closely approximating to kinship fostering in which the foster-parent expects to have the domestic services of the child.[4]

In these southern Ghana samples a substantially higher proportion of girls than boys is sent to non-kin foster-parents. Some of these girls are learning trades like baking or sewing, while others are acting as 'housemaids'. The fact that they were considered as being 'reared' by their mistresses may be related to the domestic nature of the skills they were learning, and to the undoubted fact that their training involves helping their mistress in household work as well as sometimes learning a particular skill.

In southern Ghana neither boys nor girls are frequently sent to grandparents to rear. The contrast with the figures for Gonja is pronounced, and the difference with the West Indian samples is extreme (see Chapter 11). There is a regular tendency for girls in all samples to go more frequently to their grand-

Table 7-2. *Generation of relationship between child and foster-parent in three southern Ghana societies: Boys*

	Fanti	Ewe	Krobo	Totals
Grandparents'	7 (21%)	2 (28%)	0 —	9 (11%)
Parents'	19 (57%)	4 (57%)	24 (60%)	47 (59%)
Siblings'	5 (15%)	1 (14%)	12 (30%)	18 (22%)
Unrelated	2 (6%)	0 —	4 (10%)	6 (8%)
Totals	33 (99%)	7 (99%)	40 (100%)	80 (100%)

mothers than boys to their grandfathers. This, as I suggested in discussing the Gonja data, seems likely to be related to the domestic nature of the training for the fostered girls.

The majority of the boys in the southern Ghana samples went to a 'sibling' of either the father or the mother (59%). This preference for a foster-parent of the parental generation appeared in some of the Gonja samples but here it is much clearer. For the girls in the southern Ghana sample the parental generation also provided the largest class of foster-parents (40%). The next largest group, for both boys and girls (22% and 24% respectively), went to an elder sibling (own or classificatory). These proportions are much higher than the 6 per cent average for the Gonja samples and probably reflect the fact that older siblings in the south who are educated or have learned a trade are more likely to be seen as able to contribute to a child's development than older siblings in the less complex world of northern Ghana where age and adult competence are still highly correlated.

While southern and northern Ghanaian samples reflect a similar preference for selecting foster-parents from the parents' own generation, in the north there is a relatively greater emphasis on sending a child to a grandparent, and in the south on making use of siblings and unrelated foster-parents. At the time these children were being fostered, between 1910 and 1950, northern Ghana scarcely

Table 7-3. *Generation of relationship between child and foster-parent in three southern Ghana societies: Girls*

	Fanti	Ewe	Krobo	Totals
Grandparents'	8 (24%)	8 (30%)	3 (7%)	19 (18%)
Parents'	17 (51%)	7 (26%)	17 (39%)	41 (40%)
Siblings'	5 (16%)	8 (30%)	12 (28%)	25 (24%)
Unrelated	3 (9%)	4 (14%)	11 (26%)	18 (17%)
Totals	33 (100%)	27 (100%)	43 (100%)	103 (99%)

Table 7-4. *Generation of foster-parent: Comparison of northern and southern Ghana: Combined samples*

	Foster-parent is of:								
	Grandparents' generation		Parents' generation		Child's generation		Not kin		Total N =
Gonja	80	(39%)	104	(50%)	12	(6%)	11	(5%)	207 (100%)
Southern Ghana	28	(15%)	88	(48%)	43	(23%)	24	(13%)	183 (100%)

participated in the economic differentiation and educational stratification of present-day society. The south, on the other hand, had already begun to enter the age of social and technological change. In seeking to understand the shift away from grandparents as foster-parents in favour of siblings and strangers, the critical factor is the balance between fostering as a reflection of rights vested in kinship roles, and fostering as a mode of training. Both these aspects co-exist in traditional Gonja fostering (Chapter 2). However, with a shift to sibling and non-kin fostering, the element of kinship rights becomes secondary to the educational functions of fostering. A child is not sent to an elder sibling (and certainly not to a stranger) because they have a right to a lien on its labour and companionship. On the other hand, this was a significant element in the request for a foster-child in traditional Gonja. In the modern world of southern Ghana, rights vested in kinship roles are competing with the need to help children make their way in the new occupational and social milieu. Indeed, the shift probably reflects the diminishing role played by the senior generation in helping youth to become established in the adult world. Instead of age in itself leading to positions of importance, relatively restricted skills, especially those based on advanced education, become the critical factor. Not only does age fail to bring advantages, it is more often the young people who have modern skills. Nevertheless in all the Ghanaian samples there is a pronounced emphasis on fostering by parents' siblings, which reflects the persistence of reciprocal rights and obligations acknowledged between both full and classificatory siblings.

I have argued that traditional fostering by kin, while it fulfilled many specific functions which varied with the form of each society, also reflected the strength of claims that kin could successfully make on one another. As the skills demanded for full participation in an increasingly diversified economy grow more complex, with success in school of growing importance on the one hand and many new crafts on the other, it is no longer equally possible for all adults to provide the model and the training which are necessary for the child to take his place in society. Where no kinsman is available, an arrangement for the child's training must be made on another basis. The usual pattern is that the child's labour over a period of several years pays for the training he receives, though a lump sum

Fostering contrasted

may be given to the teacher at the beginning or at the end of the training period. In this transformation of the traditional institutions of fostering, two aspects are emphasized by the actors: the experience is sought for the child as a way of helping him prepare for a more successful adulthood; the labour of the child is a major part of the recompense for the training received, but money may pass either to the 'teacher' or to the parents, in lieu of the kinship obligation which would once have sufficed. If there is a highly educated member of the family, a teacher, a clergyman or one who is in some other kind of important job, he will often be asked to take on children, since it is felt that he is in a position to give them a better training than others; it is not only specific skills that are sought but a facility with the written and spoken word and with Westernized ways.

8

Modern apprenticeship: response to differentiation

In Chapter 6 we were concerned with the incidence of parent-role delegation in the non-urban population for three southern Ghanaian groups. The Krobo have a named institutionalized pattern of delegation of parent roles, but in all the survey communities the sending of children to relatives, and sometimes to non-kin, occurred; about 30 per cent of all children were partially reared apart from their jural parents.

A common theme in the arrangements for boys was training in an occupational skill. However, formal apprenticeship was little stressed by those interviewed, and there was a strong preponderance of kin among those taking over the training of boys. Only 8 per cent went to non-kin in the Sibling Sample (Table 6-4b); the proportion of Ga boys sent to non-kin among those fostered 25 years ago was roughly similar, 10 per cent. However, among the urban Ga boys fostered within the past 25 years, this figure nearly triples, with 28 per cent going to non-kin. There is evidence from recent studies of apprenticeship that training by non-kin has become very much more common within the past few decades in Ghana and Nigeria, particularly in the cities.

There is a small but excellent literature on apprenticeship in West Africa, mainly on Nigeria; Lloyd's early paper (1953) was followed by studies by Callaway (1964; 1973), Koll (1969) and Peil (1970; 1978). With the exception of Lloyd's article, all are based on extensive surveys. Callaway undertook a complete survey of all the indigenous craft enterprises and small industries with permanent premises in Ibadan (Nigeria) in 1961–3. In the course of this, 5,135 enterprises were found and 250 apprentices, and later 225 proprietors, were interviewed. Additional case studies were made in individual enterprises in Kano, Zaria, Maiduguri, Benin, Enugu, Onitsha, Lagos, and in several rural towns and villages throughout Nigeria. Koll used a 10 per cent random sample of Ibadan craftsmen, locating 1,427 masters, of whom he was able to interview 1,262.

Callaway's survey produced a total of 5,135 enterprises, while Koll's 10 per cent sample five years later, suggests that the figure should be closer to 14,000. While an increase in the number of enterprises during the period between the two studies would be consistent with the very rapid increase in the kinds of

188

businesses, an increase of this magnitude is unlikely. Rather, it is almost certainly the definition of 'enterprise' adopted by the two researchers which accounts for most of the difference. While Callaway limited his enquiry to those enterprises occupying permanent premises, Koll used the United Nations 'international standard industrial classification (manufacturing and personal services)' together with the criteria of 'visibility of workplace' (which excluded enterprises going on within the walls of a compound) and 'working for own account'. Anyone familiar with West African towns will recognize the importance of temporary stalls, tables and benches set up by the wayside or around the outskirts of markets and stores. Such people bring their goods and equipment in the morning and take them home at the end of the day. For this, less capital is needed and it may well represent a stage in the establishment of a more successful business.

Apart from the difference between figures for total enterprises in Ibadan reached by the two studies, there is an equally striking difference between the number of apprentices located. Callaway found that 61 per cent of all craft units contained apprentices while in Koll's survey only 35.5 per cent did. Here again it is likely that apprentices will be less often attracted to the one-man-and-his-table type which Koll included, and that business occupying permanent premises are more apt to employ apprentices. Rather than taking one of these studies as 'correct' and the other as 'wrong', we should see them as tapping somewhat different levels of craft and service activity.

Peil's work is not based on random samples, and hence does not permit an estimation of total numbers either of enterprises or of apprentices. The first study, the only one in Ghana, was based on 120 Accra craftsmen selected to represent both traditional and modern occupations, and included interviews with 233 apprentices. Later Peil carried out a further study in Lagos (Nigeria) of 426 self-employed craftsmen, which enquired into their own apprenticeship history and their employment of apprentices.

Callaway was working on the problem of unemployment among school-leavers. He sees apprenticeship as a response to the inability of what he calls the 'high-earnings economy'[1] to provide wage or salaried work for most of the large body of school-leavers whose ranks are swelled annually (1973:1). Peil also notes that apprenticeships are in great demand among school-leavers in Ghana, and that masters prefer apprentices who have been to school. However she points out the discrepancy between the needs of developing countries for skilled workers and their resources for training these. Not only is the number of technical schools limited by availability of staff and finances, but there is evidence that even the few who graduate from them have difficulty getting work of the sort for which they are trained. They are too highly qualified to find a place in the small-scale indigenous businesses, and most eventually take other work (Foster 1965:294-5; Pfefferman 1968:113; Peil 1970:137). All these writers comment on the striking prevalence of individual apprenticeship to a practising craftsman as the major contemporary mode of recruitment to craft, trading and service occupations. Callaway estimated that there were 'some 2 million apprentices throughout Nigeria' and compared this figure with 'the present total of half-a-million wage and salary earners in government, the professions, and in the larger industrial and commercial firms' (1964:2).

Koll is particularly interesting in setting his analysis of apprenticeship in the context of the greatly increased occupational differentiation in the colonial and post-colonial period, and in linking this to social stratification. He extracts from the literature a list of crafts referred to as 'traditional' in the nineteenth-century Yorubaland (see Table 8-1).

Table 8-1. *List of crafts cited as traditional in accounts of nineteenth-century Yoruba (from Koll 1969:13)*

Barber, hairdresser	Ivory carver	Spinning
Basket, mat-maker	Jewelsmith	Tailor
Bead-worker	Leather-worker	Tanner
Blacksmith	Potter	Weaver
Calabash carver	Rope maker	Woodworker
Dyer	Soap maker	

Koll links this level of occupational specialization, which is well above the level of simple subsistence economy, to the essentially urban nature of nineteenth-century Yoruba settlement. Everyone farmed, but farms lay outside the towns, and specialists were concentrated inside. People depended on specialists for their products, and money was a widespread medium of exchange. The royal court and the demands of defensive and aggressive warfare also added to the forces towards specialization. The Yoruba pattern is similar to the Fanti and Krobo 'town states' along the littoral of pre-colonial and colonial Ghana. Political status was anchored in kin groups (Lloyd 1965), and some descent groups tended to specialize in a particular occupation. This is clearest for blacksmiths, but men of a compound might also specialize in silver-smithing, wood and calabash carving, or weaving, while the women would be dyers or potters (Lloyd 1953:34).

Lloyd writes that apprentices are usually between the ages of 15 and 20 and unschooled. It is an indication of the speed of change in modern Nigeria, that only ten years later Callaway sees apprenticeship as the refuge of unemployed school-leavers. An earlier phase of this process of change is recorded by Lloyd as the shift from a time when occupations were linked to the lineage, and training was by father, and secondarily by father's brother, sibling or mother's brother, to the taking of unrelated apprentices for fees. It is presumably because he was told that traditionally non-relatives would not be trained, that Lloyd states that apprentices and journeymen are not found in traditional Yoruba society. Here he seems to be equating apprenticeship with the contractual training of a non-

190

relative, and he writes as though contracts were always made at the initiation of an apprenticeship. However Callaway, Koll and Peil have all found the use of contracts to be extremely variable. They are rare in the more traditional crafts, even where non-relatives are being trained, and locally common in some of the more recently introduced occupations.

Lloyd links the breakdown of the lineage monopoly of crafts and the training of outsiders to the influx of new crafts. The men who know these are young, and, having no sons to train, must accept outsiders if they are to have the assistance of an apprentice. Here I think there is a problem with Lloyd's model of Yoruba craft production, which is based on the single craftsman with perhaps one or two youths helping him. He specifically contrasts it to Nadel's accounts of *efako* work units among the Nupe in which a number of kinsmen cooperate in production. Lloyd links this individuated production unit to the simplicity of tools and techniques. However some of the new crafts use complex tools and relatively elaborate techniques. There is thus a direct incentive to take on apprentices in order to train assistants. Moreover, as Lloyd himself notes, a craftsman may lose custom if he is away from his shop; an apprentice can remain in the shop to see customers, giving the master freedom to move around when there is no work.

However, it is clear that the pressure to train apprentices also comes from the youths who wish to enter the new occupations, and cannot gain their training from father or kin because these men belong to a generation of farmers and traditional craftsmen. All the surveys report a very low level of continuity of occupation from father to son among current craftsmen. Koll's data on continuity of occupation are the most detailed, and certainly support his contention that 'The present generation of Ibadan craftsmen have chosen their occupation not because of their families' traditional attachment to a particular craft, but as a response to conditions in the labour market and to the customers' demands for new goods and services' (1969:31).

Age of craftsmen

Callaway found that 65 per cent of the small businessmen and craftsmen he studied were under 40 years of age, with almost half between 30 and 39. Koll's figures show an even higher bias towards youth, with 74.5 per cent of his craftsmen below the age of 37, and half between 25 and 36.[2] Of particular interest is his finding that 12 per cent of the independent craftsmen were below the age of 20. As he notes, this supports their assertion that a man is free to set up independently as soon as he has completed his apprenticeship, and become a master in his own right. The relative youth of these independent craftsmen and businessmen is significant in relation to the recent introduction of many of the crafts, and the consequent scarcity of older men (and those occupying the kinship statuses of father and grandfather) who are in a position to pass on skills. Callaway

Table 8-2. *Relationship between respondent's occupation and that of father (men) or mother (women) (from Koll 1969:31)*

Occupation of respondent's father or mother[a]	Number	Per cent
Same craft	111	8.8
Different craft	84	6.6
Farmer	750	59.4
Trader	204	16.2
Fisher, hunter, tapper of palm wine	6	0.5
Government employee	35	2.8
Private enterprise employment	7	0.6
Muslim priest	8	0.7
Other	21	1.7
No answer	36	2.7
Total	1,262	100.0

[a] Women made up 11% of the sample.

also notes that, of the 225 businesses he studied, only 10 had been inherited. With few exceptions the rest were established by their present owners, and are being run by them.

Spatial mobility

All three researchers comment on the high level of spatial mobility represented by masters and their apprentices. In Accra Peil found that for goldsmiths, carpenters and tailors (all crafts that are either traditional or 'modern', but not 'new' according to Table 8-3), 25 per cent or fewer of the apprentices came from Accra, while between 58 and 65 per cent came from non-urban areas (i.e. those with populations of 10,000 or less). For the 'new' trades the proportion from Accra was much higher: fitters (45%), radio repairmen (58%) and printers (85%). Only 23 per cent, 15 per cent and 8 per cent respectively came from non-urban areas. A large part of this difference is almost certainly accounted for by the unfamiliarity of rural youths with such new occupations.

Callaway found that only 30 per cent of the apprentices he interviewed came from Ibadan province. Most of the remainder came from other parts of Yorubaland. However, 11 per cent had migrated from the Midwest Province, 7 per cent from the Eastern Province and 3 per cent all the way from Northern Nigeria. Koll does not give information on the origin of apprentices, but does so for the independent craftsmen. He found that about half came originally from Ibadan province or from the city itself, the rest being immigrants from farther afield. This corresponds closely to Callaway's figure of 47 per cent of proprietors from

Table 6-5. *Comparison of craft and service occupations practised at different periods in Yoruba towns*[a]

Crafts reported for nineteenth-century[b] 'traditional'	Crafts considered 'modern' in 1950	'New' crafts reported in 1967 (Ibadan)[d]	
Barber, hairdresser (2)	Goldsmith[c]	Auto electrician	Sprayer
Basket, matmaker (2)	Guilder smith (cheap brass ornaments)	Baker	Upholsterer
Bead-worker (3)	Silversmith[c]	Battery charger	Vulcanizer
Blacksmith (8)	Tinker	Blacksmith/machines	Watch repairer
Calabash carver (6)	Gunsmith	Camera repairer	Welder
Dyer (5)	Sawyer	Cornmiller	Mattress maker
Ivory carver (1)	Carpenter	Drycleaner/hand	Turner
Jewelsmith (6)	Tailor	Drycleaner/machines	Rubber-stamp maker
Leather-worker (7)	Barber, using scissors, comb and clippers	Electrical mechanic	Office cleaner
Potter (5)	Builder	Pepper-grinder	Gardener with shop
Rope maker (1)	Shoemaker	Motor mechanic	Typewriter repairer
Soap maker (3)	Washerman	Photographer	Sewing machine repairer
Spinning (1)	Bicycle repairer	Sieve maker	Book binder
Tailor (3)		Sign writer	Beautician
Tanner (5)			
Weaver (8)			
Woodworker (6)			
From Koll 1969:13	From Lloyd 1953:35	From Koll 1969:122–4	

[a] Of course none of these lists is complete. For some reason printers do not appear on Koll's list of Ibadan occupations, though they are a major occupational category for Peil in both Accra and Lagos. Similarly some crafts have disappeared, such as soap making.

[b] Numbers in parentheses indicate number of sources citing each craft (out of 8).

[c] Although Lloyd lists these as modern, it is likely that they are included under Koll's heading 'jewelsmith' in the nineteenth-century list.

[d] Lloyd's list refers to three Yoruba towns ranging in size from 17,000 to 50,000. As Peil notes (1970), very large urban communities provide quite special conditions for occupational structure and differentiation. Thus some of the crafts appearing in the list for the 1960s in Yorubaland, no doubt were practised in the urban centres of Lagos and Ibadan in the early 1950s when Lloyd wrote.

outside the Ibadan district. The higher figure for apprentice immigration than for their masters suggests a ripple effect, with spreading knowledge of new crafts drawing apprentices from further afield. There would thus seem to be a phased transmission of crafts from the urban centres. Immigrants from rural areas come mainly to learn the longer-established crafts. Those learning the very recently imported skills come mainly from other urban centres or from the same town. As crafts become more established, and their practitioners move away from the original centres to avoid competition for customers, youths in outlying towns and rural areas learn about them and may then seek masters in the urban centres with those who grew up there.

While spatial mobility from rural to urban areas is clearly a very important factor in the discontinuity of occupations between generations, it is itself a consequence of the 'explosion' of new occupations which has taken place in West Africa, beginning with the colonial era, and vastly increased since independence. Those who learn newly introduced occupations cannot learn them from parents or other kin. How are these new occupations introduced? To deal with this fascinating question properly would take a separate study, but the major sources can be indicated. These are institutions: the army, technical colleges, mission schools, clinics, libraries; large firms which train their employees on the job (railways, the big car importing firms, the few manufacturing enterprises); and individual innovating entrepreneurs who tend disproportionately to be expatriate, but may come from Europe, the Near East, the West Indies, or elsewhere in West Africa. Koll mentions the central role of a few Sierra Leonian metalworkers in establishing modern metal-working trades. West Africans who have themselves trained abroad are an increasingly important source of dissemination of new skills. In the London study of West African families (Chapter 10) we found men training as television repairmen, broadcasting technicians, in advertising, film-making, accounting, etc. Those who on their return successfully set up their own businesses, as most wish to do, will no doubt soon begin to train others.

Whatever the source of new crafts, their rapid spread is undeniable, though difficult to document clearly. Some indication can be given by comparing the three lists of craft occupations given in Table 8-3 which represent the nineteenth-century crafts considered traditional in Yorubaland, those judged by Lloyd to be 'modern' in the early 1950s, and those not previously mentioned which appear in Koll's very careful census of independent craftsmen in Ibadan carried out in 1967 (Koll 1969:122–4). Even in the 1950s Lloyd found that those practising the 'modern' crafts had to learn them from unrelated masters, or from working in a firm or institution. With the number of introduced crafts more than doubling (even on this admittedly rough estimate) by the late 1960s, the need to look beyond the kin group for a teacher was clearly inevitable; as indeed was the very substantial movement of apprentices from rural and outlying urban areas into the cosmopolitan centres in search of masters.

194

Relationship to master

It is only against the background of the very rapid multiplication of new crafts that the relationship of apprentices to their master in contemporary West Africa can be understood. There are several issues here which should be kept separate for clarity. First, there is the question of the relation of kin groups to occupation. In writing about the traditional Yoruba pattern of recruitment to crafts Lloyd says that traditional crafts were restricted to one or more particular descent groups who only trained their own members. Knowledge of craft skills was part of descent-group property, and only members had a right to share it.[3] With the introduction of modern crafts, descent-group monopoly ceased to operate, not only for the modern crafts, but for some of the traditional ones as well. Thus in Yoruba Ibadan in 1967 it was only the blacksmiths and weavers who continued to recruit from among their kin. Lloyd implies (though his later work suggests that this may not be intended) that a descent-group monopoly is generally characteristic of traditional African social structure, with the Yoruba simply a convenient example. However, data on other moderately differentiated traditional systems shows that while some do restrict occupational specialities in this way (although their kin groups are not unilineal, the Dagomba seem to be another case, see Chapter 5), others, like the Gonja, do not. The conditions for descent-group monopolization of craft skills may be rather special, since both economic differentiation and descent groups are required, but the former often undermines the latter (see Chapter 4, and Evans-Pritchard 1962). In Ashanti (though matrilineal) and in Gonja (though cognatic), it was the duty of the father to provide his son with the basis for assuming an effective adult role, as it is among the patrilineal Yoruba (Lloyd 1953). This duty does not seem to vary with the kin-group structure of a society. What clearly do vary are the constraints and resources available for fulfilling this obligation, the implications of which form the focus of Chapter 12.

The second issue involved in interpreting the material on relationship of apprentices to their masters concerns the nature of an ideal arrangement, assuming it were possible. Lloyd states flatly that 'A son is trained by his own father, or in the absence of his father, by his father's brother or his own elder brother' (1953: 33). This is repeated by Callaway and Koll as necessarily applying where recruitment to a craft is within the kin group. However it is not clear that it has been documented in the field. Among the Gonja of Daboya, where there were large compounds within which most men were taught weaving, fathers avoided teaching their own sons, sending them to a relative whose skill was recognized, and taking other men's sons to train in their stead.[4] While there is no basis for assuming that the Gonja pattern obtained in traditional Yorubaland, there is also no basis for assuming that fathers 'naturally' trained their own sons in all West African societies. Indeed, this seems most unlikely, in view of the widespread character of traditional fostering, and the equally widely held view that parents are not the best people to rear their own children, specifically because they tend to be too lax with the discipline felt necessary if a child is to develop a good character. Lloyd himself mentions that it was common for sons to be sent to their maternal kin to learn the craft practised by that lineage, and that this was justified because 'the boy will have some craft blood in his veins' (1953:33). And Fadipe (1940), cited in Koll (1969), noted that children were given as pawns (security for loans made to their kin) to craftsmen to learn a trade and work for their master. Thus it appears that even among the traditional Yoruba a father did not necessarily train his own son, even when otherwise able to.

The main implication of both these aspects of the relation of kinship and recruitment to occupational roles is that it is not justified, and may be positively misleading, to assume a universal *status quo ante* in which occupational roles were restricted to kin groups and fathers taught their own sons if they were able to. Clearly, the meaning of contemporary patterns of recruitment to occupational roles is relative to the kind of change it represents. I shall argue in Chapter 12 that in the widest terms there has indeed been a shift from recruitment within the local kin group and training by the father to the modern, impersonal, formal apprenticeship to strangers, to training in an institutional setting or by a firm. But that this has very often been mediated by a phase in which occupational roles were not tied to kin groups, and in which children were sent to relatives or friends outside their family of orientation to be reared, training in an occupational role being part of growing up and working within a setting where family and occupational roles were not segregated. The model of a leap from the closed intimacy of the nuclear family embedded in a kin group, to the impersonal world of Western industrial society is misleading, and does not reflect the sort of transition which occurs with progressive internal stratification and differentiation and the move into the modern world economy.

The data from the Fanti, Krobo and Ewe surveys showed that many children are not reared by their own parents, most of them going to close kin, and a few to unrelated foster-parents. Some of those going to kin are sent specifically in order to learn an occupational skill. Others go to further their formal education, to fulfil parental obligations – of love or duty – or because their parents are having difficulty with them and feel that a relative may do better. Most of those going to non-relatives appear to do so in order either to learn an occupational skill, or to further their formal education. But of the apprentices studied by Callaway, Peil and Koll, how many are learning with kin and how many are with non-relatives? Koll was studying independent craftsmen, and has little direct information on apprentices. He notes that in Ibadan blacksmiths and weavers are recruited by kinship (but they may still have been taught by a relative other than a parent). Of 1,211 craftsmen, 1,111 had been taught by a 'master' while the remaining 100, or 8 per cent, had been taught by either mother or father. But again we do not know whether the 'master' was a relative or not.

Table 8-4. *Relationship between master and apprentice: Proportion of masters who were trained by and who have trained kinsmen (from Peil 1978:7)*

Trade	Per cent trained by kinsman	Per cent having trained kinsmen
Carpenter	60	67
Goldsmith.	57	46
Blacksmith	38	55
Shoemaker	31	60
Tailor	29	50
Mason	25	30
Painter	25	50
Fitter (auto mechanic)	21	39
Photographer	20	44
Printer	17	46
Watch repairer	15	21
Electrician	12	50
Radio repairer	0	7

In writing of apprenticeship in Accra, Peil gives most information with reference to a previous factory study in which, of those workers who had been apprenticed, one-quarter were trained by kin, another one-quarter learned on-the-job in the factory, and half were apprenticed to an unrelated master. In other words, of those privately apprenticed, one-third were trained by kin. Of those trained by kinsmen, the largest set had gone to a relative of their father (38%). More had been trained by a sibling than by the father himself.[5]

Consistent with the earlier point that kin-group structure does not directly determine training for adult occupational roles, she reports that very few of the matrilineal Akan had been trained by maternal kin. The father's obligation to train his sons was still expressed in a bias towards sending sons to paternal relatives. She comments generally that apprentices appear to be trained more often by kin in rural areas than in towns. This fits with the finding in the southern Ghana surveys that, of small-town populations, only 13 per cent of children reared away from home had been sent to non-kin.

The clearest information is given in Peil's paper on self-employed craftsmen in Lagos (Table 8-4). Although in this table no distinction is made between those trained by a parent and those trained by other kin, the implication in the text is that fathers formed a relatively small proportion. The single most striking finding here is that in only one of these trades were no masters taught by kin, the exception being the relatively recently introduced craft of radio repairing. In only three crafts were less than 20 per cent of the masters trained by kin, and these again were in the category of new crafts: printers, electricians, and watch repairers. Two of the crafts stand out with around 60 per cent of the masters

197

having been trained by kin. Goldsmithing is an ancient skill, although not apparently formally restricted to kin in the same sense as blacksmithing. Carpenters are a well-established modern craft, with many masters available to train apprentices, and hence relatively many kinsmen available to choose from.

The other significant finding is that in every case but one, the printers, more masters have taught kin than have been taught by them. At the very least this shows that apprenticeship to kin is not disappearing, for in most cases it will be several years after his own apprenticeship finishes that a man begins to take apprentices himself. And if we consider Koll's finding that only one master in three takes apprentices, the implication is that these high percentages of masters having taught kin must allow for many who taught no one at all. The higher proportion of apprentices taught of course reflects the fact that a man is himself apprenticed only once[6] but may take many apprentices during his career as an independent craftsman and thus has many 'chances' to train a kinsman. But it also is consistent with the increasing numbers of men practising the new crafts who are available for training kin, i.e. the increasing likelihood that a youth who wants to learn one of the new crafts will have a relative who practises it and who could act as his teacher.

Apprenticeship as a path to economic independence

Writing at the beginning of this century, and looking back at the previous one, Quartey-Papafio saw apprenticeship among the Ga of Accra as having become necessary when 'Europeans and others came into the country and a good many other trades [besides farming, fishing and blacksmithing which he has already discussed] came into use in the Colony, e.g.: Carpenters, Bricklayers and Masons, Washermen, Coopers, Stone Plasterers and such other trades and crafts as are known to people of more advanced stage in civilization' (1913:419). It therefore became necessary to apprentice some sons to people engaged in these new trades. Quartey-Papafio's account lays great stress on the rules binding master and apprentice. As long as these trades were carried on within the jurisdiction of the Ga Mantse (the paramount chief),

apprenticeship appears to have assumed the aspect of perpetual servitude. There was no certainty as to when an apprentice would become really free from his customary obligations to his master. For the master's liabilities are still exactly as they were in the days of yore, when there were only two principal trades known among the Ga people (farming and fishing). These liabilities were as follows:

1. The ward is to live with the master at his house; but may make occasional short visits when necessary to his own parents.
2. The master is to provide for his ward food, lodging, clothing, and other necessaries of life, with liberty to use his tools, so that he may learn his trade.

198

3. The master is liable and answerable for all misconduct on the part of the ward, and for all debts due by him whilst he lives in his house as his ward.

4. The master is the proper person to obtain a wife for his ward with the knowledge and consent of his parents and family.

The ward on his part has to give all his earnings to the master. Even after his marriage the master was still expected to look after his ward and to continue to do so until his death. In fact, the relationship between the ward and master was in the nature of an insurance for future support and maintenance of the ward by his master. [And, one might add, of the master by his ward's earnings] (1913:420).

This was the situation while apprenticeships were carried out within the jurisdiction of the Ga Mantse. But beginning in the middle of the nineteenth century, Accra craftsmen began to be needed in the European settlements in Nigeria, the Cameroons and the Congo. Once trained, apprentices went to work in these other colonies for long periods. They became resentful of their master's rights over them and their pay. As Quartey-Papafio puts it, 'the ward wanted greater independence' (421). The masters then made a new set of rules, as follows:

1. When the ward goes to the Bights for the first time he is to hand over all his earnings to his master on his return. Out of these earnings, the master may give some drink to the parents of the ward.

2. When he goes to the Bights for the second time he is also to hand the whole of his earnings to his master on his return. But the master now is to hand a small portion of these earnings to the parents of the ward.

3. When the ward goes to the Bights for the third time he is again to hand the whole of his earnings to his master on his return. This time the master must divide these earnings into three parts, giving one-third to the ward and one-third to the parents (421).

After the third trip the ward had no further obligation to give up any of his earnings. He might also marry through his own family. Nor need the ward consult his master before making decisions. The relationship between them 'is now one of intimate friendship born of gratitude supposing, that is, that the reminiscences of the past are pleasant enough to warrant it' (421). A further rule was made by craftsmen in the trade: any ward who failed to hand over all his earnings on any of the first three trips to the Bights must, with his parents, pay a lump sum of £32 to the master which cancelled further obligation. At the end of the nineteenth century £32 represented a large sum, and must therefore have been a very severe penalty. In some cases, Quartey-Papafio writes, the custom had arisen of compounding for the post-training obligations to the master all at one time by a prior payment of £30. 'This amount is then paid to the master as a fee for teaching the ward his trade as soon as his tuition is complete' (422). It is interesting to note that this sum is about the same as that reported by Callaway for apprenticeships of five years in many trades in Ibadan fifty years later. Peil found Accra fees higher. They ranged from an average of £35 for carpentry to between

199

£50 and £63 on average for goldsmiths, tailoring and fitting, with radio repairing averaging £104. Peil remarks on the stability of fees – with little change in her Lagos study between amounts paid by masters and those they charged to their apprentices. But it is astonishing that Accra fees should have no more than doubled in fifty years. The amounts of fees appear to have become customary and in a sense detached from the cost of living, which would be consistent with the function of the first fees in terminating the obligations of an apprentice to his master, when these obligations originally extended until the master's death. In this context it is striking, but hardly surprising, that both in Accra and in Ibadan the ending of an apprenticeship is referred to as 'freeing' the apprentice.

The first of the Ga rules was that 'the ward is to live with the master at his house; but may make occasional short visits when necessary to his own parents'. This rule takes on added meaning when linked to the apprentice's obligation to turn over all his earnings to his master, and the master's duty to look after his ward until his death. It marked, in fact, a transfer of *potestas* from father to master. For traditionally a son continued to hand over his earnings to his father as long as he lived,[7] just as the father had the obligation to see that his son married, and to look after him until his own death. Quartey-Papafio's account suggests that it was the inability of the masters to control their wards when working away that initially forced a limitation of the obligations to the master after three trips to the Bights, and ultimately led to a convention whereby diffuse rights of *potestas* were transformed into the specific right to a stipulated sum of money. Something of the old attitude remains in those crafts in which the 'freeing ceremony' includes drinks and a libation. Here witnesses and the gods are being notified in a pan-West African idiom that the obligations between master and apprentice are at an end.

However it is important to distinguish between the rights and obligations of mutual support between a man and the youth he has trained, and their jural identity. There would have been no question of the Ga apprentice of this time becoming a member of his master's patrilineage, of being eligible for offices held by his master's lineage or of his inheriting lineage property. These rights were conveyed once-and-for-all with birth-status identity. The obligations owed to the father can now be seen in a new light, as a result of the father's training and sponsorship where the youth remains in his father's household, learning and participating in his father's occupation. Where the youth was apprenticed to another man, into his care and tutelage, he no longer owed these duties to his father but to his tutor and sponsor. It is critical to note that on the master's death the ex-apprentice returned to his own patrilineage compound and took up his place as an adult lineage member.

The progressive attentuation of the obligations owed to the master, and their eventual transformation into a single money payment reflect the greatly reduced control of the senior generation over adult males, resulting from working abroad. In other words, it was only possible to enforce strict control over the earnings of adult men when backed by the local politico-jural system. Fathers today bemoan the same loss of authority over their adult sons that is described for a master and his apprentices. Nadel documented it for Nupe where the agricultural cooperative work group ceased to hold adult brothers and sons together because the reciprocities on which their membership was based could no longer be maintained. The *efako* head could no longer afford to pay the taxes and marriage costs for members because the amounts had risen so much while the income from farming had not kept pace. There was no legal force which bound *efako* members to remain in the group, once the balance of responsibilities had broken down. There remains a moral obligation to help support one's father, but the son no longer has to live under his authority.

Masters today may still be held responsible for misdemeanors of their apprentices, and quite often for their food and shelter. Partly this is a matter of convenience on both sides, for apprentices from other towns in particular, and for masters who want the maximum 'after-hours service' from their apprentices, for running errands and acting as watchmen for the workshop. But it also reflects the continuing diffuse nature of the master–apprentice relationship. The contract quoted by Lloyd (1953) makes the father 'submit his son' to the future master; the son is to be 'under the mastership' of the bricklayer named in the contract. The master promises to 'faithfully teach' the son and to 'carry out his feeding affairs'. But no longer is complete *potestas* transferred. The father remains responsible for 'all other expenditures such as clothing' and agrees to pay the fee should his son desert his master. Significantly, the son does not sign this document, only the master and the father, for they are the ones taking and transferring responsibility.

All those researching into craft enterprise and apprenticeship comment on the eagerness of apprentices to set themselves up as self-employed craftsmen. How soon this independence is possible depends partly on the cost of tools, and partly on the opportunities available for paid employment as a journeyman, which provides the main source of initial capital (Callaway 1973:17). Peil found that one-third of the tailors and photographers interviewed had been in business for themselves by the time they were twenty, although one-half of the blacksmiths and three-fifths of the printers were over twenty-five (1978:11). The figures for the mean number of years before self-employment show surprisingly little variation between trades, the averages ranging between 1 year (for carpenters, painters, photographers, masons, shoemakers, and radio repairmen), 2 years (for tailors, goldsmiths, watch repairmen, and blacksmiths), 3 years (for fitters and electricians), with printers taking substantially longer, an average of 5 years (1978:10).

A freed apprentice can sometimes get paid employment at his craft, either with his ex-master or in another workshop, and in this way save to purchase tools. But the evidence is consistent that there are relatively few journeymen in relation to the number of apprentices. Callaway found about 10 per cent, while Koll's figure of 192 works out at 15 per cent. Peil gives data on the percentage

Table 8-5. *Self-employed craftsmen: First job after completion of apprentice-ship, by craft (from Peil 1978:10)*

Craft	Per cent first job:				
	Self employed %	Wages, own craft %	Other %	Total %	N
Carpenter	80	15	5	100	30
Painter	80	5	15	100	20
Photographer	70	12	18	100	40
Mason	70	25	5	100	20
Tailor	68	10	22	100	60
Shoemaker	67	14	19	100	21
Goldsmith	41	46	13	100	39
Watch repairer	40	5	55	100	20
Radio repairer	36	32	32	100	22
Printer	34	54	12	100	61
Fitter	33	41	26	100	39
Blacksmith	33	5	60	100	40
Electrician	21	54	25	100	24

whose first work was as self-employed craftsmen, and the percentage who first worked for a wage in their own trade. Here there is substantial variation, as indicated in Table 8-5.

There appear to be two quite different constraints on the number of journey-men in a given craft. In some, the chances of working as a journeyman are very low, while in others it is relatively easy to set up on one's own. Which of these two factors operates in a given craft one cannot tell, because only craftsmen who were successful were interviewed. In those crafts where it is both difficult to get journeyman's work, and difficult to become an independent craftsman, many apprentices may drop out of the craft altogether.

In striving for independence, freed apprentices resemble the Ga apprentices at the beginning of the century. And indeed they resemble Tallensi sons who elude their responsibility to work for their fathers by establishing bush farms in margi-nal land, Nupe craftsmen in those crafts not requiring close cooperation between skilled workers, who exercise their rights to leave the *efako* of their father and establish an independent unit of their own, and Gonja youths of Muslim and Ruling estates who withdraw from the father's authority in order to 'roam about' visiting kin, perhaps hunting or trading, on their own account.

It is a strikingly consistent pattern in traditional West Africa that sponsorship is linked to a man's first marriage. Ga apprentices could only marry with the help of the master; Tallensi youths had to have bridewealth cows from their father's herd; the *efako* head in Nupe was responsible for meeting the expenses of the first marriages of *efako* members; in Gonja, where the absence of bride-wealth might appear to make marriage relatively easy, parental sponsorship was necessary if the girl's family were to agree. Even a foster-parent could not arrange the marriage of a protégé without consulting the parents. Fathers made use of their control over a son's marriage in different ways. So long as the son had no wife he was unable to maintain a separate household, and so was dependent on his membership in the household of either his father or another senior kinsman. Therefore delay of a son's marriage was one way of retaining his economic services. Once married, although a son might continue to live in his father's household, it was recognized that his interest and loyalties became divided.

Ability to maintain a separate household without a wife varies between societies; it is less of a problem in an urban money economy than in one based on subsistence farming. It is also easier for a man to be economically self-sufficient in a market economy where labour can be sold and domestic services purchased. These changes have led to changes in paternal strategies in regard to son's marriages. In Daboya, fathers feared that their sons would leave to seek their fortunes in the south, and were suggesting that they marry younger than before so that their new responsibilities might keep them at home. In towns and cities, sons are anxious to find work or learn a trade so they can support themselves independently of their families. Significantly, however, since a wife is no longer a prerequisite to adult status and domestic autonomy, men in towns are less anxious, indeed less willing, to tie themselves in marriage.

In accounts of West Africa there is also a consistent theme of tension between father and son which in part centres on the son's desire for independence and the father's acknowledged right to the son's labour and loyalty as long as he lives. Some societies have formalized this point of tension by institutionalizing the progressive reduction in a father's claims. The Nupe *efako* member has the right to claim his share of the group's assets and then secede. Such is the recognized right of the Gonja youth to 'roam about', though as with the revision of Ga apprenticeship rules, this 'right' is perhaps largely a recognition of the impossibility of constraining adult males against their will. The Tallensi often allowed first sons to establish an independent compound during the father's lifetime. But the critical fact about this struggle for independence is that it is both a struggle for economic independence – the son seeking to employ his strength and skills for his own purposes rather than entirely on behalf of the father – and a struggle for autonomy, in the sense of independence from paternal authority. In traditional societies, and to a large extent today where son and father remain in close proximity, this is a struggle for relative rather than complete independence. The son always remains obligated to his father, always owes him respect and obedience, is always obliged to support him in adversity. But the drive is a strong one, and small gains are major victories.

I see the great weight attached to kinship authority in these West African societies as connected with the fact that political authority was built on kinship authority. A man who is head of his own household has also a political status. As economic independence is a prerequisite of domestic independence, so it is also a prerequisite of political status.[8]

This greatly valued independence from authority seems to underly the striving for economic independence as a self-employed craftsman. It makes working for wages at one's craft a second-best that is tolerated in order to gain capital for the establishment of one's own workshop. But not as a career.

The significance of this striving for independent self-employment lies partly in the frequent resort to apprenticeship as a necessary step on the way. But it also takes on meaning in the context of an argument put forward by Verdon (1979) that apprentice-based craft workshops will never 'develop' into expanding industrial enterprises, however much government assistance they are given with loans, equipment and management training.[9] Verdon maintains that apprenticeship involves the master in a diffuse relationship with the apprentice in which the master is obliged to 'faithfully teach' him his trade 'to a sound standard' for a stipulated number of years. This obligation holds whether business thrives or is slack. Further, Verdon points out that apprentices seek out masters, not the other way around. In this situation, the masters have no control over their labour force. They cannot increase it in response to a sudden increase in demand for their produce. They cannot lay off workers when the market declines. Many observers have commented that workshops seem full of youths doing nothing, and accounts of apprenticeship always decry the amount of non-productive work (sweeping up, doing the master's washing) that apprentices do. In addition, each apprentice freed is a potential competitor, since the master's obligation to teach his craft 'to a sound standard' produces a replica of himself, though of course without his experience and contacts.[10] Koll's figures on the number of apprentices trained by twelve craftsmen in one cluster of workshops make clear the level at which this replication is occurring (Table 8-6).

Verdon stresses the contradiction between a master's dependence on his apprentices for labour and his inability to adjust his labour force to the demands of the market. Given more resources, craftsmen might use them to buy machines, but they would also take on more apprentices who would seek them out because of their evident success. These apprentices would eventually leave, to be replaced by others. But there is a limit to the number of apprentices one master can supervise and support, and in effect this places a limit on their aspirations for expansion. Apprentices are preferred to journeymen because they cost less (and often pay for their training). They also enhance the master's status, for they appear as 'followers' and 'clients' and give his workshop an air of prosperity.

Journeymen, on the other hand, are not a docile labour force. Peil comments that the journeymen interviewed 'felt exploited' and tried to become independent as soon as possible (Peil 1978:10). They only want to work for a year or two, until they have the capital to establish an independent workshop. To the employer oriented to the diffuse relationship between master and apprentice,

Table 8-6. *Craftsmen in one Ibadan workshop cluster: number of apprentices trained (from Koll 1969:45)*

Craft	Age	Present number of apprentices	Passed out apprentices[a]
Mechanic	42	15	60
Battery charger	28	3	1
Sprayer	42	8	10
Mechanic	30	15	6
Mechanic	37	25	30
Mechanic	25	12	4
Blacksmith	35	1	—
Welder	—	—	—
Straightener	30	2	2
Mechanic	—	35	8
Blacksmith	—	3	4
Welder	—	5	3
Total		124	128

[a] Apprentices not completing their training not included.

this temporary involvement of journeymen seems like disloyalty, and breeds distrust. Apprentices are easier to control, and more dependent.

It seems likely that it is in an important sense the apprentice's drive to become an independent craftsman in his own right which underlies the inherently small-scale nature of craft workshops in West Africa. Wage labour as a journeyman may be a necessary means to an end, but it is not the goal itself.

9

Creole wardship: response to hierarchy

West Africa's colonial experience differed from that of the east and south of the continent in never including a European settler population that alienated land and created a white/black caste system within the country. But there are two West African countries which have developed extreme status hierarchies based on Western culture and values but contained within the black population. Both Sierra Leone and Liberia were created around a nucleus of freed slaves returned from the New World, who were later joined by 'Liberated Africans' (as they were known in Sierra Leone), that is, men, women and youths released from slaving ships captured at sea. In each case the original settlement was established by people who had lived and suffered in the New World, for whom English was a first language and Christianity the true faith. Some had been born free, others gained their freedom through the Revolutionary War, their own efforts or kind masters. They were sent to establish a colony in Africa where not only would they be self-supporting but, their sponsors hoped, would bring civilization to the dark continent. Those who were sent to Liberia considered themselves to be Americans who had been driven from 'the land of our birth and childhood memories' by prejudicial laws and bigotry. They did not see themselves returning 'home', and regarded the natives as 'uncivilized' people to whom they were naturally superior. Clarkson, who supervised the bringing of 1,190 negroes from Nova Scotia to Sierra Leone in 1791 wrote to his superiors that:

I have told them that I shall form a very unfavourable opinion of those who may show an inclination to be servants to any gentlemen, when they have an opportunity of becoming their own masters, and valuable members of society if they please, and that in short, the character of the black people for ever after will depend on the manner they conduct themselves, and that the fate of millions of their complexion will partly be affected by it (J. Clarkson quoted in Porter 1963:27).

Having thus been handed the 'white man's burden', along with their freedom and a few acres of uncleared land, the immigrants began the task of establishing their own countries.

It is perhaps hardly surprising that in each case there evolved an exclusive

206

elite culture based on Western religion, language, and education in which farm-ing and manual work were stigmatized and avoided at all costs, in favour, ini-tially, of trade. But soon this too was seen as demeaning in Sierra Leone and descendants of the original settlers felt that they were destined only for the pro-fessions of law, medicine or the church. Fraenkel comments insightfully that the exaggerated stress on Western dress (suits and top hats regardless of the tropical heat), manners and morals, and the aloofness from the native population, were almost forced upon an immigrant group which, unlike other colonists in Africa, was not distinguished from the natives by the colour of their skin. Convinced of their fundamental difference and superiority, this had continually to be demon-strated.

In both Monrovia and Freetown, the Creole population (descendants of freed and recaptured slaves) formed an exclusive upper class, living in a Western style, marrying only among themselves, running the economy and holding the impor-tant jobs in the church, education, law and government. In Sierra Leone, which was governed as a British Colony until 1960, increasing provisions for local par-ticipation were made beginning in the nineteenth century. Arthur Porter's study of the development of Sierra Leone, entitled *Creoledom*, is essentially an account of the successive processes of assimilation by the settler elite first, of the Libera-ted Africans taken off the slaving ships, and then of the natives of the protec-torate.

While the settlers lived in Freetown, on the coast, the Liberated Africans were established in rural villages so that they could grow their own food and form their own communities. However, they were quick to see the possibilities of trade between the native villages and Freetown, and many enterprising Liberated Africans moved into Freetown and established successful businesses. They belonged to Christian churches (though they were sometimes not allowed to join those of the original settlers), and their children went to mission-run schools. Gradually the Liberated Africans adapted the Creole form of Western lifestyle, bringing to it their own contributions in ritual and cuisine. One of the most important mechanisms in this process of adaptation was what at the time was called apprenticeship. Porter says:

The apprenticeship system set the stage for the later fosterage or adoption of children which formed a central feature of Freetown society from its earliest days. Those who were apprenticed in the homes of Settlers were able to learn how to behave in the ways of the favoured group. . . . Some of the Liberated African children passed from apprenticeship to adoption, and were given the family name of the respective Settler family. Others took the family names of their masters, though they were never adopted, and remained domestics in the respective households (Porter 1963:37).

Unfortunately it is not at all clear what was meant by apprenticeship. It certainly meant placement with a master who could teach a useful trade, which clearly involved joining the master's household. But Porter suggests that others were simply placed in Settler homes as servants and to be 'civilized'. Fraenkel's account of the early days of Liberia also stresses the importance of the placing of children in the homes of the Settlers. However, in Monrovia, the original settlers greatly outnumbered the Liberated Africans who subsequently joined the colony. There seems to have been little difficulty in assimilating the latter. The children who were placed in Settler homes were, instead, those of the indigenous tribal peoples. Although they were occasionally adopted, they were mainly used as domestic help. In 1838 this practice was regulated by law as a form of apprenticeship, and the master required to provide clothing and some schooling. Fraenkel concludes: 'This custom was, over the ensuing century, to prove of the greatest importance in the process of assimilation of the tribal people into the community of Americo-Liberians' (1964:12).

Sierra Leone was founded by a group of Englishmen who formed a company devoted to both philanthropic and commercial ends. Very soon the Missionary societies began to play a major role in the development of the colony. In addition to building churches they ran schools; churches were often used for services on Sunday and school during the rest of the week. Education was regarded as an important means by which civilization would spread, eventually throughout Africa. Originally there were separate schools for Settlers and Liberated Africans. Commenting on this division in 1840, an Inspector of Schools wrote:

In a colony expressly founded among other objects for the removal of all those exclusive ideas and hateful distinctions of caste which have been fostered by slavery, the best means that could be adopted are in this way used to renew and maintain them. The Creole children receive rapidly those ideas of their own superiority to which all are so prone. The young Liberated Africans, who have been emancipated from the greatest degradation and misery found themselves still humbled in their own esteem and that of others as an inferior race. These distinctions are further encouraged by the Apprenticeship system and they are continued through life (Quoted in Porter 1963:90).

Five years later the English Governor noted that the schools had been 'opened to all classes' but that the Creole population preferred paying for better teachers in the Missionary Society schools, while the Liberated Africans were unable to do so, and so attended only the free Government ones (Porter 1963:91). New schools were founded, including fee-paying Mission secondary schools, but gradually the Liberated Africans' success in trade and commerce enabled them to send their children to these better establishments.

The tribal peoples remained, however, quite outside this world until the twentieth century. In a book devoted to the first hundred years of Sierra Leone, Ingham wrote that the 'country people' formed a class below the Creoles. They were their servants, and might engage in sexual liaisons, but never marriage. Parties of visiting chiefs and their followers might come to see the governor or traders to conduct business, but both sides kept to themselves. However, tribal children began to replace the Liberated Africans as wards of Freetown Creoles.

208

There was thus a trickle of country people into the ranks of Creole society. But such mobility required that the ward take his master's name, and 'pass' as Creole, which his rearing in a Creole household enabled him to do, at least so far as knowledge of the required lifestyle was concerned, if not with the same degree of prosperity. Tribal children were placed with Creole families by their parents in the hopes that the children would become established in Freetown society, and that they would then be in a position to help their relatives. As the affairs of government were conducted in English, it was a great advantage to have a kinsman who could speak that language and who knew whom to go to.

As the tribal people became more aware of the internal workings of Freetown society, they began to realize that some degree of literacy was also necessary if a youth was to get a non-manual job. They started to insist that if they sent a child to a Creole family, he must go to school as well as work in the house.

During the twentieth century many more schools have been built in rural Sierra Leone, including secondary schools. But two factors conspire to maintain the deficit in educational opportunity between Creole and tribal children. First, there is the obvious difference in the ratio of schools to children. In proportion to numbers of children there are a great many more schools in Freetown than in the rural areas. Furthermore there are significant differences in quality both between rural and urban schools, and between government and private schools. There is still a hierarchy of schools, with those at the top requiring high fees. Thus children of the urban elite have a double advantage in the quest for education. In addition, Creole children grow up in literate, English-speaking homes, which makes school a smooth continuation of their earlier childhood experiences. For the tribal child, school marks what must be a strange disjunction, for here he meets for the first time not only the English language, but reading and writing and arithmetical calculation and formal abstract reasoning (G. Cohen 1976; Gay and Cole 1967). The importance assigned to getting a good start in school can be judged from the recent increase in fee-paying nursery schools which Creole families now feel are necessary if their children are to get the most from the expensive primary schools they attend, which in turn lead to places in the few prestigious secondary schools that make possible a University place, in Sierra Leone or in England. A successful secondary-school career is of course a prerequisite for professional training which is still felt to be the highest occupational goal.

The desire to have one's children enter the professions has been a characteristic of Sierra Leone society since the nineteenth century. When a Liberated African succeeded in becoming wealthy as a successful merchant, he still had to validate his social position among the Creole elite. Such newly rich men tried to give their children the access to Western culture which they themselves had lacked, principally by sending them to be educated in England. The professions of medicine and law were nearly always their goals.[1]

Wards in Creole society today

The placing of children with families in Freetown and Monrovia as wards is so widely accepted there that it seems to require little comment from ethnographers. Banton in his study of contemporary Freetown (1957) noted that formerly many tribal people, seeking an education for their children, placed them with Creole families as wards, which often led to the child adopting the name of the fostering family and 'passing' as Creole in order to enter the labour market and to achieve high status in Creole society. But since the 1930s educated youths have been able to get clerical jobs without passing as Creole, and Banton was of the opinion that 'passing' had virtually ceased. If this is so, it corresponds to a sharp decline in the power and status of the Creoles themselves, brought about by the gradual broadening of the base of educated clerks and professionals on the one hand, and on the other by the extension of the franchise to tribal peoples and thus the transfer of effective political power from the tiny Creole minority to the tribal peoples.

Yet the incidence of wards continues to be high in Freetown itself; and ethnographic references suggest that the placing of children outside the natal family of orientation is common in rural areas as well. It has been reported for the Mende (Little 1951), the Limba (Finnegan 1965), the Temne (Gamble 1963), the Fula (Butcher 1964), and the Sherbro (Hoffer 1974). Banton gives figures for the presence of wards in Creole and tribal households in Freetown which show that wards are much more likely to be in Creole households.[2]

For Monrovia, Fraenkel examines a sample of 400 households from eight dif-

Table 9-1. *Presence of wards in Creole and tribal households in Freetown (from Banton 1957:206, Tables 45 and 46)*

Type of household	Number of households	Number of wards	Per cent of households with wards[a]
Creole			
Male headed	40	10	25
Female headed	23	9	39
Tribal			
Male headed	162	4	2
Female headed	12	2	17

[a] I have expressed the number of wards in relation to the total number of households for each category as a per cent of households having wards. In fact it is not possible to tell from Banton's material whether there were some households with more than a single ward, so this may not be strictly correct. The intention is merely to give a basis for comparison between Creole and tribal wardship.

Table 9-2. *Incidence of wards in eight residential areas in Monrovia (from Fraenkel 1964:117)*[a]

Residential area	Houses in sample	Houses with wards	Number of wards		Wards as percentage of total population
			M	F	
Vaitown	50	34	47	41	20
Kwi Street	50	20	27	6	12
Bassa Community	50	13	10	6	5
Bishop's Brook	50	11	11	2	5
New Krutown	50	6	7	1	2
Loma Quarters	50	5	7	0	3
Old Krutown	50	2	3	0	1
Claratown	50	1	0	1	0
Total	400	92	111	57	6%

[a] The table is actually headed 'Wards, foster-children, servants and small boys' and includes 'wards and other children *unrelated* by kinship to the households in which they were living'. (Italics in original.)

ferent residential areas, largely containing members of only one or two tribes. As Table 9-2 indicates, although 92 out of the 400 households contained wards (23%), in fact two-thirds came from only two areas. One was Kwi street which she describes as 'middle class', where 'almost all the wards were children of illiterate families who had been sent to educated ones to learn "civilization"' (Fraenkel 1964:117). The other, Vaitown, is particularly interesting. Not only does it have by far the highest percentage of wards (one in five of the total sample population) but the residents of Vaitown are Muslim, largely illiterate in English, and considered to be outside the Creole culture. They are also unique in Monrovia in being a thriving community of craftsmen and their apprentices. Here, in other words, those recorded as wards are not learning 'civilization' but occupational skills. Fraenkel's definition of ward excludes children related in any way to their sponsors. She notes that because of this definition, there are few Kru wards recorded, although many Kru children are sent to relatives.

Kru criticise other tribes, notably the Vai, for their practice of sending children away to be brought up by strangers, and many consider this a greater disgrace than having an illegitimate child. On the other hand, some of the educated Kru claim that this prejudice has retarded the process of 'civilization' among the Kru and accounts in part for their late entry, compared with the Vai, into 'civilized' society' and positions in government. For this practice has long been of major importance in enabling children of illiterates to get an education, and most persons of tribal origin who now have prominent positions in government were in fact taken into 'civilized' households in this way. In their generation, this normally meant Americo-Liberian or missionary households, but the process is a cumulative one so that today many households taking such children are themselves made up of tribespeople (Fraenkel 1964:116).

Fraenkel's data are particularly valuable because they make clear not only the importance of placing children with non-kin as a means of cultural and social mobility, but also the existence of many other forms of parental-role delegation as well as this educational fostering.

Further light is thrown on wardship in Freetown by Gaynor Cohen's recent study of education and social mobility (1976). She found that while children were living in non-parental households among both Creoles and tribal peoples, different patterns were clearly recognizable for these two groups. The Creole wards were far more frequently sent as a result of family crisis, and they were nearly always with kin. Indeed, Creole children tended not to describe themselves as wards at all because they were living with kin. Tribal children, on the other hand, were found living both with kin and with non-relatives, and much less often as a result of family crisis. A census of one 'non-high-status' school found that 43 per cent of the 369 children were wards. In contrast, in a high-status girl's school only 25 of 175 students (14%) indicated that they were wards. The major reason for the fostering of tribal children was to further their educational opportunities, and this often meant moving from their natal village to a town with a primary school, and then later into Freetown. Consistent with this, they were often living with sponsors who had more education than their own parents. Both in Freetown and in Monrovia, many tribal children now go not to the Creole but to tribal families who have themselves entered the middle-class world of the educated, professional and white-collar elite. It is unlikely that the placing of tribal children as wards with elite families would have proved such a popular and successful avenue of social mobility had it not been seen by the tribal people themselves as simply yet another form of traditional patterns of parent role delegation.

* * *

This section has sought to bring together material on the several institutionalized forms of delegation of parent roles in West Africa. There were a number of common themes, and in the final chapter a basis for ordering these is suggested. But perhaps more immediately striking is the variety. From Dagomba *zuguliem*, to Mossi *pogsioure*, to Hausa client fosterage, to Creole wardship, the societies of West Africa have elaborated particular institutions which serve their immediate needs.[3] It should be clear that what has been described is but a few instances of an open set. My purpose has not been to include all possible forms of delegation of parent roles, but rather to explore some of the factors involved in this rich variation. In the next section the focus is shifted to the question of the conditions under which these forms of role delegation appear. The empirical base is a

212

study of immigrants in London who came from many different West African societies. To the extent that there are common features of West African social structure and culture, these people shared them. They also shared conditions of life as impoverished students in a foreign city. Very many were parents with children in London. The formal problem is whether and in what ways their definition of parent roles reflected West African forms.

In West Africa the delegation of parent roles does not occur in all societies. Is it only members of traditionally fostering societies who used this form in England?

PART III

Beyond West Africa

10

The quest for education

With CHRISTINE MUIR GROOTHUES

Ann (not her real name) aged nine, a Ghanaian girl fostered nearly all her life by a white professional English couple in suburban Surrey, can stay in their care, Sir George Baker, President of the High Court Family Division, decided recently. He said that he could not bring himself to send her back to Africa, where her real parents wanted to take her . . . 'My answer in the best interests, present and future, of this girl - despite the blood tie, the race, despite colour, is that I cannot bring myself to send this child to Ghana, and I, as well as the girl, would feel a rankling sense of injustice were I to do so', he said. (*The Times*, 5 December 1972). Judge Baker had begun his summing up by saying:

The reason why I am giving this judgement in open court is that I think the public, and particularly potential foster parents, ought to know of the practice, indeed custom, of West Africans and other coloured people who come to this country, which is that the husband is a student, often a perennial student, the wife works and the children, particularly those born here, are fostered out privately, often for many years, and often as a result of newpaper advertisements or cards in shop windows or by the introduction of friends. The children are brought up in and learn our British ways of life. When a strong bond of attachment and love has been forged between the children and the foster parents, the natural parents take them away, even tear them away, to go with them to West Africa or elsewhere. There is overwhelming evidence before me of this practice, and there have been two other cases before Judges of the Family Division in the last few weeks (*The Times*, 5 December 1972).

Ann was placed with English foster-parents when she was three months old. Two months later, when it became clear that the foster-parents assumed they would adopt her, Ann's parents took her home. After reassurances they allowed her to return to the foster-parents, but when she was four the foster-parents again pressed for adoption, and Ann was again removed by her parents. Her father then wrote to the foster-parents: 'I must make it clear to you that (Ann) belongs to us and nothing can separate us and the baby, not all the riches in the world. The child is ours, and will be ours forever and take it from me that you will never see her again.'[1] Later an agreement was reached and the foster-parents

217

understood that Ann was to stay with them until she was 18, and finish her education. When Ann's parents later decided to return to Ghana and wanted to take her with them, the foster-parents took action to retain custody over the child. On hearing in court that Ann must remain in England, her parents were very upset, her father saying that since they were Akans (a matrilineal people) his wife's relatives would hold him responsible for returning without their child; that he dared not return without Ann (*The Times*, 5 December 1972).[2] Like the High Court judges, social workers have assumed that West African parents in England 'for one reason or another are either unwilling or unable to provide a home for their children' (C. Hill 1970:87). Estimates of the number of West African children in English foster-homes vary from 2,700 (*West Africa* 25 December 1965) to 5,000 (Ellis 1971:21). Since these children are usually placed in English families by private arrangement, there is no way of knowing what proportion of the families are registered with the local social services, and hence no basis for accurate figures. However, one indication of the significance of fostering among West Africans in England is the finding of Holman (1973) that 60 per cent of the children in a sample of 143 private foster-homes in the Birmingham area were West African. Since, according to the 1971 census, there were then only 880 people in Birmingham who had been born in West Africa in a total population of over one million, the proportion of West Africans being fostered is clearly very high. Indeed, we found in our London study that many families had been forced to look as far as Manchester and Birmingham for suitable foster-parents. Significantly, Holman found no other immigrant groups which regularly fostered children. In the group of 296 West African families we interviewed in London, exactly half had placed one or more children with English foster-parents at some time, although only one-quarter currently had a child being fostered. It would seem that fostering is 'normal' for West Africans in England.

These cases of contested custody over West African children, and the frequency with which they are placed with English foster-parents, raise a number of questions about West Africans in Great Britain: who are they, and why have they come here? Why are they willing to let other people rear their children if they care so much about them? Is the West African conception of parenthood different from our own? And perhaps most fundamental of all, what is the meaning of the judge's assumption that not only he, but the Ghanian child Ann, would feel 'a rankling sense of injustice' if she were sent back to West Africa?

There are relatively few West Africans in England, compared with several of the other minority groups. In the 1971 census the total number of those born in the three largest Commonwealth countries of West Africa (Nigeria, Ghana, and Sierra Leone) was 46,065. This figure of course represents adults born in their home countries. The census also gives figures for children born in this country of parents born abroad, and 19,440 were born here of parents born in all parts of Africa. Some unknown proportion of these are children of West African parents. This is probably an under-representation because census figures

218

inevitably include only those recorded on census forms. Those who originally entered England on visitors' or students' permits, and who have since taken a job or ceased to study, are not likely to wish to be officially recorded and may avoid the census taker. It is impossible to estimate how many West Africans have remained here after their permits expired. However, the figure of 46,065 from the 1971 census is almost certainly too low, even for adults.

The popular stereotype of West Africans in this country is that they are students, here for university degrees or technical qualifications unavailable in their own countries. This is a view that is held by West Africans themselves, though they often add that many are not very serious students. In 1970, as part of a larger study, we carried out a survey of all the West African families living in selected enumeration districts in four inner London boroughs. The results surprised us, for we found that in our sample of 296 families, 96 per cent of the men said that they had come to England in order to obtain professional or technical qualifications. As our sample was based on married couples with children, we included no student hostels; yet nearly every man we spoke to considered himself to be a student and gave this as his reason for coming to England. It is true that in answer to further questions many explained that they had been unable to continue as full-time students due to the responsibilities of supporting a family. The most common pattern was one of alternating study and work, with some periods of half-time or evening study combined with a job. Despite this, many had succeeded in obtaining preliminary qualifications ('O' and 'A' levels) and in entering degree courses or specialist professional and technical courses (in law, accountancy, engineering, and the like). Some had completed these and were waiting until their wives finished their training before returning home. Sometimes both of them worked, after they finished their studies, until they could save enough to buy a car or other major item of equipment that was difficult to obtain at home. A number had even gone on to get a second qualification, adding economics to law, or a business course to a qualification in accounting. West Africans in England do indeed seem to be students, and if they are forced to pause in their studies from time to time in order to support themselves and their families, they are doggedly persistent in returning to their education. This persistence is the more surprising when one realizes that three-quarters had been here for six years or more, and over 40 per cent for at least eight years. The men are thus substantially older than most English students, with 80 per cent over 35 years of age.

Education and occupational stratification in West Africa

Even when working full-time, and not enrolled in any course, West Africans often prefer to describe themselves as students. The significance of the role of student can only be understood in the context of contemporary West Africa.

Centuries of Western trade, followed by Christianity and Colonial rule, have

219

set in motion processes which in turn have led to the flow of West Africans seeking qualifications in England. The major and most far-reaching change has been in the economic structure of society, and particularly in the occupational system. Where previously nearly everyone farmed, and chief and citizen (and slave) shared much the same style of life, by the mid-twentieth century an occupationally differentiated and clearly stratified social system was emerging. Salaries of clerks were many times the yearly income of an ordinary farmer, while business men, civil servants or members of the professions lived in large Western-style houses, had many servants, drove large expensive cars, and sent their children to private schools. Unlike Europe and Asia, privilege here was not mainly the result of landed property, but usually followed from the income attached to occupations in the modern sector of the economy. And the key to occupational mobility was education.

It is impossible to overstress the suddenness of these changes. Following exploration of the coast in the fifteenth century, European forts became a focus of trade at many points along the West African coast. Enclaves of African middlemen grew up around the forts, and as early as the eighteenth century some of the wealthier families sent sons to be educated in Europe to enable them to keep accounts and deal as equals with the foreign merchants. But there was virtually no contact with the peoples beyond the coastal strip until the mid-nineteenth century. The following 100 years of colonial rule still saw relatively little change. There was never a European settler population in British West Africa (malaria and the apparently impenetrable high forest made the costs too high). But enough administrators and soldiers were sent from Britain to carry out the work of governing. So there were, even in the early twentieth century, relatively few occupations within the Westernized sector of the economy.

This situation was reflected in the provision of schools. Most jobs then allocated to Africans could be carried out with only a primary education, and in 1920 there were in Ghana only three secondary schools with a total enrolment of 207. Despite a colonial policy of improving facilities for education, expansion did not begin to keep pace with demand. A report on admission to government secondary schools in Eastern Nigeria in 1960 notes that whereas in 1944 there were 513 candidates for 28 places, in 1950 2,800 candidates were seeking the 112 available places, and in 1958 there were 9,000 applicants for 140 places. At the time of this report there had been requests for 28,000 application forms for the 1960 entry (Wareham 1962:62). Foster wrote of Ghana in the 1960s that 'the academic secondary school has become increasingly vital for social mobility, since it commands entry to nearly all significant roles within the public service' (which accounted for 60% of all wage and salary employment). Secondary education was 'also a prerequisite for employment by the larger commercial companies' (1965:197).

If the difficulty of entry into secondary school was a serious obstacle to occupational mobility, a second hurdle appeared at entry into sixth form.

The quest for education

Foster's (1965) study of education in Ghana showed that only a few secondary schools had a sixth form. Furthermore, these were all government, or government assisted schools, and it was virtually impossible for students from private secondary schools to get a place. Since their number was so small, those who successfully completed the sixth-form course were practically assured of a place at university. But for pupils in the private secondary schools (which made up 86 of the total of 101) both sixth-form accreditation and higher education were effectively ruled out. While we neglected to ask those we interviewed in London whether they had been able to secure a sixth-form place in West Africa, the proportion who began their studies here by taking 'O' and 'A' level courses supports the strong inference that this bottleneck in the educational system was often responsible for their coming to England to study.

When the West Africans we talked to arrived in England, during the early or middle 1960s, higher educational qualifications were the key to occupations carrying the greatest rewards in both wealth and prestige. With a civil-service or professional position virtually assured, a period of study abroad seemed a good investment. This was doubly so because the new West African elites - who ran the colonies under the British, and took over their governments on independence - were the educated occupants of professional and bureaucratic positions (Lloyd 1966). One trained not only for an occupational career, but also for entry into the governing stratum of these newly independent countries.

The policy of West African governments towards training in the professions has radically changed in the early 1970s. The opening of a number of new universities and professional schools has made it possible to become a fully qualified doctor or lawyer without leaving Nigeria or Ghana, and resources have been concentrated on improving the training available at home, rather than on scholarships to send students abroad. Indeed, doctors and lawyers who do train abroad are now required to take additional courses to acquaint them with the medical and legal problems particular to their own countries. However it seems likely that it will be many years before there are sufficient places in the West African universities for all those seeking to qualify in these and other professions. Perhaps a more effective restraint on the numbers seeking to train abroad will be the growing scarcity of openings in government employment for those with higher qualifications. What seemed like an insatiable demand for qualified personnel in 1960 (Hollander 1962), had become in the mid-1970s a glut of secondary-school leavers in relation to the jobs available, and fewer and fewer openings for university graduates in the government offices which formerly supplied the majority of all white-collar and professional employment. It has also become more difficult to enter Britain as a student. Since 1968 immigration officials have been required to seek evidence that a would-be student had a place at a recognized school or university, to satisfy themselves that he is capable of following such a course and that he has sufficient financial support to see him through his studies. Such requirements would have turned away many of the

221

students we talked to in our study, since they often arranged their courses after arriving in Britain, and few had sufficient funds for more than the first few months.

This, then, is the background to the steady stream of West Africans who have come as students to Britain from Nigeria, Ghana, The Gambia, and Sierra Leone since the Second World War. The colonial administration presided over the transformation of their countries' political and economic structures, and by the coming of independence some qualification through higher education was the *sine qua non* for participation in the emergent elite which replaced expatriates in government and commercial firms as the dominant class. There is a further thread to untangle. For it is not accidental that the people of these countries come for preference to England.

Language is of course a tremendously important factor, since, in the ex-British colonies, at least the later years of primary education, and all further education is in English. But in addition there was the conviction that life and training in England held some kind of extra virtue. The most probable origin of this view is to be found in the years of colonial domination, when judges, administrators, soldiers and technicians who were English held both power and the knowledge on which it seemed to be based. Thus until very recently many West Africans felt that a lawyer or doctor trained in England must be more skilled than one who had studied at home. Such a person, a 'been-to' (been-to England), was likely to be given preference in competition for a job, and in promotion, and in any case received added respect from colleagues, friends, and kin. Now, for many reasons, the trip to England is losing its mystique; perhaps at the same time that it is becoming both more difficult and less necessary for occupational advancement.

This search for educational qualifications has brought thousands of West Africans to study in England, but while living here they have made a practice of placing their children in English foster-homes. Judges and social workers assume that this must mean that the parents either do not care about their children, that they reject them; or that they are unable to care for them through poverty or incompetence. Such a judgement follows logically from our own views concerning the 'natural' expression of parenthood as succinctly expressed by Judge Baker: 'The practice of fostering for the convenience of the natural parents is contrary to our ideas and social beliefs, and particularly the belief that a young child should if possible spend its early formative years with its own natural parents or at least with its mother' (Re 'O' *The Times*, 5 December 1972).

West Africans in London

In an attempt to understand both the determination of West Africans to study abroad, and the pressures and traditions which led to the placing of their children with English foster-parents, we carried out a dual-focus study of West

Africans in London between 1970 and 1972. Our first problem was to find some way of getting a sample which was, even in a crude sense, representative of West Africans who come to England.[3] This required quite a large sample, but the information was necessarily relatively superficial. To balance this we included a second phase in which Christine Groothues worked intensively with 20 couples, half of whom were from Ghana, and half from Nigeria.[4]

Among the most striking findings of the survey were the universality of the intention to study in England, and the length of time which the men had already spent here. Despite this, only two per cent planned to remain here permanently. We have seen why the ambition to gain qualifications abroad is so important in contemporary West Africa, but the length of time involved seems to be far longer than originally planned for. This in turn has a number of consquences for life in London. But why should it take so long to complete studies?

First of all, there is the obvious problem of finances. Only 11 per cent of the families depended mainly on grants, loans or help from relatives. As we were interested in families with children, we did not include student hostels in our survey; had we done so the proportion of government-sponsored students would have been higher. A further six per cent received supplementary help from some outside source. The remaining four-fifths have no outside support at all. Relatives at home, although a potential source of help, are rarely able to support a student once he is over here, even if they have been largely responsible for financing the trip itself and expenses during the first few months. Only five per cent of our survey sample listed relatives as a major source of financial support, though many mentioned that they had sent money at first and still occasionally sent small amounts. Because the civil war in Nigeria impoverished many families there, the flow of money was often in the other direction. Relatives at home tend to think that money is easily found in England, and they expect to see something of it, even before the migrant returns.

With such a high proportion having to be self-supporting it is not surprising to find that two-thirds of the men in the survey were currently working, nearly all of these full time. Only one-quarter were devoting all their time to studies. But the picture is yet more complicated. The typical pattern is alternating periods of full-time study with periods of work-plus-study when a shortage of funds makes full or part-time employment necessary. While 43 per cent were both working and studying at the time we talked to them, an additional 34 per cent had done both at some time during their life in England. Less than one-quarter had never tried to combine work and study.

The men we spoke with varied greatly in how clearly defined their goals were. Several of those in our intensive sample came intending to do a particular course, set about getting the necessary 'O' and 'A' level qualifications, enrolled for the course, and completed it with no apparent indecision as to the best plan of action, even when there were difficulties and delays for other reasons. Others, however, came intending to do 'business studies', medicine or engineering and

223

found for one reason or another that this was impossible. It is significant that they did not then give up and go home, but found some other, more realistic vocation for which they could train. Again this often meant a period of preparation before actually beginning, but men seem to be willing to think and plan a long way ahead in order to be able finally to return home with a qualification that will ensure good career prospects. Mr Achebi,[5] for instance, originally intended to study medicine in Yugoslavia. He found the language a serious problem and, when with the outbreak of the war in Nigeria his grant came to an end, he came to England where his wife was already studying. Although he did two 'A' levels here, he still could not get a place in a medical school, and when finally convinced of this decided to do law. He has passed the first year examinations but failed the Part I, so is now preparing to sit this again. He feels that, although he managed to complete his 'A' levels by correspondence course while working, his law studies have suffered from the lack of concentration this involves. He is very anxious to find a foster-mother for his two small boys so that he can work nights and do full-time studies during the day. At present he has to be at home during the day because his wife is working in an accounts department in conjunction with her training in accountancy.

Many men find that they must first obtain 'O' and 'A' levels to satisfy matriculation requirements before they can begin the course they have chosen. When Mr Bankwah first came to England, he had to begin by doing 'O' level English and then the three 'A' levels he was advised were necessary for university entrance. After this he began to study law, but gave this up as a 'useless subject'. In 1971 he began a degree course in economics. He had worked in the family business for some time before coming to study in the United Kingdom and keeps in touch with this by trips home in the vacations. From his business interests he receives enough, together with what his wife earns (working overtime in a toy factory) to study full-time and work only during the vacations.

Because of the pattern of part-time and interrupted education, a man often finds his stay in England lasting far longer than he originally planned. Loneliness, together with the prospect of a long delay before he is ready to return, may lead him to send for the wife he left behind in West Africa. Among the survey families there was a mean difference of two years between the length of time the husband and wife had been in this country. From the husband's point of view there are probably two main reasons for asking his wife to join him. One, obviously, is to relieve the loneliness and provide a few home comforts in a land where food, climate, and language are all foreign. Another reason is that by getting a job in this country, she may enable him to give up working, or to work only part-time, and thus to give more time to his studies.

Of the 296 wives in the survey, 45 (15%) had come on their own to study or train and had married while in this country. The proportion of our intensive sample which came independently of their husbands is even higher; six or nearly one-third, had come on their own to train in England, and then married here.

The quest for education

But many of those who were already engaged or married also came to study. About one-quarter of the survey wives accompanied or followed their husbands with the intention of studying in this country, and a further 30 per cent joined their husbands expecting to both work and train. In all, 70 per cent of the survey wives came to the United Kingdom hoping to obtain a professional or technical qualification of some kind. The proportion in our intensive sample is very similar: three-quarters of the wives came intending to train or study, though in this group, too, many knew they would have to work as well.

Women in West Africa are famous for their enterprise as traders and their industry as farmers. Although women's economic roles vary appreciably from one society to another, in the societies of the coast and forest belt which send migrants to England, a woman assumes that she will work in addition to looking after the household and the children. The question is not whether she will work, but at what? Thus when a man brings a wife to this country he is securing not only companionship and a homemaker, but both he and his wife assume that she will work as well. Often her earnings are an important, or even essential, contribution to the family finances.

Among the twenty couples of the intensive study, only one of the five women who did not make a major contribution to the family budget was not working at all. She had been nursing full-time until a difficult pregnancy, and in fact, resumed full-time work just at the end of the study. The others worked full or nearly full-time, but, because their husbands were earning more, their own contribution was proportionately lower. None of the wives in the intensive sample was only a housewife and one woman whose four young children kept her at home taught herself to sew, and then worked her way up to a well-paid machinist's job.

But, although they know they must work, West African women come to this country with their own ambitions. What do they hope to learn? About 20 per cent of the survey wives intended to enter a profession, nearly always nursing; another 20 per cent were thinking in terms of secretarial work, while a further 20 per cent planned to prepare for setting up a business. This last group is largely made up of women doing dressmaking, hairdressing, catering and domestic-science courses. The choices are the same for the intensive sample. Nursing is the most commonly chosen career among those who came to study on their own and married in this country. Although some of the wives in the intensive sample who followed their husbands hoped to become nurses, the need to earn money to help their husband's studies, and the arrival of children had led them to switch to a less demanding course of study.

Perhaps equally revealing of the commitment of this group to educational goals is the fact that of those wives in the intensive sample who initially came to join their husbands without having specific plans for study, all but two have, in fact, taken courses – in hairdressing, wig-making, English and typing. One of the remaining two had plans for intensive study when her husband finished his course. Clearly, although they are wives and mothers, and also working, these women have their own goals and see a period in this country as giving them a chance to further their own education, whether they came initially as students or as wives with responsibilities for helping to support the family. This determination to achieve some form of educational qualification while in England was readily expressed. One woman compared the motives for coming to this country with the competition between villages at home, each seeking to do better than the other. In education 'the best' is thought to be English and, by coming to this country to train, she said 'you can topple your rival on your return with ease'. Another wife remarked that: 'People who come to England are proud when they return, and you feel you're missing something.' These sentiments also affect the men who come to study in this country, and indeed are very important in their decisions to do so. But whereas all the men were here to better their prospects by training, there would seem to be no *a priori* reason why their wives should share this ambition. Nor were these merely optimistic hopes. Fourteen out of the twenty wives in the intensive study had already completed qualifications in this country.

The delay–companionship–responsibility cycle

Broadly speaking, these West African families are of two kinds. One kind is the recently married, where either the couple met in this country or the wife came over as a new bride. The second kind of family was already established when the husband decided to study in the United Kingdom. The wife remained behind at first, but joined him later. A common arrangement is for children who are already in school to stay behind with relatives in West Africa. If there are younger children, they may accompany their mother when she comes to join her husband, or they may remain with a grandmother or other relative at home. One-third of the families in the survey had left at least one child behind, while another 13 per cent had sent one or more children home from England. In contrast, only 6 per cent had brought a child to join them after both parents were settled here.

Such a pattern is confirmed by the age distribution of the children of West Africans in this country. The largest group is in the infant and pre-school category, while the primary and secondary-school age groups are relatively small. This is the sort of distribution one would expect from a young married population. Yet 80 per cent of the husbands are over 35 years old, and only 14 per cent of the wives are under 25 years old, usually the most fertile period for women. As this distribution of child ages suggests, there are strong pressures on both kinds of family to have children while in England. In the newly established families, the relatives back home are naturally anxious to be assured that the marriage will be fertile, and the partners themselves share this concern. While many couples are fully aware of the difficulties involved in raising small children while trying to work and study, they are also anxious to begin a family before they are any older. Ironically, the tradition that a West African woman should be able to rear a large family while pulling her full weight either on the farm or in trading leads these women to feel that they ought to be able to manage even under the changed circumstances of life in London. It is expected of them and they expect it of themselves. The pressures on an established family to continue having children may be only slightly less severe. As the years go on and the date of a return home is still not certain, so the couple grows older, and the remaining years of childbearing dwindle. If they are to have even a moderate-size family, they cannot just miss out six or eight years.

This situation in which West African couples so often find themselves may be described as the 'delay–companionship–responsibility cycle'. It is a pattern of interrelated role conflicts involving husband and wife which ultimately affects the children. When the husband finds his training will take several years, he sends for his wife, or arranges to marry. The wife comes to join her husband in England to help, both as companion and wage-earner, but she brings along her own set of needs and ambitions. Now there are two people trying to combine work and study. At the same time, the creation, or reunion, of the conjugal couple leads to the birth of children which makes still more difficult the balance between work and study, and greatly increases the difficulty of finding suitable accommodation. The added difficulties mean further delays in completing courses and training programmes. This is likely to mean another child, more responsibilities and yet more delays.

Strategies of childrearing

An English couple confronted with a similar set of role conflicts will almost certainly resolve them by the wife giving up her studies to care for the children, while a combination of parental support and government grants finances the husband's continued studies. If they are particularly fortunate, there may be a grandmother or aunt near enough to look after the children so that the wife can continue to study, at least on a part-time basis. But the wife is expected to be ready to give up her career for her children's sake if there is any conflict between the requirements of the two.

Given this contrast between English and West African responses to the same kind of problem, it would seem that mothers' aspirations for their own training were likely to be a central factor in the resort to fostering of young children. However the picture is not so simple. Our data from the intensive sample suggest that there is no very strong link between the decision to foster and the determination of a mother to complete her training. Of those whose studies were completed before the birth of children, about half nevertheless subsequently fostered a child; the same number used neither foster-parents nor daily minders. Of those whose training was not completed, nearly all made use of either fostering or daily minding, but the same pattern holds for those who had no clear career plans on coming to this country. There is however a link between foster-ing and the wish to complete training in particular cases. Mrs Boateng says that their daughter was fostered at the age of nine months because she could not manage to work full-time and keep up with her evening classes as well as caring for the baby. And when Mrs Kotoko found that she was pregnant, although still not finished with her midwifery training, she immediately set about looking for a foster-mother, as she never even considered the possibility of giving up her training when she had so nearly reached the end.

The frequent use of foster-parents and daily minders by women who are not strongly career oriented reflects several other factors which also influence choices about child care. Among the constraints which operate in this way, poor accom-modation and the father's efforts to complete his qualifications are without doubt important. But we have also seen that nearly all mothers work. Some, indeed most, do so for financial reasons, and if young children threaten to inter-fere they must be entrusted to someone else's care. Thus Mrs Ikoye is very anxious to have the two youngest boys at home, despite the fact that they are very satisfied with the foster-parents with whom they have lived since infancy. But they cannot manage without the wages she brings home, and as the boys are not yet in school she would have to give up her job to look after them during the day. Similarly, when Mrs Idusi came to England specifically in order to support her husband through the remainder of his studies, their son was sent immediately to foster-parents so that she could take a full-time job. He remained there until old enough to start school, and is now at home since he can stay with a neigh-bour until Mrs Idusi gets back from work.

But if some children are fostered because the mother must work in order to support the family, in other cases women work because they want to. Often, as with Mrs Bentum, this seems to be associated with having achieved a high level of skill and holding a responsible job. She finds her work in Whitehall as a steno-graphic secretary extremely interesting. When her first child was born she nursed her for three months and then sent her home to her mother in Ghana. The second child, a son, stayed longer, and was sent first to a daily minder, and then to a foster-parent before they decided that he too would be better off with his grand-mother. Mrs Bentum says she cannot imagine giving up her work to look after the babies, and as her mother is very pleased to have them this is not necessary. She would certainly find it difficult to combine their care with her present job, as she not infrequently works until ten at night. Mrs Molomo was fully qualified as a nurse before she married, and when her daughter was born she stayed home for only a month before beginning to seek nursing jobs through an agency. The child was placed with a daily minder who was most carefully examined before the arrangement was completed. Mary Molomo was soon back to working vir-tually full-time, and though she says this is because they are trying to arrange a mortgage on their new house, she also adds that she could not imagine staying at home with the baby all day.

The quest for education

Even women who have few skills to exercise seem to need the outlet of a job. They also value the major household goods which this enables them to buy: washing machines, refrigerators and almost always a sewing machine. But women also need to feel some degree of independence from their husbands. As one wife put it: 'I cannot always be asking him for money to buy my toilet articles, I must have something of my own.' In addition, it is important to remember that women in West Africa are expected to contribute actively to the domestic economy. Thus Mrs Obemi struggled to keep up with her factory sewing throughout a difficult fourth pregnancy in five years until she became ill. In referring to this she said simply that it was her duty to do what she could to help with the family finances.

Conjugal roles and child care

Since all mothers work, this factor alone cannot be used to explain why some couples foster children and others do not. And it seems that women's aspirations for gaining qualifications while in England are not directly related to the use of fostering. Nor is it simply a matter of the age of the child, with parents of infants sending them to be fostered, while those with school-age children can manage with them at home (although this pattern does appear). There are two main ways in which couples cope with pre-school children at home. They may send them to a women who looks after children during the day, a daily minder. Or they may so synchronize their schedules that one or the other of the parents is always at home. Examples from the intensive sample of how spouses coordinate their schedules are a husband who works on the night shift in a factory while his wife is a secretary during the day, and several cases of women who do night nursing and thus are able to be at home during the day while their husbands are working or attending classes. It should be noted that husbands who share the responsibility for seeing that someone is always with a young child do not necessarily do anything about the maintenance of the household. The man on night shift tries to sleep during the day, and does only the minimum necessary to keep the toddler clean and fed. Husbands whose wives are working at night will, of course, get up with the children if they cry, but often do not expect to do anything more. However, one man feeds and dresses the children before his wife gets back.

All women 'must' work, as they see this as part of a wife's responsibility. Those with infants and pre-school children can only work if they can find some way of caring for the children while they are away. If the husband is willing, and if his regime of study and work allow, he can often fill this function. But if the husband's commitments are such as to make such a careful meshing of schedules unworkable, then some other course must be found. Many of the survey couples said they had tried to get places in local-authority nurseries for their children, but had been unsuccessful. Our impression is that local authorities do not treat such requests very seriously, perhaps because they feel the wife should be at home looking after the children herself. Seven per cent (20) of the 296 survey couples had been able to place a child in day nurseries, and of these four per cent had also made use of foster-parents.

In a classic study of London families, Bott (1957) suggested that there was a significant difference in the pattern of conjugal relations with different styles of extra-family networks. Her categories were based on the extent to which a couple carried out the various activities of marriage and family life jointly, either taking turns or working together; or where their roles were segregated, each having a separate sphere of competence and responsibility. Bott found that those couples whose pattern of task performance was segregated tended to spend their leisure time separately, each with kin or friends of the same sex who knew one another. The network of each spouse was 'connected'. Each spouse would depend on his or her friends for assistance and companionship in the activities for which they were responsible, rather than turning to the other partner. Those couples with a joint activity pattern had common friends, but these tended to be unknown to each other; their network was 'unconnected'. Friendship activities - dinners, outings - involved husband and wife together and jointness was carried over into leisure pursuits. Husband and wife turned to one another for assistance in domestic activities rather than to kin or friends of the same sex outside the conjugal family.

In traditional West African societies the division of virtually all spheres of activity into 'male' and 'female' is pronounced, and this is nowhere clearer than in domestic matters. Women cook, wash clothes and care for children as a matter of course, in addition to their work as traders or farmers. In the homes of the modern elite servants do most of the domestic work, and thus jointness in roles is unnecessary. While some leisure activities are shared, many are not. The husband has his career, and the wife either a career or some kind of job which occupies her during the day. Their home is a common ground on which they share interests, above all in their children (see Oppong 1974 and Harrell-Bond 1975). Thus in traditional West African societies, and often still to a notable extent, conjugal roles are highly segregated, in terms of both interests and task performance. When West Africans who have spent some time in Europe return home, they often comment on the difference between this pattern and life abroad where 'we did everything together'. One of the things we looked at in our work with the couples of the intensive sample was the organization of domestic and leisure activities and the kinds of social networks within which these couples moved.

There were quite clear differences between couples from Ghana and those from Nigeria in the organization of conjugal roles; these are related to the different types of descent system followed by each group, and the consequent differences in traditional marriage roles. However, the case material suggests that at least some of those couples who share responsibility for decisions, child care,

230

family expenses and leisure activities here in England are doing so because their customary alternative sources of assistance and support are absent. Their roles are joint-under-duress, rather than as a result of fundamental changes in ideas about how responsibilities ought to be shared. In one case, for instance, while the wife was ill her husband took care of the baby, did all the shopping, house-work and cooking, but once she recovered they reverted to the pattern of the wife having responsibility for domestic chores and children, with the husband helping with the shopping at weekends.

Patterns of leisure-time activities are particularly revealing. Over half of the couples (11/20) had highly segregated leisure roles, with only four being fully joint. Generally, friends tend to overlap to a considerable extent, since both know many people from home who are also in London. But each spouse tends to have some friends not shared by the other – either school or work friends from home, or people from current or past study and work situations in England. Husbands rarely take wives along to sporting events and pub sessions with friends from work, and one husband who had a band treated this part of his life as en-tirely separate from his family. On the other hand some of the Nigerian couples attended meetings of their home-town union together, and couples from both countries often had friends and relatives from home who celebrated a birth or wedding or the achievement of a degree, or who had to be welcomed or sent off home with a party. Even here, however, the husband would often attend while the wife stayed at home with the children. This was likely to be her own choice, for, with job and studies and the house to look after, women tended to be very tired most of the time, and to prefer a quiet evening at home to a large gather-ing where they would feel called upon to participate fully. Husbands' social net-works also extend beyond those of their wives because men are freer to attend parties and gatherings uninvited; if they know someone who has been invited they may go along with him, but a wife is not included in such an arrangement.

We were surprised by the number of couples who had relatives in Britain. Only one of the twenty couples in the intensive study did not have at least 'distant cousins' from home who were also in London at the time of the study. While there were quite frequent visits, unless these relatives were living close by there was very little exchange of services. Although this is contrary to the West African ethic of kinship solidarity, it is perhaps hardly surprising in view of the full and complex lives which both men and women lead here. Anyone, man or woman, who is in London is likely to be trying to work, study and raise a family in some combination, and thus to have little time to help out kin with similar problems. The fact that relatives tend to be dispersed, and not to live in the same neigh-bourhood (unless, as sometimes happens, they are sharing a house) adds to the difficulties of helping out. Transport is a perpetual problem, both because of the extra time involved and because of the cost. Couples with cars tended to share significantly more leisure activities than those without. This isolation is, for many couples, compensated for by extensive use of the telephone for keeping

Table 10-1. *Relationship between child-care arrangements and conjugal role structure: Intensive sample*

Conjugal role structure	Arrangements for child care			
	Fostering	Daily minding	Parents only	
Joint	1	1	3	
Intermediate	5	1	2	
Segregated	5	2	0	
Totals	11	4	5	N = 20

in touch, and information circulates rapidly among relatives and those from the same home community.

We tried to select the couples of the intensive sample in order to have equal numbers who had fostered a child, and who had reared their children entirely at home. This turned out to be more difficult than we anticipated, because many couples try a series of arrangements due both to changing circumstances and to the difficulty of finding one with which they are satisfied. In the end we found that of our 20 couples, 11 had used foster-parents at some time, while of the remaining 9, 4 had placed their children with a daily minder. Only 5 of the 20 couples had never used either form of child care. In Table 10-1 the degree of conjugal role segregation is related to the kind of arrangements made for child care. Although with such small numbers we can do no more than indicate trends, it is striking that none of the couples with highly segregated roles had reared their children entirely at home, while only one of the five couples scored as having fully joint conjugal roles sent a child to foster-parents. This could be interpreted in either of two ways: it may be that couples with highly segregated roles cannot manage to synchronize their schedules and share responsibility sufficiently to allow them to keep a child at home while both parents are working or studying. When there is no sharing of responsibility and tasks, and the mother is working and possibly also studying, she may simply be unable to cope with a child as well. Since West African conjugal roles are, traditionally, highly segregated, this may be a common source of pressure on West African parents to place a child with foster-parents. The other interpretations of this pattern would be that parents who have defined their conjugal roles in terms of sharing tasks and responsibilities are those who have also adopted the view that it is harmful for a child to be reared by anyone other than his own parents. Both these attitudes chacterize the stereotype of the modern Western family where companionate marriage and close bonds between parents and children are idealized. It seems likely that both these interpretations may be correct, and that both kinds of pressure are influencing decisions about child rearing.

Conclusions: Educational fostering as a cultural paradigm

We have tried to show why education in England is so important to ambitious West Africans, and to indicate the kinds of problems they encounter in trying to secure it. But there remains the question of why West African couples so often attempt to meet the conflicting demands of earning a living, studying, and rearing a family by placing young children with foster-parents. English families do not see this as a possible solution to similar problems, nor do other immigrant groups; Pakistani, Indian, Irish, and Cypriot families all appear closely to resemble English families in this respect.[6] West Indian families do make considerable use of daily minders, but rarely send children to foster-parents (see Chapter 11). It is here that West African traditions are crucial. Explanations of fostering by West Africans in England must be seen in terms of fostering as a cultural paradigm for the education of children.

Earlier chapters have shown that in many traditional West African societies children are sent to be reared away from home in order to learn adult skills and sound moral values. In the more complex West African societies, both traditional and modern, specialized skills are learned in apprentice-fostering. Today, families from rural areas place children with city people as housemaids or wards. And there is a well-established practice of sending a schoolchild to live with a teacher or clergyman in order that he may receive help with his studies. All these forms of fostering are based on the underlying premise that parents are not necessarily the best people to rear their own children, and may very well not be able to provide them with the opportunities and advantages available in a foster-home. Thus, the West African parent sees private fostering arrangements in England in a very different light from the English child-care officer well-versed in child psychology from Freud to Bowlby. Faced with crowded living conditions, and the demands of work and studies on both parents' time and energies, English foster-parents appear able to provide their children with just those positive advantages that they themselves came here to seek: familiarity with English culture and language and a basis for later social mobility. Judge Baker's supposition that the Ghanaian child Ann would feel a 'rankling sense of injustice' if she were sent back to West Africa suggests that many English people also feel that an English upbringing conveys special advantages. It is hardly surprising that couples who have come to this country in order to receive an English education are eager to provide their children with the same opportunity.

11

West African and West Indian immigrant families

Many different forms of delegation of parent roles occur in West Africa, both in societies little subject to modern economic and political influences, and in urban centres where new occupations and formal schooling have transformed the old life. The delegation of parent roles has proved highly adaptable to changing conditions. In the last chapter we saw that when West Africans spend periods of several years in London, they still find ways of delegating the rearing of their children, and again the form has changed to fit the constraints of their present situation. This chapter raises two questions. First, how general is the resort to English foster-parents among immigrants in the United Kingdom? Perhaps the West Africans are simply adopting a common response to the problems of immigrant life in London. The West Indian immigrants provide an ideal group for comparison because, having come originally from Africa, they are often said to share a common cultural heritage. Further, as blacks they share the same problems of discrimination in housing and jobs which add to the difficulties of life in London.

The second question follows from the first. If there appears to be a common underlying theme in the different forms of delegation of parent roles among West Africans, which is not shared by other immigrant groups, even by West Indians, what is the basis for the differences between them?

Many reports on West Indian domestic and kinship organization also include a reference to sending children to kin to be looked after. Typically an infant goes to his mother's mother or perhaps to a mother's sister and is often brought up to regard this foster-mother as his mother, using 'mother' as a term of address for her, and calling his own mother by whatever term her siblings use (see R. T. Smith 1956:143; Clarke 1966:142, 179; Spens 1969:278ff.). These accounts suggest that the rearing of children by kin in the West Indies tends to be the result of the inability of the parents to provide proper care (whether because they have no joint home, or because the mother must work full time), a situation that I have called crisis fostering in discussing the West African material. However, there are also hints of purposive fostering in the West Indies; Clarke speaks of 'schoolchildren' who are ostensibly taken into a household to help in

234

exchange for food, clothing and a chance to go to school. One such child she encountered was treated much like the other children in the house – all of whom helped with chores – but she alone did not go to school (Clarke 1966:177). Among the Black Carib of Guatemala Gonzalez describes the sending of young boys to families in town where they take an increasing share of jobs around the house, and learn both literate skills and town ways (Gonzalez 1969:54ff.). Again, Horowitz refers to children staying with kin in cases where their parents are living together on Martinique (1967:49). But on the whole the picture is one of fostering as a means of coping with children of dissolved or non-residential unions. Indeed, M. G. Smith (1962b:80) writes as though this was the only circumstance under which children would be sent to be reared by kin, and treats fostering in the way he does household composition, as a reflex of the mating forms.

In both West Africa and the West Indies, then, children are sent to be reared by kin when the family of orientation cannot, for some reason, manage. And in both areas, fostering is used as a means of widening the education of a child, of providing relatives with companionship and assistance, and of strengthening ties with kin who are relatively well-off. In the West Indies it appears to be crisis fostering which is most prominent, while in West Africa purposive fostering is more important.

The question of whether the West Indian institution is a 'survival' from West Africa via the slaves brought to Caribbean plantations is not relevant at this point. I am concerned with analysing the present constraints and supports of behaviour, whatever its origin.

Although people from these two regions seem to have very similar institutions in respect of the rearing of children by kin, they behave very differently when they come as immigrants to the United Kingdom. In the last chapter we showed the very high percentage of West African children sent to English foster-parents. Less direct information from several sources indicates that West Indians virtually never send their children to English foster-parents (though the local authority may occasionally place children of disturbed or broken homes with their own foster-parents as a welfare measure). Instead, West Indian mothers prefer to send their young children to a 'nanny' who takes several children into her home from early morning until six in the evening. Payment is on either an hourly or a weekly basis and the mother is expected to do all the laundry for the child and often must provide food. These women are also known as 'daily minders'. Many of the women who do daily minding are themselves West Indian and it appears that many of the children sent to them are also West Indian.

The problem I wish to pose here is this – why should two groups with apparently similar institutions at home for rearing children outside the natal family of orientation react in such different ways to the constraints of living in an urban environment abroad? In order to be able to answer such a question, we must look more closely at both traditional and contemporary fostering in the West

Indies, as well as at the circumstances of life in London for both groups of immigrants. It may be that the parents of each group are seeking different goals in coming to England, and, more immediately, have different reasons for delegating the care of their children to others. Or the choice between forms of child care may simply be one of economics: one mode or the other may be more expensive and require more resources. Or it may be that we have been over-hasty in seeing the traditional forms as they appear in West Africa and the West Indies as essentially similar. Perhaps they function rather differently at a basic level, and in the immigrant situation this difference gives rise to the variations in adaptations to the new environment which we have found.

West African fostering in different contexts

In earlier chapters I have considered the distribution of children in fosterage in a number of very different West African contexts: first, we saw that in Gonja society, where education and occupational differentiation are very little affected by industrialization, children go almost always to kin. Exceptions are found only among boys, who sometimes are sent to Koranic teachers and occasionally to office-holders. Forty per cent of the children go to a foster-parent of the grandparental generation, while about half go to kin of the parental generation – that is, to a parent's real or classificatory sibling.

The second context was contemporary southern Ghana where apprentice fostering is becoming important. Here 'masters' are sought among kin for preference, but differentiation of skills may make this impossible. Apprentice fostering affects both boys and girls, but exists side-by-side with fostering for more diffuse objectives. Children are also sent to educated relatives in the hope that they may receive both an improved education and perhaps advantages in securing work later. Here foster-parents are seldom of the grandparental generation, and children most often go to a 'sibling' of the parent, or, in a substantial number of cases, to non-kin.

The final situation in which we have found fostering of children by West African parents is among the temporary immigrants to London. Here the children are much younger, reflecting the absence of domestic help or relatives in the household to assist with the care of infants and toddlers. There are no relatives available to serve as foster-parents in London[1] and children all go to strangers, and indeed to English couples who care for them in exchange for a weekly payment.

These data reflect a clear progression from fostering by kin to fostering by strangers which shows a close similarity to apprenticeship. They also suggest (Chapter 7) a decreasing reliance on the grandparental generation in situations in which fostering is viewed as a means of securing skills or advantage for the child. Admittedly the situation of immigrants to London is an extreme one, but

236

perhaps all the more revealing for that, especially when contrasted with the response of West Indians to objectively similar circumstances.

Fostering in the West Indies

There are a few references in the ethnographic literature on the West Indies to the sending of children to live with kin even though their natal family of orientation is still intact and forms a co-residential unit. Gonzalez writes of the 'loaning' of children between compounds as sometimes based on kinship ties and this seems to include children of intact families (1969:52-3). Sanford also refers to 'loaning' of children and it seems likely that in some of these cases the parents are living together (1971:100). Horowitz specifically mentions that parents may send a child to a relative from an intact conjugal household (1967:49). There are also clear indications that children are sent to stay with non-kin who are in a position to offer them a better start in life than their own parents. Edith Clarke's data from three very different communities in Jamaica show a substantial proportion of children living with neither parent; over the three communities the average is 18 per cent (see Table 11-1). Nearly one-third of these fostered children are living with non-relatives. In the poorest community (Mocca) almost half the fostered children are with non-kin, while nearly all those from prosperous Orange Grove are with relatives. But although Orange Grove children are seldom sent out to live with non-kin, Clarke reports that more unrelated children come to live in Orange Grove homes than was the case in the other communities studied (1966:178).

The sending of children to middle- and upper-class white and Creole families in the hopes that they will receive an education and assistance in finding a secure occupational niche is also reported by Gonzalez for the Black Caribs of Guatemala (1969:53ff.) and Sanford for the Carib and Creole population of a British Honduras community (1971:94-5; 1975).

Table 11-1. *Children of families of three Jamaican communities who are being fostered: Per cent with kin and with others (from Clarke 1966:Appendix 5)*

	Fostered children living with:				
	Kin		Non-kin		Total Children fostered
	No.	%	No.	%	
Orange Grove	20	90	2	10	22
Sugar town	65	72	25	28	90
Mocca	14	54	12	46	26
Total	99	72	39	28	138

Yet, despite these references, purposive fostering with kin and with strangers seems to account for a relatively small proportion of the children who are reared apart from both their parents in the Caribbean area. Again from Sanford's figures, 59 per cent of her instances of 'child keeping' (205 cases) I would classify as crisis fostering, with another 13 per cent (46 cases) as probable crisis fostering. If we include the latter group, then something like 72 per cent of her cases were due to the inability of the parents to rear the child themselves (Sanford 1971:82). As Sanford points out, this classification is based on reasons given 'after the fact' and cannot but represent bias of some sort. Unfortunately there are few figures of which I am aware which enable a distinction to be drawn between crisis and voluntary fostering in the Caribbean area.[2]

The burden of the descriptive material on the West Indian area is also that children are most often placed with a pro-parent because their parents have no home in which to care for them. These may be children of transient unions, 'outside' children whose presence in a conjugal household is not welcome, or children whose parent or parents must work in a city or abroad, and cannot care for them as well; but for some such reason the parents cannot cope and some pro-parental figure has to be found.

The multi-functional quality of fostering in the West Indies is precisely what we find in traditional West African societies, and the adaptations in West Africa to Western industrial changes are echoed in those described for the Caribbean. Yet the working out of the pattern is subtly different. Not only does a relatively higher proportion of crisis fostering seem to characterize this area, but fostering among kin seems more likely to mean the rearing of a child by a parent's own parent rather than, as in West Africa, by a wide range of classificatory relatives, particularly parents' siblings.

It is in societies based on cognatic descent systems, or with weak unilineal descent groups that fostering appears to flourish in West Africa. West Indian societies are cognatic, with a few weakly unilineal (e.g. M. G. Smith 1962a). Despite this similarity, the range of kin which participates is wider in West Africa than in the West Indies. What is interesting for the comparison of fostering in the two areas is that these collateral kin are, in West Africa, seen as having a claim on children to foster. Furthermore, they are ready to acknowledge requests to take children which are phrased in terms of kinship ties.

Sanford refers to anxiety over dependability of kinship bonds among the Creole and Carib peoples of British Honduras (1971:108). But the bonds of which she is speaking are those linking primary kin, that is, full and half-siblings and parents and children. And given the dispersal of half-siblings in different households in the town, and extended absence of fathers and the periodic absence of many mothers, this is not perhaps surprising. It is a case of a dispersed core, with very little in the way of backing-up institutions. The comparable situation in rural West Africa finds the paternal half-siblings usually located in a single compound (this will be the case with maternal half-siblings in a matrilineal system like Ashanti). The same compounds contain a number of elementary families, linked by senior members of a kin group who usually recognize one person as their formal head. This person in turn represents the compound to the community, acting on behalf of the individual members on such public occasions as life-crisis rituals or serious litigation.[3] Should the child's own family of orientation break up, there is a double safety net – on the one hand there are the two on-going residential groups in which the parents have birth-status rights, into either of which he will be welcomed, and on the other there are the kinsfolk living elsewhere who have a claim on him, and an obligation to care for him if this becomes necessary. Fostering does sometimes occur within a residential complex of several domestic groups. In Gonja, this happens most often when an elderly woman is assigned one of her granddaughters as a companion and a runner-of-errands. But on the whole fostering occurs between compounds, and very often between villages. By this I mean that the parents are living in a different compound or village from that of the foster-parent, and that these are their regular homes. In Gonja, and I believe in other West African societies too, the fostered child moves between fixed points (domestic groups, though not necessarily based on a conjugal unit), and these fixed points are embedded in a nexus of wider institutions, kinship, jural, ritual, political, into which the child is introduced in a systematic way, and as a person with a birth-status identity linking him permanently to one.

To an outsider, it seems as though the fostered child in the West Indies has only his foster-home as a secure base.[4] And further, that however strong the bonds between parent, child, and foster-parent, this is in effect an isolated unit. Even where domestic groups are gathered into larger aggregates (as among Black Caribs in Guatemala, Gonzalez 1969), there is not the pattern of extra-domestic institutions into which these larger groups are themselves integrated.

Thus fostering in West Africa leads the child out from the domestic and local group of the parents, but this remains his primary base and he (or she) remains the child of this compound, of this village, of these particular parents. One minor index of this continuity in Gonja is that kinship terminology does not alter with fostering. The child and the foster-parent use the same kin terms as before, and the child continues to call only his own parents by the fond terms for 'mother' and 'father'. The major index of the lack of change in status through fostering is that a man is eligible for no new offices by virtue of residence with his foster-parent, and remains eligible for whatever offices were open to him in his natal community; inheritance is not altered by fostering relationships, though a fond foster-parent may give gifts *inter vivos* to a foster-child.

In contrast, there seem to be two themes in West Indian fostering. First, the child may be sent 'outside' to unrelated foster-parents, usually in a quasi-servant role, but with the intention that he learns urban middle-class ways and gets an education. If this is successful, then as an adult he will be in a good position to support his parents. There may be a breaking of ties with natal kin, and an

attempt to 'pass' into middle-class society. If the child fails to secure an education or effective occupational skills, he will be thrown back onto his own kin
and class. The second theme is the fostering grandmother. Here the child is
returned to the mother's home, which may or may not still be her primary base.
If the mother has established a separate conjugal household, it is likely to be
with a man who is not the child's father, and the majority of writers on the West
Indies seem to agree that 'outside' children are not welcome in the conjugal
home (see especially Clarke 1966:174). If, as in Sanford's community in British
Honduras, the parents are both away working, there *is* no conjugal home to
which the child can relate. The result appears to be a very strong relationship
with the fostering mother. Several authorities have noted that she is apt to be
called 'mother' while the real mother is referred to by her name, and treated as a
'sister'. Sanford suggests that it can go much farther than this. Writing of a
woman who reared a younger brother and sister, she says:

This woman receives from her younger siblings the reverence and the regular
acquiescence to her authority over them that a mother would receive . . . Their
attitudes are almost a caricature of the respect for authority which is a strongly
evidenced characteristic of social relations in Stann Creek. No matter that they
are both quite old and responsible themselves, their sister is the elder and she is
loved, feared, and obeyed in all respects as if they were children. She is their
psychic mother (133–4).

Yet Sanford insists that the 'keeping' of children by Creole and Carib peoples
in British Honduras is not a form of adoption, and gives as evidence the fact that
the mother's right to reclaim her child is recognized as overriding any promise
she might have made to the fostering parent (1971:92–4, 125). Interestingly
enough this is discussed in the context of the treatment of parent and foster-
parent by the grown foster-child. A girl who sent gifts only to her foster-mother
and not to her real mother was criticized for forgetting the woman who bore her
and looked after her in infancy. Sanford remarks that she would not have been
able to withstand these criticisms if she had been living in the community, but
as she was working abroad they did not affect her. Another woman affirmed
that if either of the two boys she had reared should turn out well (i.e. become
well-off), she would see to it that the mother shared in her good fortune. As
these examples suggest, it appears to be the fostering mother in the first instance
who benefits from the assistance of grown children, but the mother is seen as
having a residual claim, though this may be difficult to enforce, and may depend
on the goodwill of the foster-parent.

Such dual responsibility can be seen as arising, on the one hand, from the
moral obligation which links genetrix (and genitor) and offspring, regardless of
their subsequent relationship, and, on the other, from the reciprocities of rearing
which arise from the dependency of infancy and childhood, and the emotional
and moral claims this makes on the child in adulthood. The same dual obligations exist for the West African foster-child, but there are two important dif-

ferences in their form. First, the moral obligations towards his biological parents are augmented by the fact that they also provide him with his place in adult society, since this is (or was in traditional times) implicit in birth status. This very strong pull back to one's natal kin is recognized by the Gonja who say that a son will always return eventually to live with his father. Anyone could provide instances of this happening, even in middle age. These rights and obligations arising out of bestowal of birth status are best seen as *status reciprocities*, and differ fundamentally from ties generated through the rearing process (Chapter 1).

Second, there seems to be much less emphasis on children as a form of security in old age in West Africa. With Sanford, I suspect that this may be because of the insecurity of the West Indian situation, rather than because West African parents do not look to their children for comfort in old age. But in the African context there is a wider range of relatives with whom one may find support, and, perhaps more important, old age in many societies is a time when both men and women are highly respected for their wisdom and skill.[5] Nor, in most traditional societies were adult sons likely to disappear regularly for the major part of their working lives. In the West Indies both the migration of young adults out of the country, or to distant centres of employment, and the absence of a strong extended kin group, leave the older folk without a sure means of support and companionship in old age.

In the West Indies, then, the fostering of children appears to be associated with a narrow range of kin ties; the foster-child is often without an alternative home and grows up very strongly identified with his foster-mother. Her home is his home; there is little to pull the foster-child back to his own parents, although he owes them respect and support too; and finally, adults, particularly women, may depend very greatly in old age on the support of their youngest 'child', who is very likely to be a foster-child. Indeed, it would seem that by fostering her daughters' children, a woman can effectively so extend her own period of child-rearing that it lasts not until middle age, but through to old age. Sanford speaks of women 'building their empires as mothers' by appropriating their daughters' children (1971:99; see also Clarke 1966:180–1).

The importance of the grandmother as foster-parent in the West Indies can be seen in Table 11-2. The figures for British Honduras and Jamaica also reflect the pattern of sending children to non-kin, presumably in apprentice or educational fostering. The other point to note from Table 11-2 is the very low proportion of foster-parents of the parents' own generation. There are some cases in each sample, but the figures are very low in comparison with those for grandparents.

West Indians in London

These comments are based on a pilot study carried out by Dr M. T. Spens and a West Indian (Dominican) assistant in a London suburb where there is a small Dominican enclave. They draw also on reading of West Indian ethnography, and

Table 11-2. *West Indian fostering relationships: Generation*

	Foster-parent is of:				
	Grand-parental generation	Parents' generation	Child's generation	Not kin	Total N =
Dominican rural village[a]	130 (89%)	10 (7%)	–	6 (4%)	146 (100%)
British Honduras coastal village[b]	156 (55%)	34 (12%)	6 (2%)	89 (31%)	285 (100%)
Three Jamaican communities[c]	74 (54%)	21 (15%)	2 (1%)	39 (29%)	136 (99%)

[a] From M. T. Spens (1969).
[b] From M. Sanford (1971) I have omitted category 'other kin' (N = 64) in calculating percentages, as this could not be assigned to any generation. The figures in the above table thus represent percentages of those classifiable by generation from Sanford's data.
[c] From E. Clarke (1966) Appendix 5. I have considered only children living with neither parent. Two cases have been omitted as they could not be classified by generation.

on Spens' close knowledge of Dominica. They must, however, be considered as tentative findings rather than as the results of a full-scale study.

The trip to England is in a sense but a further extension of the emigration in search of work which takes West Indians from the farm to the local sugar plantation, on to the towns and cities, or perhaps to the fruit, tobacco or sugar estates on other islands or the mainland of central America. Puerto Ricans holding US passports go to the United States in search of work. Those from the ex-British colonies come, or used to come, to England. Many, both men and women, leave a child behind with a mother or sister, and some men come promising to bring over wives and children. Those who reunite their families in England often add to them, while others find a spouse and start a family. The jobs they are able to get are those which English workers avoid. They generally work as industrial cleaners, railwaymen, bus conductors, or unskilled and semi-skilled factory workers – jobs which pay poorly and require few skills. Since both husband and wife are almost certainly committed to sending money home regularly, both must work.

The pattern of illegitimate first (and often second) pregnancies is very clear among the families in the pilot study. Seven out of nine women had borne their first child before marriage, and three were still not married several years later. Illegitimacy among first-born is not equally characteristic of all Dominican women, however. Again and again these women explain that they came to England because they had a child (or several children) to support and they could not do this successfully on the island. Thus emigrants to London appear to be selected from those who have difficulty meeting their responsibilities under the conditions of low wages and high unemployment on Dominica. Mothers of illegitimate children are prominent in this group, and probably account for the large majority of single women who come to work in England. All those in the pilot sample had left their illegitimate children with kin in Dominica. One of the women had come with her husband, but again for much the same reason – to work and earn a better standard of living. This couple left their first child behind with the wife's mother so that they could both work full time. This is exactly the reasoning given by single women for leaving a child with its grandmother: 'If I had to look after the child I couldn't work so much, and that is why I came to England.'

But for the single woman with a child to support, work has an added meaning: she must send money to the woman in whose care she has left the child. This person is almost always the mother's mother. The money is seen as fulfilling two obligations. In the first place, the care of her child places an extra burden on the grandmother. And secondly, the daughter feels responsible for helping the mother herself with cash if she possibly can. There is, however, a subtler pressure on a woman to contribute to her child's support: if she is the one who provides money for daily necessities and for such extra expenses as the clothes and celebration of First Communion, then she has a much clearer claim to the child's affection and loyalty later on. She has been a proper mother, even though circumstances forced her to leave the child to be reared by others. This is of very great importance in the mother's eyes. One woman whose mother died just before she left for England had left her daughter with the child's godmother. She did this very reluctantly, and insists that she has always continued to send money for her support, because the godmother would like to adopt the girl, and she does not want to lose her. In another case the mother had sent money for the maintenance of her son while he was being looked after by his father's mother. She was careful to continue these payments in order to retain her rights in the child, and later was able to take him to live with her.

A woman feels differently about the child she has left with her own mother. My impression is that this is usually a temporary arrangement in the beginning, 'until I am able to send for the child in England'. Whether the grandmother views it in this way is unclear. Significantly, two of the women in our sample had encountered serious resistance from their mothers when seeking to bring to England the child left in their care. Both had left the child for some time longer, and one ended by having to return to the West Indies to resolve the matter there. Thus the mothers do not from the first consider that they are turning a child over to its grandmother 'for good'. However, this is often the outcome of fostering by the maternal grandmother, either because she effectively resists returning the child, or because the mother is never in a position to send for it.

243

The grandmother's position is very much strengthened by the fact that a child left with her in infancy grows up knowing her as its mother and calling her 'Mama', while calling its own mother by her first name and often treating her like an older sibling. Interestingly enough, this even happens when the mother is present in the household. One of the Dominican women in London had lived with her mother after the birth of her first child, going out to work while the grandmother looked after the baby. The child grew up calling the grandmother 'Mama' as its mother did, and calling the mother by her first name, as the grandmother did. The mother describes the situation as 'like I was the big sister'. It didn't worry her at the time, and after some years she left her son with his grandmother to come to England where she married and had two more children. When the boy joined her in England he still refused to call her 'Mama' and at this time she minded very much and tried unsuccessfully to change the pattern which had been established in his infancy. There is another instance in our small pilot sample of this same pattern – a son who grew up calling his grandmother 'Mama' and who in this case refused to admit that his own mother *was* his mother.

Women are very ambivalent about 'losing' a child to their mother in this way. On the one hand they feel extremely grateful that the grandmother was able to care for the child at a time when they could not do so. This places the mother doubly in her own mother's debt: firstly there are the reciprocities of rearing built up during her own infancy and childhood; now there is a second set which links child, mother and grandmother. In this situation the continued residence of the child with its grandmother in adolescence and adulthood is seen as one way of looking after the grandmother in her old age, one way of fulfilling the obligation felt towards her. One of the women in the pilot study, still unmarried with four children, said that she sometimes regrets having had so many children, as: 'No man will marry you with four children. They are scared of the responsibility.' However, she went on to say that whenever she thinks like this, she remembers her mother and how she needs the children, and what a help they are to her. The eldest boy is now 17 and has a job, and in addition makes a vegetable garden for his grandmother. The others fetch wood and water and run errands. She expects them to look after her mother in her old age. So she is glad she had the children, since her mother needs them. 'But', she added, 'they must also give me some sort of respect as well.'

And here is the crux of the matter. A child who feels primary obligations towards his grandmother and treats his mother 'like a big sister', cannot be depended on by the mother in her later years in the same way as the child she has reared herself. The reciprocities of rearing are laid down between child and grandparent, not between child and parent. And concern about whether children will care for their parents in old age is very real.[6] Mrs M's first child was born in Dominica, and acknowledged by the father who could not marry the mother as her family was 'lower' than his. The girl had been raised by a sister of Mrs M's mother, and even now is staying with her since Mrs M's husband does not want the child in their home. Mrs M is pleased that her daughter shows great fondness and respect for her foster-mother, but she only hopes 'that R. . . will not neglect me in my old age, when she is bigger and able to help herself'. The Dominican interviewer comments that in her opinion the girl will not let Mrs M down because she is conscious of her mother's goodness towards her. The interviewer is here referring to the fact that Mrs M has always sent money to help with her daughter's maintenance and kept in touch with her.

The concern over whether a child will feel obliged to care for a parent in old age when reared by someone else is most clearly seen when the foster-parent is not the maternal grandmother. This is probably because the mother feels a strong obligation towards her own mother, which she can fulfil through her child, and also because the bond between mother and grandmother is close enough that the child identifies the two and can reasonably be expected to give the mother too 'some respect when she is old'. But when the foster-parent is a step-mother or godmother, then women become really anxious that they will lose their right to the child's sense of obligation in old age. In one of the sample families, the husband and wife had virtually separated but still occupied the same house. The mother was determined to try and maintain this arrangement as otherwise she feared she would lose her children. She wants to look after them when they are small so that they can care for her when she is old. She thinks they will do this, except perhaps the eldest girl who is against her.

None of the West Indian children in the pilot study had been sent to English foster-parents, and indeed London informants specifically deny that they would ever do this. Sending very young children to a 'nanny', that is, a woman who looks after them locally during the day, is a fairly common practice. Ideally, women prefer to stay at home when their children are very young, but this is not always possible. Some who must work manage by taking an evening job when the husband can be at home with the children. Others make use of either West Indian or English daily minders ('nannies') with whom they leave the children from early in the morning to 5 or 6 in the evening. School-age children are often 'latchkey' children who return to an empty house and may even be expected to start the supper for a working mother.

Economic aspects of fostering and daily minding in London

To what extent is the preference of West Indian parents for daily minding rather than fostering with English families a matter of economic necessity? The range of costs for daily minding in London (at 1970 prices) starts below that for fostering, but there is an area of overlap. The less expensive foster-parents charge no more than the more expensive daily minders. There are additional costs in both forms of care; for daily minding, food (usually supplied by the parents), laundry, and twice-daily fares on bus or underground, and, of course, clothing; for fostering, occasional lump sums for clothes, new shoes, etc. and the expense of visits.

245

It is worth noting that although the West Africans in London are on the whole much better educated than the West Indians, the jobs they are able to find are frequently the same. Both tend to take unskilled or semi-skilled jobs in transport, the post office, or factories. Hence many West Africans are not materially better off than West Indians. Although virtually *all* West Africans are in London as students, only 11 per cent of the extensive sample were mainly supported by either loans, student grants or money from home. The families in one of the two groups in the intensive phase of the West African Immigrants study, the Ibo, were receiving no money from home and were instead trying to send money to kin who had lost homes and jobs as a result of the Biafran war. Overall, the Ibo families tended to delegate their parental roles less frequently than the others, but this applied equally to fostering and daily minding. Despite their financial straits, there were Ibo families who fostered their children in English homes.

When discussing the relative advantages of fostering and daily minding with West Africans the choice generally turned on factors other than expense. Daily minding was preferred because parents could check up on the minder's standard of care, and for convenience if there was a good minder near the mother's place of work. It was disliked because of crowded conditions, poor care and constant travel. Fostering was disliked due to difficulty of checking on the foster-parents' care of the children (parents are expected to give notice of visits beforehand), and because of the difficulty and expense of frequent visits. Fostering was preferred to daily minding because of the 'home atmosphere' – the children were thought to get more attention and be treated more like own children by a foster-parent; there was no need to take and fetch the children every day (often in the dark and cold); and the mother was free in the evenings to study or work the night shift.

Fostering can be considerably more expensive than daily minding, and a few West African families are undoubtedly better off than virtually all West Indians. Yet these differences do leave a considerable area of overlap, where there are West Africans who are as hard up as the typical West Indian family, but who still prefer to foster their children rather than send them to a daily minder. While there is probably an economic element in the choice between the two modes of care, impoverished West African parents do foster their children. Nor can this factor account for the explicit rejection of English foster-homes by West Indian parents.

Comparison of contemporary patterns of fostering in West Africa and the West Indies

We noted that there were two themes, one dominant and one subordinate, in West Indian fostering. The main theme is the caring for a child by the maternal grandmother when the mother is for some reason unable to do so herself. The

West African and West Indian immigrant families

Table 11-3. *Comparison of northern Ghana, southern Ghana and West Indian fostering relationships, by generation of foster-parent. (From totals of Tables 7-4 and 11-2)*

	Foster-parent is of:								
Population	Grand-parents' generation		Parents' generation		Child's generation		Not kin		Total N =	
Northern Ghana	80	(39%)	104	(50%)	12	(6%)	11	(5%)	207	(100%)
Southern Ghana	28	(15%)	88	(48%)	43	(23%)	24	(13%)	183	(100%)
West Indies	360	(63%)	65	(11%)	8	(1%)	134	(24%)	567	(100%)

secondary theme is the sending of a child to non-relatives in apprentice fosterage. Both are reflected in the summary figures for the West Indies in Table 11-3 (drawn from the totals of Table 11-2) where by far the majority of foster-parents are found in the grandparental generation, while the next largest category consists of non-kin. This pattern contrasts strongly with the relative lack of emphasis on the mother–daughter–granddaughter chain in West Africa. If we take the southern Ghana situation as reflecting a degree of occupational and social differentiation roughly equivalent to that in the West Indies,[7] we find that the majority of related foster-parents are in the parents' generation, that is, they are collateral rather than lineal kin. While the figures suggest that the resort to non-kin in apprentice fosterage is less pronounced in the Ghanaian samples, observations do not entirely support this finding. This may be because non-kin fostering is increasing rapidly at present, while the figures refer to the childhood of informants who were adults in the mid 1960s. Fostering by non-kin is definitely more common in southern Ghana than in the north where several samples had no instances, and the overall incidence is substantially below that in the south, and markedly lower than the figures for the West Indies. We have suggested that this is probably related to the greater occupational and social differentiation in the south, itself a response to increasing urbanization and industrialization.

But why should there be such a striking contrast between the West Indian preference for fostering by maternal grandmothers and the West African pattern of sending children to collateral kin of both parents? The analysis of West Indian material has indicated that two factors are critical in accounting for this bias. On the one hand, mothers are very often in need of someone to care for an infant while they work or establish a stable conjugal union. The woman on whom a mother has the strongest claim for such service is her own mother. On the other hand, older women are extremely anxious about what will become of them in old age, and one kind of provision they can make is to continue 'mothering' children after their own period of childbearing has ended. The children they have

247

the strongest claim to are pre-marital children of daughters (and less often, of their sons). Finally, the needs of daughter and mother coincide: the former is seeking to gain an additional child, the latter to delegate the care of an infant.

The dynamics behind the sending of children to be reared by their parents' siblings in West Africa is entirely different. Parents believe that they are likely to spoil their own child, while a relative will be more demanding. The purpose of (non-crisis) fostering is the education of the child as well as the fulfilment of kinship obligations which are recognized between full and often between classificatory siblings. To the extent that foster-parents in the grandparental generation are seeking domestic services rather than supplying training in adult skills,[8] then the preference for collateral kin also reflects the educational aspect of fosterage.

Finally, it should be emphasized that only very rarely are men stipulated as foster-parents (or 'keepers') in the West Indies, while the West African data show a rough balance between male and female foster-parents. This I take to reflect the essentially *nurturant* role of West Indian fosterage except where older children are sent to non-kin. The utilization of male foster-parents in West Africa corresponds to their function in *training* boys both in adult skills, and in manly virtues.

The differences reflected in Table 11-3 result in a distinctive 'shape' to fostering in West Africa and in the West Indies which may be summarized as follows:

West Africa	*West Indies*
Strong element of purposive fostering by kin	Emphasis on crisis fostering by kin, purposive fostering by non-kin
Most foster-parents are in parents' generation (i.e. collateral kin)	Most foster-parents are in grandparental generation (i.e. lineal kin)
Male foster-parents common	Male foster-parents rare
Model of fostering stresses the claims of foster-parent	Model of fostering stresses the needs of parent and child
Fostering kin are not necessarily primary kin of parents	Fostering kin tend to be primary kin of parents
Fostering links siblings' children (lateral linkage)	Fostering links generations (lineal linkage merging mother and her mother with the child)
Fostering does not change birth-status identity; status reciprocities unaltered	Fostering may change birth-status identity informally; no status reciprocities operate

Comparison of child-care arrangements by West Africans and West Indians in London

What then can we say about the observed difference between West Indians who refuse to consider placing their children with English foster-parents while in England, and the West Africans who favour this form of arrangement? We have seen that both groups must make some arrangements for their young children to allow them to pursue the goals for which they have come so far. And while economic factors would favour a higher incidence of fostering among West Africans than among West Indians, these factors are not sufficient to account for the complete rejection of English foster-parents by the latter group. Further, it is clear that both groups share the premiss that delegation of some aspects of the parents' roles may be in the best interests of both parent and child.

I would suggest that the difference lies in the cultural meaning of fostering to the two groups. For West Indians, the rearing of a young child by another woman involves the transfer of at least some (if not all) aspects of 'motherhood', with all the loyalties and obligations that arise out of childcare in the early years. So long as this transfer is used to reinforce the ties between a woman and her own mother, it is tolerated as necessary, though we have seen that feelings here may also be ambivalent. But to risk the loss of a child to a complete stranger – which is the implication of sending it to live with another family – this is simply unthinkable. The care offered by English foster-parents is not seen as offering any advantages to compensate for the threat to ties which the child will feel obliged to honour as an adult.

For West Africans, the meaning of fostering is different. Traditionally children were not sent away as infants, and a foster-parent is not seen as a substitute mother, but rather as providing character training and instruction. Where fostering occurs between kin, it is recognized as fulfilling (and creating) rights and obligations, but these in turn reinforce existing ties of a secondary nature rather than create a new set of primary ties (as happens between the West Indian child and the foster-parent who becomes a 'psychic mother'). The delay of fostering in West Africa until the child 'has sense' at six or seven is consistent with this pattern of augmenting existing ties rather than creating a new set of primary bonds. Early rearing reciprocities are already established between the mother and child, and reinforced by status reciprocities linking the child to both parents. Only the later reciprocities of rearing based on training in adult skills remain as a basis of bonding. When the parental roles are under strain in an immigrant situation, the West African response is also consistent with the traditional pattern. The roles of father and mother are seen as firmly established and not as liable to threat in a caretaking situation. The fostering experience is perceived as providing a service to parents and their children, and as being primarily educational and custodial in function (since no kinship obligations are involved in fostering by strangers).

12

Parenthood and social reproduction

It is time to pull together a number of themes underlying the various studies in this book: one such theme is the very stress on parenthood that characterizes West African societies; another is the rich variation in the specific institutionalized forms of delegation of parent roles; another is the recurrent puzzle as to why in some societies all parent roles are filled by one set of parent figures while in others some roles are delegated to pro-parents.

It is useful to begin with an apparent paradox: There are two major features of West African parenthood which are strikingly distinctive, and yet which appear to be contradictory. Any attempt to describe the basic themes of West African parenthood must confront this contradiction. For a consistent and obtrusive theme in the ethnographic literature of West Africa is the stress placed on parent–child relationships. This is reflected on many levels: in the great desire for children, in the strong bonds between parents and their children; in the many specific institutions concerned with allocating rights over children, and over women's childbearing powers; in such other institutions as the parental curse, the oath, the many forms of ancestrally focussed religion in which parental anger is projected and seen as responsible for misfortune; and, by no means least, in the forging of political institutions in the idiom of descent which uses one or another parent as a link between the domestic and the wider politico-jural domain (Fortes 1958, 1969). Indeed, it is probable that the strength of parent–child relations is in part due to the way in which parenthood is built upon in defining and legitimating supradomestic institutions. But to put it simply, in West Africa, parenthood *matters*.

The second major distinctive theme concerns the extremely wide-spread occurrence of a variety of practices - pawning, crisis and voluntary fostering, 'housemaids', educational fosterage, wardship, apprenticeship - which in one form or another involve the delegation of parental roles to others. These patterns of delegation of parenthood are not simply occasional statistical anomalies in the otherwise even flow of nuclear-family life. On the contrary, in each case they are formalized institutions, with beliefs, rules and sanctions elaborated, which, in

250

addition have sufficient incidence to form a significant aspect of childrearing in a given society. This proliferation of pro-parental institutions would seem to further emphasize the significance of parenthood in West African societies; parental roles are clearly currency of high value where social transactions are concerned. At the same time the stress on filial piety, and the parental rights and child resources which this represents, raises the question of how parents can be brought to part with rights over and custody of their own children. And this is the paradox: If parenthood is indeed as central to and in a real sense as sacred in West African society as the evidence suggests, how does it happen that the same societies have generated institutions dependent on the giving up of parental rights? And I would stress that these pro-parental institutions involve a child of anywhere from four to as old as ten years going to live with the pro-parent, until adulthood.

There is another tantalizing aspect of parental-role delegation in West Africa: Why is it that some societies have institutionalized the delegation of parental roles while others totally reject any such practice? Fortes' figures for the Tallensi show that of a sample of 170 children, only 2 per cent were living with neither parent (1949b:136). The regional comparison in Chapter 4 showed that many other northern Ghana societies also expect that children will be reared by their own parents.[1]

Further, among societies which have institutionalized fostering some send children only to kin (Kru) or mainly to kin (Gonja, Dagomba, Mossi) while there are others in which children are placed with strangers as well as with kin (Vai, Ibadan Hausa, Kanuri, Fanti, Ewe, Ga, Krobo). At first this suggests that there might be three different kinds of societies in West Africa: those in which no parental roles are delegated; those in which some roles are delegated to kin; and those in which some roles are delegated to strangers. There are interesting reasons why this cannot be the answer. In the first place, societies in which children are sent to strangers continue to send children to kin – so this represents a further elaboration of parental-role delegation rather than the substitution of one form for another. More significant, what members of a given society do about parental-role delegation seems to depend very much on the conditions in which they are living: Fraenkel writes of Creole families who have their own children at boarding schools abroad, send their illegitimate children to private schools in Monrovia, and allow their fostered children (wards), usually unrelated, to attend local schools, though perhaps not very regularly. These Creole families do not send their own children to other Liberian families to rear (Fraenkel 1964). But Creole families might well be among those West Africans studying and working in London who place their children in English homes from an early age, often until they are old enough to attend primary school. These families which foster in England include Ibo who do not traditionally foster children in West Africa. And indeed most of those who fostered their children in England said, in answer to our query, that they could not imagine any circumstances under which they would do so on returning to West Africa, 'since there is no one there better able to care for them than we are ourselves'.

This variation in the patterns of parental-role delegation in the same society under different conditions rules out the possibility that delegation is the result of some special definition of parenthood specific to certain societies. As the many cases of Ibo fostering in London make clear, there must be a basic West African conception of parenthood which is consistent with the delegation of certain aspects of parental roles under certain conditions. It must then be the conditions giving rise to role delegation that vary between societies, rather than the fundamental cultural definition of parenthood. Enid Schildkrout has noted that, in Kumasi, migrants from several different ethnic groups exchanged children in various fosterage arrangements, although linguistically and culturally they had little in common. She too suggests that this can only be understood if there is a common cultural definition of parenthood which transcends the boundaries of particular societies (Schildkrout 1973). I will return to the question of the nature of such a 'basic West African conception of parenthood' at the end of this chapter. But first we must pursue the paradox by looking more closely at the many forms of role delegation discussed in earlier chapters and at their systematic variation in relation to several structural constraints.

Varieties of fostering

My first experience with the delegation of parent roles was the Gonja institution of *kabello* - the rearing of boys by a male relative (*nyinipe*) and of girls by a female relative (*tchepe*). The Catholic priests who were working on Ngbanyito translated the terms for foster-child as 'servant'; to them the child's contribution to the domestic economy was the defining characteristic. But the Gonja insisted to me that the reason they sent their children away to kin was that it kept the kinsfolk in touch and ensured that the children would know their relatives in other towns. This was most directly put by the homily that 'a child must know both the mother's place [town] and the father's place [town]; the mother's people and the father's people'. Which interpretation is correct?

This question is raised in a more insistent form by the proliferation in West African societies of institutions which centre on the delgation of parent roles: the Dagomba *zuguliem*, and the rearing of princes by eunuchs; the Mossi *pogsioure*, and the sending of first-born sons to grow up with their maternal kin; Kanuri apprentice fosterage, and the placing of sons with politically important men; Hausa fostering of first-born children, the fostering of girls to link women in seclusion with the outside world, and complex forms of client fosterage; and the many modern forms of placing children with pro-parents - as housemaids, wards or apprentices; and in England the regular use of English foster-parents for infants and young children by West African families. Earlier chapters have shown how each of these forms can be 'explained' in particularistic terms arising

252

out of the special circumstances of the given society. Mossi and Hausa have a strong avoidance rule governing contact with first-born children, therefore they 'must' send them to be raised elsewhere; Gonja and Dagomba princes are at risk from jealous rivals if they remain in their paternal home, therefore they 'must' grow up in a safer place; Hausa women cannot leave their compounds to buy food or trade, therefore they 'must' have foster-daughters to help them when their own are grown up; Accra and Freetown housewives have too many responsibilities to be able to do their own domestic work, so they 'must' have wards and housemaids; a Ga or Fanti farmer-father cannot teach his son to repair radios or drive a lorry, therefore the son 'must' be apprenticed to another; and West African students in London cannot both work and study if there are babies to be cared for, so they 'must' send them to English foster-parents.

While persuasive reasons for each of these forms of delegation of parents' roles are readily offered by the participants, if one remains at this level there are as many reasons as there are particular forms. But are these really all quite different, independent institutions? Or is there some underlying common factor which 'explains' – on another level – why these societies delegate parental rearing roles when others in West Africa and indeed in many parts of the world do not? In order to begin to resolve this question, we must first see whether it is possible to order the patterns of parent-role allocation in West Africa in some systematic way. To balance the accounts already presented of the various forms of parent-role delegation, it is necessary to look briefly at parent-role delegation in segmentary societies like those analysed in Chapter 4, in which children were not sent away in long-term fostering.

1. Many accounts follow Fortes' classic paper 'Social and psychological aspects of education in Taleland' (1938) in describing how a boy learns to farm from his father, while a girl learns domestic skills from her mother. Children grow gradually more skilled and more responsible until they marry and establish domestic groups of their own. This might be described as the *father–son/mother–daughter* model of parenthood. Here all parental roles are the responsibility of a single pair of socially defined parents.

2. Several societies are characterized as following the father–son/mother-daughter model, but with children often going for visits to grandparents, during which time they are under the authority of, and trained by, the grandparent. Usually such visits are made to maternal grandparents or to mother's brother, since father's parents live with, or near to the child's own father and mother. This might be termed the *father–son/mother–daughter (visiting)* model of parenthood. Parents still perform all the parental roles, but occasionally share nurturance and training with close kin on a temporary basis.

3. There are a number of societies in which daughters are sent to very

253

close kin - an elder sister, a mother's mother - because of claims for assistance made on the basis of the kin tie. For instance, a girl may be sent to help her older sister when she first marries, or when she bears her first child. Daughters may also be sent to maternal grandmothers as companions and to help with domestic chores. It is likely that some accounts of pure father–son/mother–daughter rearing are incomplete, and that many if not most societies in West Africa have a pattern of daughters sometimes going to live with older female kin who need assistance. This might be called the *father–son/modified mother–daughter model*.

The various forms of institutionalized allocation and delegation of parent roles already discussed can be usefully grouped under the following headings.

4. There are some societies, matrilineal and double descent systems, in which the descent system splits paternal roles between father and mother's brother. In such systems children are usually reared by the father, but civil status/identity links them to their maternal kin and the mother's brother holds jural rights over them. In crises the mother's brother may also rear (train and sponsor) his sister's sons. Mother–daughter socialization is not affected by a mother's brother's claims, since daughters are reared by their mother in any case. The normal pattern is for father–son socialization (Rattray 1923; Fortes 1950). In these matrilineal and double descent systems alternative claims by mother's brothers to rear boys are contained within roles already exercising jural authority over the child, and we might term this a *shared mother's brother, father–son/mother–daughter model.* In terms of formal allocation of parental roles, the mother's brother is the source of status entitlements, while the father is responsible for training and sponsorship. (Nurturance, as is virtually always the case, is the primary responsibility of the mother.)

5. In those societies, like the Gonja, where kin of both parents are seen as having rights to rear children the result is *kinship fosterage*. Here both parent/child and foster-parent/foster-child roles are explicitly recognized. Boys are fostered as frequently as girls and there tends to be an explicit 'philosophy of education' which stresses the advantages of character development in sending a child to be reared away from home; parents are assumed to be inclined to spoil their own child through reluctance to employ proper discipline. Civil-status identity is unchanged by delegation of rearing, and continues to link the child to his original social parents. It is usually the training role which is delegated to kin, but sometimes sponsorship is undertaken by the foster-parents as well.

254

In many societies where kinship fosterage is common, other more functionally specific forms of parent-role delegation are also found.

6. Ethnographies of West African societies frequently mention the pawning of children, where they are sent to live with a creditor as surety on a debt (see Chapter 6). This in fact results in what amounts to *debt fosterage*. The cause of the arrangement is the parent's debt. But the *de facto* consequence is that the child is reared by a pro-parent during the period when she or he is learning adult role skills, and indeed it is the labour of the child in performing these role tasks which serves as interest on the parent's debt.

7. The placing of children with those who hold special occupational roles in order that they may learn these occupations occurs in the more highly differentiated societies. Among the Dagomba the *zuguliem* combines fostering by kin with training in special drumming and singing skills. Among the relatively more highly differentiated Hausa and Kanuri, boys join specialists in a variety of crafts as well as going to traders and Koranic scholars. Although the arrangement is specifically intended as a means of learning a specialist role, the relationship of the youth and his teacher is a diffuse one. The boy gives whatever help is required, both in the craft itself, and in farming, running errands, or carrying messages; in return he learns whatever economic and social skills are characteristic of the household. When a youth is placed with a mentor who occupies a special political, religious or economic role, it is assumed that he will learn, if he is keen and respectful, how to manage all aspects of that role. Further, it is understood that the teacher will take some measure of responsibility in helping him to get established on his own in adulthood. Because this model combines the diffuse responsibilities for training and sponsorship which characterize kinship fosterage, with an explicit emphasis on education in the more formal sense, it is useful to term it *apprentice fosterage*.

8. In some societies fostering is used to establish political alliances between a chief and his subjects. This takes many different forms, from the highly informal occasional practice in Gonja, to the placing of Dagomba princes with their fathers' eunuch courtiers, to the highly formalized Mossi *pogsiouri*. It appears to have been a common practice in the Hausa states and Bornu. Here we are dealing with *alliance fosterage*.

Apprentice fosterage sometimes takes on the additional character of alliance fosterage, where for instance parent and foster-parent cement their business relationship by the apprenticeship of a child of one to the other (see A. Cohen 1969 and Tahir 1976).

255

The types of parent-role delegation so far considered are drawn from accounts of traditional West African societies and there is no reason to suppose that Colonial administration, Christian education or the world market economy have significantly contributed to their form. This quite clearly cannot be maintained of those which follow, though the continuities with prior forms seem obvious.

'Wards' in Liberia and Sierra Leone are children placed with elite families, usually in the capital city, to work in exchange for an opportunity to learn elite ways, and sometimes to attend school. This appears to be a very long-standing practice, and the term in fact covers three rather different forms of role delegation which often appear separately in contemporary West African urban centres.

9. In Ghana the girls who live in other people's households to do domestic chores and look after children are known as housemaids. They may be kin (this tends to be preferred) or they may be from the home village, and thus known to the family, or they may be strangers. If not kin, some payment is usually made to the parents. If the housemaid is a relative there will be an expectation that she be allowed to go to school, but frequently they are expected to remain at home all the time since they are responsible for young children. There is a regular pattern of girls being brought from rural areas into the city to be housemaids. Here the parents hope that their daughter will learn 'city ways'. This use of domestic work as a means of access to a higher socio-economic stratum may be called *service fosterage.*

10. The great proliferation of new occupations in recent years has produced a situation in which there are very few opportunities for formal training, and few kinsmen as yet in a position to pass on their skills. The most common solution has been some form of *apprenticeship*, in which the youth works for a master for some years, during which time he learns 'the secrets of the craft'. A money payment is frequently, though not always, required by the master, who may or may not take responsibility for helping the trained apprentice become established in his own right. Where a youth is formally apprenticed to a kinsman *apprentice fosterage* conveys the combination of formal training and diffuse kin-based obligation which is involved.

11. With the growing importance attached to literacy in English and to occupations based on a Western education, those in professional and whitecollar occupations, particularly teachers, have immense prestige as controllers of the new system of knowledge and hence of the positions to which it grants access. There has thus grown up the practice of *educational fosterage*; the sending of children to live with those who are educated, frequently, but not always, relatives. Creole wards tended to be non-Creole – either Liberated Africans or from the tribal people.

Very often nowadays it would be possible for the child to attend school at home, but the parents hope that by living with educated people it will be easier for the child to successfully complete school. They also hope that the fostering family will feel an obligation to act as sponsor when the child finishes school, either by assisting with further education or by finding a suitable, white-collar, job.[2]

12. The placing of infants and young children with English families by their West African student parents (Chapter 10) constitutes what might be called *nurturant/educational fosterage*: 'Nurturant' because the manifest purpose is to care for the child in healthy surroundings with more attention than the parents are able to provide; but 'educational', too, since the parents seek out English foster-parents who can enable the child to learn English as a first language, and give it an easy familiarity with English culture.

These different ways of delegating parental roles can be seen to fall into three sets. First, there are those where the rearing and sponsorship roles are performed by the child's social parents, unless a crisis occurs which makes this impossible. Visits to close kin and occasional exceptions do not affect the norm about who should rear children. These are unitary parental rearing forms (1–3).

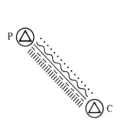

Where P ⬲ = parents*

C ⬲ = child*

—————— = bonds of bearing / begetting

∿∿ = birth-status identity

– – – = nurturance reciprocities

······ = training reciprocities

‖‖‖‖‖‖ = sponsorship reciprocities

* For some purposes it is necessary to differentiate between parents and/or children by sex. Where this is not critical no distinction is made for the sake of clarity of presentation.

Figure 12-1. Unitary parental rearing model

Then there are the forms involving distribution of parent roles among kin. These are the kin sharing forms (4 and 5). Finally, there are the forms of parental role delegation to non-kin (forms 6-12). We have seen that systems of this third sort

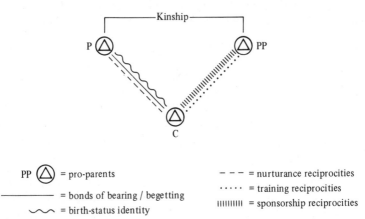

Figure 12-2. Kin rearing model

are found both in so-called traditional West African societies (Kanuri, northern Hausa) and in societies strongly influenced by the literate-Christian ethos and/or the modern economy (Ibadan Hausa, Monrovian and Freetown Creole, modern Ga, Ewe, and Fanti).

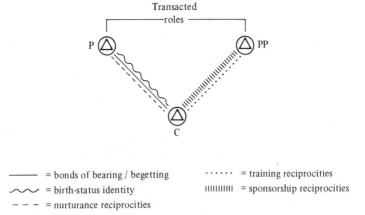

Figure 12-3. Non-kin rearing model

258

Parenthood and social reproduction

These three models of distributing parent roles are related to other institutions in certain regular ways. First, those societies in which allocation of parent roles is restricted to the jural parents tend to be stateless systems characterized by unilineal descent groups (see Chapter 4). On the other hand, societies in which one or another form of institutionalized delegation is common have some kind of centralized political structure. They may be kingdoms in which descent groups are weak or non-existent, like the Dagomba or Hausa; they may be kingdoms like Gonja where kinship is bilateral although descent groups continue to play a part in some commoner enclaves (Vagala and the Tampolensi); or they may be small, coastal town-states like the Ga and Fanti where descent groups were the basis of a form of representative government. The relevant factor is the change in the nature of unilineal descent groups in the context of a state system with its more complex exchange systems, division of labour, centralization of the control of force, and hierarchy of social groups.

Second, societies in which delegating parent roles is normal and institutionalized tend to be internally differentiated, in terms of the kinds of status identity conveyed at birth (e.g. Gonja estates), or of occupations, or of lifestyle and socio-economic status, and often in all these ways.

These regularities raise three complementary questions:

1. What is it about segmentary societies that leads to a concentration of parent roles?

2. What is it about internal differentiation which is associated with the delegation of some parent roles?

3. What accounts for the distinction between kin-rearing models and non-kin rearing models?

The major locus of factors critical in answering these questions lies at the level of the social structure. But before exploring further the nature of segmentary societies and the internal differentiation found in varying degree in centralized systems, it is necessary to turn to another set of influences on the allocation of parent roles. These arise from the very exercising of parent roles. And it would be wrong to see parenthood as entirely determined by external 'system' factors. Family life has dynamics of its own, and these dynamics make a given parental strategy more adaptive under certain external system conditions than under others. When this happens systematically, the result is institutionalization of one of the particular forms of role delegation we have found. The particular dynamics which are discussed here have emerged from in-depth studies of a few African societies; there are no doubt others which could be added. This account is not intended to be definitive, but rather to rough in examples of one sort of constraint on parental-role strategies.

Dynamics arising from activating parent roles

Intergenerational tensions

It can hardly be accidental that recent contributions to the understanding of intergenerational tensions - especially those between parent and child - have come from students of the West African family. What is it then about the West African family which has made the study of intergenerational tension there so fruitful? Not, I think, anything about parent–child relationships themselves, nor to do with polygyny, but rather, as the classic studies show, it is the embedding of the elementary family within a descent group polity which strengthens its power over its members, and in so doing magnifies certain tensions between them. Fortes (1949b; 1959; 1961) and Middleton (1960) have shown how the authority of elders over the younger generation, which also reinforces the father's authority over his son, is reflected in beliefs about the importance of obedience and respect for one's elders and the projection of these beliefs onto ancestors in seeking explanations for illness and misfortune. But these are not simply passive beliefs. They structure relations within the family, and between members of the lineage. Among the Tallensi (as with many West African peoples) sacrifices which are vital to the welfare of the descent group and the community may not be performed while there is quarrelling within the lineage. Tensions must be formally resolved for the good of the group. Middleton has shown how elders use their power to speak with the ancestors to control dissident members of the local descent group. Elders claim their words to the ancestors as the cause of their subordinates' illness and misfortune, and thus obedience and respect are the only sure way to health and prosperity among the Lugbara.

In his study comparing LoDagaba and LoWiili of northern Ghana, Jack Goody has shown the central role played by tensions surrounding the inheritance of property within the local descent group. Major sacrifices tended to be offered by sons in the latter group and by sister's sons in the former, and this corresponds with the transmission of wealth, including the cows used in sacrifices - for inheritance is patrilineal among the LoWiili while wealth passes to matrilineal kin among the LoDagaba. Such a major sacrifice by the heir can be seen either as the return of the property to its original owner, or as an attempt to expiate the guilt felt over the anticipation of, and perhaps even gratification felt on, the previous holder's death (J. Goody, 1962).

In many West African societies the intensity of interpersonal, and particularly close intergenerational, relationships is reflected in the institutions of ancestor worship, the fear of the parental curse, in patterns of witchcraft accusation and particularly in institutionalized avoidances between a man and his first-born son (see Chapter 5).

What is particularly interesting here is that while there are many West African societies in which there is formal avoidance between a man and his first-born son – Tallensi, Gonja, Mossi, and Hausa are all clear cases – only those societies having other forms of institutionalized delegation of parent roles handle this avoidance by sending the first son to grow up with other kin. Of itself the avoidance is not sufficient stimulus for sending children away from home. Fortes has described the way in which the Tallensi manage it through ritual prohibitions. But where delegation of training and sponsorship are accepted as ways of allocating parental roles, then first-born sons (and indeed first-born daughters among the Hausa) are often placed with foster-parents.

The general point is that there are powerful centrifugal forces between close kin which would, if unchecked, act to separate the generations. The major constraints on dispersion of close kin in the traditional segmentary systems, lay in the significance of the descent group as a political unit, indeed as the only political unit. Thus descent group membership was identical with civil status, and to break away from one's lineage was to become a stateless person without protection of one's kin, without right in land or access to the shrines which alone ensured health and fertility.

In simple differentiated states, the population density is often low (and access to land thus no problem), and descent groups tend to be weak or non-existent, with ties to kin distributed among several communities. At the same time, centralized government usually guaranteed safety of travel. Some, though not all, of the rights of citizenship are linked to residence in village, rather than to kinship. Here, where the kin group is dispersed, and no longer the sole determinant of civil status, there are fewer constraints balancing the centrifugal force represented by tensions between close kin. In these systems there is often a recognized period in late adolescence and early adulthood during which youths 'roam about' visiting kin in other towns, trying their hand at hunting or trading, and generally seeing the world before settling down to the responsibilities of adulthood. The Gonja phrase is *ba ji kalumbo* – they walk about. However, the Gonja say that a man will always eventually return to his father's home town, because it is there that his people, and his prospects lie. Only in his father's town may a man hold office, and only there will he be likely to succeed to the headship of a local kin group which also provides a recognized position of authority (see E. Goody 1973, ch. 11). In other words, in this simple differentiated state, civil status and kinship ties still provide a valued form of identity, and access to significant statuses. But the major economic resources are not monopolized by the kin group, and the pattern of intergenerational relationships is much more open than in the segmentary polities. These relational dynamics centering on holder–heir and successor-incumbent tensions, and the succession of the generations grow out of, or are exaggerated by, what I have called the status entitlement aspects of parenthood, rights to office and property.

The dynamics of informal learning

The rearing roles are also a source of dynamic in the structuring of parenthood. Closely related to intergenerational tensions is the nature of teaching in pre-literate societies as it has been studied in northern Ghana. Fortes again has provided the classic account in his 1938 paper, where he outlines the three fundamental learning processes, mimesis, identification and cooperation. Children learn from older children, from their parents and from other adults; and they learn in two major contexts (which often merge). Children are from the very beginning expected to make a contribution to the domestic and agricultural economies according to their abilities. Girls are given a broom or tiny water pot, or set to watch their younger siblings; boys have the job of gathering in the chickens, and later the goats, and cows, and are set to scare birds from ripening grain long before they can do the heavy work of farming. These tasks make a real contribution to meeting the needs of the household, and Fortes concludes that 'the child's training in duty and skill is always socially productive and thus psychologically worth while to him; it can never become artificial or boring' (Fortes 1970: 243-4). So the first major context of learning is that of adult occupational roles, scaled down to the child's strength and understanding. The second context is play, and Fortes shows how in play mimesis and identification reinforce the skills and the cognitive schemata on which learning and development depend.

This Mimesis/Identification/Cooperation model is important for understanding informal education, in part because it fits so well and describes so clearly much of what is occurring. But, more than this, it allows us to understand the kinds of contraints placed on informal learning; to recognize the conditions under which informal education is most effective. Specifically, there must be provision for mimesis, identification and cooperation. One of the striking features of the institutions which have grown up around the delegation of rearing roles for children and adolescents is the diffuse definition of the role responsibilities. Even where a child is sent to learn a specific occupational skill, he or she is often expected to live with the teacher, to show proper filial respect and obedience, and to carry out a range of domestic tasks which have no obvious relationship to the skills being taught. (I once asked a youth learning to drive a lorry what he did for his master – meaning, what aspects of care of the lorry, collecting passengers' fares and so on, he was responsible for. His answer was that he did his master's washing, fetched his meals, and swept the room.) The teacher–pupil relationship is part of a wider rearing relationship between pro-parent and child (or adult/child or superior/subordinate), and not functionally specific to the particular skill being taught; just as the child learns by 'watching and doing' rather than by formal instruction and artificial exercises.

This stress on close involvement between teacher and pupil leads inevitably to its own kind of tension which is only partially moderated by the fact that mimesis, identification and cooperation also occur in relation to peers and several adult figures, and not with a parent alone. For the fact that the 'teacher' role is one aspect of the parental-role set means that it is combined with roles of nurturant-socializer, holder of domestic authority, controller of adult resources and spokesman for the ancestors. And the teacher/father is also the one who mediates between his son and the rest of the community as head of the lineage segment or family in which his civil status is vested. Since informal education is built on a multiplex relationship with those who serve as teacher/model, when this role coincides with other parental roles as well, the relationship is inevitably intense, and centrifugal forces augmented. This follows from the nature of the set of parental roles as it has been outlined, and from Fortes' Mimesis, Identification, Cooperation model. But it is far more than a deduction. It is often made explicit in discussions about training. In Gonja, for instance, there is a recognized preference among weavers for sending a son to learn the craft from a relative, since it is felt that the father would not be a good teacher. Brothers may exchange sons, and no shift of residence, meals or other responsibilites may be involved, save that the youths are not learning from and working for their fathers.

Control over resources vested in the kin group

In segmentary polities the major productive resources are rights in land, rights in capital (usually cattle, sometimes special currency such as cowries or brass rods) and rights in persons – rights to defence and labour from men of the kin group, and rights to control and dispose of the fertility of daughters, sisters and wives. It seems probable that the ability of the domestic family in segmentary systems to contain the centrifugal forces tending to push youths out of the local lineage and domestic group of their parents is linked to this pre-emptive control by the descent group over productive and reproductive resources; and, I would add, over the civil identity of its members. In productive systems which rely on labour from youths and young men, there is a potential problem in securing enough labour from youths, as well as with retaining them as members of the domestic productive unit in adulthood. For under some conditions the youth can threaten to withdraw both his labour in the present and his membership of the family productive unit in adulthood. Such a threat is probably seldom explicit, but unless the domestic family is part of a group which holds pre-emptive rights over major productive resources, or over specially valued resources, there is little to prevent a young man from moving out to establish his own productive unit. The residence of adolescent and adult sons apart from their fathers in central Gonja (E. Goody 1973, chs 10 and 11) illustrates this very clearly.

Many West Africa societies meet this problem by making relatively light demands on youths. This is quite a different pattern from that met in training girls, who are in a subordinate role by sex as well as age, and will in any case marry out of the domestic productive unit.[3] The Gonja, for instance, do not force a boy to go to the farm, or at least they will be cautious about adding force to persuasion. If a youth persistently refuses to go to the farm, he is left to sit in the village, to find employment 'more suitable to his character'. Typical ethnographic accounts of the contribution of boys to farming elsewhere note that they scare away birds from ripening grain, and fetch water for the men who are clearing, hoeing, or making mounds – the really heavy work. It is often suggested that up to the age of 16 or 17 a youth is not strong enough to do more. Yet I have seen boys of 11 and 12 working alongside the men in a cooperative hoeing party, where food and beer are brought into the fields, and songs and joking add zest to the work. If the goal were the maximum amount of output from each member of the domestic group, then boys (in contrast to girls) could in fact work much harder than they do in Gonja. It seems that there is a greater concern with long-term relationships between men and their adult sons, than with extracting the most possible work from adolescents. 'If you force a boy to farm, he will leave you later' I was once told. And, even more explicitly, in studying weavers' training of their children, it was explained that if boys were forced to work at the weaving sheds too young, they would come to be rebellious. It was better to leave a boy of 7 to 10 or 11 to roam about with his friends. When he was ready he would ask to join the weavers. This is the more striking as younger boys – of 5 and 6 – are cajoled into helping with a number of tedious but simple tasks. At this age they are still biddable. But to insist on help from older boys would lead to conflict and confrontation, and the weavers have come to feel that in the long run it is better to forego the child's help at this period, since he will in adolescence almost certainly return of his own free will. This for two reasons. First, because it is a matter of pride to adolescent boys to be able to weave with their elders. And second, because this has been the only way they can get shirts and trousers, shoes and cash and ultimately a wife.

Another common pattern, in northern Ghana as elsewhere on the continent, is for youths to be given tasks which allow them a large measure of autonomy. Herding of small stock, sometimes of a few cattle (large herds are usually placed in the care of a 'Fulani' herdsman) or the responsibility for keeping birds out of growing grain are all tasks in which a number of boys can combine work with games, often also learning to use a bow and arrow and to trap small animals. These are also occupations in which the boys have little supervision, but are left to themselves, often from early morning until nightfall. Thus there is a minimum of friction between men and their sons over economic tasks so long as the grain ripens and the goats and cattle don't stray. Another index of the delicate power balance between parents and youths is the parents' recognition of the rights a boy acquires by virtue of his work. Fortes has neatly documented this for the Tallensi (1970:228).

The elaborate age-set systems of east and south African cattle-keeping peoples can also be seen as a way in which the young men are allotted the task of caring for the society's major resources – cattle – without themselves as yet having rights in the herd. By withdrawing entirely, and leaving the youths to establish their own miniature society the parental generation avoids open conflict. The Nyakusa age-set villages are an extreme example, but many systems have rules prohibiting young men who are herding and guarding cattle from sleeping within the villages or, as among the Samburu, from eating food cooked by women. That the young men do not simply go off with the cattle and establish their own separate communities is due to their dependence on their elders for wives and entry into the higher ranks of the age-set system, both of which are valued resources in these societies.

The paradox of adolescent labour

It is difficult to assess just how important a contribution older children and adolescents make to subsistence production, for the reasons outlined above. Labour is likely to be the most important scarce productive resource in systems based on extensive cultivation without modern technology, under which heading I include the plough as well as irrigation, use of fertilizers, etc. (see J. Goody 1976). Yet in Gonja youths are said not to be capable of the major farming tasks, and there are serious constraints on exerting too much pressure on them to work for the family productive unit. (It is probably not accidental that in segmentary polities, working for future in-laws is often an important part of the transactions which gains a man rights in his bride.) In petty-commodity production, iron-working, pottery, and weaving, the assistance of unskilled youths is also valuable, and can be a crucial factor in releasing adults for more highly skilled work. Indeed, in craft production, as in many modern trades, there is less emphasis on strength and stamina than is the case in subsistence agriculture, and more need of many hands for relatively simple, but repetitive work for certain phases of the productive process. To the extent that this is the case, child and adolescent labour become more valuable, despite the greater skill needed to complete the product. (Tailors, weavers and butchers all organize their work so that less-skilled aspects can be delegated to unskilled youths. I suspect that this would also prove to be true of other crafts if they were considered from this point of view.)

The paradox of adolescent labour arises from the fact that in certain conditions parents seem to get relatively little work out of their own sons, at least during late childhood and early adolescence – say between the ages of 8 and 16 – even in 'scarce labour' systems. It is when sons are sent to be trained by relatives, or are apprenticed to strangers, or placed in houses of the elite as wards, that they really work very hard indeed. This would seem to be related to the tensions arising from various aspects of the parental role which I have already noted. And it goes some way to explaining the related paradox that in simple

Beyond West Africa

differentiated states in West Africa, parents are willing to forego the labour of their sons as they must do in sending them to foster-parents. For the obvious 'explanation' of fostering as a way of rationalizing the distribution of adolescent labour between households fails to account for the fact that the people who receive foster-children are often those who have least need of assistance, while those sending them may thus lose the only help available (see E. Goody 1970b for cases).

There are other strands to the explanation of parents' willingness to lose the labour of adolescents, which have to do with the dispersal of kin who can make claims on one another's children, and with the consequences of socio-economic and political differentiation which distinguishes the simple differentiated states from segmentary polities. Here I am concerned with the dynamics of parental-role allocation which grow out of the nature of parental roles themselves.

The dynamics of respect

One of the central idioms of social relations in West African societies is respect for one's seniors, and this is equally true within the kin group and in the political sphere. This concern for recognition of relative status, and the according of respect to all those deemed senior has been institutionalized in ancestor worship, in greeting and gift-giving rituals, and forms of address, in many ceremonies of precedence, and indeed is evident in many kinship terminologies. In Ngbanyito, for instance, the only distinction among relatives of one's own generation which must be made is that between those younger and those older than oneself. Sex need not be indicated, but age relative to ego is always important. And towards one who is older, even by a day, one must show obedience and respect, and above all never show anger or disagree. The typical sanction for lack of respect to a senior kinsman or kinswoman is that the ancestors will 'hear' them complaining of this shameful treatment and punish the offender, whether the insulted kinsman wishes this or not. The extreme sanction for disrespect from a child is a parent's curse, which again (in Gonja at least) need not necessarily be intended by the parent, for 'the spirits see into the heart of the one who is insulted by his child and see how unhappy he is made, and they will not agree' (i.e. they will punish the child).

The preoccupation with respect is just as much a central feature of community and political relations as it is of relations between kin.[4] Nor is this resemblance accidental. For the giving of respect is an essentially political act. This is very clear in M. G. Smith's account of gift-giving to political superiors in the Hausa emirate of Zaria (1955:11 and *passim*). The head of a large kinship group had, in traditional societies, by this very fact also a political role in the community. And conversely, any holder of office who has no followers to demonstrate their loyalty by the public rendering of respect cannot hope to be accorded the prestige to which his office entitles him. No doubt followers are always a key element in the development of political authority,[5] but in systems of extensive cultivation where labour is scarce, the labour a man can command directly influences the amount of land he can cultivate, and hence his wealth. In the absence of plough, wheel or modern means of harnessing energy for productive effort, labour rather than land or capital becomes the critical limiting factor in production. Under these conditions the number of people who work for one is directly related to both wealth and status. Since the payment of respect implies obedience, those who tender respect can be called upon for assistance. (Though in most cases this will never be tested.) The link between respect and labour is also seen in the common rule that a chief should not himself work on the farm; instead he ought, the Gonja say, to remain in his council hall to receive the greetings of his subjects, supplicants and strangers.

One of the consequences of delegating the training or sponsorship of a child is that the pro-parent receives the deference and respect of that child, as well as controlling his labour. Furthermore, in becoming a dependant of his pro-parent the child adds to the number of those who are seen to be his followers and supporters. There is thus a quasi-political element in the rearing of other people's children which is occasionally, as with the placing of children with important officials among the Kanuri (R. Cohen 1967) or the Mossi institution of *pogsioure*, given institutional recognition (Chapter 5).

Even where this political element is not explicit, it often remains as an underlying theme. In Gonja, poor relations may place a child with a chief as his horse-boy, not only to give the youth a chance to make useful contacts at court, but to show their own respect for the chief, and as an acknowledgement of his right to make claims on their children. (And of course with a son as the chief's horse-boy other members of the family can be sure of hospitality at court, and perhaps an ear for their troubles.) More generally, the claiming of rights in relatives' children (or occasionally, as among the Mossi, in subjects' children) is an assertion of rights in resources. If the claim is successful, it is evidence of superior authority – or power – and at the same time initiates a relationship of pro-parenthood which sets up counter-rights and ultimately counter-claims framed in the same idiom of respect.

Social structural constraints on strategies for allocation of parent roles

We are now in a better position to ask why it should be that segmentary polities are characterized by unitary parent roles, and what it is about centralized states which, in West Africa, is associated with the elaboration of so many different forms of delegation of training and sponsorship. The answer to the third question, concerning the conditions which make the delegation of rearing roles to non-kin effective, follows from the first two.

267

Beyond West Africa

Segmentary societies

In societies which anthropologists have tended to call 'acephalous' or 'segmentary', citizenship, the rights to basic resources, and relations with communities outside one's own, all depend on lineage membership. For example, where descent is defined patrilineally, the lineage group in turn depends on retaining control over its males, who are themselves both a productive resource and the basis of political relations of defence and attack, of feud and war, as well as of its daughters whose marriages must bring in bridewealth if sons are to have wives. Such a situation is overdetermined. A man cannot assume adult status, with full access to land, shrines and a wife, except as an agnatic member of his lineage community. Therefore to send him outside this community for training or sponsorship cannot enhance his adult status, and may both weaken his own community and threaten that into which he is sent. Where access to full adult citizenship and productive resources is channelled through lineage membership, only the family of jural identity can provide these resources.

There is an important escape clause in many patrilineal societies which allows men to borrow resources from their mother's local descent group. The mother's home may also serve as a refuge for a youth who quarrels with his agnates. The significant thing about this strategy is that, while allowing some play in an otherwise rigid system, the right to use land is provisional and the maternal descent group retains control. Further, even if a youth decides to settle permanently with the people of his mother's descent group, there are critical ways in which he may not assume full rights of the sort any lineage member is entitled to. Among the Tallensi, for instance, these disabilities are linked to the all-important sacrifices to lineage ancestors which only descendants through men may perform. The Tiv say that when a man settles in his maternal home, it takes five generations until his descendants build up a full set of agnatic links, with the rights and duties this entails. This is a particularly clear way of expressing the difference in birth-status rights of the children of male lineage members and a woman's child.

While the training or sponsorship of children by non-lineage kin would place them at a disadvantage in relation to lineage resources, they could of course be reared by the father's agnates (in a patrilineal system) or by mother's uterine kin (in a matrilineal one). In fact this does not seem to happen in segmentary societies. This may well be due to lack of difference in status and resources held by members of the same descent group, particularly where inheritance is lateral, between brothers, so that the children of all the brothers have equal rights to parental resources. Furthermore, rearing by lineage kin typically would mean that the child remained in the same place. In a patrilineal system a boy would be exchanging a mother's care for that of a classificatory co-wife, often considered a dangerous situation; and he would very likely be farming the same fields whether he was reared by a father or father's brother. It is interesting,

268

however, that in centralized systems where resources tend to be more differen-
tially distributed youths are sometimes sent to kin within the lineage (Ga, Krobo
and Mossi).

West African segmentary societies are characterized by a balance between the
centrifugal forces represented by holder–heir and incumbent–successor tensions
(reflected in parent–child respect and avoidance) and the ambivalence generated
by informal learning on the one hand, and the constraints imposed by the
anchoring of civil status and access to valuable resources in the descent group on
the other. The precarious nature of this balance is often reflected in descent-
group fission and migratory drift. But the domestic group remains the basic productive unit, and typically fission occurs between domestic groups or at a higher
level in the lineage. Parents and their children remain living and working together.

Simple differentiated states

If the relationship between segmentary societies and rejection of fostering is
based on the pre-emptive role played by the local descent group in claims to
citizenship, protection of rights and productive property, resources and adult
status, then what are the significant changes in centralized societies related to
the delegation of parental roles? It would be wrong, both theoretically and empirically, to offer a simple equation between absence of lineages and presence of
fostering. There clearly is a link of this kind, but not a direct one, as indicated
by the co-existence of patrilineages and institutionalized fostering among the
Mossi, Ga, and Krobo.

As I tried to show in Chapter 6, lineages play a different role in the small,
coastal town states than in the segmentary systems of the north. First, in the
coastal states there is a politico-ritual division of labour such that the relationships between lineages are governed by functional interdependence, with the
elders of the different lineages jointly forming the government.[6] Typically there
are courts and a system of appeals for the protection of individual rights, and a
framework for mobilizing the men of all the constituent lineages for defence, or,
exceptionally, attack. Military mobilization was sometimes on a lineage basis,
but among the Fanti the military companies (*asafo*) recruited their members on
the basis of patrifiliation, thus completely cross-cutting the matrilineages. There
are thus supralineage institutions of government, justice and warfare which limit
the actions of the constituent lineages and their individual members. The same
is true of the Mossi commoner descent groups. The lineage structure is important
because it defines access to political, military and religious offices, and is in some
cases a main focus of residence. But these structures are nonetheless significantly
different from those in stateless systems.

On the economic level, individuals have different occupations and prosper to
different degrees, which again affects lineage structure. In the coastal states this
differentiation is clearly related to the long-standing influence of external

market forces. Individuals were involved in trading, brokerage, in acting as middlemen between producers, long-distance traders and European merchants, and in all the myriad services that arise to facilitate international marketing; the result was a considerable degree of socio-economic differentiation.

In contrasting the role of lineages in stateless societies with their role in centralized systems, the crucial factor is the extent to which the lineage pre-empts all aspects of adult status and achievement. With political centralization in the state systems, and with greater economic differentiation, new occupational roles appear, and the opportunity for political alliances and the establishment of dependency relationships with powerful figures all become significant factors in social life, and hence in getting established successfully as an adult. These new occupational and political opportunities may occur within or outside the lineage, and within or outside the more diffusely defined field of cognatic kinship. If parents are limited to seeking assistance in the training and sponsorship of a child from among their lineage kin, they will be in a strong position to *claim* such help, but the range of opportunities secured may be relatively narrow. If, on the other hand, claims may be validly made on a wide range of relatives, then opportunities for occupational, political and social mobility will be substantially increased.

Where social differentiation is combined with a weakening of the pre-emptive control by descent groups on key resources as in the centralized states, then parents may seek to arrange more advantageous forms of training and sponsorship than they themselves can provide. At the same time, political centralization results in greater ease of travel and the traditional West African savannah states were, apparently without exception, associated with centres of local and long-distance trade. Thus weakening of descent groups, political centralization and economic efflorescence often occur together.

Nevertheless, an individual's claims on the basis of birth-status entitlement are still significant – for office, placement (i.e. identity), and inheritance of property. There is thus a premium placed on retaining these rights, even though the descent group tends to weaken.

The most significant feature of these centralized systems is internal differentiation. This appears in many different forms: ethnic heterogeneity, spatial dispersion, occupational differentiation, political stratification. In the simpler savannah states this differentiation is accompanied by open connubium – that is, marriage between individuals of different positions in the system. The result is that claims on kin continue to be of primary significance, but kin are not grouped into corporate unilineal descent groups, with joint rights in a clearly delimited set of resources – but, rather, dispersed among ethnically, occupationally, and politically differentiated groups which are often themselves spatially scattered. Men can make claims on child resources of collateral kin, and a parent is presented with choices about which of the available skill or patronage resources he wishes to assert specific claims to by means of delegation of parent

270

roles. And, given choice plus dispersal, the asserting of claims based on birth status is no longer a quasi-automatic process dependent on seniority and age, as in segmentary systems. Instead, if claims are to be made on resources vested in or managed by kin other than own parents, some positive act must occur. The norm of joint rights in corporately held property, office and status remains very strong. Yet these claims tend to overlap since they are defined by cognatic rather than unilineal kinship. It is therefore important to reinforce *de jure* rights with freshly created obligations. It is just this which fostering does, through the generation of rearing reciprocities. The parent's sibling who has lived for years in a distant town becomes, through fostering, a pro-parent whose own children are more like brothers and sisters than distant cousins. And when either the parent or the foster-parent dies, the siblings and their children have shared experiences as well as shared rights to serve as a basis for settling the inheritance.

In societies with institutionalized kinship fosterage, the domestic group is still closely identified with the productive unit, but the basis of recruitment to the domestic group shifts from pre-emptive rights in women's reproductive powers (as in segmentary systems) to the assertion of claims on the child resources of the (non-localized) kin group. Children's labour is a valued resource in itself, but a parent will forgo his own rights to his child's labour either because of the strength of kinsmen's claims (usually supernaturally sanctioned), because of the potential advantages to the child, because delegating the rearing of a child is one very effective way of managing the constraints of parent–child avoidance, or, perhaps most usual, a combination of these factors.

The delegation of training and sponsorship roles in simple differentiated systems thus has multiple functions. But the fundamental characteristic is that children are sent to kin, and that the transaction represents, for both parties, an effective assertion of claims to resources in children; to their companionship, labour, and to the rights to which the rearing relationship gives rise. Adults thus seek control over the human resources to which their kinship statuses entitle them; parents seek the best training and sponsorship arrangements for their children. And, with differential rewards to offer, followers can indeed be attracted. The result is a dynamic propelled by the twin, and complementary, forces of the less-well-endowed seeking advantage, and the better-off seeking followers. Yet this is still conducted within the nexus of kinship and in the idiom of kinship rights and obligations; it is a system based on claims validated through kinship.

The coastal town states: An intermedial category

In their explicit stress on the claims and obligations of kin in the allocation of parent roles, the Ga and Krobo resemble the simple differentiated states. Yet they also participate in the more functionally specific forms of parent-role delegation which characterize more complex and hierarchical states (see below).

Beyond West Africa

In the coastal town states where lineages acted as the basis for representative government both local endogamy and in some cases marriage within the lineage counteracted the tendency towards open kin groups. Endogamy was sometimes explicitly designed to retain resources within the lineage segment, and Field reports that it occurs in families that have become rich or have particularly valued offices (1937). As this suggests, market forces have resulted in marked differentiation within the local community. Rearing of children by kin existed in institutionalized form among the Ga and the Krobo in the mid-twentieth century. It is not clear whether delegation of parent roles was traditionally institutionalized in Ewe and Fanti society.[7] At the time of the surveys reported in Chapter 6 (1964–5) children of all four societies were frequently reared by kin and a small proportion were being sent to non-kin. Although the survey communities were not 'urban' in terms of population size, southern Ghana in the mid-twentieth century was an urban society in terms of the economic interdependence of its constituent communities.

Whereas the emphasis in the simple differentiated savannah states like Gonja and Dagomba is on the rights to rear children of kin (often backed by supernatural sanctions), in the coastal town states more stress is placed on the benefits to the child and sometimes to the parents. Azu's account of traditional Ga fosterage scarcely mentions rights to rear children but is very explicit about the service and training aspects. However, kinship sentiments remain central to the dynamic. As one survey informant said, 'I reared my sister's child out of love'.

More complex hierarchical states

It has been argued that, in the simple states, the dynamic maintaining parental-role delegation, and underlying the several specific functions it can be shown to fill, is the pressing of claims based on kinship rights: claims to resources on the one hand, and to child labour and companionship on the other. But the ethnographic material is rich with forms of training and sponsorship which do not depend on kinship. Does this mean that we were misled about the importance of kinship, or perhaps that these other forms are quite different and unrelated to kinship fosterage? No, for the confusion is resolved if instead of thinking in terms of a dichotomy between segmentary systems which do not delegate parent roles, and centralized ones which do, one looks more closely at the variations among the centralized states. For what seems to be happening is that as they become more internally differentiated and more hierarchical, the placing of children with kin continues, but is augmented by various functionally specific institutions which draw upon non-relatives. How this happens is best understood by looking at the most complex West African societies.

In comparison with the simple states of northern Ghana, these systems involve greater differentiation in wealth, socio-economic status, occupations, political power and style of life. *Cultural* differences are highly significant for ranking purposes, and ranking is a general preoccupation. Among the traditional complex hierarchical systems in West Africa, it is usually only the ruling group which retains effective descent groups. Inheritance appears to be biased towards lineality (father to son) rather than laterality (between brothers), and effective claims can only be made on close kin. Social mobility is a central feature of these systems in West Africa (unlike their highly stratified equivalents on the Indian sub-continent). This means that the dynamic of parental-role allocation is often governed by the need to seek training and sponsorship for a child *outside* the kin group, in order to take advantage of opportunities – political, economic and occupational – not controlled by kin.

To some extent the difference between what I have called simple differentiated states and the more complex hierarchical states is one of degree. And indeed the scale of complexity and hierarchy does not end with the Hausa Emirates and the kingdom of Bornu in the savannah, or with the modern urban Creole societies of the coast. Still greater occupational and socio-economic differentiation occurred in medieval Europe, in the Middle East, in India and China, and of course in modern industrial society. But even if this distinction between simple differentiated states and more complex hierarchical states seeks to specify variation in the less complex end of the overall scale, it is about differences which are of major importance in understanding West African systems.

The two critical features of the more complex West African states appear to be those concerned with political hierarchy and the division of labour. Not only are there many occupations besides farming, hunting and fishing, but even in the rural areas most men have some occupation in addition to farming. This is clearly shown for the Hausa (by M. G. Smith) and for the Kanuri (by R. Cohen). Today in both societies it is related to requirements for cash as well as agricultural produce for rural subsistence. This in turn is associated with the existence of wage labour: a man can sell his labour for money if he has no occupational skill. Both in the pre-colonial Hausa emirates and in pre-colonial Bornu, the central authorities levied taxes on individual craft production. In the colonial period English, French and German colonial policy used taxation as a way of forcing manpower into the labour market. It is impossible to say whether this was a conscious policy in traditional pre-colonial states, but it would seem that taxation and a market for labour may have also existed there. A further interrelated characteristic of the more complex traditional states was production for sale. Not only was petty-commodity production for local consumption common, but near the major trading centre of Kano there was production for long-distance trade of cloth, leather, and metal goods.

There are two quite different sets of more complex hierarchical systems in West Africa. One consists of the northern state systems strongly influenced by Islam; the other set includes urban coastal, and particularly Creole, societies in which the complexity and hierarchy are in part a response to the introduction of Western education, Christianity, and close involvement in the world market,

273

and with modern industrial – and hence occupational – institutions. Where colonialism, Christianity and the world market economy have introduced marked differentiation into formerly segmentary systems and simple states one would predict that institutions would appear which provided access to these resources and opportunities, in a way functionally analogous to the traditional institutions of alliance fosterage and apprentice fosterage found in traditional complex hierarchical states and utilizing the same kind of 'currency' as these traditional transactions. And indeed several such institutions have been described: apprenticeship, the placing of 'tribal' children in Creole households as 'wards', the practice of sending girls from rural areas to work as housemaids for city families, and the widespread practice of 'educational fosterage'. The most recent addition to this list of modern forms of parental-role delegation is the placing of West African children with English foster-parents in Britain in nurturant/educational fosterage.

Despite their obvious differences, more complex traditional kingdoms and modern urban coastal society share a relatively complex division of labour, and involvement in a market economy. It seems probable on the basis of existing evidence that the final stage in which transactions over the training and labour of children are expressed in monetary terms has, at least until very recently, occurred only in the coastal system long exposed to the world market economy. Even there the use of money to secure training is relatively recent (see Chapter 8), while the payment of English foster-parents appears to have begun in the late 1950s.

The shift from kin to non-kin training and sponsorship

In complex systems when the family holds few resources and does not train its own children there are fewer centrifugal forces pushing children out of the parental domestic group than in segmentary systems and simple states, and also fewer constraints binding children to it. There is less basis for claims on children as a form of resource vested in the kin group than in simple differentiated states because kin groups are weaker, and there is often little to be gained from sending children to kin, since the resources and opportunities controlled by kin are likely to be much the same as those controlled by the parents themselves. But the introduction of such major differentiating factors as urban life, skills of crafts, trade and scholarship, appointive political office and patron–client relations, creates new resources and opportunities which are highly significant for effective entry into adult roles to which parents and kin may not have access.

Two changes in the weighting of family roles appear in the more complex systems to support the shift to non-kin training and sponsorship made possible by the complexity of the social structure. There is some evidence that holder-heir tensions may take different forms, since property tends to pass from a man to his children rather than laterally to adult brothers before dropping to the son's

274

Table 12-1. *Paradigm of West African parental-role allocation, with examples drawn from text*

	Parental-role allocation	Type of polity	Examples:	
			Societies	Type of parent role delegation
I	Unitary parent roles	Segmentary societies	Ibo, Tallensi, LoWiili	None – temporary sharing as in types 1–3
IIA	Parent roles allocated among kin	Matrilineal and double descent societies	Ashanti	Jural status and reciprocities to MoBr; Rearing roles to genitrix and genitor
IIB	Parent roles delegated to kin	Simple differentiated states	Gonja, Dagomba	Kinship fosterage, apprentice fosterage to kin (drummers and fiddlers, Dagomba)
			Ga (traditional), Krobo	Kinship fosterage, apprentice fosterage to kin
IIIA	Delegated – kin and also non-kin	More complex hierarchical states: traditional	Hausa emirates, Kanuri, Songhoi	Kin fosterage (first-born; other), apprentice fosterage, alliance fosterage, educational fosterage (Muslim)
IIIB	Delegated – kin and also non-kin	Rural and semi-urban areas within modern market	Fanti, Krobo, Ewe	Housemaids, apprenticeship, educational fosterage; but primarily with kin
IIIC	Delegated – kin and also non-kin		Accra, Lagos	Apprenticeship, housemaids, educational fosterage (Christian)
		More complex hierarchical systems: modern urban West Africa	Ibadan	Hausa alliance, fosterage, apprenticeship
			Monrovia, Vai, Creole	Wardship (educational fosterage), apprentice fosterage by kin
			Freetown Creole	Wardship (educational fosterage), housemaids
		Europe	London immigrants	Nurturant/educational fosterage

generation as in segmentary systems, and also in the simple states. The elaborated rules of rights of adult sons in Hausa *gandu* and Nupe *efako* are most easily understood in these terms. Lineal inheritance throws greater stress onto the father–son relationship than in those societies in which a man's son does not inherit his property directly. At the same time, training and sponsorship become more important in the establishment of adult roles, since the elaborated division of labour offers more occupational alternatives, and sons did not necessarily follow their father's occupation; and the complexity of political and economic patronage make it highly advantageous to have links outside the immediate kin group.

The appearance of forms of training and sponsorship which are not linked to kinship reflect, then, two important differences in comparison with the simple states: First, rights to resources that are controlled by kin are more narrowly defined, and a relatively smaller proportion of resources and opportunities are in fact controlled by kin in the complex systems; and second, the scale of differentiation and hierarchy is much greater in comparison even with simple differentiated systems, to the point where there is clear disjunction; thus there is often a rural–urban component in the differentiation as well as radical differences in life-styles. This is as evident in traditional complex differentiated systems such as Hausa and Bornu as in the Creole communities of Freetown and Monrovia and the modern urban centres of southern Ghana and Nigeria.

In the simple states, differentiation may occur within the kin group, with one segment prospering more than the others and some falling behind. This is to some extent balanced by the continuing claims of all members on joint resources; strongest claims are those between siblings and the children of siblings. However, both in the traditional more complex states of the savannah and in the modern urban centres of the south, differentiation tends to become at once more individualized (since claims of siblings' children are less readily recognized) and horizontally stratified. While there is a possibility of movement between strata, on the whole, members of a kindred share the same life chances. Endogamy reappears, but here it is status-endogamy, with the wealthy marrying their children to others equally well-off and the children of the poor restricted in their selection of spouses by the exclusiveness of the better-off (Tahir 1976).

Conclusions

I began this set of studies with a framework for looking at parent roles, as a way of facilitating comparison between societies. The argument that has been developed holds that the strategies which parents adopt to accomplish the several tasks of parenthood are strongly constrained by the social system in which they live. What seems to work best in one kind of society may be a mistake in another. However, strategies which are efficient for meeting the tasks of parenthood will also have other implications, and strategy choices are likely to be made in terms

276

of multiple advantages wherever possible. Thus placing a child with a kinsman in a simple state may not only secure desirable training and sponsorship, but may also reaffirm the parents' claims on this branch of the family when it comes to help in meeting debts or getting backing in suit for political office. The weaker and more dispersed kin groups become, the more necessary it is to find ways of reinforcing links with kin if they are to be made the basis of claims for support. Kin fosterage is here seen as a means of picking out certain links and building new, optative, relationships upon them. As status reciprocities become less dependable as a basis for support, rearing reciprocities may be managed so as to reinforce them.

If claims to assistance and support must be *created*, then the question becomes how this can be most effectively accomplished? The strongest claims are those based on both status reciprocities and the reciprocities built up through the rearing relationship. But in societies in which status reciprocities are weak or non-existent (such as the West Indies) rearing reciprocities alone may have to bear most of the load. One of the interesting features of societies characterized by kinship fosterage is that there are reports of the same parents receiving children and sending them out. This seems to be irrational, yet is it really so? For there is a sense in which children reared by the parents who begot and bore them may take for granted the care bestowed on them. It is as though the parents have an *obligation* to look after their own offspring. This is not true of foster-parents. Instead, all accounts appear to agree that this relationship is readily perceived as one of reciprocal services. It is as though the element of choice which comes into play with the seeking out (or accepting) of a child places the whole relationship in the realm of intention. The pro-parents sought responsiblity for the child, and the child in turn must acknowledge obligations to them. In this sense it may be that fostering children creates a stronger claim on them than they would acknowledge to their own parents.

In West African simple states people depend on other people in myriad ways. The giving of a child to kin to rear serves to provide services while at the same time acknowledging the existence and legitimacy of the claims of kin – and thus supporting a system of claims from which the child-givers will later be able to benefit. What potentially clouds the picture is that in the simple states kinship fosterage is based on this diffuse, delayed reciprocity between kin, but it in turn provides the model for placing children with non-kin in functionally specific forms of training and sponsorship. These forms emerge in response to the constraints of political and economic institutions which become increasingly demanding as polities become more centralized and hierarchical, and as the economy becomes more differentiated with a complex division of labour.

The interest of the West Indian material lies in the lack of mesh between the available forms of training and sponsorship and the political and economic institutions of the wider society. There is very little a parent can do to place a child advantageously in West Indian society, though lodging with schoolteachers is a favoured pattern, and, significantly, carries with it the expectation that the schoolchild will look after the teacher when she is old.[8] But as there is little means of access to advantageous positions in the external system, in which parents themselves occupy only marginal positions, in the West Indies status placement cannot serve as a means of access to resources. This throws the whole weight of the construction of reciprocities onto the reciprocities of rearing, with the consequent reluctance to part with a child except to the mother's own mother. There is no safety net of status reciprocities to fall back on.

From the viewpoint of the social system, the placing of children with kin functions to reinforce selectively some kin ties, and to reaffirm the legitimacy of claims on kin in general. As such it can only be effective within a system in which claims on kin have meaning. The rearing relationship itself does generate reciprocal claims, but in the absence of a wider 'claim system' these tend to be highly particularistic, as in the West Indies.

From the point of view of the parents' strategies for fulfilling the tasks of parenthood, the two major sets of constraints are those arising from the dynamics of the parent roles themselves, on the one hand, and those produced by the social structure on the other. If there are no central institutions, then all calculations must be made in relation to one's own descent group. Or if the central institutions are effectively closed except to kin as in the type case of the Hindu caste system, then again options are restricted. The placing of children outside the family for training and sponsorship appears characteristic of those societies in which descent structures no longer pre-empt all adult resources and roles, and in which differentiation and hierarchy are sufficient to encourage selective placement.

Two general questions about the nature of West African parenthood were raised at the beginning of this chapter. Attention was drawn to the apparent contradiction between the great importance attached to parenthood, and the widespread practice of sending children to grow up away from home. And it was pointed out that the delegation of parent roles had recently appeared in societies in which it was not traditional, suggesting that it was a response to particular constraints, and that there must be a general definition of parenthood in West Africa which facilitated delegation when conditions made it attractive. The answers turn out to be related.

The framework for the analysis of parent roles in Chapter 1 distinguishes between birth-status identity, linked to social paternity and anchoring the individual to the key institutions of his society, and the rearing roles which assign responsibility for nurturance, training and sponsorship. It is an absolutely consistent finding that delegation of rearing roles has no effect on birth-status identity in West Africa; indeed, it is said that there is no such thing as adoption in West Africa,[9] which is another way of affirming the immutability of birth status. If the various institutions which place children outside their natal home

278

to grow up with others are put in terms of the parental role framework, it is evident that it is always the rearing roles which are delegated, while birth-status identity remains unaffected. The paradox thus dissolves, for the very firmness of the continuity of birth-status identity acts as a guarantee that 'merely' delegating the rearing of a child cannot lead to its loss. The complications arising from the use of English foster-parents by West Africans in London (Chapter 10) reveal clearly that the parents simply cannot imagine that they would lose their rights to a child even though it has lived for several years with foster-parents.

And here perhaps is the key to the particularly West African conception of parenthood which underlies and facilitates the proliferation of pro-parental institutions there. As it is recognized that an individual is once and for all time a member of the kin group through which he is socially identified as a legitimate member of his community, parents are free to respond to changing constraints of family dynamics and the external system in managing the delegation of rearing roles. With the significant exception of selling a child into slavery, there was, in traditional systems, nothing they could do which would alter their child's adult membership in his society. As the child's social identity was fixed by legitimate birth, once and for all, other parental roles might be managed in the most advantageous way without jeopardizing this. Thus traditional Ibo trained their sons themselves, while they lived in a world in which descent-group membership determined civil status and economic resources. But in modern Nigeria where opportunities in the home village are limited, Ibo are ready to place their sons with teachers and craftsmen in the town. The allocation of parent roles changes in response to external system constraints.

While this formulation may seem obvious, it raises a further interesting question. For as thus far proposed, the West African definition of parenthood 'determines' the possible range of adaptations to external constraints. The meanings attached to birth-status identity and the rearing roles determine what parental strategies are seen as beneficial and indeed as possible. (This rather abstract formulation may be clearer if one substitutes the current Western definitions of parent roles. We see nurturance and socialization as necessary elements of 'true parenthood' and thus are able to argue, like the English foster-parents, that parents who do not fill these rearing roles 'cannot really deserve their children' – for us they cease to *be* parents. But given West African definitions of the parent roles, this is no longer true.)

The question is, 'Are meanings primary in determining social behaviour?' For this is what such an analysis thus far implies. However, if we look instead at the range of West African societies, from segmentary polities to simple states, to traditional complex systems, to modern coastal urban society, it is clear that what appears to be a fixed West African definition of parenthood does in fact change. The change is very slow, and seems to lag behind the institutional conditions which eventually do modify ideas and meanings. But 50 per cent of the

West African parents in our London study did not place their children with foster-parents, and indeed, 25 per cent used neither daily minders nor foster-parents. And in conversation such parents gave very Western meanings to their understanding of nurturing and training their own children. Perhaps an even more forceful proof that meanings do in time change in response to structural constraints is the West Indian definition of parenthood, which denies the validity of allowing distant kin to rear a child because this risks the loss of claims on the child as an adult. When they first were taken to the West Indies from West Africa the ancestors of contemporary West Indians must have shared the West African understanding of parenthood. But after centuries of living in conditions which did not permit the re-establishment of meaningful anchorage in the wider society, but, on the contrary, reduced dependable relationships to those with primary kin, parenthood has taken on a new meaning consistent with the social structure in which people must live.

There seems little point in debating the primacy of meanings or of structure. At a given time meanings determine how the social structure is perceived and utilized. But when the constraints of that structure make old meanings maladaptive, these are not blindly kept intact. They are recast so as to permit new ways of adapting to the new structural constraints. The interesting and difficult questions have to do with how such changes in meaning come about. The studies reported here suggest that there is indeed a conceptual lag, with the cultural paradigms generated in response to a given set of structural constraints initially retained when constraints alter. Thus the paradigm based on joint rights in descent-group resources which characterizes the unilineal descent polities remains in force when descent groups disperse in simple states. It is the conviction of having *rights* in the children of kin which propels the claims on which systems of kinship fosterage are based. Presumably it is when such rights can no longer be defended as reciprocal, even on a delayed basis, that they cease to be acknowledged *as rights*. And of course, where differentiation and hierarchy are well-advanced, there is little that poor relations can do to reciprocate. At this point transactions become subject to calculation of equity. Masters take apprentices in exchange for a fee and the right to their labour for a fixed period.[10] Mistresses pay housemaids; school boys pay boarding fees; and immigrant parents pay English families to nurture their infants. But the contrast between West Indian and West African strategies in London suggests that for many West Africans the paradigm of legitimate delegation of rearing roles is still in effect, even though the West African social structure which produced it is far away.

I have purposely refrained from making comparisons outside West Africa with the exception of the West Indian immigrant pilot study. There is evidence that Dark Age Scandinavian, Irish, Welsh and Anglo Saxon societies recognized the fostering of children outside the natal family as a regular form of training. There are later parallels in the English practice of placing the children of the well-off in noble households (alliance fosterage) and the practice by craftsmen of apprenticing their own children to others. The findings that a high proportion of English children spent their adolescence outside the parental household in the sixteenth and seventeenth centuries in various forms of service fosterage is also directly analogous. (See for instance Macfarlane 1970: and Laslett 1965.) These cases would appear to fit in with the formulation that the placing of children in other families for training and sponsorship occurs as the division of labour becomes more complex, thus creating a range of occupational alternatives, and where political hierarchy places a premium on the establishment of relationships of clientship with the powerful (who also need followers). However I do not wish to raise here the inevitable questions as to the comparability of European and African economic and political institutions that would be implied in such a comparison of the response of kinship strategies to institutional constraints in the two areas. The parallels are strong, but they should be argued independently of the attempt to establish a set of models and processes for the West African material.[11]

Appendix I: Data from the Kpembe study

i Background data: Matrices

When the TAT material had been coded, a record was compiled for each child which included demographic data, rearing history, interview responses and TAT scores. The full analysis in the Report considers the interrelations between demographic and family history variables (Matrix A); for those children who were fostered, the relations between variable aspects of fostering (Matrix B); and finally, the interrelations between demographic and fostering variables (Matrix C). These three matrices are included here without discussion to provide a background to the analysis of the projective material. It should be stressed that, of all the analyses, the most conclusive was that which looked at the relationship between sex and the TAT variables. The clearly differing responses of boys and girls to the Aggression and Affiliation indices is one example of this.

Table AI-1. *Matrix A: Demographic variables*

	Sex	Father's estate	Mother's estate	Age	School experience	Parents living?	Parents married?	Number of full siblings	Rank in sibling group
Sex		.20	.06	.13	.39 (.001)	.13	.12	.10	.12
Father's estate	.20		.30 (.05)	.23	.11	.19	.32 (.05)	.20	.17
Mother's estate	.06	.30 (.05)		.29 (.05)	.10	.22	.27 (.10)	.11	.09
Age	.13	.23	.29 (.05)		.36 (.05)	.30 (.05)	.37 (.01)	.29 (.10)	.07
School experience	.39 (.001)	.11	.10	.36 (.05)		.06	.10	.15	.15
Parents living?	.13	.19	.22 (.05)	.30 (.10)	.06		.97 (.001)	.33 (.01)	.22 (.10)
Parents married?	.12	.32 (.05)	.27 (.10)	.37 (.01)	.10	.97 (.001)		.44 (.01)	.29 (.10)
Number of full siblings	.10	.20	.11	.29 (.10)	.15	.33 (.01)	.44 (.01)		.68 (.001)
Rank in sibling group	.12	.17	.09	.07	.15	.22 (.10)	.29 (.10)	.68 (.001)	

Associations are expressed in phi values.
The probability value, 'p', is given in brackets where p = .10 or less.

283

Table AI-2. *Matrix B: Fostering variables*

	Crisis foster- ing	Subse- quent trauma	Inclu- sive trauma	Age at foster- ing	Dura- tion foster- ing	Prox- imity foster- ing	Fostering relationship	
							Laterality	Generation
Crisis fostering		.12	.75 (.001)	.07	.16	.23 (.10)	.02	.07
Subsequent trauma	.12		.47 (.001)	.02	.08	.33 (.02)	.13	.16
Inclusive trauma	.75 (.001)	.47 (.001)		.08	.21	.41 (.01)	.11	.26 (.05)
Age at fostering	.07	.02	.08		.19	.10	.12	.02
Duration fostering	.16	.08	.21	.19		.11	.02	.06
Proximity fostering	.23 (.10)	.33 (.02)	.41 (.01)	.10	.11		.02	.23 (.10)
Fostering relationship: Laterality	.02	.13	.11	.12	.02	.02		.43 (.001)
Generation	.07	.16	.26 (.05)	.02	.06	.23 (.10)	.43 (.001)	

Associations are expressed in phi values.
The probability value, 'p', is given in brackets where p = .10 or less.

284

Data from the Kpembe study

Table AI-3. *Matrix C: Demographic variables by fostering variables*

	Sex	Father's estate	Mother's estate	Age	School experience	Parents living?	Parents married?	Number of full siblings	Rank in sibling group
Whether fostered	.17 (.10)	.24 (.10)	.26 (.05)	.11	.12	.22 (.05)	.22 (.10)	.06	.03
Crisis fostering	.26 (.05)	.22	.24 (.10)	.03	.13	.61 (.001)	.69 (.001)	.31 (.05)	.32 (.05)
Subsequent trauma	.08	.22^a	.25 (.10)	.15	.18	.00	.12	.22 (.10)	.15
Inclusive trauma	.39 (.01)	.24	.13	.23	.12	.58 (.001)	.57 (.001)	.32 (.05)	.27 (.10)
Age at fostering	.13	.14	.12	.28	.13	.05	.09	.49 (.01)	.36 (.05)
Duration fostering	.04	.24	.10	.54 (.001)	.41 (.02)	.16	.31 (.10)	.08	.24
Proximity fostering	.21	.16	.19	.31 (.10)	.12	.33 (.02)	.29 (.10)	.23	.28
Fostering relationship:									
Laterality	.03	.28	.06	.28 (.10)	.05	.04	.32 (.05)	.20	.12
Generation	.08	.19	.23	.08	.20	.30 (.05)	.24	.16	.28 (.10)

Associations are expressed in values of phi.
Probability values, 'p', are given in brackets where p = .10 or less.
^{a} The low numbers in two of the six cells of this table do not strictly speaking allow the calculation of phi. It has been included for the sake of completing the matrix.

ii Brief definitions of TAT indices

The indices which survived the stages of scoring and analysis are listed below, with brief definitions. The full, scoring definition is given in the Report.

Need Affiliation	Concern over establishing, restoring or maintaining an affective relationship with another person; friendship.
Need Achievement	Concern with success in competition either with other people or with some standard of excellence ('fame', 'success').
Physical Aggression	Imagery concerning actions which harm others physically.
Verbal Aggression	Cursing, oaths, abuse or criticism.
Supernatural Aggression	Injury or harm (expressed fear of injury or harm) from supernatural agencies.
Aggressive Threat	Threatening or aggressive actions, such as theft and ostracism.
Extreme Aggression	Imagery referring to serious injury or death.
Moral Traits	References to vices and virtues: lying, stealing, greed, being quarrelsome, being 'good' or 'bad'.
'Proud Child'	Concern with obedience and deference behaviour; explicit reference to child who is 'proud' or 'naughty'.

Appendix I

Harmavoidance	The reaction of withdrawal, and the tendency to avoid painful and threatening stimuli. This is used as an index of anxiety.
Child–Adult Orientation	Whether the balance of stories leant towards adults or towards children.
Outcome	Whether the balance of the outcomes of the stories was positive or negative.
Failure	Number of references to failure, over all the stories.
Role-Task Orientation	Number of instances over all stories of references to sex-role-appropriate tasks.
Nurturance Codes	References to the giving or receiving of assistance, help in trouble, food, care. Nurturance was scored separately in terms of the following providers of care.

Nurturant Female
Nurturant Male
Nurturant 'Parent' (labelled)
Nurturant Peer
Nurturant Supernatural Figure

Nurturance Summary Score	This measure takes into account all references to nurturant behaviour, regardless of agent.
Anxiety Nurturance	Explicit fear about or concern over the quality or absence of care.

Adult Sanctions

Physical Punishment	Hitting, beating as sanctions by adults.
Rejection	Rejection, neglect as sanctions by adults.
Verbal Abuse, Criticism	Abuse or criticism as sanctions by adults.
Introduced Actors	The number of actors present in stories but not attributable to the picture cues.

Denial Codes
Denial Female
Denial Male
Denial Threat Hostility
Denial Food

Scored for four characters/themes, specified for each picture cue. 'Denial' was scored when clear cue was judged present, but no reference appears in story.

Hunger Codes

Deprivation Index	References to deprivation of food, the need for food, or attempts to overcome obstacles to getting food.
Goal Index	References to food as a goal of action, or desire; help in getting food.
Deprivation minus Goal (similar to Atkinson-McClelland's *Food Need Score*)	References to deprivation, need for food, but deduction made for references to food as goal, help in getting food.

Social Distance Codes

Positive Social Distance (Approach score)	The tendency to react positively by approaching, interacting, or cooperating with others.
Negative Social Distance (Avoidance score)	The tendency to react negatively by avoiding, being hostile or refusing to cooperate with others.
Neutral Social Distance (Passivity/Withdrawal)	Failure to interact with others, passivity in specified relationships, as where there is description only.

Sources of indices based on TAT material

Need Affiliation:	Scored on basis of Manual prepared by Heyns, Veroff, and Atkinson, pp. 205–18, and Smith and Feld, pp. 735–76 in Atkinson (ed.) 1958.
Need Achievement:	Scored on basis of Manual prepared by McClelland, Atkinson,

286

Data from the Kpembe study

	Clark and Lowell, pp. 179–204, and Smith and Feld, pp. 693–734, in Atkinson (ed.) 1958.
Aggression Codes:	Scored on basis of code derived from familiarity with stories and
Extreme Aggression:	Murray's analysis of the aggression drive in Murray *et al.* 1938.
Moral Traits:	Scoring defined by Goody and Tahany.
'Proud Child':	Scoring defined by Goody.
Outcome:	Scoring defined by Goody and Tahany.
Failure:	Scoring defined by Goody and Tahany.
Harmavoidance:	Scoring derived from definition of need Harmavoidance, and illustrative material in Murray *et al.*, 1938.
Role Task Orientation:	Scoring defined by Goody and Tahany.
Denial Codes:	Scoring defined by Goody.
Introduced Actors:	Scoring defined by Goody.
Nurturance:	Scoring based on need Nurturance as defined by Murray 1938, but modified to take into account identity of nurturant figure.
Anxiety Nurturance:	Scoring defined by Goody and Tahany.
Adult Sanctions:	Scoring defined by Goody and Tahany; definition of rejection partly based on Murray 1938.
Hunger Codes:	Scored on basis of outline presented in Atkinson and McClelland in Atkinson (ed.) 1958, pp. 46–63.
Social Distance Codes:	Scoring defined by Goody and Tahany.

Due to the fact that the boys' and girls' pictures were not identical, there are some indices on which their scores are not directly comparable. When this is the case, I have controlled for the discrepancy either by standardizing the scores for the number of stories told by each subject or by weighting the scores themselves. It is only in the comparisons of boys' and girls' scores that this presents a problem, as in the subsequent analysis the two are treated as separate samples.

There is a further problem of the extent to which the indices are independent of one another. The simple answer is that they are not, for they have been derived from a single body of imaginative material. I have tried to define each index as it relates to different kinds of behaviour, but they inevitably overlap to some degree. Where my aim has been to build up a composite picture of Gonja boys and girls, or of children who have had different sorts of childhood experiences, the independence of these projective measures is not of prime importance. For the testing of the hypotheses, it is only necessary to compare measures which do not overlap.

Reliability of indices

For three of the indices, need achievement, need affiliation, and the hunger codes, it was possible to have all the scoring done twice, with discrepancies reconciled by my recoding the material yet a third time. The proportion of judgements on which the two initial coders agreed varied between indices. For need affiliation it was 81 per cent for the boys' stories, and 85 per cent for the girls'. For the hunger codes agreement was even higher – for boys 90 per cent and for girls 84 per cent. Both these indices would appear to have been successfully defined in that reliable judgements could be made on the material, even though this was from a culture unfamiliar to the coders. The level of agreement between coders for the scoring of need achievement was substantially lower: boys' stories, 64 per cent, girls' stories 67 per cent. This relatively low agreement reflects our difficulty in being clear about what constituted true achievement imagery in the Gonja idiom.

Appendix I

Unfortunately resources of time and money did not allow the double scoring of the later indices. I worked closely with N. Tahany throughout, as we attempted several measures which proved unworkable, and careful evaluation of the effectiveness of each code was necessary. Despite this limitation on the reliability of the later indices, it still seemed worth trying to use them, particularly as this aspect of the study must in any case be seen as exploratory.

iii The pictures used for the Thematic Apperception Test, and two sets of stories told by Kpembe children to these pictures

In Kpembe the telling of stories (*aserkpang*) is a favourite pastime of children of both sexes from an early age. Toddlers are carried along by older siblings to the evening gatherings where often no one over fifteen or sixteen is present. Boys are more likely to take the role of narrator than are girls, but anyone who knows one of the many traditional stories may tell it. The audience sits silent, unless the story is one which has its own song as refrain at certain well-known points. Stories may have as characters people, or animals, or spirits, and often include a mixture of all three. Many have implicit morals, and some end with '. . . and that is why today there is (rain, heat, millet porridge, etc. etc.), before there was none'. Others implicitly conclude with admonitions against laziness, pride, etc. So regular is the ending of a story with a moral that we found several cases where the child had added a moral precept at the end which had nothing to do with the story! It is necessary to mention this, lest the reader think the Gonja are obsessed with morality. This would be especially misleading in the context of story-telling, as the atmosphere is free, relaxed and gay.

It was inevitable that children asked to tell stories about our picture cards at first fell back on the familiar form of traditional stories. The testers did their best to explain that we wanted them to make up a story of their own – 'one that only you know', they were told. While it does sometimes happen that elements from the traditional stories have been introduced, this tends to be done in an individual way. The following examples can illustrate the resulting combinations far better than explanation. But over the ninety-seven subjects' story material, the use of traditional forms proved a problem in only a very few cases. Interestingly enough, it is in standardized beginnings (Here is my story. There lived a man/woman/child), and endings, that the traditional form is most apparent. We have many note-books full of the traditional *aserkpang* stories, but in content they are almost entirely different from those told in response to TAT pictures.

Before analysis of the story materials was begun the names of the children were replaced by numbers, so that familiarity with the subjects would not influence coding judgements. In presenting these examples, however, I have looked up the names, and written a few comments about the circumstances of each child to serve as an introduction to his or her stories. The pictures which served as cues for the stories are also given in this appendix; these were drawn by Anna Craven, from photographs taken earlier in central Gonja.

Moru's stories

This is Moru, a boy of nine. Moru has a withered leg and a quick temper, but he is an affectionate and extremely bright boy who is liked and respected by his companions even though he often cannot keep up with their games. His father is a son of the Divisional chief, but himself holds no office. His mother, a member

288

Figure A-1. Boys' and girls' picture I

of a neighbouring tribe, was away on a 'visit' for most of the time I was in Kpembe. I learned later that she had left Moru's father permanently. Moru is the third of four full siblings, all but the youngest, boys. He adores his father who is often impatient with him, and refuses to send him to school 'because it is too expensive'. Instead Moru does his best to tag along when his father goes to the farm, and when the yams began to mature, he proudly brought home some from a little plot of his own.

I. 'This is my story. There lived a certain man and his wife. That woman too did not want to be cooking in the noon, but only in the night. One day all her colleagues cooked in the day time but she refused and went to roam. By the time she could come, it was dark. Then she started cooking in the night. When she was pouring soup, a scorpion stung her. Then she left the food and went to the room. And she would not eat. But the husband came and slept and it was *kati kati kati* [tossing and moaning]. And he said, "What is wrong with you?" And

289

Appendix I

Figure A-2. Girls' picture II

she said, "A scorpion stung me when I was pouring soup." And he said, "*n!hing*, that is how it is and you said you want cooking in the night". So a woman who cooks in the night should stop cooking in the night. That is the end of my story.'

II. 'My story goes this way. There lived some six children and their mother. Where as the mother went for water they too went to the farm. When they returned from the farm, their mother had not returned from the river. And they came and sat like that, and looked for the place their mother had gone. And they got up and came and were sitting looking for the place they will go and get something and come and eat. And this one went and stood by his companion and said to him, "Let's go to the farm we shall go and get a yam and come and

Figure A-3. Boys' picture II

eat. If it waits a little [in a little while], they will come; We don't know the place they are gone." They were standing when they saw the mothers coming. And one ran and went and met them, and came home. He was coming to the house, here is his father too and this one too ran and came and met him. When they just brought those yams everybody ran and went and took his [own]. This one says "this is for me", this one says "this is for me"; one too did not get and he went and stood quietly and broke out his cries. And wept like that, and his father came and asked him "Why?" And he said, "They took yams and did not give me." And he said, "All right, all of you should put in what you have taken; it is not for you. They want to cook and everybody will eat. Not because of you [only] that I brought them. If you wanted that, why did you not bring your yams?" And all the children put in and went and stood quietly. That is why farming is very good. Here is the end of my story.'

III. 'Here is my story. There lived a certain child. He also hated people a lot.

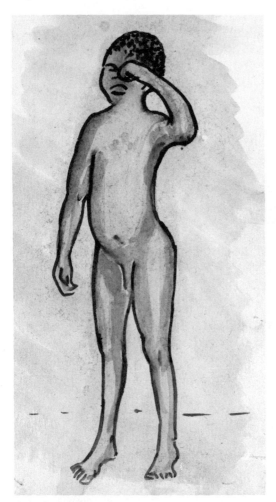

Figure A-4. Boys' picture III

The mother did not like his ways [did not like him]. One day and he got up and went and caught his younger brother and beat him for no reason and his mother asked him, she said, "why do you do that?" And he said, "If you play [annoy me], I shall beat you too." And the mother kept quiet. And he came to the house and came and said, he said that he is feeling hungry. And the mother kept quiet and was in the room. And he got up and went and gave the mother a punch in the stomach, *laab*. And the mother drove him and he ran weeping, weeping. And a certain child went and saw him, and stood and was making rough [teasing]. And he said, "I am not a boy they tease. If you just do, I shall just beat you. Do you know why I am weeping, coming?" And he caught the boy and beat him well. And the child's mother came and saw him, and said "Why

Figure A-5. Boys' picture IV and girls' picture III

do you beat him?'' And he said he was teasing him and she said, "Well, what did he make you?'' [do to you] and he said, "If you play, I shall beat you yourself. I am not such a child. I walk making bad things. I am not such a child. So everybody does not like me.'' And the woman left him alone quietly. He was going and went and met a certain bad boy who said "Why are you weeping?'' And he said it was because his bowels hurt him. And he caught him and beat him very, very well and took him and sat. The boy got up and was going and went and met a certain man coming, and the man said, he said "Why are you weeping?'' And he said, "My mother drove me.'' And he led him to the house quietly; he should go and sit down. In a few minutes the boy went and stole the man's one pound. And ran. That is why a bad boy is not good. This is the end of my story.'

293

Figure A-6. Girls' picture IV

IV. 'Here is my story. There lived some four boys. They too had their farms. And they went to the farm. And went and dug their yams and came. They saw a house with nobody there. And everybody took out one yam and put it on the fire, and they were cooked all right. Everybody also marked his. And they took and ate. The small one's [yam] was not big and he said that he was not satisfied and he stole his companion's and ate. And his companion came and caught him and said "Well, have you not got yams?" And he said that he was not satisfied. And they said, "Take one of your own [and cook it] and if you will not do that, do not take ours and eat. Everybody has got his own farm." And the boy said:

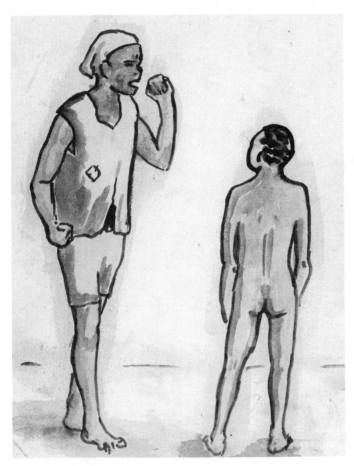

Figure A-7. Boys' picture V

"Well, mother shall be coming." And the mother came and he told her. And she said, "When you bring your yams [you show that] you love me." And he said, "It is true what you say" And she said: "Well if you don't love me any more, go out and find you a wife and come [back] and she will come and be cooking for you." "Because you have got me, I cook for you." And he went out but he did not get the person who will cook for him. And he came and went to the road and went and found stones and sticks and placed on top [made a fire]. And he took his small calabash and took it and placed it on and put in his yams. He thought that a calabash also does not break. There was a certain bad boy. He also steals very much. And he took something and placed on top and in a few minutes, the calabash exploded and his one yam was in the fire. And he got up and he was weeping and packed his yams and took them and went and met a certain woman, and the woman said: "What is wrong?" And he said, "I am very

Figure A-8. Boys' picture VI and girls' picture V

hungry, and I don't know the one who will cook for me." And the woman went
and cooked for him and he ate and finished and beat the woman's children. And
he said that they should come and accompany him to the toilet; and they were
accompanying him and he went and beat them and killed them. And passed on
and was running going, and went and met a certain man and he quietened him.
And he played [the fool on him] begging a penny saying, "Wouldn't you give
me a penny? Wouldn't you give me a penny?" And he said: "Do I grow money?"
"Do you know me?" [are we friends?]. And he said: "If I do not know you,
why am I begging you a penny?" And he said "Where do you know me? Go
away." And he got up and followed the man. And the man went and sat in a
room and the boy got up and went and sat begging a penny, begging a penny

Figure A-9. Girls' picture VI

and the man got up and went and brought him a penny. He got up and was going and went and met a certain boy selling bread and he said "I like bread." And the child took the bread and gave him and he said, "Let me look and take a good one." And he added two and took his penny in addition and ran and went and was eating. And a certain child came and met him and said that he liked him. And the first boy said "Look at your stomach and look at mine. You are satisfied, you have got mothers [his own mother and other women also called mother]." And he said "Is that how you want to be? I shall go and tell in the house." And the boy just ran quietly and stood against a wall. That is why when you are beating a child, he runs and stands against a wall weeping. That is the end of my story.'

297

V. 'Here is my story. There lived a certain bad child. A certain man is also coming from farm. And he came and was annoyed. Red monkey had come and dug up his yam. And the child went and asked him, "Why are you annoyed like that?" "And if I am annoyed, have I brought my annoyance to you?" And he said, "Just *do* me here [trouble me]. You say you are spoilt." With his fist ready: "Come and let's fight." And the child stood and opened his eyes on him [stared rudely]. And he was bringing his fist and the boy said, "Just beat me. Do you think that I have no brother? Look at him standing lean like." And the man said: "Look at me that you have insulted." And he ran after the child like that and the child ran and went to the house. And the man followed and went and squatted in front of his father [greeted the father respectfully]. "I was walking and came and this child went and stood playing me the fool." And his father caught him and beat him well. That is why badness is not good. Here is the end of my story.'

VI. 'Here is my story. There lived a certain man and his wife. The woman too did not like wearing a cloth; she sits naked.

One day she just came and was sitting like that and some children were running coming and just came and met her sitting down naked with her husband. And the children just got up looking at her. *Woo-woo.* And the husband just got up quietly and just took his whip and drove all the children and they went to their houses. And he went and caught them and whipped them well. And he came and was sitting conversing to his wife, saying: "Have you seen? That is why women wear cloth. You don't want to wear and when they ask you, you say I don't give you money. The money you get too, you go to spend it. O.K. sit there. You are the one the children are hooting at, not me. As I am wearing my shirt like this, do you also wear." And she said, "I did not even beg you." [I didn't ask you to help me]. And he said: "Sit down. I don't like you even. Only because of your cooking food for me [that I want you here]. I can also cook too. Is it because a man is not a woman? [that you think I cannot]. If you want, you can go." And the woman got up and entered the room and packed all her things, and stole her husband's money on top. And the husband went and looked in his room and found his money was stolen. And he got up and followed her. And asked her, "Let me look inside these your things." And she put them down. And the woman played her trick and put her money in her waist band. And the man said, "As you did not steal my money, where did you get the waist band?" And she said she bought it. And he said, "What money did you use in buying it?" And she said "With the one you gave me", and he said, "Where have you got the penny?" And he said, "Undress." And she undressed and the man inspected the waist band and said, "What is inside?" And he took out his money. And he said "Go!" And she was going and some children met her and hooted at her again. That is the end of my story.'

Afishata's stories

This is Afishata. She is twelve, daughter of an office holder of the Ruling estate; her mother, Miama, is also of the Ruling estate. Her parents separated four years ago, although they both still live in Kpembe. She lives with her mother, who runs the domestic affairs of the compound of the Divisional chief, Afishata's maternal grandfather. Her mother has three children, now adult, by a previous marriage, and in addition Afishata has a single full sibling, an elder brother, who lives with their maternal uncle in another village. Her mother has with her a foster-daughter of 15, her brother's child, and has recently been sent a four-year-old granddaughter to rear. Afishata has never attended school and is known for her flirtatious nature and her aversion to work. As this suggests, there is a streak of wilful stubbornness underlying her gaiety.

I. 'Here is my story. There lived a certain woman and her three children. In the morning she would get up and make food while the children slept in the room. As they were going on like this, one of the daughters married. After she was married [and went to her husband's house], her "marriage companions" [Young unmarried girls who keep a new bride company in her unfamiliar surroundings, and help her with her work.] came and said they should all go for firewood. And the girl told them, "When I was in my mother's town, I did not go for firewood. If I were to go out in the sun, my body would melt very quickly. My mother took shea butter to make me. [Shea butter is like lard in consistency; it melts in the sun but is reasonably firm in cold temperatures.] And my mother said as she used shea butter in making me; if I spoil it is not good. My mother said that if I marry, I must not go out in the sun, but stay in the room and cook."

Therefore, if you have a child, you should teach her how to cook, and teach her every type of work.'

II. 'This is my story. There lived a man, and he had two wives. One was called Adisa and one Hawawu. He liked Hawawu a lot, and didn't love the other. And he went to the farm and dug yams for Hawawu to carry home. He gave Hawawu a good path, and gave Adisa a bad path. [This does not mean that the husband actually sent them by different paths, but, metaphorically, that he treated one well and the other badly.] As they were going home there was a bad thing [This bad thing might have been an evil spirit, a witch, or a wild animal. This is really the point of the story. It is not clear whether Adisa is a witch who turned herself into 'a thing' and caught Hawawu, or whether it was a spirit of the forest, or a wild animal. If the latter, it is likely that lion or bush cow or some such beast would have been specified.] on the path, and it caught Hawawu. The mother of Hawawu didn't see her so she asked Adisa, "Adisa, where is my child?" And she replied, "Hoi! as I am here I am [supposed to be] everyone's enemy. I have no man [husband], I have no child. He went to the farm, and he gave yams to his Hawawu, and I went and found firewood and came back; and something went and caught Hawawu." Therefore, when you have two wives, love them both. Do not only love one.'

III. 'This is my story. There was an old woman. She was there with her two girls. They [all] went to look for firewood one day, and their mother went [on ahead] to the farm, leaving them in the forest. They were there in the forest and the mother could not see them. She looked for them in vain, and stood and said: "Where have my two girls gone?" The mother liked the older girl a lot, more than the other. Therefore, if you have two children do not dislike one and love one.'

IV. 'Here is my story. There was a certain man with his two youths. And one he liked very much, even though he wasn't good. And one day he said: "We will go to the farm." And he sent the one he liked very much to sleep in the room [while the other went with him to the farm]. And he said: "All right, as I like you so much, you can stay and rest here, and cook some food for us, and we will go to the farm, and come back." And when they went to the farm and returned, they found that he had not cooked. And the man said: "My child, today what is it you have done to me? I favoured you, and told you to stay behind and cook while we went to the farm. All right, go and bring water so that I can bathe." But the youth refused. He said he would not draw water for him. And the man said: "What is this! I used to like your behaviour, but now I do not like it. [*m'ma sha fo ba asheng* = "I don't like your things." It can mean either "I don't like your ways, your behaviour" or "I don't like you"] And I no longer prefer you to your brother."

Therefore, if your father is there [living], you should follow him and go everywhere that he goes [do what he tells you and not expect special attention and privileges].'

V. 'Here is a story. A woman and her husband were sitting. As they were there, they didn't lock their room, for they had no key. One day, someone entered the compound, and the husband said, "Where are you from?" and he answered he had come to find a key to put in their room. And she said, "In our town, that is how we sleep. We have nothing which needs to be locked up. And always we sleep this way." And he said, "It is your wife I want." And the husband answered, "For my wife, if you go to every town, you will not find her equal."

Therefore, if you want to sleep peacefully, lock your room or it will be spoiled.'

VI. 'There was a woman and her two children. She cooked sweet food and gave to one. Every day when she cooks food, she does not give the other one. She does that every day and then the loved child became sick. When the child was sick, they asked the woman, "What is wrong with your child? Will you not send him to the farm?" And she answered, No she would not send him. She was giving the child food when the child become like something. He became like a snake. And he was lying in the room. And they said, "What is this?" And the other one said, "Every day she cooks sweet food and gives him, and takes bad food and gives me, and I eat." So if you and a person are in a house and you cook your food, you should share and you and he eat together.'

iv Scores on selected TAT indices

Sample size and level of difference required for 'trend' are specified on each table. The tests used are as follows:

χ^2 Where this is used the distributions were split at the median, or a 'none'/'some' split was made.

$c\chi^2$ This is χ^2 corrected for continuity, where N is less than 40, or where the expected frequency in one cell drops below 5.

K-S   This is the Kolmogorov–Smirnov test (of whether two samples could have been drawn from populations with the same distribution). See S. Siegel 1956:127ff.

Fisher: The Fisher exact probability test. Where small sample size allowed, Finney's table of critical values was used, and here probability levels are expressed in interval form. Exact probabilities are only given where the full calculation was made.

p   The level of significance used with the K-S test, as well as that for χ^2 and $c\chi^2$, is based on critical values of χ^2. I have interpolated to obtain the figure for p = .15.

df   Degrees of freedom: Usually df = 1. Where degrees of freedom are greater than 1, this is indicated.

NS   Literally, Not Significant.

Data from the Kpembe study

As discussed in detail in the Report, I have reported two levels of findings. Where the difference between samples reaches a level of significance of $p = .05$ or better, this is stated as a 'difference' or a 'significant difference'. However, where there are several independent measures of the same variable (as where sets of pictures, or individual pictures, are analysed separately) the *pattern* of differences can be as informative as a single 'significant' finding. I have therefore set criteria for a trend in such cases, where, often due to small sample size or low numbers in particular cells of a table, the level of p does not reach .05. I have reported as 'trends' or 'tendencies' analyses where: (i) the difference between samples reaches a per cent previously determined in relation to the sample size; (ii) where $p =$ between .20 and .06.

Table AI-4. *Need affiliation scores for boys and girls compared*

Boys: $N = 46$
Girls: $N = 51$
Total: $N = 97$: Level of difference for trend $= 10\%$

Need Affiliation

Boys'	Girls'	
Picture I	*Picture (I)*	Girls tend to respond to picture of woman cooking with affiliation-related imagery more than boys.
Diff. $= 15\%$		
K-S $\chi^2 = 3.15$		
df $= 2$ $p = .20$		
Picture II	*(II)*	Different pictures used for boys' and girls' sample.
Not analysed		
Picture III	*(VI)*	This is the picture of (like-sex) child (?) crying. Both boys and girls responded to this cue with affiliation imagery about one-third of the time.
No difference		
Picture IV	*(III)*	Girls are more likely to respond to picture of family returning from visit/farm with affiliative imagery than are boys.
Diff. $= 15\%$		
$\chi^2 = 5.73$		
$p = .05$		
Picture V	*(IV)*	About one-fifth of the girls respond to the picture of (like-sex) adult admonishing/threatening (like-sex) child, with affiliative imagery, but none of the boys do. This difference is probably significant, but due to low numbers K-S and χ^2 inapplicable.
Diff. $= 20\%$		
No test made		
Picture VI	*(V)*	Girls are more likely to respond to picture of couple sitting, talking, with affiliative imagery than are boys.
Diff. $= 20\%$		
K-S $\chi^2 = 9.70$		
df $= 2$ $p = .01$		
Need Affiliation Summary		Over all six stories, girls are more likely to have high need affiliation scores than are boys. (The difference would be more pronounced if picture II had not been included in the summary. This is a 'peer group' for the Boys' set, and boys' affiliation responses are very high on this cue. The girls' picture II shows a couple quarrelling, and affiliation scores are low for this cue.)
Diff. $= 10\%$		
K-S $\chi^2 = 6.63$		
df $= 2$ $p = .05$		

Appendix I

Table AI-5. *Aggression scores for boys and girls compared*

Boys: N = 46
Girls: N = 51
Total: N = 97: Level of difference for a trend = 10%

Pictures were divided into three sets, those presenting an 'aggression cue'; those presenting a 'threat cue'; and those which were 'aggression-neutral'.

Responses to each set of pictures were scored separately, and are reported separately below.

Stories were separately coded (in these three sets) for imagery of physical aggression, verbal aggression, supernatural aggression, and extreme aggression. This last category contains references to death and severe maiming which were sufficiently extreme to warrant separate treatment.

Physical Aggression
Aggression cue
Diff. = 25%
K-S χ^2 =5.79
df = 2   p = .10

Boys tend to respond to aggression cue with physical aggression imagery more frequently than do girls.

Threat cue
No difference

Aggression-neutral cues
Diff. = 15%
K-S NS

Boys tend to respond to aggression-neutral cues with physical aggression imagery more often than do the girls.

Verbal Aggression
Aggression cue
Diff. = 45%
K-S χ^2 = 20.73
df = 2   p = .001

Boys are very much more likely to respond to aggression cue with verbal aggression imagery than are girls.

Threat cue
No difference

Aggression-neutral cues
Diff. = 20%
K-S χ^2 = 3.77
df = 2   p = .20

Boys tend to respond to aggression-neutral cues with verbal aggression imagery more than girls.

Supernatural Aggression
Aggression cue
No difference

Threat cue
No difference

Aggression-neutral cues
Diff. = 10%
K-S χ^2 = 6.84
df = 2   p = .05

Girls respond to aggression-neutral cues with imagery of supernatural aggression more often than do boys.

Aggressive Threat
Aggression cue
No difference

302

Data from the Kpembe study

Table AI-5 *(cont.)*

Threat Cue Diff. = 25% K-S χ^2 = 5.93 df = 2 p = .10	Boys tend to respond to threat cue with imagery of aggressive threat more often than girls do.
Aggression-neutral cues Diff. = 35% K-S χ^2 = 10.26 df = 2 p = .01	Boys are significantly more likely to respond to aggression-neutral cues with imagery concerning aggressive threat than are girls.
Extreme Aggression *Aggression cue* No difference	
Threat cue Diff. = 10% χ^2 = 2.38 p = .15	Girls tend to respond to the threat cue with extreme aggression imagery more than boys.
Aggression-neutral cues No difference	

Table AI-6. *Nurturance index scores for boys: frequency of mention of nurturant males in relation to position in sibling group*

Eldest siblings mention nurturant males less often than youngest siblings: Difference = 30%, p = .10

Eldest siblings mention nurturant males less often than middle siblings: Difference = 65%, p = .001

First sons consistently see male figures as less nurturant than do middle or youngest sons.

---

v Interview used in Kpembe study

Section I. Parents' background

Name
Age
Sex
Compound of current residence
Father's name
Father's village
Mother's name
Mother's village
Father now living where? (indicate here if dead)
Mother now living where? (indicate here if dead)
Are parents still married?
Father's religion?

303

Was parents' marriage a 'kinship' marriage?
Was parents' marriage arranged?
If arranged, by whom arranged?

Section II. Sibling-Rearing Sheet

(These questions were printed as column headings across the length of a foolscap page. The child was asked who was the very first child of his/her mother and father, who was their next-born, and so on. The names of these full siblings were written down the side of the Sibling Rearing Sheet, and the questions heading each column asked of each full sibling in turn. The information for Ego was thus placed in the context of his/her full siblings' rearing histories.)

Column 1. Name of all Ego's full siblings in order of birth.
Column 2. Where born?
Column 3. By whom reared?
Column 4. Where lived? (residence accounted for from birth to present)
Column 5. Where now?
Column 6. When last seen by Ego?
Column 7. Did this sibling rear any child of another full sibling?
Column 8. Did another full sibling rear any child of this sibling?
Column 9. Was any child of this sibling reared by others?

School attendance, and class reached, was noted by each sibling's name in Column 1.

Section III. Questions initially asked in interview

1. Was your father the first husband of your mother?
2. (Only if 'no' to Question 1)
   What town was her first husband from?
   Did they have any children? Do you ever see them?
3. (If more than one previous husband)
   What town was the second husband from?
   Did they have any children; Do you ever see them?
4. If child's parents are not still married, has mother re-married?
5. (Only if 'yes' to Question 4)
   What town was the subsequent husband from?
   Do they have any children? Do you ever see them?
6. If you could live anywhere at all, where would you *really* like to live?
6a. With whom would that be?
7. If someone gave you £1, just gave it to you for nothing, what would you do with it?
8. What person in your family (*basa*) do you think you most resemble? In what way?
9. Is there anything you remember particularly from when you were small?
10. (For girls) If you were going to go into Salaga market for the day, just to see things, not to do any work, who would you like to have to go with you? Tell me the names of two friends you would like to have come along.
    (For boys) If you were sent to spend the day in the farm scaring birds from the grain, what two friends would you like to ask to come with you? (Boys sent to guard the grain play miniature drums, sing, and play tag, and generally fool around.)

Data from the Kpembe study

Section IV. Additional questions

(These were added later, about half-way through the data gathering phase.)

11. If two girls (boys) were together in a household, and one was the daughter (son) and the other the foster-child, how do they treat them, just the same? Or differently?
    (probe – 'In what way?' or 'How do you mean?' – then, if necessary, directed probes for treatment related to (a) work, (b) food, (c) discipline.)
12. If you could be with a foster-parent, or with your own (same sex) parent, which one would you choose?
13. When you have your own child, will you raise him/her yourself, or send him/her to a foster-parent? Why?
14. If you could go and stay with any of the following, which would you choose?
    (For boys) father's younger brother, father, mother's brother[a]
    (For girls) mother's younger sister, mother, father's sister.

The interviews were conducted in the vernacular by the author. The re-interviewing of those who were not initially asked the final four questions was done by Anna Craven.

vi Observations on Kpembe adolescent girls

The analysis of the story imagery, described in Chapter 3 and this Appendix, was carried out with no knowledge of the identity of the story tellers, and indeed all the stories to a picture were coded for a given variable at the same time, identified only by numbers. However, as a part of the analysis, I wrote accounts of the children in each of the compounds of the core neighbourhoods, using both the notes taken during the study and interviews with each child. Here the focus was on individual children as they interacted with peers and parents. As a further perspective on the impact of the fostering experience, profiles of eight Kpembe girls are presented here. There is not space enough to include all the children in the two core neighbourhoods; instead I have used a sub-set consisting of the teenage girls in Ewurajipope. Following the individual profiles, each has been scored from the observational data on some of the main variables used in assessing story imagery. This makes it possible to look at these variables in terms of individual children in the context of their daily lives.

Of eight teenage girls in this section of Kpembe in 1965, five were living as foster-children and three were with their own parents. These girls shared two central problems: they were expected to do a good deal of work in the household – cooking, washing clothes, fetching water and firewood; and they were becoming involved in the pleasures and conflicts of courtship and impending marriage. Most comments on them relate to these areas. The two who were in

[a] There is a single vernacular term for all brothers of a mother, and all sisters of a father, hence these are single choices. In *Ngbanyito*, however, one must distinguish between older and younger brothers of the father, and older and younger sisters of the mother. In each case it was the younger relative who was given as a possible choice, as there is a less authoritarian relationship with those younger than the parents than with older aunts and uncles. The implication of 'father's elder brother' or 'mother's elder sister' is of someone who is like a family head, and has authority over the parent as well as the child.

school had both remained with their parents, and for them school experience is an additional major factor to be taken into account. Comments are also drawn from responses to questions on the interview schedule.

Hawa (age 18, of the Ruling estate). Her parents never married; her father met her mother in Togoland while on treck with the Medical Field Unit. Her mother was later married in Banda, and bore a daughter, and is now married at home in Togoland with four more children. Hawa has not seen her mother for several years, but keeps in touch with her half-sibling and her mother's sister who live in Banda. Hawa came to stay with her father's mother, Adama, at the age of three and a half, and has remained with her ever since. Her earliest memory is of taunting Adama with being a witch, for which she was spanked. While I was in Kpembe, Hawa was married to a young man whose courting she had encouraged. However she decided that this was a mistake and refused to live with him. She was going through a difficult time, as all her kin were trying to persuade her to give the marriage a try, arguing that if she did not no one else would marry her, and that she must face the fact that it was time she married; she could not remain a child forever. At this time Hawa was extremely difficult. She refused to do housework at all. She was blatantly rude to her foster-mother, picked fights with the other teenagers and generally made herself thoroughly disagreeable. Indeed, her behaviour was exactly that which the Gonja describe for a *kabi jigge*, a spoiled child. Ironically, it is precisely this situation which being reared by a foster-parent is intended to avoid. Here, however, one could argue that having gone to Adama at an early age, and seldom seeing her own mother, she had in effect become Adama's daughter, and an only daughter at that. Against this must be set the fact that Adama had raised five sons, and other foster-daughters, and, while not a difficult or irritable woman, was not the sort to indulge a child. Hawa's early memory of taunting Adama suggests that the element of confrontation in their relationship, which was very evident during my stay, was probably of long-standing. It is also consistent with Hawa's generally spirited style.

Fatimabi (age 14, of the Muslim estate). From her father's village of Tari, she was sent to her mother's mother in another section of Kpembe when she was about five. She remained there until her grandmother died, about four years ago. By this time her father had also died, and her mother remarried, though she has now returned to her own kin in the village of Labunga with a child of the last marriage. Fatimabi was sent to her mother's 'younger sister' (MoMoBrDa), Dongiche, in Kpembe when her grandmother died, and has remained with her ever since. Fatimabi apparently has very ambivalent feelings about her own mother. In answer to the interview questions, she said that a foster-child is better treated than an own child; that she would rather be *kabita* because she doesn't like to stay with her own mother; Dongiche's son Soale says that her mother treats her badly. Fatimabi would foster her own children but 'doesn't know' with whom. But in response to the question about where she would most like to live, replied 'Kpembe, with mother'; and when asked to rank possible mother figures in terms of who she would like to live with, she placed her mother first. In this context it is interesting to recall Soale's earlier comment on foster-children in his own interview: they are not well-treated, and no one would buy them any cloth except for a rag. It is certainly true that Fatimabi wears the oldest and most worn cloth I have ever seen hang together on a body. She is a very shy and modest girl, who speaks only with persuasion and works very hard. She makes a striking contrast with Zenabu, who also lives in this compound.

Zenabu (age 17, of the Ruling estate). Her mother has always been married to her father, and they are still together. Zenabu is the third of nine children, and the only one to have been sent as a foster-child. Her *tchepe* is her mother's older maternal half-sister, Selamata, whom she joined when she was about 6. Most of her childhood was spent with Selamata in Kumasi, a major city in the forest south of Gonja. There she helped with trading as well as housework, and she seems to have enjoyed this life. Zenabu also shows a mixture of attitudes towards fostering. She would prefer to live in Kpembe, 'if not with my mother, then with Selamata'; and she would prefer to be an 'own child' rather than foster-child. Yet she said enthusiastically that she would send her own daughter to Selamata to bring up, and in choosing among mother's younger sister, father's sister and mother, placed her mother last as the person she would want to live with; mother's older sister (which Selamata is) was not among the options. In answer to an indirect question about the advantages and disadvantages of being a foster-child, she volunteered 'if I stay at home, I will refuse to do what they ask me so I will never learn'. Very much the 'party line', but it was offered spontaneously (note her shift from the impersonal to first person in replying). Zenabu is in fact a strong-willed character, and she has probably often been told that she needs disciplining. Given her enthusiasm for sending her own child to her present foster-parent, she cannot be taken as 'anti-fostering'. Yet she clearly would like to live with her own mother.

On another occasion I asked her who a foster-child confides in, her foster-parent or her own mother. She answered that she would confide in Selamata because she feels shy with her mother, but she could talk to Selamata. Zenabu is a big, hefty girl, outgoing and pleasant, if ribald. I heard after leaving Kpembe that she had become pregnant and was not going to marry the father. She went back to her mother's house to have the baby. As I was not there, it is impossible to say whether this was because of her desire to be with her mother, or because Selamata could not look after her and the baby properly with all her trading activities and trips. Without these, it would have been possible. During the time I lived in Kpembe, an old woman in Selamata's compound was looking after an ex-foster-child who had come back with her first baby. This woman stayed with her ex-foster-mother, although her own mother was living in another compound in the same section.

Afisha (age 13, of the Muslim estate). Afisha's mother married her father as a young girl, and they are still married, living in Yapei. Afisha has only one surviving sibling, a brother who is in Bole (western Gonja) as a foster-child with his father's younger brother, learning the Koran. Neither she nor her brother have lived with their parents for many years, although she saw her brother a year ago when she was there on a visit at the same time as he. Afisha was first fostered in Daboya by a much older half-sister of her father. A year ago, this woman's married daughter had to move from Daboya to Kpembe when her husband was transferred there as clerk of the local council. At that time Afisha was passed on to the daughter, Mimuna, to help her with the three young children, and came with the family to Kpembe.

In answering questions in the interview, Afisha repeatedly answered 'I don't know', as some much younger children, although she is quite intelligent enough to understand. She said she would like to live 'in all towns, I don't know', as though she had given up establishing a fondness for any one particular town, or had decided that her wishes had little to do with the matter. She named three companions instead of the two asked for, and all three are slightly older adolescent girls from the same section. She does not in fact spend any time with these girls (she appears to have little free time); nor did any of them choose her. But she seems to be saying that she would like to join in their activities if only she could. She is the most outspoken of all the girls on the questions about attitudes to fostering. On every question she is consistently negative. She *knows* that an own child is always favoured, and that the foster-child never gets anything until the own child has it already. She would definitely not foster her own child and would prefer to be with her own mother.

Afisha is a stable but not very happy child who is apparently reacting to too much movement and too little affection. At least so far as her verbalized attitudes go, she does not like being a foster-child and longs to be with her own mother. But she does not show anxiety in her demeanour nor over-dependence in her questionaire responses, although the number of 'don't knows' is problematic. She is oriented towards her peers as best she can be, living in an isolated position on the edge of the section (she lives in the clerk of council's house which most people leave in respectful solitude); and she has little time for making friends.

None of the girls so far mentioned have been to school, and all are foster-children. This is consistent with the fact that fewer girls do go to school, and that in Kpembe most adolescent girls were being fostered. The next two girls were both living with their parents and were in the third class in Middle School.

Adama (age 15, of the Ruling estate). Adama went for a long visit to an 'elder brother' in Kumasi during the summer holidays and thus did not participate in the formal part of the study. However, I saw enough of her to be able to record that she is a pleasant, open girl who enjoys school, partly for the freedom it gives her from chores at home. She talks vaguely about being a teacher but, as she was not selected for secondary school, this will be difficult to accomplish. Her other interest is the singing and clapping games which the girls of the section play in the evening, and which are an occasion for the youths to gather round and joke with them. In short, she likes fun and does not much like housework, but manages to do enough of both to satisfy herself and others. Adama's household is particularly interesting in that it appears to approximate closely to the Western norm of parents living with their three children, aged 15, 8 and 3 years. However there are another three children living elsewhere as foster-children; two, a boy and a girl, are with their father's father and his classificatory mother respectively in another village; the third, a girl of six, has been with her father's paternal half-sister in a different village for about a year. All three visit Kpembe every few months, and the other children go to see them in the villages. It is worth noting that the high rate of fostering in this family is unrelated to any family crisis. The failure to send any children to maternal kin is probably due to their mother's lack of relatives (it is possible that her mother was of slave descent).

Wuria (age 15, of the Commoner estate). Wuria's mother, Zenabu, married her father as a young girl and they were still together, though I learned that they had separated about three years after the study was completed. They had nine children, of whom two died in infancy or early childhood. Five, all girls, were sent as foster-children. One, Wuria, protested strongly although her foster-mother, a 'sister' of her father's mother, was in the same section of Kpembe as her own parents. At first she refused to go, and, when taken by force, cried and refused to eat. Her father offered to bring her anything she needed that her *tchepe* did not give her, and to send her food from home. She remained inconsolable and after four weeks was allowed to return home. At the time of the study, at 15, Wuria is shy, tense and moody. She appears to be a lonely girl who still finds her main companionship among her younger siblings. Her earliest memory was of being afraid of frogs because they leapt about. She still does not want to be a foster-child and would not send her own children to be fostered 'for fear of beating'. While I was talking to her there was a nervous twitch under one eye the whole time, although she had known me in the village for four months and had played Wari (a 'board' game) with me several times. She is a striking contrast to her younger sister, Amamita, who, at the age of ten, has been a foster-child of her mother's mother for several years. They move between Agona (in Ashanti to the south), Tamale and Kpembe. In Agona, Amamita has to carry water for sale for her grandmother, but she enjoys the bustle of the town and in response to the interview question immediately said she would like to live in Agona. Judging by the quickness with which she grasped the meaning of the questions, and the rapidity of her answers, she is highly intelligent. This is supported by her general demeanour about the village; she is a ring-leader in plots among the younger children and generally full of impish vitality. All her responses seem to indicate a sense of independence. She does not think she resembles anyone in her family; she would not take anyone with her on an expedition to Salaga. (Other children who did not give any names of children they would like to have accompany them, said either they 'didn't know of any' or that they had no friends. Amamita said she preferred going on her own.) She however was chosen by her older sister, Wuria, her younger brother, Sulemana, and by several other girls from quite distant compounds.

Mariamu, of the Ruling estate, is 15 and lives in the household of the divisional chief, the KpembeWura. This household is managed by the chief's daughter Miama, who has retired from marriage and returned to look after her aged father. Miama has reared Mariamu, who is a daughter of her full brother who lives in another town. Her mother lived with her father for a while, but they did not marry. Mariamu remained with her mother until she was seven, when her father came to take her away to his sister in Kpembe. Mariamu is very matter-of-fact about being a foster-child. 'Of course I do more work than if I were with my own mother. I cannot refuse if my *tchepe* asks me to do something. She has become my father (i.e. because my father gave me to her, and because she is my father's own sister). I cannot do anything that would hurt my father.' She is not in fact as obedient as this, and I have heard Miama berating her more than once. However, there is a lot to be done in the divisional chief's household and, as Miama is partly crippled, most of the work falls to Mariamu and to Miama's own daughter, Afishata. 'I do more work than her own child', was Mariamu's view. She is very consistent about preferring to be a *kabita* both for herself ('so that I will not become spoiled') and for a future child. She would send her child to her older half-sister. Significantly, perhaps, her first choice of a parent figure to live with is neither mother nor father's sister (with whom she now is), but her mother's younger sister. Mariamu is a distinctly independent child, full of spirit but very pleasant. I think she is much more of a handful to Miama than her rather over-conforming answers suggest. (I was once told that all foster-children become liars because they want to please their foster-parents – and perhaps also interviewers?) Her abrupt removal from her mother does not seem to have cowed her, nor resulted in obvious over-dependency.

Miama's daughter, *Afishata* (age 12, of the Ruling estate) is the youngest of her five surviving children, and, unlike some of the others, has never gone to school. Miama became very ill while married to her second husband, and was finally brought back to her father's house to die. To everyone's surprise she recovered, but remains weak and partially crippled with curvature of the spine. She has stayed in her father's house, rather than returning to her husband. Afishata's earliest memory is of 'praying to God that the next day I would be healthy'; this apparently obsessive concern is almost certainly related to the great anxiety surrounding her mother's extended illness. She believes that own children and foster-children are raised in the same way, and that if there is trouble with laziness, whichever of them is the elder will be punished more. (In her own household, there is a foster-child slightly older than she is, so, in her experience, age and fostered status coincide.) Although Afishata would rather be with her mother than with a foster-parent, she would send her own child to be fostered, either to her sister or to her mother's sister, 'so it wouldn't become spoiled'. This pattern of inconsistent responses was very frequent. It seems to indicate that the girl herself wishes to stay with her mother, but that she acknowledges the validity of the cultural view that children often become spoiled if they remain with their mothers; that is, both responses are 'true'. Afishata is one of the two children whose stories are given in full here. Although she is not living as a foster-child, her stories are consistently preoccupied with the theme of sibling rivalry: three are about parents who favoured one child more than another; one about a man who favours one wife more than another, and another about a bride whose mother has spoiled her by failing to teach her how to work. She seems to be very preoccupied with conflicts about work and favouritism. In this context it is significant that not only is there an older fostered girl in the household, but her mother has recently received a new foster-child, a little girl of about five. The mother gives her new charge considerable attention, and she is often to be found sitting on Miama's lap. It seems that even children remaining at home are closely affected by the practice of fostering. However, Afishata can not be too seriously disturbed by competition with the foster-children for her mother's affection, as she chose the older one, Mariamu, for a hypothetical companion on the trip to Salaga.

Discussion

It is difficult to evaluate a set of accounts of eight girls coping with the problems of being a Kpembe teenager; each one seems so individual. What I have done in Table AI-7a is to score each on a number of key variables on the basis of the interview and field notes. They have also been given a score on their attitude to fostering which reflects the balance of the answers to several related questions as well as any additional information in the notes. One pattern, which is fairly clear and hardly surprising, is that girls who have problems with dependency and anxiety tend not to be the ones who have problems with settling down to culturally specified sex and work roles. The two girls with high scores

Data from the Kpembe study

Table AI-7a. *Rating of Kpembe teenage girls on attitudes to fostering and difficulty in various areas of adaptation, based on observations and interviews*

Name	Whether fostered	Age	Attitude to fostering	Dependence	Anxiety	Peer relations	Sex role	Work role	Total
Hawa	Yes	18	N.A.	0	0	2	2	2	6
Fatimabi	Yes	14	Ambivalent	2	2	1	0	0	5
Zenabu	Yes	17	Ambivalent	0	0	0	2	1	3
Afisha	Yes	13	Negative	0	2	2	0	0	4
Adama[a]	No	15	N.A.	0	0	0	0	1	1
Wuria	No	15	Negative	2	2	2	0	0	6
Mariamu	Yes	14	Positive	0	0	0	0	1	1
Afishata	No	12	Ambivalent	1	1	1	0	1	4

Scoring: The 'difficulty' scale runs from 0 (for no difficulty) to 1 (for some difficulty) to 2 (for marked difficulty). The scores on attitudes to fostering are based on the consistency of responses to the several questions on different aspects of fostering. 'Ambivalent' means that some responses were positive and others negative.
[a] Adama was away during the formal interviewing so there is no schedule for her.
N.A. = Not ascertained.

on difficulties with these roles are both unanxious, independent and indeed high spirited. They are also the oldest girls in the set, and for them the constraints of marriage and domesticity are looming close. However, it is interesting that both these girls are with foster-parents who do not seem to have been able to steer them through this difficult period without conflict.

The two girls who score highest on anxiety and dependence are very different from each other. Fatimabi is a twice-fostered child whose first foster-parent died, whereupon she was sent to her present *tchepe*. During the time she was living as a foster-child her own father died, and her mother first remarried and then left the second husband. Her own mother is said by others to treat her badly. Here is a girl for whom life has been objectively hard. She has responded by withdrawing into herself and overconforming in her responses to demands made on her by others. Wuria, on the other hand, seems to have been a very anxious child from an early age. She was afraid of frogs, terrified of living in a foster-home, and has remained, in mid-adolescence, very dependent on her family. There may of course be factors in Wuria's life to account for her long-standing pattern of anxiety: her father is known as a drunkard and ne'er-do-well; two older sisters died in adolescence, while she was small. In any case, it is clearly not the experience of fostering alone which accounts for the high anxiety/dependence scores of either Fatimabi or Wuria.

Of the six girls for whom explicit opinions on fostering are available, three expressed both positive and negative views in different contexts. This is a true reflection of the complexity both of individual feelings, and of the situations in which fostering becomes significant. What you feel is best for your child, or is your duty, is not necessarily what you personally would prefer. Of the two girls who were strongly negative about fostering, one was a twice-fostered child (this seems always to create problems), and the other a child who had refused at an early age to be fostered and had grown up with her own parents. The one unequivocally positive response is from a fostered girl who has an unusual

Table AI-7b. *Ranking of Kpembe teenage girls on total difficulty scores and fostering status*

Name	Difficulty score	Whether fostered
Hawa	6	Yes
Wuria	6	No
Fatimabi	5	Yes
Afishata	4	No
Afisha	4	Yes
Zenabu	3	Yes
Adama	1	No
Mariamu	1	Yes

amount of work to do, but who lives in the compound of the divisional chief and clearly enjoys being at the centre of activity. There is no neat relationship between the experience of being fostered and the attitude towards fostering as an institution.

In Table AI-7b the eight teenage girls have been ranked in order of the degree of difficulty they seemed to be experiencing. The striking pattern here is that of the two girls with the highest 'difficulty' scores, one was a fostered child and the other reared by her parents, while at the other end of the scale, of the two girls with lowest 'difficulty' scores, again one was fostered and the other reared by parents. There clearly is no sharp distinction between the adolescent adjustment of fostered and parentally reared girls in this sample.

Appendix II: Data on the southern Ghana surveys

i Characteristics of Survey Communities

In the terminology of the Ghana census of 1960, communities of less than 1,000 are hamlets, those between 1,000 and 5,000 are villages, between 5,000 and 10,000 they are considered towns, and over 10,000, large towns. One of the four surveyed communities, Tefle, is therefore a village and the rest are towns (Table AII-1).

The proportion of men employed in non-agricultural work in the four survey communities is compared with that for the men in a 10 per cent sample of rural hamlets from the same Local Council areas in Table AII-2. The levels of non-agricultural employment are strikingly different between the survey towns and the sample of rural communities. The only exception is Anomabo in which many men are engaged in fishing for the market; there the men from rural hamlets show only a slightly higher level of non-agricultural employment. For the other three survey communities the level of non-agricultural employment is between 36 per cent and 55 per cent higher than the rural hamlets.

Another index is the extent to which adults have attended school. In part this is a consequence of the simple presence of schools. All the survey communities have had primary schools for many years, and all have middle schools, either in the town or nearby. The striking difference in Table AII-3 between the proportion of adults with at least some education and the proportion of children who have attended school reflects the gathering momentum towards universal primary education since Independence in 1957. But the figure of one-third of

Table AII-1. *Population of four surveyed towns (Ghana Census 1960)*

	Males	Females	Total
Tefle	697	772	1,469
Anomabo	2,432	2,991	5,423
Odumase	2,147	2,372	4,519
Somanya	4,398	4,860	9,258

all adult men with at least some education is high in comparison with rural areas, even in southern Ghana. This is best shown by comparing figures for education for the four survey communities with those for the rural areas around them, as in Table AII-4.

Table AII-2. *Comparison of per cent in non-agricultural employment in four survey communities and in sample of rural hamlets from same local council areas: Males*[a] *(Ghana Census 1960 II:36ff., 206ff., 298ff.*[b])

Four survey communities	%	Rural hamlets	%
Tefle	70	Tongu	15[c] (10)
Anomabo	30	Mfantsiman	23
Odumase	70	Manya-Yilø-Osudoku	16[c] (4)
Somanya	52		

[a] The census definition of being employed is very wide and includes not only those who receive a wage for their work, but also those who work on their own farms whether or not they sell their produce; those temporarily out of work due to seasonal factors, illness or labour disputes; family workers who worked, even if without remuneration, for at least one week in the past month; as well as domestic servants, apprentices and members of the armed services (II:XIV–XV).

[b] A 10 per cent random sample of hamlets and scattered households, i.e. those not part of any village or town, was taken for the Local Council Areas of each of the survey communities. Both Odumase and Somanya are in Manya-Yilø-Osudoku Local Council Area.

[c] There was a single case in which a large proportion of men were engaged in non-agricultural (etc.) employment. Although it is impossible to tell from the census data these exceptional cases were probably due to some local small industry. The proportion as it would be without the exceptional case is given in parenthesis.

Table AII-3. *Per cent of males and females with at least some school experience: Adults and children between 6 and 13, for the four sampled towns (Ghana Census 1960 II:48, 228, 312)*

		Ewe: Tefle %	Fanti: Anomabo %	Krobo-Manya: Odumase %	Krobo-Yilø: Somanya %
Adults (15 and over)					
Per cent with some schooling	M	32	29	66[a]	47
	F	11	9	35[a]	13
Children (6–14)					
Per cent with some schooling	M	68	48	76	68
	F	37	39	58	47

[a] Secondary schools and teachers' training college bring in students over 15 from other communities, artificially inflating the Odumase figures for 'adults'. The Basel Mission has been active in Kroboland since 1856, and together with other Christian denominations has established a widespread network of primary and secondary schools. When they were driven from Krobo mountain, the Manya Krobo, whose paramount was very friendly with the Mission, settled at Odumase which became the headquarters for the Mission's work in Kroboland.

Data on the southern Ghana surveys

Table AII-4. *Comparison of rural and small-town literacy: Per cent of population over 15 with at least some school experience. Sample of hamlets in local council areas of four survey communities*[a]

	Males %	Females %
Survey communities		
Tefle	32	11
Anomabo	29	9
Odumase	66[a]	35[a]
Somanya	47	13
Rural hamlets		
Tongu	35	3
Mfantsiman	17	1
Manya-Yilø-Osudoku	26	4

[a] The Odumase figures are inflated (see note to Table AII-3).

ii Additional Tables from Survey Data

Table AII-5. *Relative frequency of purposive and crisis fostering in independent sets of fostered children representing three generations: Parents, children, and grandchildren: Fostered Sample*

Type of fostering	Set of fostered children based on:			
	Parents of Sibling groups: Parents' generation	Children fostered by parents: Siblings' generation	Children of the siblings: Children's generation	Total
Crisis	11 (27%)	20 (30%)	15 (36%)	46 (30%)
Purposive	30 (73%)	49 (70%)	27 (64%)	106 (70%)
	41 (100%)	69 (100%)	42 (100%)	152 (100%)

Table AII-6. *Incidence of crisis in family of orientation for Fostered Sample by ethnic group*

Crisis during childhood?	Fostered child is:			
	Fanti	Ewe	Krobo	Total
None	49 (63%)	30 (86%)	53 (42%)	132 (55%)
Parents divorced	4 (5%)	0 –	12 (10%)	16 (7%)
Parent(s) died	25 (32%)	5 (14%)	61 (48%)	91 (38%)
	78 (100%)	35 (100%)	126 (100%)	239 (100%)

315

Table AII-7. *Whether child attended school, and how far, by ethnic group:*
Fostered Sample

	Fanti	Ewe	Krobo[a]	Total
No school	35 (40%)	21 (50%)	20 (31%)	76 (39%)
Primary school	34 (38%)	17 (40%)	25 (39%)	76 (39%)
Middle school or more	20 (22%)	4 (10%)	19 (30%)	43 (22%)
Total for whom school known	89 (100%)	42 (100%)	64 (100%)	195 (100%)
Schooling not ascertained	39	4	138	181

[a] The comparatively low proportion of Krobo who had not attended school is almost certainly related to the very high proportion of Krobo for whom information on schooling is lacking (two-thirds). As schooling is a source of prestige, those with nothing to be proud of are most likely not to have answered this question.

Table AII-8. *Relationship between fostering and school attendance for male*
siblings

	Was this sibling fostered?		
Did this sibling attend school?	Yes	No	Total
Yes	42 (55%) (53%)	33 (45%) (60%)	75 (100%) (55%)
No	38 (61%) (47%)	24 (39%) (40%)	62 (100%) (45%)
	80 (100%)	57 (100%)	137 (100%)

Table AII-9. *Relationship between fostering and school attendance for female*
siblings

	Was this sibling fostered?		
Did this sibling attend school?	Yes	No	Total
Yes	26 (54%) (37%)	22 (46%) (33%)	48 (100%) (39%)
No	45 (50%) (63%)	45 (50%) (67%)	90 (100%) (61%)
	71 (100%)	67 (100%)	138 (100%)

Table AII-10. *Payment of school fees: Fostered Sample*

No school	76
School, parent paid	26
School, foster-parent paid	38
School, payment of fees not ascertained	55
School attendance not ascertained	178
	373

iii A Note on Divorce

It is unlikely that the low figure for divorce is altogether explained by the very complex legal situation concerning divorce in Ghana, but this may be a factor for the Christian families. There are three different ways of getting married in Ghana: with customary rites (which of course vary from one ethnic group to another), in a Christian church service, and by Ordinance. Relatively few marriages in southern Ghana were of the latter two types prior to 1965 (when this survey was made). An Ordinance marriage required a fully legal divorce, and indeed was avoided by many for this reason. Most Christian denominations did not allow divorce, and many insisted on monogamy. The parents of the full sibling groups in the Sibling Sample were about half Christian (46, or 43%) and half not (47, or 44%). For some reason a large proportion of the 15 Ewe respondents did not answer this question (10, or 60%). I suspect that this may be because of the great pressure in many Ewe communities to be Christian. Those who are not may find it difficult to admit to a stranger. There is also the further resistance of a son or daughter to admitting that they have left the church of their parents. In any case it is probably reasonable to suppose that Christianity may have exerted a pressure against divorce in about half of the sample families of orientation.

It is possible to check this figure for divorce by looking at the answers to the question, asked of women only, on current marital status. While there are many reasons for distorting replies about parents' marriages and even one's own previous marriages, there were always other people about during the interviews I conducted, and it would have been difficult for respondents to deny commonly known facts about their current marital status.

This table suggests a solution to the puzzle. For one-third of the women reported that they were not currently married, but had formerly been so, yet they did not describe themselves as either widowed or divorced. There are a number of reasons why this could have happened. I found among the Gonja that many women left their husbands to return to their natal kin once their childbearing years were over. Marriage was in effect defined as a condition related to the sexually active years for women, and thereafter alternative statuses such as sister, father's sister, senior woman in the kin group, became more attractive and more relevant. It is impossible to know from these data whether those women responding that they are 'not married now' had retired from marriage in the same way. Another feature of Gonja 'divorce' was that when women had to return home to their kin for some reason such as an illness or a funeral, it was expected that the husband would come, or send someone to bring them back. If this was not done, the separation gradually slid into a permanent state. For older women, this was unlikely to be followed by remarriage. They became 'forceably retired', to elaborate on the idiom which English-speaking Gonja have adopted.

Table AII-11. *Incidence of crisis in the families of orientation of the Sibling Sample*

| | Crisis during childhood? | | | |
	No crisis	Parents divorced	Parent(s) died	Total
Number	54	9	43	106
Per cent	51	8	40	99%

In either of these circumstances it is understandable that a woman would not consider herself divorced. She had not been thrown out, nor had she left in anger. Indeed, retired wives often return to the conjugal home for funerals and other ceremonies, particularly if the welfare of adult children is involved. But, for the present analysis, the problem is the effect of this liminal marital state on the domestic family in which the child is growing up. The problem is further complicated by the fact that marriages may be much more unstable now than they were in the first half of the century; indeed there is considerable evidence to support such a suggestion (Oppong 1974). So the situation in 1965 may not tell us much about that in 1920 or 1940 when these adults were growing up. On the other hand, in Gonja the twin patterns of visits home becoming separation and retirement from marriage, appear to be long-established, and not a recent response to the disruptions of modern life. Finally, where respondents are talking about conditions affecting their own childhood, or that of their own children and siblings' children, their perception of the state of a parents' or sibling's marriage ought to be taken seriously as data about how it felt to be part of that family.

Table AII-12. *Current marital status of women in Sibling Sample*

	Number	Per cent
Currently married	26	43
Widowed	4	7
Divorced	2	3
Never married	2	3
Not married now	19	31
Not ascertained	8	13
	61	100%

Notes

Introduction

1   M. G. Smith's analysis (1955) of the composition of households in rural
Zaria (Hausa, northern Nigeria) revealed the presence of 'adopted' children. Some information is available about their relationship to 'adoptive'
parents, and it seems probable that a form of kinship fosterage is practised
here.

1. A framework for the analysis of parent roles

1   And incompleteness. For one is left to define for oneself the difference
between members of the transactional series. Further, while one appre-
ciates Goodenough's wish to establish definitions which are applicable cross-
culturally, the refusal to consider content of parental roles, but to deal only
with transactions (succession, delegation, sharing, pre-emption) when each
of these transactions can concern 'some or all' of the undefined rights linked
in some way to mothers and their husbands, leaves the reader with very little
idea of what is meant by parenthood. Attempts to apply this paradigm have
not proved very successful (see Schildkrout 1973).

2   The limiting case seems to be that where the social identity of 'siblings' is so
strong that physiological as well as social paternity is merged, as in fraternal
polyandry or the unusual, but recognized, Tallensi institution of deputing a
lineage member to beget a child for an impotent man. Even a Trobriand
man, who is believed to have no physiological relationship to the children
he begets, treats children born to his wife while he is her sexual partner differently from those she bears while with someone else. For he has a special
relationship with those children for whom he 'opened the womb'.

3   Milan Stuchlic pointed out to me that in modern Western societies there are
occasionally transactions concerning begetting where the mother's word is
taken, together with circumstantial evidence, to determine paternity for the
purpose of assigning responsibility for contributing to the support of an
illegitimate child. It is significant that such examples as one can find are
either deviant within the society where they occur or else are very rare (see
also note 2 above).

4   The significance of girls' puberty rites in matrilineal systems is further discussed in Chapter 6.

319

5   For example, in Ceylon (Yalman 1967), in black communities in the Caribbean (R. T. Smith 1956; Clarke 1966), and in slum communities in the United States (Hannerz 1969; Stack 1974) and Mexico (O. Lewis 1961). There are some interesting exceptions to the restriction of lack of concern about the legitimacy of offspring to the underprivileged among some highly privileged groups. Illegitimate children of the nobility in England asserted their paternity by prefacing their biological father's surname with 'Fitz. . .' which was understood to mean 'the illegitimate child of. . .'. These strategies, institutionalized in varying degree, seek to secure the advantages of physiological kinship which the rules of the society would replace with rights derived from 'legitimate parentage'.

6   See E. Goody (1978a) for a discussion of some of the implications for learning.

7   There are a great many examples of this type of delay, for example, in Nadel's discussion of witchcraft accusations between men and their sister's sons (1952), and La Fontaine's analysis of Gisu male initiation (1960).

8   *Notes and queries* (1951), Gough (1959), Leach (1961), J. Goody (1956a), W. H. Goodenough (1970b).

9   No exhaustive systematic comparison has to my knowledge been carried out, but these systems which link 'real' parenthood to rearing seem to be limited to societies in which civil/kinship status determined at birth does not link the individual to any corporate kin group. That is, it is not a matter of rearing relationships *displacing* identity based on descent, since this is not significant.

10 The classificatory use of parent terms may be extended not only to close kin of the parents, but to other members of the descent group and their spouses. The parent terms are also the most widely used of all kin terms for the purpose of metaphorical manipulation. Male authority figures are often referred to, and even addressed, as 'father', and political authorities tend to be termed the 'father' of their people. The use of the terms 'mother' and 'father' probably carry a unique affective load. Perhaps this is why, in Gonja, it is considered a declaration of hostility to fail to use the term for 'mother' to a mother's co-wife. She has a residual responsibility for the children of her husband's other wives, and a right to be addressed as, and treated as, a mother. Gonja children often resolve the conflict this arouses by adding her name to the word for mother: *niu Hawa*, mother Hawa. Another distinction is made by using a baby term, *mma*, for one's own mother, and the formal term *niu* for classificatory mothers.

11 At different times I have used both 'purposive' and 'voluntary' to describe fostering which is arranged in accordance with the general norm that kin of both parents have a right to rear children of a union. Both terms are appropriate, but each emphasizes a different aspect of the Gonja institution. As implied by the term 'purposive', the Gonja view fostering arrangements as fulfilling certain useful functions for those concerned. However I shall argue that these manifest functions – companionship, labour, character building – are not those which caused fostering to become institutionalized among the Gonja. So in one sense 'purposive' is a misleading term, since on another level fostering is culturally enjoined. The same reservation applies to the term 'voluntary' which was initially used to emphasize the contrast with crisis fostering arising from demographic constraints. Having noted these problems, I shall continue to use the two terms interchangeably.

Because moral and legal rights and obligations seldom coincide exactly, the individuals who act voluntarily and those who come forward in a crisis may not be identical. In Gonja there is a high correspondence, and the institutional charter is the same for purposive and crisis fosterage.

12 Marvick 1974:266 and note 35; Flandrin 1979:204–5. Ariès concludes that there were virtually no infants left in Paris (Ariès 1962:374).

13 There was a further set of constraints related to the very high level of infant mortality, especially in cities where sewage disposal and pure water were serious problems. Marvick (1974:265) cites infant-mortality rates of between 25 per cent and 75 per cent for the first year of life. Despite the equally high death rates of French infants placed with wet-nurses in the country, the distress of an infant's death must have been lessened if s/he died away from home, a relative stranger.

14 L. Lambert (1608:418), quoted in Marvick 1974:264; P. Coustel (1687, I:68).

15 Ross speculates that 'The child returning from the *babia* [wet-nurse] therefore [i.e. because the family was apt to be large and complicated] might have to compete for the attention of his mother' (Ross 1974:197). But he offers no actual evidence that this was a problem.

16 The *peculium* was a sum of money placed by his pater at the disposal of the adult who was still under *potestas* and thus unable legally to own property on his own account. It fits the functions we have indicated for sponsorship, allowing the young man to establish his own household and thus to gain a measure of independence even though legally a jural minor.

2. Kinship fostering

1 For detailed references to the allocation of parent roles in other West African societies, see Part II, especially Chapters 4, 5 and 6.

2 In a state with an area of some 15,000 square miles, encompassing groups of differing ethnic and linguistic affiliation, some variation in form and content is to be expected. I have somewhat different, but overlapping, information from central, northern, eastern, and western Gonja, and where variations are significant this fact is noted in the text. This chapter makes no attempt to discuss regional differences: it is in the nature of an overview. Some calculations have been made for certain samples and not for others; information is more complete for some samples than others. No negative results have been omitted.

3 The date in this and the following tables are assembled from several sources. The western Gonja women's sample is based on a stratified random sample of all the compounds in the old town of Bole. All adult women in twenty-four compounds were interviewed. The men's sample from western Gonja used in Table 3 consists of all the full brothers of the women interviewed in the Bole sample. The women's sample from northern Gonja consists of all the adult women in nine Daboya compounds non-randomly selected to represent Muslim and ruling estates. The men's sample from northern Gonja is based on all the full brothers of the Daboya women interviewed. The men's samples from western and central Gonja (Busunu) are based on all the men in randomly selected compounds stratified to represent Muslim, ruling, and commoner estates. The sample from eastern Gonja includes all the men of the Muslim section of Kpembe, plus all the men in randomly

selected compounds in one of the sections of the town dominated by the members of the Singbung gate of the Kpembe ruling estate. There were no refusals, although some permanent residents were absent on extended visits. The sample from central Gonja (Gbuipe) consists of all the fostered children living in the village at the time of our census. The 'successful' men in both eastern and western Gonja were all those in the three categories discussed who were present in the two towns at the time the interviewing was done.

4   See J. Goody (1967) for a discussion of the Gonja political system.

5   It is perhaps equally plausible to argue that the fostering experience would serve to make a woman less dependent on close emotional ties and for this reason better able to tolerate the inevitable strains of married life. Although the trend of the divorce ratios in northern Gonja is in the direction of more stable marriages for fostered women, in the absence of any significant difference between the ratios for the fostered and non-fostered groups, there is no confirmation of such a hypothesis.

3. The Kpembe study

1   During the study I was struck by the embarrassment of some of the children when given pencil and paper and left to draw a picture 'of themselves'. However it was not until the analysis stage that I realized that it was regularly those children with no schooling who had failed to produce coherent pictures. Children who had never been to school seemed to believe that they did not know how to use pencil and paper 'correctly'.

2   In addition Jerry Kagan has pointed out that we failed to standardize the length of story unit coded, so that children telling long stories have more opportunity to score on all the indices, while tellers of short stories are correspondingly likely to have fewer scores on all indices. Unfortunately, there is no way of correcting this short of recoding all the material. However there is no reason to suppose that the error this introduces is systematically related to fostering.

3   During the 1956–7 fieldwork I had tried to use doll play with Gonja children with the same mystified response. At that time I felt that it would be possible to teach the children to play with the dolls, but was doubtful whether their play would then reflect their own ideas or my teaching.

4   By structural determination it is meant that a given pattern of behaviour is a response to the experiences of filling particular roles. I specifically do not mean here 'cultural determination' in the sense that there is a cultural norm/idea/paradigm that organizes behaviour. Behaviour is a function of *both* social structure and cultural paradigms, and the two interact. However in this case I am discussing the consequences of living as a Gonja boy or girl, as a first-born or later-born. The experience of a role is obviously shaped in part by the way that role is culturally defined. But the fact that there are common aspects to role definitions across cultures argues that cultural meanings are not the only factors involved. This distinction is considered again in the final chapter.

5   I have not changed the name of the divisional capital in which this study was carried out, since there are many Gonja, some of whom helped in the study, who could easily identify it. But names of sections of Kpembe have been altered as have all names of individual children who participated in the study.

322

6   See, for instance, McClelland's discussion of the effect of entrusting children to slaves (1961:128).

7   There is no evidence in this material as to where the 'normal' level would fall.

8   Perhaps more striking is the relatively high proportion of fostered girls who did not answer where they would like to live, but said with whom they would like to be instead. But while the proportion so responding is 10 per cent higher than among the boys, it does not really differ from the proportion of parentally reared girls who respond in terms of person rather than place. So this is as much a difference between boys and girls as between fostered and parentally reared children.

9   Mastery here is of the environment and their main activities.

10 The single exception I came across was an instance of 'educational fosterage', where a kinsman had undertaken to put the girl through school.

11 Of course they also vary as to how authoritarian they are and whether they set high standards, but less so in my opinion.

12 It is only fair to say the Gonja fathers tend to be more indulgent and less demanding of daughters than of sons.

13 School, a European education, introduces yet another factor into the discussion which is central to a final understanding of the contemporary situation but cannot be dealt with here.

4. The circulation of women and children in northern Ghana

1   The mechanism at work here has something in common with the attempt of friends in some Western cultures to perpetuate their necessarily evanescent relationships by acting as godparents to one another's children, and by joking references to marriage between their offspring.

2   In respect of the selected variables there is little difference between the LoWiili and the LoDagaba (whom we refer to collectively as the LoDagaa); but, since our recent information was collected from Birifu (LoWiili), we will draw the contrast with this latter group.

3   While ideally a ratio of sibling to conjugal residence would be calculated for each woman over her lifetime and would represent the time spent with 'brothers' and with husbands, this ratio 'A' is in practice difficult to obtain and for comparative purposes virtually impossible to extract from published data. Less satisfactory (because of the assumptions entailed), but more practical, is ratio 'B' which compares the number of women living as wives and as 'sisters' in N households at a given time. In calculating ratio 'B' it is necessary to do so separately for each of several significant age cohorts in order to take into account differences in circumstances affecting young, middle-aged, and old women.

4   By pattern we refer to the relative frequency of divorce at different periods of a woman's life. The assumption here is that there may be different factors affecting stability of marriage at different times (see Fortes 1949a; E. Goody 1962). (See Chapter 2 and E. Goody 1973 for Gonja divorce ratios.)

5   Residence with a husband in old age is slightly more common in eastern Gonja than in the central or western part of the country. But here women are at pains to explain that although they may live in the same house, they are no longer 'married', that is, they no longer sleep with or cook for the 'husband'. There is, for women, something incongruous about being old and being married.

6   A LoWiili girl will sometimes go to help her elder sister as a nurse girl (*biyaal*) to look after a young child, if there is no one else in the house to help. The same institution is reported for the Kusasi and the Kasena. For the purposes of this comparison (Table 4-2), we have not reckoned this practice as a type of fostering, partly because the girl goes in the capacity of sister rather than as child, partly because of the instrumental character of the institution and its relatively brief duration and partly because the crucial factor for this argument is whether or not boys are fostered, and, if so, whether foster-parenthood is a function of lineage membership or not; girls have to move in any case because of marriage. (See typology in Chapter 12.)

   A very young child whose mother has died is taken by her kinsfolk to be looked after until she grows up (J. Goody 1956a).

7   How widely marriage and fostering are spread is directly related to population density and the distance between villages. Population is thinner, villages more widely separated and the distances involved in marriage and fostering are greater in central Gonja than in the east. Western Gonja occupies an intermediate position in this respect (see E. Goody 1973).

8   This statement refers to northern Ghana. There is some reallocation of children within large Mossi compounds in Upper Volta (Lallemand 1976) which I discuss in the next chapter.

9   In some groups in northern Ghana, e.g. the Builsa, the Kasena and the Kusasi, the widow is encouraged to remain in her dead husband's house, but she cannot marry there; instead, she takes lovers from among his distant lineage 'brothers' and breeds children to the dead man's name in a form of widow concubinage.

10 Exceptions occur in two types of situation. Where the marriage was between kinsfolk, an elderly woman who has no nearer relations may remain in her dead husband's house, partly as widow, partly as kinswoman. Where the widow is of slave origin and has no kin, she also stays in the house. Some Muslims allow marriage to a dead patrilateral parallel cousin's wife, but not to a brother's wife. The wives of divisional chiefs were supposed to remain with his successor, but he had to be from a different dynastic segment than the previous chief – i.e. was not a kinsman.

11 Gifts of money to the parents of the bride are becoming larger in eastern Gonja. In the west the traditional scale of gifts still obtains. Throughout the area the fixed legal payment is 12s. and 12 kola nuts.

12 Where orphans are placed in the custody of the parent's heir we speak of proxy-parenthood, since the heir replaces the parent in a whole variety of domestic and descent group roles.

13 Ardener makes a useful distinction between demand-sensitive and demand-insensitive systems of marriage payments (1962:78).

14 Tallensi divorce is clearly very high in the experimental phase. Fortes writes that 70 per cent of women had been married more than once, in some cases a subsequent marriage being leviratic (1949b:85 note); and that in a sample of over 100, no man over 30 'failed to experience one or more unsuccessful and usually short-lived marriages' (84). But if only fertile marriages for which bridewealth was paid are counted, the ratio of marriages ending in divorce to all marriages is 7 per cent, i.e. relatively low (85 note). This figure corresponds to what we have called the middle and terminal phases of marriage. The figure of 7 per cent is not entirely satisfactory as it excludes barren marriages. For comparative purposes it would be desirable to com-

pare the percentage of all 'correct' marriages ending in divorce, in addition to the percentage of all fertile correct marriages so terminated. But the concept of a 'correct' marriage again raises analytical problems.

15 We have altered the rubric of section 5, since more work needs to be done on the inheritance systems of these groups before we can be certain about the position described earlier as 'double'.

16 In northern Ghana where descent groups are found within centralized states it is within linguistically distinct subordinate peoples. In southern Ghana there are small 'town states' which incorporate ethnically distinct elements into a polity based on descent-group representation. Although here the structure of the centralized polity is different from that in northern Ghana, the two types of system both have a centralized governmental structure which pre-empts political initiative and the use of force and leaves the descent groups to manage mainly domestic matters. The southern Ghana systems are discussed in more detail in Chapter 6.

17 'Grandparents are entitled to the services of the first-born son and daughter of their eldest son. These children will leave the home of their parents (supposing the eldest son to have 'gone out' and built his own compound) as soon as they can walk, and go to live with their grandparents, until they marry. They will, however, visit their own parents from time to time' (Rattray 1932:I, 263).

'It is not uncommon for Nankanse children to be brought up in the maternal uncle's compound, with the full consent of the natural parents. "Your mother's mother often loves you more than your mother. You may take anything you like at your uncle's compound and be familiar with his mother, calling her 'old grey hairs'. A child may continue to live at his uncle's house until he grows up, and may marry and continue to live with his uncle after marriage" ' (I, 273).

18 A second theoretical aspect concerning the relationship between divorce rates and the system of kinship or descent is discussed in the original article (J. and E. Goody 1967).

19 The high marriage payments of urban Ghanaians are basically wedding expenses; the high payments of the Kanuri are not 'jurally' high as they vary between 5 and 100 pounds (R. Cohen 1961) and the high payments in Egypt were an indirect dowry for the bride (Lane 1871:I, 204).

20 This discussion of bilateral systems is pursued in E. Goody 1973.

5. Traditional states: responses to hierarchy and differentiation

1 See Eyre-Smith 1933:26; Rattray 1932:ii, 565; Manoukian 1952:58; Staniland 1975:34–5.

2 There is no discussion of marriage policy among occupational groups except for the fiddlers. Thus it is not possible to judge how often *lunsi* girls marry men from other *lunsi* families. Nor is it clear whether a child would be claimed in this case.

3 Diviners are the one exception to this generalization. Significantly the sanctioning agency is the divining spirit itself, which enters the descendants (either through men or through women), of previous diviners. That is, the men of the diviners' kin group take no initiative, and merely respond to the diagnosis that a particular individual has been chosen by the spirit.

4 Gonja first-born observances are very mild and consist essentially of the

prohibition on eating from the same bowl. Neither first-born son nor daughter may call to their mother from outside when she is in a room. The Gonja have no explanation for this last observance, but it does suggest a sensitivity to the possible reversal of authority roles. A parent ought to give orders to a child, not the other way around. A first-born daughter should not sit on an upturned mortar of the kind that women daily use to pound both grain and yams in preparing the family's meals.

5　This seems to have been more of a problem where the master was also a kinsman.

6　*Yaro* (pl. *yara*) in Hausa means (1) a boy; (2) a servant; (3) a dependant. All three meanings would have applied to boys living as apprentice-clients (*yara*) in a merchant's house.

7　The text is ambiguous here. It reads 'nearly 20 per cent of all fostered male children in the survey were of this type' (87). There were 46 fostered male children, of which 20 per cent would be 9. However, 31 of the fostered male children were with foster-mothers, not foster-fathers; presumably these were fostered as infants, when men have little to do with children, and possibly as the result of the mother's divorce or widowhood and consequent remarriage. Nine is three-fifths of the 15 boys fostered by men, which is the base implied in the text.

8　The obligatory avoidance between a Hausa father and mother and their first-born makes it very difficult for them to live in the same household. Reciprocal fostering by siblings of each other's children is thus in the nature of an obligation. I have placed less weight on this avoidance than might seem warranted, since fostering of first-borns is by no means always part of institutionalized fostering.

9　Cohen's figures for fostering are unusual in that men foster as many girls (15) as boys (15). He himself writes that it is normal for men to foster boys and women girls, and makes no comment on this discrepancy. But if, as he also suggests, the landlord is anxious to foster clients' first-born children, who will presumably be girls about as often as they will be boys, and, if he is also anxious to have 'daughters' whom his clients can marry, then fostered daughters would be as valuable as fostered sons. Fostered girls are no doubt placed with his wives for care and instruction, just as girls fostered directly by the wives would be.

10　A further source of fostered daughters is the children of the numerous prostitutes who live in the Hausa quarter. Prostitutes are not allowed to foster children, and find it difficult to rear their own children, preferring to have them fostered. However, Hausa prostitution is a unique institution, in large part a reflex of the high divorce rate and the seclusion of wives. Women move from the status of wife to that of prostitute and back again (A. Cohen 1969:51–70).

6. Contemporary patterns in southern Ghana

1　See for example Quartey-Papafio (1913).

2　For the mid-twentieth century Christensen gives population figures of 2,000 for the smallest and 34,000 for the largest, and lists 19 Fanti 'states' which never formed a single organized federation (1954:8, 14).

3　The circulation of offices has been discussed in theoretical terms by J. Goody in the introduction to J. Goody (1966) and for the Gonja of northern Ghana in a paper in the same volume.

4 See Azu (1974) for a discussion of the forces weakening the Ga lineage.

5 *Awøba* is derived from an Akan word meaning 'security, pawn, hostage'.

6 The Krobo preference for pawning boys rather than girls is consistent with the pattern of retaining control over daughters either by marrying them within the minor lineage or by refusing to accept marriage payment for them.

7 This is a striking example, because Azu has just said that children are often fostered because their own parents are unlikely to punish them when they ought to. Foster-parents may also be tender hearted!

8 There are of course exceptions. But the exceptions appear to be cases in which the parents feel that some particular sort of training can be better supplied by foster-parents. The Krobo professional felt his brother could provide better character training. Our London families valued the exposure to English language and culture which their children received in English foster-homes.

9 In Anomabo and Tefle I was introduced into the community by a well-known member of the dominant ethnic group, and worked with a local assistant who was also fluent in English. I used a crude form of quota sampling, aiming at interviewing both men and women: young adults, middle-aged and elderly people. The only regular criterion was that each interviewee be a native of the town and of the ethnic group identified with it. Before interviewing each ethnic group I discussed with my assistant the relevant vernacular terms and went over the questionnaire to be sure that no major problems of misinterpretation existed.

The Krobo survey was organized by Gladys Azu after I returned to England. I sent her a sampling plan which selected streets at random, and then took every tenth house and required that all the adults living there be interviewed. While admittedly crude, this procedure at least avoided leaving the choice of informant up to the interviewer, and attempted to randomize bias. The main weakness of the material lies in its narrow focus. The interviews with Ewe and Fanti were necessarily conducted through an interpreter, and the central question, once the constitution of the informant's sibling group had been established, was 'Who reared . . . [each sibling in turn]?' Although this was further broken down by periods in infancy, childhood and adolescence, a full exploration of the rearing situation was not possible. Informants were adults, and the information thus refers to childhood of from 25 to 65 years ago.

10 The figure of Odumase is inflated by the presence of secondary and teacher-training institutions which have many students over the age of 15, used as the cutting point in the census.

11 The data on which these comparisons are based come from the 1960 Ghana census. The critical material is summarized in tabular form in Appendix II.

12 The total Fostered Sample was 373, of which 25 (%) could not be clearly identified. The proportions given are for the remaining 348.

13 When comparisons are made between the three ethnic groups, the very different size of the three samples makes it misleading to relate them in the same way to means for the sample as a whole. There were only 16 Ewe interviews, compared with 60 for the Krobo and 30 for the Fanti. For this reason findings are generally expressed as proportions of the responses for the given ethnic group, rather than in terms of the contribution which a given ethnic group makes to the total figure for a given response category.

14 The 'length unascertained' category may contain more instances of short-term fostering as those children who stayed in the household for a shorter time would tend to be less clearly remembered. On the other hand, it is not surprising if adults cannot say much about the children reared by their own parents, perhaps before they were born. And indeed dispersed employment, where kin may be working in widely separated parts of the country, creates new conditions under which they may well not know the details of one another's arrangements for child-rearing.

15 This apparent shift from fostering by kin alone to the inclusion of non-relatives is discussed more fully in the next chapter. In the Krobo case, it is unlikely that when they lived on Krobo mountain there could have been unrelated adults in this tightly knit and isolated community available to act as foster-parents.

16 With Krobo and Fanti particularly, the interviewers' knowledge of the community may have led them to rate members of 'important' descent groups as having higher economic status than was justified, but concrete criteria were used (ownership of house, car, radio, business) and extreme discrepancies, i.e. an error of two categories, are unlikely.

17 Although there were 14 respondents for whom the traditional rights of descent group were not indicated, it is highly likely that had these individuals been members of important descent groups they, or the interviewer, would have been sure to note it. There were also 11 respondents for whom it was not possible to estimate economic standing.

18 See an excellent discussion of this issue in Azu (1974).

19 The table giving these data is in Appendix II. Information on schooling is missing for two-thirds of the Krobo fostered sample, so less confidence can be placed in this figure.

20 This point is nicely documented in Gaynor Cohen's study (1976) of education and wardship in Sierra Leone Creole society.

21 The detail on children fostered by the parents of the Sibling Group is insufficient to allow analysis of the reasons for fostering beyond the distinction between crisis and purposive fostering.

22 The weavers of Daboya, discussed in a forthcoming paper, appear to be a partial exception to this generalization.

7. Fostering contrasted

1 Though by no means unique, see studies of fostering and adoption in Eastern Oceania in Carroll (1970) as well as the Caribbean material (Chapter 11).

2 There is another, equally important question with which I am not concerned here. What accounts for the fact that fostering is institutionalized in some West African societies, while it appears to be absent from others? This question is discussed in Chapter 12.

3 Ages can only be roughly guessed at from Busia (1950), my main source on this point. The youngest girls may be ten or eleven.

4 These two tables, and therefore Table 7–4, differ slightly from the versions previously published because I discovered, in returning to the data, that I had originally included one sub-sample for which the data were based on a question that biased the responses towards foster-parents of the parents' generation. This enhanced the contrast between generational distribution

of the northern and southern Ghana samples. But on recalculating the table without this sub-sample the difference still remains substantial.

8. Modern apprenticeship: response to differentiation

1   The high-earnings economy of Ibadan comprises the professions (including government administration); the larger commercial firms; the few modern industries; a number of successful private traders (men and women); and several profitable, privately owned enterprises of medium size in baking, in building and construction, in transport. The low-earnings economy includes the multitude of small-scale traders, the minor manufacturing units, small-scale printing, transport, and contracting businesses (Callaway 1973:1–2).

2   Again these differences are consistent with the bias of Callaway's sample towards more established businesses (occupying permanent premises).

3   This does not make the Yoruba a caste society, since most people had no occupation that was restricted to the descent group but were simply farmers. Nor were the craft-owning descent groups ranked as in the prototype of caste systems, Hindu India.

4   This is treated in detail in a forthcoming paper on the weavers of Daboya.

5   No figures are given for how many were trained by a sibling, but of the masters interviewed (1970 paper), of those who had trained a kinsman, only 14 per cent had trained a sibling.

6   Unless he learns a second skill.

7   A secondary-school teacher in northern Ghana, married with a number of children confided to me in 1964 that he still handed his pay to his father 'from respect'. The father returned most of it to him for the support of his family. It is very difficult to know how widely this duty is still honoured, because it is recognized to be 'old fashioned' and modern men don't like to admit it.

8   This argument is developed in *Contexts of kinship* in relation to the Gonja, but seems to me self-evident for West African societies generally, except for those at the highest levels of differentiation and stratification, although even here there are strong vestiges.

9   Verdon points out that there is a widespread assumption that this development is a 'natural' process if only the right resources are made available (see Callaway 1973:46–7).

10   There is a persistent anxiety among apprentices that their master is keeping secrets back and not teaching them everything. It is difficult to know whether this really happens, or whether it is a reflection of the general West African linking of knowledge with power and particularly with the power to exclude the uninitiated. Once a master gained the reputation for withholding important knowledge and skills from his apprentices, he would soon cease to have any apprentices at all. One is reminded here of Miner's observation concerning the influx of outsiders into the craft of slipper-making, traditionally reserved for the Arma of Timbuctoo. Non-Arma were able to learn the craft because they disregarded both the supernatural sanctions on their participation, and the possibility that the inferior craftsmen who were willing to teach them had been unable to give them all the skills of the craft. If there is economic incentive enough, even the withholding of 'secrets' will not deter apprentices (see Miner 1953:55–9).

9. Creole wardship: response to hierarchy

1 Porter lists many examples (1963:113).
2 'A juvenile, other than a servant, is classed as a ward if he lives in a household no member of which is a parent of his' (Banton 1957:203). In Banton's Table 43 (p. 203) there are 40 wards recorded for 211 households, male headed. This would give a figure of 19 per cent for the sample as a whole. However, this table is not broken down by Creole and Tribal identity.
3 The reification of 'societies' is a convenience here which is perhaps permissible since this problem of the generation of specific institutions is the subject of the last chapter.

10. The quest for education

1 Transcript: Re 'O' (a minor) High Court, Family Division, before the President Sir George Baker. 4 December 1972. Transcribed from the tape by the Mechanical Recording Department.
2 Transcript: Re 'O' . . . in the Family Division before Baker, 4 December 72; Appeal in the Court of Appeal (CA) before Davies and Megaw (Lord Justices), and Sir Seymour Karminski, 26 February 73.
3 For the first phase of the study we had originally hoped to be able to locate lists of West Africans living in London from which we could draw a representative sample for interview. However this proved impossible as all available lists were either incomplete or seriously biased. In the end we decided on an essentially pragmatic approach. Four Central London boroughs known to contain concentrations of West Africans were selected for study. Using the results of the 1966 ten per cent sample census, we were able to rank the enumeration districts within each borough in terms of the proportion of residents born in Africa. All enumeration districts with 5 per cent of more African-born population were taken as the universe for the survey. The interviewers then went to each address in these enumeration districts and listed the country of origin of the heads of all the households (being especially alert for multiple occupancies). The sample consists of all households in this census which met our criteria of two West African parents who had at least one child with them in this country. (On the basis of this census we estimate that between 80 and 85 per cent of the West African couples living in these boroughs had at least one child with them.) We were finally able to interview about 70 per cent of the sample or 296 couples. There are obvious limitations to the selection of a sample in this way and generalizations beyond the residents of the four boroughs studied can only be tentative. Information from these interviews will be referred to as based on the survey.
4 The couples for the second phase of the study were located through informal contacts and some of them with the assistance of the Commonwealth Student's Children's Society. The couples were selected so that half were from a major Nigerian ethnic group and half from a Ghanaian one; with each of these two sub-samples, half of the couples had fostered a child and half had never done so. Extensive notes were kept on visits to these couples over a period of several months, and background information systematically collected from each. Pseudonyms are used in referring to the couples who contributed to the intensive phase of the study, and details have been altered

where these seemed likely to permit identification. By now the majority have probably returned to West Africa. The purpose of the second phase was to gain an insight into the mechanisms which underlie patterns of work, study and the care of children. Here we were not concerned with generalizing to a wider population so much as with understanding how different factors interact to create the pattern of West African life in London.

5   All names are fictitious.
6   See the collection of studies of immigrant groups in England edited by Watson (1977). According to these accounts, no immigrant groups other than those from West Africa send children to foster-parents.

11. West African and West Indian immigrant families

1   In fact a surprising number of West African couples do have one or two relatives in the UK, but as they are also here in order to study and must work to support themselves, they are not available as foster-parents.
2   To do so on the basis of whether or not the child's parents are living together at the time of enquiry is not satisfactory, since in at least some cases the family of orientation is likely to have dispersed following the fostering arrangement.
3   See Fortes 1969, chapters 9 and 10 for an especially clear account of the compound as a mediating structure in Ashanti.
4   This is partly a function of the age at which a child is sent to foster-parents. In West Africa this tends to be around 5 to 7, often referred to as the time when a child begins to 'have sense'. In the West Indies, on the other hand, the pattern seems to be to place an infant with a foster-mother in order that the mother can work to support herself and the child, and be free to try and form a stable union. In the latter case, the child knows no other home than that of the foster-parent, though the mother may visit it regularly.
5   The coming of Western technology and education is altering this rapidly. When wisdom is learned at school, the elders are at an increasing disadvantage.
6   It was Dr Spens who made me realize the depth of this.
7   Southern Ghana lacks, of course, the racial differentiation which plays such a central part in West Indian stratification. I would not wish to imply that this is not of great importance in determining the available avenues of social mobility in the two culture areas, but the West Indian data come from black and coloured populations, and thus the discussion is necessarily limited to this stratum.
8   This assumption is only partly warranted in a West African context. A father's father may still be relatively young and actively engaged in his trade. On the other hand, many grandparents are sent foster-children to provide companionship and small services when they become old and infirm.

12. Parenthood and social reproduction

1   The wider identification of non-fostering societies is very difficult from ethnographic literature, because of the risks in taking no mention of fostering as equivalent to rejection of fostering. Many ethnographers do not enquire about residence of children, and classificatory kinship terminology means that such information is likely to come to light only accidentally. Further,

the distinction between purposive and crisis fostering is impossible to make without special enquiries.

2   Fiawoo has recently described how successful women traders in Accra place their children with Protestant families in one of the Accra suburbs known for its good schools. Such an arrangement secures for the child a 'normal' family life (which a busy businesswoman finds it difficult to provide), adult role models of highest moral standing (known for their devotion to the church) and access to good state schools (not readily available in the city centre). Here the fostering family is paid for their service (Fiawoo 1978).

3   The exception to girls marrying out is societies which practise uxorilocal marriage, or duo-local marriage as in traditional Ga and Ashanti. Here there tends to be a formal puberty ritual which makes a public break in the girl's status as a child-dependant, and establishes her, not only as a legitimate bearer of children, but also as an adult woman of whom full economic participation is expected. (See Brown (1963) for evidence of association between puberty rituals for girls, uxorilocality and women's productive roles. See also, Richards (1956) for explicit statement of change in expectations for girls' productive and domestic contributions following puberty ceremony among uxorilocal Bemba.)

4   I have elsewhere discussed in detail the role of greetings in expressing respect in both domestic and political contexts in Gonja, and the ways in which formal indications of respect have become institutionalized as means of securing certain goals – wives, office and secret knowledge (E. Goody 1972).

5   See L. Mair's discussion of the role of clientship in the development of centralized political systems in East Africa (1962).

6   In Durkheim's terms, this reflects a shift from mechanical solidarity in segmentary societies to an organic solidarity in the centralized systems.

7   Despite a very high level of kinship fosterage, the Ewe did not have special terms for foster-children or foster-parents, nor did they have a formal fostering ideology. M. Verdon, personal communication.

8   Janice Justus in personal communication.

9   The limiting cases are informative. They concern slaves (who have been permanently cut off from their natal kin by force); and very occasionally the incorporation of strangers from abroad who can bring no vestige of their birth-status identity with them, since it is anchored in their own society.

10 One contract I encountered stipulated a sum of money which was to be paid to the apprentice by the master if the former remained for the full period of five years; but the same sum was due to the master from the father of the apprentice should the term not be completed.

11 A related problem has led me to refrain from comparison with the considerable corpus on delegation of parent roles in Oceania. There, it would be necessary to make a working model of economic and political structures as well as the descent systems in terms comparable to those used for West Africa. Only then could a meaningful comparison be made between the two areas. This is a perfectly possible task, to which a number of important contributions have recently been made. But it must be the subject of a separate study.

Bibliography

Abernethy, D. 1969, *The political dilemma of popular education: An African case*. Stanford
Acquah, I. 1958, *Accra survey*. London
Amherst, H. W. 1931, 'Report on the constitution, organisation and customs of the Nanumba people'. Ms., Dept of Social Anthropology, Cambridge
Ardener, E. 1962, *Divorce and fertility: An African study* (Nig. soc. econ. Stud. 3). London
Arensberg, C. N. 1959, *The Irish countryman*. (2nd edn) Gloucester, Mass.
Ariès, P. 1962, *Centuries of childhood: A social history of family life*. trans. R. Baldick, New York
Atkinson, J. W. (ed.) 1958, *Motives in fantasy, action and society*. Princeton
Atkinson, J. W. and D. C. McClelland 1958, 'The effect of different intensities of the hunger drive on thematic apperception'. In J. W. Atkinson (ed.), *Motives in fantasy, action and society*. Princeton
Azu, D. G. 1974, *The Ga family and social change*. Leiden
Banton, M. 1957, *West African city: A study of tribal life in Freetown*. London
Barnes, J. A. 1949, 'Measures of divorce frequency in simple societies'. *J. R. Anthrop. Inst.* 74:37–62
Bascom, W. 1955, 'Urbanization among the Yoruba'. *Am. J. Sociology* 60:446–54
Bede, the Venerable 1968, *A history of the English church and people*. Harmondsworth
Binger, L. G. 1892, *Du Niger au golfe de Guinée*. 2 vols. Paris
Birney, R. C. 1958, 'Thematic content and cue characteristics of pictures'. In J. W. Atkinson (ed.) *Motives in fantasy, action and society*. Princeton
Blair, H. A. 1931, 'An essay upon the Dagomba people'. Ms., Dept of Social Anthropology, Cambridge
Blalock, H. M. 1968, 'The measurement problem: A gap between the languages of theory and research'. In Blalock and Blalock (eds.), *Methodology in social research*, New York
Blalock, H. M. and A. B. Blalock (eds.) 1968, *Methodology in social research*. New York
Boder, D. P. 1940, 'The adjective-verb quotient'. *Psychol. Rec.* 3:309–43
Bott, E. 1957, *Family and social network*. London
Bowlby, J. A. 1960, 'Separation anxiety'. *Int. J. Psycho-analysis* 41:89–113
Brown, J. K. 1963, 'A cross-cultural study of female initiation rites'. *Am. Anthropologist* 65:837–53

Bibliography

Brown, Susan Drucker n.d., 'Fieldnotes on the Mamprusi of northern Ghana'

Busia, K. A. 1950, *Report on a social survey of Sekondi-Takoradi*. London

Butcher, D. A. P. 1964, 'The role of the Fulbe in the urban life and economy of Lunsar, Sierra Leone'. Ph.D. thesis, Edinburgh

Callaway, A. 1964, 'Nigeria's indigenous education: The apprentice system'. *Odu U. of Ife J. of African Studies* 1:1–18

1973, *Nigerian enterprise and the employment of youth*. Nigerian Institute of Social and Economic Research. Monog. 2. Ibadan

Cardinall, A. W. n.d., *The natives of the northern territories of the Gold Coast: their customs, religion and folk-lore*. London

Carroll, V. A. (ed.) 1970, *Adoption in eastern Oceania*. Honolulu

Christensen, J. B. 1954, *Double desent among the Fanti*. New Haven

Clarke, E. 1966, *My mother who fathered me*. (2nd edn) London

Cohen, A. 1969, *Custom and politics in urban Africa*. London

Cohen, G. 1976, 'Recruitment to the professional class in Sierra Leone'. Ms.

Cohen, R. 1961, 'Marriage instability among the Kanuri of northern Nigeria'. *Am. Anthrop*. 63:1231–49

1967, *The Kanuri of Bornu*. New York

1971, *Dominance and defiance*. Washington

Coustel, P. 1687, *Les règles de l'education des enfants*. I. Paris

Crook, J. A. 1967, *Law and life in Rome*. London

Davis, A. 1944, 'Socialization and adolescent personality'. In *Adolescence, Forty-Third Yearbook*. I. Chicago

Donzelot, J. 1980, *The policing of families*. London.

Ellis, J. 1971, 'The Fostering of West African children in England'. *Social Work Today*. 2:21–4

Evans-Pritchard, E. E. 1962, 'The divine kingship of the Shilluk of the Nilotic Sudan' (The Frazer Lecture, 1948). In E. E. Evans-Pritchard, *Essays in social anthropology*. London

Eyre-Smith, St J. 1933, *A Brief review of the history and social organisation of the peoples of the Northern Territories of the Gold Coast*. Accra

Fadipe, N. A. 1940, 'The sociology of the Yoruba'. Ph.D. thesis, University of London

Fallers, L. A. 1957, 'Some determinants of marriage instability in Busoga: a reformulation of Gluckman's thesis'. *Africa* 27:106–21

Feld, S. and C. P. Smith 1958, 'An evaluation of the objectivity of the method of content analysis'. In J. W. Atkinson (ed.), *Motives in fantasy, action and society*. Princeton

Fiawoo, D. K. 1978, 'Some patterns in foster care in Ghana'. In C. Oppong *et al.* (eds.) 1978

Field, M. J. 1937, *Religion and medicine of the Ga people*. London

1940, *Social organisation of the Ga people*. London

Finnegan, R. H. 1965, *Survey of the Limba people of northern Sierra Leone*. London

Flandrin, J. L. 1979, *Families in former times: Kinship, household and sexuality*. Cambridge (French edn 1976)

Flavell, J. H., *et al.* 1968, *The development of role-taking and communication skills in children*. New York

Forde, D. 1963, 'Unilineal fact or fiction: An analysis of the composition of kin groups among the Yakö'. In I. Schapera (ed.) *Studies in kinship and marriage*. London

Bibliography

Fortes, M. F. 1949a, 'Time and social structure: An Ashanti case study'. In M. Fortes (ed.), *Social structure*. London

1949b, *The web of kinship among the Tallensi*. London

1950, 'Kinship and marriage among the Ashanti'. In A. R. Radcliffe-Brown and D. Forde (eds.), *African systems of kinship and marriage*. London

1958, Introduction to J. R. Goody (ed.), *The developmental cycle in domestic groups*. Cambridge

1959, *Oedipus and Job in West African religion*. Cambridge

1961, 'Pietas in ancestor worship'. J.R.A.I. 91:166–91

1969, *Kinship and the social order*. Chicago

1970, 'Social and psychological aspects of education in Taleland'. In M. F. Fortes, *Time and social structure and other essays*. London. Reprinted from *Africa* 11 (1938)

1974, 'The first-born', *J. Child Psychology and Psychiatry*. 15:81–104

Fortes, M. F. and E. E. Evans-Pritchard (eds.) 1940, *African political systems*. London

Foster, P. J. 1965, *Education and social change in Ghana*. London

Fraenkel, M. 1964, *Tribe and class in Monrovia*. London

Gamble, D. P. 1963, 'The Temne family in a modern town (Lunsar) in Sierra Leone'. *Africa* 33:209–26

Garden, M. 1970, *Lyon et les Lyonnais au xviiie siècle*. Paris

Gay, J. and M. Cole 1967, *New mathematics and an old culture*. New York

Gluckman, M. 1950, 'Kinship and marriage among the Lozi of Northern Rhodesia and the Zulu of Natal' In A. R. Radcliffe-Brown and D. Forde (eds.) *African systems of kinship and marriage*. London

Gonzalez, N. S. 1969, *Black Carib household structure*. Seattle

Goodenough, R. G. 1970, 'Adoption on Romonum, Truk'. In V. A. Carroll (ed.) *Adoption in Eastern Oceania*. Hawaii

Goodenough, W. H. 1970a, 'Transactions in parenthood'. In V. A. Carroll (ed.) *Adoption in Eastern Oceania*. Hawaii

1970b, *Description and explanation in cultural anthropology*. Chicago

Goody, E. N. 1961, 'Kinship, marriage and the developmental cycle among the Gonja of northern Ghana'. Ph.D. thesis, University of Cambridge

1962, 'Conjugal separation and divorce among the Gonja of northern Ghana'. In M. Fortes (ed.) *Marriage in tribal societies*. Cambridge

1966, 'Fostering of children in Ghana: A preliminary report'. *Ghana J. of Sociology* 2:26–33

1970a, 'Kinship fostering in Gonja: Deprivation or advantage?' In P. Mayer (ed.) *Socialization: The approach of social anthropology*. London

1970b, *The Kpembe study: A comparison of fostered and non-fostered children in eastern Gonja*. Final report to the Social Science Research Council. London

1970c, 'Legitimate and illegitimate aggression in a West African state'. In M. Douglas (ed.) *Witchcraft: confessions and accusations*. London

1971a, 'Varieties of Fostering'. *New Society* 5:237–9

1971b, 'Forms of pro-parenthood: The sharing and delegation of parental roles'. In J. Goody (ed.) *Kinship*. Penguin Readings in Sociology. Harmondsworth

1972, 'Greeting, begging and the presentation of respect'. In J. LaFontaine (ed.) *The interpretation of ritual*. London

1973, *Contexts of kinship*. Cambridge

335

Bibliography

1975, 'Delegation of parental roles in West Africa and the West Indies'. In
T. R. Williams (ed.) *Socialization and Communication in primary groups.*
The Hague

1978a, 'Towards a theory of questions'. In E. N. Goody (ed.) *Questions and politeness.* Cambridge

1978b, 'Some theoretical and empirical aspects of parenthood in West Africa'.
In C. Oppong *et al.* (eds.) 1978

Goody, E. N. and C. Muir 1972, 'Report on SSRC-funded study of West African families in London'. Mimeo

Goody, E. N. and C. M. Groothues 1977, 'The West Africans: The quest for education'. In J. L. Watson (ed.) *Between two cultures.* Oxford.

Goody, E. N. and C. M. Groothues 1979, 'Stress in marriage'. In V. Saifullah Khan (ed.) *Minority families in Britain.* London

Goody, J. 1956a, *The Social organisation of the LoWiili,* London

1956b, 'A comparative approach to incest and adultery'. *Br. J. Soc.* 7:286–305

(ed.) 1958, *The developmental cycle in domestic groups.* Cambridge papers in social anthropology 1. Cambridge

1962, *Death, property and the ancestors.* London

(ed.) 1966, *Succession to high office.* Cambridge papers in social anthropology 4. Cambridge

1967, 'The over-kingdom of Gonja'. In D. Forde and P. Kaberry (eds.) *West African Kingdoms in the Nineteenth Century.* London

1968, 'Descent groups'. In *International encyclopaedia of the social sciences.* New York

1969, 'Adoption in cross-cultural perspective'. *Comp. Stud. Soc. Hist.* 11:55–78

1976, *Production and reproduction.* Cambridge

Goody, J. and E. N. Goody 1966, 'Cross-cousin marriage in northern Ghana'.
Man (N.S.) 1:343–55

1967, 'The Circulation of Women and Children in Northern Ghana'. *Man* (N.S.) 2:226–48

Gough, E. K. 1959, 'The Nayars and the definition of marriage'. *J. R. Anthrop. Inst.* 89:23–34

Graft, J. C., de 1964, *Sons and daughters.* London

Greenberg, J. H. 1946, *The influence of Islam upon a Sudanese religion.* Monogr.
Am. Ethnol. Soc. 10. New York

Hammel, E. A. 1968, *Alternative social structures and ritual relations in the Balkans.* New York

Hannerz, U. 1969, *Soulside: Inquiries into ghetto culture and community.* New York

Harrell-Bond, B. 1975, *Modern marriage in Sierra Leone.* The Hague

Hill, C. 1970, *Immigration and integration.* Oxford

Hill, P. 1969, 'Hidden trade in Hausaland'. *Man* 4:392–409

1972, *Rural Hausa, a village and a setting.* Cambridge

Hoffer, C. P. 1974, 'Madam Yoko: Ruler of the Kpa Mende Confederacy'. In
M. Z. Rosaldo and L. Lamphere (eds.) *Woman, culture and society.*
Stanford

Hollander, E. D. 1962, 'Observations on the labour market in Ghana'. In A.
Taylor (ed.) *Educational and occupational selection in West Africa.* London

Holman, R. 1973, *Trading in children: A study of private fostering.* London

336

Bibliography

Horowitz, M. 1967, *Morne-paysan: peasant village in Martinique*. New York
Huber, H. 1963, *The Krobo*. The Anthropos Institute, Bonn
Illick, J. E. 1974, 'Child-rearing in seventeenth-century England and America'. In de Mause (ed.) 1974
Ingham, E. G. 1894, *Sierra Leone after a hundred years*. London
Jambert, L. 1608, *Traite des erreurs populaires*. Lyon
Kilson, M. 1974, *African urban kinsmen: The Ga of Central Accra*. New York
Koll, M. 1969, *Crafts and cooperation in western Nigeria*. Freiburg
Labouret, H. 1931, *Les tribus du rameau Lobi*. Paris
La Fontaine, J. S. 1960, 'Homicide and suicide in Bugisu'. In P. and J. Bohannan (eds.) *African homicide and suicide*
Lallemand, S. 1976, 'Génitrices et éducatrices Mossi'. *L'Homme* 16:109–24
Lane, E. W. 1871, *An account of the manners and customs of the modern Egyptians, written during the years 1833, -34, and -35*. (5th edn) London
Laslett, P. 1965, *The world we have lost*. London
Laslett, P. and R. Wall (eds.) 1972, *Household and family in past time*. Cambridge
Leach, E. R. 1951, 'The structural implications of matrilateral cross-cousin marriage'. *J. R. Anthrop. Inst.* 81:23–53
1957, 'Aspects of bridewealth and marriage stability among the Kachin and Lakher'. *Man* 57:50–5
1961, *Rethinking anthropology*. London
LeVine, R. A. 1966, *Dreams and deeds*. Chicago
Lévi-Strauss, C. 1963, *Structural anthropology*. New York
Lewis, I. M. 1962, *Marriage and the family in northern Somaliland*. East Afr. Stud. 15. Kampala
1965, 'Problems in the comparative study of unilineal descent'. In M. Banton (ed.) *The relevance of models for social anthropology*. London
Lewis, O. 1961, *The children of Sanchez: Autobiography of a Mexican family*. New York
Little, K. L. 1951, *The Mende of Sierra Leone*. London
Lloyd, P. C. 1953, 'Craft organization in Yoruba towns'. *Africa* 23:30–44
1965, 'The political structure of African kingdoms'. In M. Banton (ed.) *Political systems and the distribution of power*. London
1966, *The New elites of tropical Africa*. London
Lombard, J. 1957, 'Un système politique traditionnel de type féodal: les Bariba du Nord-Dahomey'. *Bulletin de l'Institut Français d'Afrique Noire* 19 (ser. B):464–506
McClelland, D. C. 1961, *The achieving society*. Princeton
McClelland, D. C., J. W. Atkinson, R. A. Clark, and E. L. Lowell 1953, *The achievement motive*. New York
Maccoby, E. E. (ed.) 1966, *The development of sex differences*. Stanford
Maccoby, E. E. and C. Jacklin 1974, *The psychology of sex differences*. Stanford
Macfarlane, A. 1970, *The family life of Ralph Josselin*. Cambridge
Mackay, D. J. n.d., 'Essay on the Mamprusi'. Ms., Dept of Social Anthropology, Cambridge
McLaughlin, M. M. 1974, 'Survivors and surrogates: Children and parents from the ninth to the thirteenth centuries'. In de Mause (ed.) 1974
Mair, L. 1962, *Primitive government*. Harmondsworth
Mangin, E. 1921, *Les Mossi*. Paris (trans. Human Relations Area File, New Haven, Conn., 1959)

Bibliography

Manoukian, M. 1952, *Tribes of the Northern Territories of the Gold Coast*, (Ethnographic Survey of West Africa, V) London

Marvick, E. W. 1974, 'Nature versus nurture: Patterns and trends in seventh-century French child-rearing'. In de Mause (ed.) 1974

Mause, L. de (ed.) 1974, *The history of childhood*. New York

Mead, G. H. 1934, *Mind, self and society*. Chicago

Middleton, J. 1960, *Lugbara religion*. London

Miner, H. 1953, *The primitive city of Timbuctoo*. Princeton

Mintz, S. W., and E. R. Wolf 1950, 'An analysis of ritual co-parenthood *(compadrazgo)'*. *Southwestern J. Anthropol.* 6:341–65

Moheau 1778, *Recherches et considerations sur la population de la France*. Paris

Muir, C. and E. N. Goody 1972, 'Student parents: West African families in London'. *Race* 13:329–36

Murray, H. A. *et al.* 1938, *Explorations in personality*. New York

Nadel, S. F. 1942, *A black Byzantium*. London

    1952, 'Witchcraft in four African societies'. *Am. Anthrop.* 54:18–29

Notes and queries in anthropology (6th edn) 1951. London

Nukunya, G. K. 1969, *Kinship and marriage among the Anlo Ewe*. London

Odoi, N. A. 1964, *The adventures of Esi Kakraba*. Accra

Oetzel, R. 1966, 'Classified summary of research in sex differences'. In Maccoby, E. E. (ed.) *The development of sex differences*. Stanford

Oppong, C. 1969, 'Education of relatives' children by senior civil servants in Accra'. *Ghana J. of Child Development* 2(2)

    1973, *Growing up in Dagbon*. Accra

    1974, *Marriage among a matrilineal Elite*. Cambridge

Oppong, C., G. Adaba, M. Bekombo-Priso and J. Mogey 1978, *Marriage, fertility and parenthood in West Africa*. Canberra

Peil, M. 1970, 'The apprenticeship system in Accra'. *Africa* 40:137–50

    1978, 'Self-employed craftsmen'. Ms.

Pfefferman, G. 1968, *Industrial labour in the Republic of Senegal*. New York

Porter, A. T. 1963, *Creoledom: A study of the development of Freetown society*. London

Quartey-Papafio, A. B. 1913, 'Apprenticeship among the Gas'. *J. of the African Society* 12:415–22

Radcliffe-Brown, A. R. 1930, 'The social organization of Australian tribes'. *Oceania* I:34–63, 206–46, 323–41, 426–56

    1950, Introduction to A. R. Radcliffe-Brown and D. Forde (eds.) *African systems of kinship and marriage*. London

Rattray, R. S. 1923, *Ashanti*. Oxford

    1929, *Ashanti law and constitution*. Oxford

    1932, *The tribes of the Ashanti hinterland*. Oxford

Richards, A. I. 1950, 'Some types of family structure amongst the central Bantu'. In A. R. Radcliffe-Brown and D. Forde (eds.) *African systems of kinship and marriage*. London

    1956, *Chisungu: A girl's initiation ceremony among the Bemba of Northern Rhodesia*. London

    1964, 'Authority patterns in traditional Buganda'. In L. A. Fallers (ed.) *The king's men*. London

Rosen, B. C. and R. G. D'Andrade 1959, 'The Psychosocial origins of achievement motivations'. *Sociometry* 22:185–218

Bibliography

Ross, J. B. 1974, 'The middle-class child in urban Italy, in fourteenth to early sixteenth century'. In de Mause (ed.) 1974

Rousseau, J. 1970, *L'Adoption chez les Esquimeaux Tununermuit.* Centre d'Etudes Nordiques, Université Laval

Sanford, M. 1971, 'Disruption of the mother–child relationship in conjunction with matrifocality: A study of child-keeping among the Carib and Creole of British Honduras' Ph.D. dissertation, Catholic University of America, Washington, D.C.

    1975, 'To be treated as a child of the home: Black Carib child lending in British West Indian society'. In T. Williams (ed.) *Socialization and communication in primary groups.* The Hague

Schildkrout, E. 1973, 'The fostering of children in urban Ghana: Problems of ethnographic analysis in a multi-cultural context'. *Urban Anthropology* 2:48–73

    1978, 'Age and gender in Hausa society: Socio-economic roles of children in urban Kano'. In J. S. LaFontaine (ed.) *Sex and Age as Principles of Social Differentiation.* London

    1979, 'Women's and children's work in urban Kano'. In S. Wallman (ed.) *The anthropology of work.* London

Siegel, S. 1956, *Non-parametric statistics for the behavioral sciences.* New York

Skinner, E. P. 1960, 'The Mossi *Pogsioure*'. *Man* 60:20–3

    1961, 'Intergenerational conflict among the Mossi: Father and Son'. *J. of Conflict Resolution* 5:55–60

    1964, *The Mossi of the Upper Volta.* Stanford

Smith, M. F. 1954, *Baba of Karo.* London

Smith, M. G. 1955, *The economy of Hausa communities of Zaria.* Colonial Research Studies 16. London

    1962a, *Kinship and community in Carriacou.* New Haven

    1962b, *West Indian family structure.* Seattle

Smith, R. T. 1956, *The Negro family in British Guiana.* London

Smutylo, T. 1975, 'Vocational training for school-leavers: The role of the wayside workshop'. Paper presented to the 1975 conference of the Canadian Association of African Studies. Toronto

Spens, M. T. 1969, 'Family structure in a Dominican village'. Ph.D. thesis, Cambridge University

Stack, C. B. 1974, *All our kin: Strategies for survival in a black community.* New York

Staniland, M. 1975, *The lions of Dagbon: Political change in northern Ghana.* Cambridge

Stephens, W. N. 1962, *The Oedipus complex: Cross-cultural evidence.* Glencoe, Ill.

Tahir, I. 1976, 'Scholars, sufis, saints and capitalists in Kano 1904–1974'. Ph.D. thesis, University of Cambridge

Tait, D. 1961, *The Konkomba of northern Ghana.* London

Tauxier, L. 1912, *Le noir du Soudan.* Paris

Taylor, L. R. 1966, *Party politics in the age of Caesar.* Berkeley

Trimmingham, J. S. 1959, *Islam in West Africa.* Oxford

Tucker, M. J. 1974, 'The child as the beginning and the end: Fifteenth and sixteenth century English childhood'. In de Mause (ed.) 1974

Verdon, M. 1979, 'African apprentice workshops: A case of ethnocentric reductionism'. *Am Ethnol.* 6:531–42

Bibliography

Wallerstein, I. 1964, *The road to independence in Ghana and the Ivory Coast.* Paris

Wareham, A. K. 1962, 'Methods of selection for the government secondary grammar schools in eastern Nigeria'. In A. Taylor (ed.) *Educational and occupational selection in West Africa.* London

Watson, J. (ed.) 1977, *Between two cultures.* London

Westermann, D. and M. A. Bryan 1952, *The languages of West Africa.* London

Wilson, M. 1951, 'Witch beliefs and social structure'. *Am. J. Sociol* 56:307–13

Winterbottom, M. R. 1958, 'The relations of need for achievement to learning experiences in independence and mastery'. In J. W. Atkinson (ed.) *Motives in Fantasy, Action and Society.* Princeton

Wolf, A. P. and Chieh-shan Huang 1980, *Marriage and adoption in China, 1845–1945.* Stanford

Yalman, N. O. 1967, *Under the Bo tree.* Berkeley

Index

341

Index

Index

Index

kinship system 18, 94–5, *see also* descent system; social system

labour, division of 13–14, 15, 70, 72, 78–82, manual 206–7, 265–7, 273, *see also* children: as labour; wage labour
labour, migrant 123, 129
Lagos 144, 188, 275
language 6, 13, 18, 209, 222
Latin America 19, 26
legitimacy 8–10, 11, 12, 147, *see also* illegitimacy
Liberia 3, 206, 208, 256
lineage 2, 11, 13, 196, 268, 269–70, 272, *see also* descent groups; descent system
London: West Africans in 4, 212ff, 234, 246, 251, 275, 279, West Indians in 241ff
Lozi 9, 109

market economy 110, 124–5, 129, 142, 144, 146, 156, 272
marriage 17, 38, 91, 92, 100–1, 107, 114, 137, 147, 150, 202, 203, 270, age of 99, 104, and birth status 11, 12, breakdown of 42, 52–3, 58, 59, 60, 99, 108–9, 166, 317–18, and descent system 2, 37–8, 47, 95–6, 107–9, 230, stability of 52, 97, 104, 105, 108
Martinique 235
men: attitudes to 59, 81–2, mobility of 95–6, occupations of 111–12, 114–16, 118, 124–5, 129–32, 150, 156, 173–4, 188–98
mobility: apprentice 192–4; social 208–9, 212, 220, 233, 270, 273, *see also* children; men; women
Monrovia 5, 207ff, 251, 275
mother: attitude of 77–8, duties of 12–14, 151, 232, role of 7, 8–10, 12–13, 248–9, *see also* wife; women
motherhood 7, 9–10, 16, 18, attitude to 81, 136–7, 227–9, 232, 240, 243, 249

Nayar 17
Ngoni 109
Nigeria 3, 4, 109, 114, 140, 188, 190, 199, 218, 220, 221, 222, 230
Nuer 17
nurturance (parental role) 1, 10, 12–13, 18, 59, 74–5, 254, 278, 286, 287, 303, delegated 23, 24, 31, 84, 134–8, 248, 257, 279, *see also* child minding
Nyakyusa 109

occupation: differentiation of 110, 118,

129, 156–7, 177, 191–4, 195, 200, 269–70, and fostering 113–17, 118, 121, 122, 123, 127, 142, 173, 177, 189–94, 236, 247, 258, 272 (*see also* specialization), and hierarchy 111–12, 132–4, 273, 276, and kin group 195–6, 255, training for 150, 190–4, 220, 221, 255, 262, *see also* apprentice fosterage; apprenticeship
occupational fosterage 113–17, 118, 141, 159, 172, 174, 178, 180, 196

parent 16, 17–18, 44, 54, 113, 121, 151, 195–6, 233, 226, 277
parental roles 1–2, 3–4, 6–16, 18, 19–22, 112, 227, 251, 254, 262–3, 276, 278–9, delegation of 2, 3, 5, 14, 19, 20–1, 25, 110, 118, 121–2, 126–7, 134–8, 141–2, 149, 159, 170, 188, 212–13, 234ff, 246, 249, 250, 252–9, 261, 270–1, 278–9, and social structure 258–9, 260ff, 267ff, *see also* fostering
parenthood 1, 3, 7, 16, 17–19, 31, 143, 149, 217–18, 222, 230–3, 250–2, 259, 262, 278–80
pastoral production: *see* farming
paternity: *see* fatherhood
'pawning': *see* debt fosterage
perception, of time and space 62, 73–4, 75–6
political power: *see* authority, political
political system 1, 2, 3, 4, 110, types of 124, 125, 128, 145, 267ff, 272, *see also* hierarchy, political; social system; society, centralized, segmentary
population density 1, 41, 112, 261
production, petty-commodity 22, 265, 273, *see also* trade
pro-parents 21–2, 31, 238, 270, *see also* foster-parents
property 12, 96, 100–1, 220, 260

rearing (parental roles) 4, 23, 227–9, 232, 262, *see also* children, rearing of; nurturance; reciprocities of 12, 19, 21–2, 29, 32, 138, 149, 179, 181, 198–200, 201, 240, 244, 247–8, 249, 271, 277, 278, *see also* children, obligations of; sponsorship; training
relationship: master/apprentice 127–8, 195–205, 262; parent/child 6, 7, 19–20, 58–9, 79, and fosterage 23, 24–5, 34, 62, 65, 69, 79–80, 114, 136–8, 271, and social structure 125–6, 250, 256, 260, 264, 276, *see also* parenthood

344

Index

religion 94, 101, 250, *see also* Christianity; Islam
residence: patterns of 1, 2, 41, 91, 95, 96–100, 102, 108–9, 112, 119, 151, 180; sibling 97, 98, 103–4, 107, 108, *see also* mobility
rituals, puberty 11, 146–7, *see also* sponsorship, ritual

school(ing) 154, 190, 314, fostering for 168, 169–70, 171–2, 177, 256, 277–8, 316, and social hierarchy 208–9, 256, *see also* education
segregation: class 206; conjugal role 230–2
Sekondi-Takoradi 171
seniority, importance of 61, 63, 81, 112, 120, 123–4, 136, 153, 159, 204
service fosterage 21–3, 139–40, 143, 170–1, 183, 184, 256, *see also* housemaids; children: as labour
sex differences 57–9, 63–4, 68, 70–1, 80–2, 86, 152, 154, 157–8, 159ff, 184–7, 248–9
sex roles 13, 44, 61, 63, 70–1, 77–8, 81, 150–2, 182–3, 184–7, 247–9, 310–12
sibling bond 52, 91–2, 99, 172–3, 180
sibling group 39–40, 181, 185
Sierra Leone 3, 194, 206–7, 218, 222, 256
skills, traditional 45–6, 112, 177, and achievement 63, *see also* craftwork
slavery 129, 134
social structure 1, 2, 3, 4, 61, 63, 91–109, 195, 203, *see also* parental roles
social system, type of: and civil status 9, 11–12, 220, 269–71, 273, 276, 278–80, and fostering pattern 40, 157–9, 241, 251, 253–60, 268–70, 274–81, and parental roles 2–5, 15–16, 20, 110, 272–4, 278–80, *see also* kinship system; society
socialization 1, 23, 40, 63, 78, 254, 279
society: centralized 2, 95, 110, 146, 258, 267, 270, 277; segmentary 2, 4, 94, 253, 263, 265, 267, 268–9, 271
specialization 110–11, and child training 113, 114–16, 117, 233, and kin groups 195, and towns 111–12, 125, 190, *see also* occupation: differentiation of
sponsorship (parental role) 1, 14–16, 19, 20, 23, 31, 110, 134, 137–8, 149, 150, 151, 202, 254, 257, 261, 267–71, 272, 274–6, 277, 278, 280–1
sponsorship, ritual 15, 19, 20, 26–8, 33–4, 146–9, 180
states, coastal: *see* town states
status 111, 132–4, 203–4, 210, 220, 272,

276, birth (parental role) 5, 8–11, 14, 15, 16, 19, 23, 28, 29, 31, 116, 147, 149, 190, 200, 239, 258, 268, 270, 278, 279, civil 10, 12–13, 17, 21, 33, 99, 146–7, 203–4, 254, 261, 268–9, and fostering pattern 3, 49–54, 165–6, 258, 270, 277–8, kinship 8–10, 12, 17, 22, 81, 190, reciprocities of 11, 27, 32–3, 241, 277, 278
system, political: *see* political system

taxation 2, 110, 111, 118, 125, 129, 273
Thematic Apperception Test (TAT) 55–7, 58, 59, 66–7, 74, 283, 285–7, 288ff
town states 3, 144ff, 190, 269–70, 271–2, *see also* West Africa, societies of: Ewe, Fanti, Ga, Krobo
towns 155–7, development of 171, 203, 313–15
trade 22, 219, and fostering 128, 138–9, 170–1, and social structure 4, 94, 110, 111, 124–5, 129, 207, 209, in West Africa 118, 220, 273
training (parental role) 1, 13–14, 16, 23, 31, 61, 77–8, 112, 113, 154, 195, 262, delegated 43–4, 45, 78ff, 85–6, 110, 113–16, 120, 127–8, 134, 138–9, 141, 149–50, 154, 171–7, 183, 186, 248, 254, 257, 261, 262–4, 267–71, 272, 274–6, 277, 278, 280–1, *see also* apprentice fosterage; educational fosterage; occupational fosterage
transactions 21–3, 258–60

United Kingdom 235, *see also* England, Europe
United States: *see* America
Upper Volta 111

wage labour 2, 110, 125, 129, 204, 205, 273
wardship, Creole 3, 4, 5, 208–9, 210–12, 256, 274, *see also* apprenticeship
warfare 118, 129, 190
wealth 38, 96, 132, 220, 260, 272
West Africa 1, 2, 3, 4, 6, 37, 110, 121, 129, 143, 148, 172, 179, 188, 195, 201, 206, 212, 220, 230, 235, 236, 238, 240–1, 247, 248, 249, 250–1, 272ff; societies of: Akan 197, 218, Ashanti 9, 15–16, 17, 37, 94, 145, 147, 148, 195, 238–9, Bariba 37, Chakalle 106, Dagomba 2, 3, 37, 45, 109, 110, 111–17, 123–4, 141–2, 173, 179, 195, 251, 252, 255, 258, 272, 275, Ewe 3, 143, 144, 145, 146, 147, 154, 155ff, 183, 196, 251, 258, 272,

345

Index

Index of authors

347

Index of authors

Cambridge Studies in Social Anthropology

General Editor: Jack Goody

* Also published as a paperback.